San Francisco Reds

SAN FRANCISCO REDS

Communists in the Bay Area, 1919–1958

ROBERT W. CHERNY

**UNIVERSITY OF
ILLINOIS PRESS**
Urbana, Chicago, and Springfield

Some parts of this book have appeared in different form in the following and appear
here by permission:
"Prelude to the Popular Front: The Communist Party in California, 1931–1935."
   American Communist History 1 (2002): 5–37, copyright 2002 Historians of
   American Communism, by permission of Taylor & Francis Ltd.
"The Communist Party in California, 1935–1940: From the Political Margins to the
   Mainstream and Back." *American Communist History* 9 (2010): 3–33, copyright 2010
   Historians of American Communism, by permission of Taylor & Francis Ltd.
"The Party's Over: Former Communist Party Members in the San Francisco Bay Area,"
   ch. 10 of *Post–Cold War Revelations in the American Communist Party: Citizens,
   Revolutionaries, and Spies*, edited by Vernon Pedersen, James Ryan, and Katherine
   Sibley, 229–54 (London: Bloomsbury Press, 2021).
Victor Arnautoff and the Politics of Art (Urbana: University of Illinois Press, 2017).
Harry Bridges: Labor Radical, Labor Legend (Urbana: University of Illinois Press, 2022).

Library of Congress Cataloging-in-Publication Data
Names: Cherny, Robert W., author.
Title: San Francisco reds : communists in the Bay Area, 1919–1958 / Robert W. Cherny.
Description: Urbana : University of Illinois Press, [2024] | Includes bibliographical
   references and index.
Identifiers: LCCN 2023046849 (print) | LCCN 2023046850 (ebook) |
   ISBN 9780252045837 (cloth) | ISBN 9780252087936 (paperback) | ISBN
   9780252056710 (ebook)
Subjects: LCSH: Communists—California—San Francisco—History—20th
   century. | Communist Party of the United States of America. San Francisco
   (Calif.) | San Francisco (Calif.)—Politics and government.
Classification: LCC HX91.C3 A52 2024 (print) | LCC HX91.C3 (ebook) | DDC
   324.2794/0750979461—dc23/eng/20240117
LC record available at https://lccn.loc.gov/2023046849
LC ebook record available at https://lccn.loc.gov/2023046850

To
Judy Nitzberg
in memory of
Leo Nitzberg and Don Watson

CONTENTS

PREFACE

This book came about somewhat by accident. Growing up in a small Nebraska town in the late 1940s and 1950s, I absorbed the anti-Communist rhetoric then prevalent in the media and my schools. My wariness toward the Communist Party (CP) lessened later, in college, in graduate school, and after, especially when I learned that some of my and my wife's friends and acquaintances—including Leo and Judy Nitzberg and Don Watson—had once been CP members. In 1996 I had an appointment as a Fulbright lecturer in U.S. history at Moscow State University. That position attracted me in part because John Haynes, the first American researcher at what is now the Russian State Archive for Social and Political History (Rossiiskii gosudarstvennyi arkhiv sotsial'no-politicheskoi istorii, RGASPI), had found relevant material there for my research on Harry Bridges. Before I left for Moscow, John was very helpful in orienting me to that archive. He also assured me that those files were among the richest sources on the 1920s and 1930s not yet used by historians of the United States.

My research at RGASPI confirmed John's comment. I found some information about Bridges (see *Harry Bridges: Labor Radical, Labor Legend*, 2023) and a great deal about the Communist Party in California. That research led to two articles in the journal *American Communist History*. I returned in 2003 to spend several weeks at RGASPI, collecting material about the California CP. My interest in the party was part of what led me to write *Victor Arnautoff and the Politics of Art* (2017). That same interest led to this book.

My dissertation and first book analyzed political behavior through voting analysis and a collective biography. My three biographies, of William Jennings Bryan, Victor Arnautoff, and Harry Bridges, have all addressed those individuals' political development. This book takes a somewhat biographical approach to political behavior, as I've followed nearly fifty individuals from the time they joined the CP, through the party's changing policies, to the point when most of them left the party, and what they did afterward. My title and subtitle make clear that this book is primarily about individuals who were open members of the Communist Party. I therefore have not rehashed the arguments about whether Harry Bridges or J. Robert Oppenheimer were members; those arguments are available elsewhere and at great length.[1]

Those individuals made this book possible by openly discussing their time as party members—they wrote memoirs, recorded interviews, gave their papers to an archive. They are, therefore, not a random or representative sample of party members. When compared to the population of San Francisco, they were better educated and less likely to have been blue-collar workers. Angela Gizzi Ward, in 1976, mused that "the C.P.U.S.A. was composed largely of professionals and intellectuals."[2] She overstated the significance of that group, but her characterization fit many with whom she was associated in local leadership. A third or more of the individuals I track in this book may fit that characterization, depending on how one defines terms.[3] That group is also disproportionately male when compared to the population in general, but insofar as data exists on gender among party members, women are well represented, with almost a third of the total. (In 1931, 20 percent of California party members were women.[4]) The appendix lists the individuals who appear most frequently, including a few who were not open party members, and may or may not have been secret members, with a brief biography and indication of where they appear in the book.

This book surveys four decades (1919–1958), but the 1930s receive more attention than any comparable time period. In part this reflects the availability of primary sources at RGASPI. In part it reflects the significant presence of the CP during those years. And in part it reflects the way that individuals thought about their participation in the CP.

Several books have drawn on the RGASPI records. Some have depicted the CPUSA as funded by Moscow and some of its top leaders as involved in espionage.[5] I found little evidence for "Moscow gold" as the financial basis for the CP in California. More typical, especially in the 1920s and early 1930s, were complaints by CP functionaries that they were scraping by on a pittance and had to raise their own meager wages. Some Californians served the Comintern as couriers or organizers in other parts of the world, but I found no evidence that those individuals engaged in espionage within the United States. Karl Yoneda described his "underground work" as covertly publishing propaganda and arranging for seamen to smuggle that printed matter into Japan. The only espionage that I found was during World War II; most of it was related to Soviet consular officials and focused on atomic bomb research at the University of California (see chapter 6), a topic treated at length by previous scholars, notably Gregg Herken in *Brotherhood of the Bomb* and the recent biographers of J. Robert Oppenheimer. Steve Nelson, the central CPUSA member in those activities, was apparently sent to the San Francisco Bay Area primarily for that work, and he left the area immediately after.[6]

There have been several excellent studies of the Communist Party at a local or state level, including those by Mark Naison on Harlem, Robyn Kelley on Alabama, Vernon Pedersen on Maryland, Randi Storch on Chicago, Gregory Taylor on North Carolina, Mary Stanton on Alabama, and Ryan Pettengill on Detroit.[7] Nearly all have focused on the party's activism during the 1930s and sometimes the 1940s.

This book takes a long view. The party members who appear in these pages joined the CP at various times—the 1920s, the 1930s, and a few in the 1940s. Most had local or state leadership roles in the party, a union, or both. A few were never more than rank-and-file party members. A few became national leaders. Insofar as sources permit, I have addressed their decision to join, their party activities, their reactions to the party line, and, for those who left, the reasons why they left and the influence of their time in the party on their subsequent lives.

For many of the years covered by this book, CP activity in the United States followed a party line that originated in Moscow, especially during the existence of the Communist International (1919–1943). For the 1930s especially, material in RGASPI suggests an iterative process: U.S. party leaders met with the Comintern's Anglo-American Secretariat (AAS) in Moscow, reported their perspective on situations facing the CPUSA, and proposed a policy; their report was discussed in the AAS and sometimes at higher levels of the Comintern; drawing on such reports and on information from the press, the AAS drafted its own report analyzing events and proposing policies, which report was sometimes discussed and approved at higher levels of the Comintern. Alternatively, the AAS or Comintern Executive Committee might take the initiative rather than U.S. party leaders, but the process was much the same. The final report of the AAS or Comintern was then discussed by the Political Bureau, the highest level of decision making in the U.S. party in the 1930s, which developed directives (the "party line") to district and local organizations. (Chapter 4 provides examples of this process.) During the mid-1930s, three Californians, one after the other, served as the U.S. party's representative on the AAS (see chapter 5). After the CPUSA withdrew from the Comintern in 1940, some direct contact with Moscow continued (see chapter 6), but even that was broken late in World War II. Nonetheless, the leaders of the U.S. party still tried to discern directions from Moscow (see chapters 7 and 8).

There were always some, including some local leaders, who exercised discretion in the local application of the party line, a situation that has sometimes been attributed to being the district most distant from party headquarters in New York City. Sam Darcy, district organizer from late 1930 to mid-1935, stands out for his efforts to adjust the party line to his understanding of reality—for which he was often admonished. In the 1950s the defendants in the California Smith Act case rejected advice from national party leaders and determined their own approach to their legal defense. Of course, there were also those who always sought to enforce the prevailing party line. And there were many who simply stepped away from the party when they found it too demanding or unrealistic. All in all, the picture I found is more complex than that presented by prominent anti-Communists of a powerful, secretive, highly organized, and tightly disciplined party apparatus—a "conspiracy"—directed from Moscow, in which CP members had a lifetime commitment to carrying out Moscow's directives.

Some historians have pointed to the number of women among party candidates for office or in party leadership positions in California and suggested that this marked the California party as unusual. However, there were clearly limits on how high a woman might rise in party leadership during the years treated in this book, 1919–1958. During those years, women served in secretarial positions in the state party, represented the party in statewide elections, and held similar positions locally, but it was not until the 1940s that a woman became head of the party organization in the city and county of San Francisco. Most women in those positions noted that they encountered problems within the party because of their gender and that serving in such positions was often seen as incompatible with having children.[8]

The party constantly lost members, a seepage that became a torrent in the 1950s. By the late 1960s more than three-quarters of the individuals I trace had resigned, been dropped or expelled, or simply drifted away. The party did not disappear, of course, but after 1957–1958 the local and state organization and leadership were very different.

From the 1920s onward, Southern California had a separate subdistrict, and the state was eventually divided into separate districts. Early in my work I recognized that the situation in Los Angeles was so complex that I could not treat both it and the Bay Area in the same book. Someone else should study Southern California's party. I have nonetheless included a fair amount of information about the party in Los Angeles during the 1920s because some individuals who first became prominent there later became significant leaders at the state or national level.

Within the Bay Area, I have concentrated on events in San Francisco, the largest city and location of the district office. When I began this book, I inquired into the FBI files of key figures, especially William Schneiderman, Oleta O'Connor Yates, and Louise Todd Lambert. I learned that it would take several years to fulfill such requests. (It took nearly fifteen years for me to receive Harry Bridges's FBI file.) At the age of seventy-seven, I decided to complete this study without those records, since I was uncertain I'd be able to wait that long. I did request five years of Schneiderman's file, and it arrived just as this book was going into copyediting, so I was able to add a bit of information based on that file. I hope other researchers will have longer timelines for their research.

ACKNOWLEDGMENTS

Given the way that research for this book has significantly overlapped with research for my biographies of Victor Arnautoff and Harry Bridges, so too my acknowledgments must duplicate some in those books. The archivists to whom I owe the biggest debt for this book include the directors of the Labor Archives and Research Center (LARC) at San Francisco State University since 1985—Lynn Bonfield, Susan Sherwood, Catherine Powell, and the current acting director, Tanya Hollis—and also LARC staff members, especially the late Carol Cuénod.

My initial research at RGASPI was possible because of my appointment as a Distinguished Fulbright Lecturer at Lomonosov Moscow State University in 1996 and was facilitated by my colleagues and students there, the attendants in reading room 413, and Datia Lotareva, my translator and research assistant in 1996 and 2003. Beth Behnam and the staff at the California State Archives in Sacramento were especially helpful during the late stages of my research when I could not travel to archives in person. Similarly, Jeff Moscaritolo searched the Upton Sinclair Papers at Indiana University for me, and Jay Driskell located materials for me at the Library of Congress. Barbe Marshall, Helen Harvey, and Silia Tahlvi transcribed my interviews.

In addition to my Fulbright appointment at Moscow State University, I received support from the National Endowment for the Humanities through a summer stipend and a yearlong fellowship, research grants from the American Council of Learned Societies, the American Philosophical Society, and several grants from San Francisco State University, all of which were for my research on Harry Bridges but also yielded material for this book.

Bill Issel, Ralph Shaffer, and Nora Lapin read drafts of part or all of this book, and I am grateful to them for their comments. I also received advice from two anonymous peer reviewers for the University of Illinois Press.

Thanks also must go to Laurie Matheson, James Engelhardt, Alison K. Syring, Leigh Ann Cowan, and Tad Ringo at the University of Illinois Press.

Finally, thanks have to go to my family for their support and encouragement: Rebecca, my wife, partner, and companion for more than fifty years; Sarah, our daughter; and our granddaughters, Cerys and Sabina.

And, of course, all errors are my own.

ABBREVIATIONS

AAS	Anglo-American Secretariat, part of the Comintern
AFL	American Federation of Labor
CAWIU	Cannery and Agricultural Workers Industrial Union, part of the TUUL
CEC	Central Executive Committee, the highest-ranking committee in the CPUSA; later called the Political Bureau (PolBuro)
CI	Communist International
CIO	Committee on Industrial Organization (1934–1938), Congress of Industrial Organizations (after 1938)
CLP	Communist Labor Party
Comintern	Communist International
CP	Communist Party; unless otherwise indicated, the Communist Party of the United States, which underwent name changes at various times
CPA	Communist Party of America (1919–1921)
CPA	Communist Political Association (1944–1945)
CPUSA	Communist Party of the United States of America, the official name from 1929 to 1944 and after 1945
DEC	District Executive Committee
DO	district organizer
ILA	International Longshoremen's Association
ILD	International Labor Defense

ILWU	International Longshoremen's and Warehousemen's Union (now International Longshore and Warehouse Union)
KGB	*Komitet gosudarstvennoy bezopasnosti*, Committee for State Security, the Soviet intelligence agency that conducted operations in the United States, between 1954 and 1991
MFOW	Pacific Coast Marine Firemen, Oilers, and Wipers Association, usually called the Marine Firemen's Union
MOPR	*Mezhdunaródnaa organizásia pómoshchi borsám revolúsii*, International Red Aid
NKVD	*Naródnyy komissariát vnútrennikh del*, People's Commissariat of Internal Affairs, the Soviet intelligence agency that conducted operations in the United States beginning in 1934; superseded by the KGB in 1954
PolBuro	Political Bureau, the highest-ranking committee in the CPUSA during the 1930s; previously the Central Executive Committee, later the National Board
PPTUS	Pan-Pacific Trade Union Secretariat, part of the RILU
Profintern	See RILU
RGASPI	*Rossiiskii gosudarstvennyi arkhiv sotsial'no-politicheskoi istorii*, Russian State Archive for Social and Political History
RILU	Red International of Trade Unions, the Comintern's organization for CP-dominated unions; in Russian, *Krasnyi internatsional profsoyuzov*, or Profintern
SPA	Socialist Party of America
TUUL	Trade Union Unity League
YCL	Young Communist League
WP	Workers Party
WPA	Works Progress Administration

San Francisco Reds

AN UNCERTAIN BEGINNING, 1919–1930

California Communists first organized in 1919. Just as at the national level, two state organizations—the Communist Party of America (CPA) and the Communist Labor Party (CLP)—broke away from the state Socialist Party. And just as most of the state's economy and politics revolved around the San Francisco Bay Area and the Los Angeles Basin, so the first Communist organizations were largely divided between those two metropolitan areas, some four hundred miles apart, then a full day's travel—fourteen hours by rail and longer by auto.[1]

The two organizations soon merged, but the geographic distance remained and was compounded and overlaid both by the party's differing bases between north and south and by the factional divisions that afflicted the national party and created internal divisions within both metropolitan areas. Not until the 1930s did the state party sufficiently overcome its internal divisions to play a significant role in California's economy and politics. However, several individuals emerged from the disarray of the 1920s to provide significant party leadership later, notably Anita Whitney, William Schneiderman, Louise Todd, and Frank Waldron, who later took the name Eugene Dennis. This chapter introduces those and other significant individuals and presents an overview of the party's first decade; the next chapter focuses on factionalism.

Going Underground in the Early 1920s

Ralph Shaffer described the early history of California Communism in three journal articles from 1967 to 1984. Able to interview several participants, Shaffer found the genesis of the California CP in the reaction of the state's Socialists to Bolshevism in Russia in 1917 and after. Those who emphasized working within the existing political system had usually dominated the California branch of the Socialist Party of America (SPA) before World War I. Those who had advocated for industrial unionism and looked disdainfully on electoral politics were more likely to embrace the Bolsheviks, a group that gained prominence during the war. In mid-1919 some of the SPA's foreign-language federation branches in Los Angeles bolted to the new CPA. Bolshevik sympathizers dominated the California delegation to the SPA National Convention in Chicago in August 1919.[2]

The California delegates were not seated in the SPA convention because of alleged election irregularities. They stormed out and marched over to the convention then organizing the CLP. Max Bedacht, a California delegate and a leader in the German Federation of the SPA, was elected to the CLP's National Executive Committee and took little further part in California developments. James Dolsen, a leader in the California delegation, chaired the CLP's constitution committee. A different California delegation, mostly from Southern California, attended the simultaneous convention of the CPA, formed largely by the SPA's foreign-language federations. The CPA was most prominent in Los Angeles, the CLP in the Bay Area, a situation likely due to the relative significance of the SPA's language federations in the two regions. In November, the founding convention of the state CLP elected Dolsen as state secretary-treasurer. Soon after, in Oakland, a mob identified as World War I veterans wrecked the office and burned the furniture and records of the CLP and the *World*, the Socialist newspaper that had gone over to the CLP. Oakland police did not intervene and carried out their own raid a few days later.[3]

In April 1919 the California legislature approved a criminal syndicalism law, aimed at outlawing the Industrial Workers of the World (IWW). IWW members across the state were soon arrested and prosecuted. Thirteen CLP leaders in the Bay Area, including Dolsen and Bedacht, were also arrested and charged with criminal syndicalism. Bedacht was extradited to Chicago, site of CLP national headquarters, to be tried on similar charges there. The remaining CLP defendants were charged with criminal syndicalism on the grounds that the founding meeting of the CLP had passed a resolution endorsing the IWW. Dolsen twice secured hung juries on that charge, but juries convicted several other defendants. The Palmer Raids, beginning in November 1919, also targeted members of the CPA and CLP. Those federal and state prosecutions drove Communist organizations underground.[4]

Anita Whitney was the most prominent among those convicted of criminal syndicalism. A founding member of California's CLP, Whitney was a native Californian, an 1889 graduate of Wellesley College, daughter of a state senator, and niece of a U.S. Supreme Court justice. After college she had worked in a New

York City settlement house and then returned to Oakland as a social worker and woman suffrage activist. Financially comfortable, though not wealthy, she was active in civic and women's associations.[5] She appealed her conviction, eventually to the U.S. Supreme Court, which in 1927 unanimously found against her, although justices Louis Brandeis and Oliver Wendell Holmes filed a concurrence that read more like a dissent.[6]

Along the way, Whitney attracted a wide range of supporters, including John Francis Neylan, éminence grise of the San Francisco Republican Party in the 1920s and early 1930s and a sometime progressive who was counsel to William Randolph Hearst. After the Supreme Court decision, Neylan persuaded

Anita Whitney in the Alameda County jail, convicted of criminal syndicalism, February 23, 1920. Photo from *California Faces: Selections from The Bancroft Library Portrait Collection,* courtesy of Bancroft Library, University of California, Berkeley.

California's governor, C. C. Young, to pardon Whitney, saving her from prison. Though not significantly involved in party leadership, Whitney was sometimes the public face of the party. Others on the left also appealed to her. In 1920 she declined a request from the state Farmer-Labor Party to stand for the U.S. Senate. California Communists took little interest in that party.[7]

In March 1919, a conference in Moscow attended by delegates from thirty-four national parties formed the Communist International, or Comintern, to coordinate, support, and provide direction to Communist parties outside Russia. During 1920 and 1921, under the Comintern's direction, the two U.S. parties merged to create the United Communist Party of America. The merged organization remained underground and created the Workers Party (WP) as its aboveground face.

Joining the Party: Six Women's Stories

Whitney was more than fifty years old, a longtime suffragist, and a member of the SPA when she joined the CLP. The party also attracted young women. Although I found only a few oral histories or memoirs by individuals who joined the party in the 1920s, the following accounts provide some sense of the differing routes that led some to the party.

Louise Todd was born in San Francisco in 1905. Her parents, German immigrants, were freethinkers and Socialists who became Communists in 1919. Todd remembered party meetings in her home when she was a teenager, including one or more involving Bertram Wolfe. She joined the Young Workers League (YWL) and recalled that most YWL members were children of party members. Todd graduated from the High School of Commerce in 1922 and found work as a secretary because her family could not afford college tuition. The YWL conducted classes and carried out actions. Todd remembered passing out leaflets to National Guard members encouraging them to turn their guns on their officers, something that, in retrospect, she considered a classic example of doing the wrong thing. The YWL, Todd remembered, was deeply involved in the factional struggles of the 1920s but did little to organize or even contact American workers. She joined the CP in late 1929 or early 1930.[8]

Rose Elaine Buchman, who went by Elaine, was born in 1906 to Russian Jewish parents in New York City. She moved with her family to Southern California in 1920, first to San Diego, then to Los Angeles. Her parents were Socialists who became Communists in 1919 and were active in the Friends of the Soviet Union, a party effort to reach supporters who were not party members. Ella Reeve "Mother" Bloor stayed at their home in 1921. Elaine took little interest in her parents' politics, but they pushed her to join the YWL, and she did. There she met her first husband, but initially they were minimally active in the YWL.[9]

Violet Balcomb was born in San Francisco in 1904, into a family with long roots in the United States. Her parents were religious, and Violet was active in the Methodist youth organization, where she encountered the Social Gospel. She learned about the October Revolution at Stanford University, where she was a history major. There she met Paul Orr, and they joined the Fellowship of Reconciliation, a pacifist organization. In 1926 they graduated (she as Phi Beta Kappa), married, and moved to New York City to study for their master's degrees at Columbia University Teachers College. In New York they absorbed more Social Gospel teachings, worked in a socialist summer camp, and began to question their religion. Interested in travel after graduation, they sought advice from George Counts, a Teachers College professor who had recently visited the Soviet Union. They then spent two years teaching English in Moscow. Upon returning to the Bay Area, they became active in the Friends of the Soviet Union, lectured on their experiences, and joined the CP in 1932.[10]

Regina "Reggie" Karasick was born in New York City in 1909 to Russian Jewish immigrant parents. She and her family moved to Los Angeles in 1912, hoping the climate would improve her mother's asthma. Her father was a cloak maker and sometime dry-cleaning shop operator. Her parents were active Socialists and moved from the SP to the CP. Reggie and her older sister, Minnie, joined the YWL as soon as they were old enough. Reggie attended college briefly after high school but left to work with CP youth groups. In 1927, at eighteen years old, she married William Schneiderman. They moved to San Francisco, where Bill was part of the state leadership of the YWL. In 1928 she attended a CP summer school where she met Francis Xavier Waldron, an instructor. She left Schneiderman, and she and Frank became partners.[11]

Dorothy Rosenblum was born in Denver in 1914 to Hungarian Jewish parents, who moved to California in the early 1920s, settling in Berkeley. There Dorothy finished high school. Her mother was a Socialist who became a Communist. Dorothy considered herself a revolutionary by the age of twelve, joined the YWL at fourteen, and worked with the Young Pioneers (the party's organization for children) while in high school. In 1931 she was arrested in Oakland for disturbing the peace by shouting the headlines while selling the *Daily Worker*. At the juvenile detention facility, she gave the name Dorothy Ray to protect her father's job.[12]

Lillian Dinkin was born in Chicago in 1914 to Jewish immigrants from what is now Belarus. Her family moved to Los Angeles in 1923. Her father was a Communist, and Lillian joined the party's youth group soon after arriving in Los Angeles. Beginning in 1928, Lillian was repeatedly arrested for distributing leaflets without a permit. She participated in major party demonstrations in February and March 1930 and was denied her high school diploma because of her political activities. She recalled, "We became expert demonstrators. We always carried a wet handkerchief for tear gas and a toothbrush and comb in case we were arrested."[13]

Though these accounts of joining the party are all from women, women remained a distinct minority in the party throughout the 1920s, and there were few women in leadership during that decade. The immigrant background of five of the six mentioned here was typical of most party members in the 1920s. Three of the six were from Los Angeles, and all three were Jewish, also reflective of patterns within the party. The three from the Bay Area were from different ethnic and religious backgrounds, also more typical of the party in that area.

Electoral Efforts, 1922–1925

In the 1922 elections, the California WP tried to conduct a write-in campaign for its candidates, but, as Shaffer put it, the results were "disastrous," producing only eighty-five votes in San Francisco and a scattering elsewhere. In 1923 in San Francisco, the party joined local Socialists in supporting George Kidwell in a special election to fill a vacant congressional seat. Kidwell, a member of the Bakery Drivers Union, had previously been prominent in efforts to create a state Farmer-Labor Party. The CP's support for Kidwell seems not to have attracted any attention. Kidwell finished third, with 13 percent of the vote.[14] Such efforts at cooperation with the SPA soon came to an end.

In early 1924 the party's weekly newspaper, *Labor Unity*, extensively covered efforts to create a Farmer-Labor Party and the development of Robert La Follette's independent campaign for U.S. president. Then the Comintern explicitly directed the U.S. party to oppose La Follette, and Charles Ruthenberg, WP executive secretary, instructed district leaders in early April: "Our Party is for the formation of a class Farmer Labor Party in the United States, but it is not for a 'LaFollette for president' movement. There is a wide distinction between support of a certain individual for the presidency and work to bring into existence a mass movement of farmers and workers for the purpose of fighting their own political battles." That position did not change even though the SPA, American Federation of Labor (AFL), and other left and progressive groups endorsed La Follette. The WP instead ran William Z. Foster for president and Benjamin Gitlow for vice president. Thereafter, often on every page, *Labor Unity* repeated, "A vote for Foster is a protest vote against war," likely an effort to undercut La Follette's promise to conduct a public referendum before any future war. Foster campaigned in San Francisco and Berkeley. After the party failed to collect the 10,000 signatures necessary to put Foster on the state ballot, *Labor Unity* advised readers to write in Nestor Mattson for presidential elector. Dolsen was unable to collect the required 697 signatures to be on the ballot for Congress, so he too was a write-in candidate.[15]

In the spring of 1925, the Southern California comrades entered candidates in two nonpartisan elections. Emanuel Levin, candidate for the Los Angeles school board, got 26,525 votes, about 18 percent of the total. The candidate for San Pedro City Council got 70 votes. These seem to have been the party's first foray into local elections anywhere in the state.[16]

Californians and Soviet Agricultural Communes

Beginning in 1919, a branch of the Society for Technical Aid to the Soviet Union was active in San Francisco. Among other activities, it recruited party members to go to the Soviet Union to help build socialism. Twenty-two members of the San Francisco Union of Russian Toilers, a party branch, embarked for the Soviet Union in early 1921. In 1922 the Society for Technical Aid recruited party members for the California Commune, an agricultural commune on the North Caucasus steppe. Some twenty-five to thirty agricultural communes were established there in the early 1920s, including several by American CP members. For such undertakings, the Soviet government provided a long-term lease on land but required commune members to bring modern American agricultural equipment and two years' worth of supplies.[17]

Many recruits for the California Commune were former immigrants to the United States from the Russian empire or Eastern Europe, but the commune had enough members who did not speak Russian that it had an English-speaking party branch. The project got off to a rocky start. A representative later reported, "The delegate sent by the commune to select a suitable location for the commune was not the proper man for such an important errand and the land selected by him was not in a location suitable for intensive farming." Commune members also faced other serious problems, especially malaria and lack of housing. Malaria was so serious that the commune moved to another location in 1923.[18]

In March 1924 a commune representative in San Francisco was seeking additional members for the fourth group to go to the commune. He reported that twenty-seven men, nine women, and eleven children currently lived there, and described the commune as consisting of nearly eleven square miles, including "five wells of good drinking water," a flour mill, orchard, two big barns, a "neglected" brickyard, and a vineyard. Most buildings, he admitted, needed "heavy repairs," but there was "a large, comfortable house" and "six smaller ones." The *kommunary* had 140 acres under cultivation and 600 acres plowed for spring planting. Their livestock included "40 oxen [steers?], 26 cows, 86 sheep, 35 goats, 55 hogs, beehives, poultry, etc." The commune boasted modern agricultural machinery from the United States, including a Best caterpillar tractor (manufactured in an East Bay plant), two Fordson tractors, a threshing machine, a binder, and two trucks— better equipment than many U.S. farmers had at the time. Those wishing to join the commune had to contribute all of their savings, with a required minimum of $250 (equivalent to nearly $4,500 in 2023), and any tools and machinery they owned.[19] The commune needed new members with particular skills. In August 1924, as a sixth group was forming, the commune was specifically seeking "a good dairyman who is able to make cheese and butter for export, a winemaker, an all-around blacksmith and several good mechanics who are able to operate tractors."[20]

In early 1926, nearly four years after the founding of the commune, the *Daily Worker* published a glowing report: the commune had grown to 140 members and, "in spite of many obstacles," was "on a sound economic basis." The account noted some continuing difficulties: "There is the task of educating our membership and drawing them more fully in to the activities of socialist construction. Our newly formed Communist nucleus is on the job and hopes in record time to liquidate all traces of illiteracy both political and ordinary." The Communist nucleus failed. Half the commune, representing twelve national backgrounds, continually wrangled with the other half, composed mostly of ethnic Russians. In December 1926 the non-Russians left for their own commune, Pioneer. The remaining California kommunary dispersed soon after, in late 1926 and early 1927, taking back whatever remained of their initial capital through state-run sales of the commune's property. The Pioneer commune dissolved soon after. Some former kommunary returned to the United States, some went to other communes, and some relocated elsewhere in the Soviet Union.[21]

Enoch Nelson chose a different route to go to the Soviet Union. He grew up in the Finnish community near Fort Bragg, north of San Francisco, where the Communist Party was active. In early 1921 he contributed regular articles about those Finnish comrades to *Toveri*, the party's Finnish-language newspaper. In 1922 he went to Karelia, the part of Soviet Russia nearest Finland, where the local language was similar to Finnish. There Enoch became a Soviet citizen and party member. He first worked in lumbering and as a *politruk*, a political instructor, whose duties were "to encourage the workers" and prevent sabotage. In 1924 he relocated to the Seattle commune in the North Caucasus, created in 1922 by a group of mostly Finnish Americans from the Pacific Northwest, but soon returned to Karelia. There he remained until 1937–1938, when he was among the two thousand or more Finns executed as part of the Great Terror.[22]

Life in the Party in the Mid-1920s

While some Californians struggled with communal agriculture on the North Caucasus steppe, the California party—District 13—wrestled with its own problems. District 13 included other southwestern states, but almost no trace of them appears in the surviving District 13 files or in the party's weekly newspapers. In 1922 District 13 reported just over five hundred members. Twenty-two were members of English branches, and the rest—the large majority—belonged to foreign-language branches, organizational forms inherited from the SPA.[23] Los Angeles had English, Finnish, Hungarian, Jewish, and Lithuanian branches. The Jewish branch was the largest. San Francisco, at various times in the early 1920s, had English, Estonian, Finnish, German, Greek, Hungarian, Italian, Jewish, Latvian, Lithuanian, Russian, and South Slav branches, none as dominant as the Jewish branch was in the south. Finnish branches flourished in Fort Bragg and Eureka, on the coast two hundred to three hundred miles north of San Francisco. The language branches typically met once or twice a month and often sponsored social events on weekends, often musical presentations by party members, which were almost always followed by dancing.[24]

The district had a weekly newspaper from May 1, 1920, until mid-May 1925, titled the *Rank and File* during its first three years, which was then renamed *Labor Unity*. Early issues carried news and ads for various left and labor organizations, including the SPA. After Dolsen became assistant editor in mid-1921, the paper became more obviously a CP organ.[25] *Labor Unity* replaced *Rank and File* on May 1, 1923, and the change involved more than just the publication's name. The paper no longer carried notices or ads for other left organizations, although there remained a few nods toward the Socialist Labor Party.[26]

By early 1924 District 13 was renting space at 225 Valencia Street, a large commercial building in a neighborhood that included housing and manufacturing. Most party meetings were held at that address. In March 1924 the party's Paris Commune meeting featured speakers, several musical numbers, and dancing. In August the party offered a debate on La Follette and Foster as presidential candidates. For the largest gatherings the party rented California Hall, owned by a consortium of German cultural organizations. There party members celebrated the seventh anniversary of the Bolshevik seizure of power with a mass meeting. Dolsen, now district organizer (DO), spoke, followed by singing by the International Chorus, composed of party members and sympathizers, and dancing. Such events came every few months, typically geared to some event or to raising funds for some cause.[27]

Despite successful events, the party faced serious financial problems. A report in March 1924 on Northern California branches found that of 504 members, only 318 had paid their dues. In September 1924 *Labor Unity* reported the result of the paper's attacks on La Follette: "Many of our readers . . . parted from us." In April 1925 one party member wrote to the national office, "Our 13th district is without any funds." The next month, the District Executive Committee (DEC) directed that the next issue of *Labor Unity* carry a statement that the paper would close down unless funds were forthcoming. No funds came forth, and *Labor Unity* closed down. Financial problems plagued the DO. In early March 1925

Dolsen asked the national office to replace him as DO and complained that he was owed over two hundred dollars in back salary, having been paid only ninety dollars over the previous two months. Noting his own "great personal sacrifices," he urged that the new DO be paid thirty-five dollars (equivalent to more than six hundred dollars in 2023), apparently per week although not specified in the source.[28]

Financial problems coincided with dissatisfaction over Dolsen's leadership, especially in Southern California. Writing on behalf of Los Angeles CP members, Emanuel Levin asked the Central Executive Committee (CEC) to remove Dolsen as DO, because his "ability as a clerk or office executive might be useful to the Party in other cities and States," but "his absolute incompetence as an Organizer has kept our organization back so long we now appeal to your committee to *remove him immediately and send us a competent man* [emphasis in original]." Levin, a former Marine, former head of the Young Men's Hebrew Association in San Francisco, former IWW member, and founding member of the party in Los Angeles, continued, "Comrade Ella Reeve Bloor has done much good organization work here . . . but when she leaves we shall again have the utter indifference of our present District Organizer to contend with." Levin complained that the DEC "has now reached a point where it knows nothing of, and cares nothing about, any place in the state except San Francisco." Finally, on behalf of his comrades, he recommended that "'Labor Unity' be discontinued, as it has no value now, as an influence on the labor movement and is a draw back [*sic*] to the Party growth in San Francisco."[29]

In March 1925 the CEC sent Tom Lewis from Oregon to replace Dolsen as DO and assigned Dolsen to take charge of *Labor Unity* and remedy the paper's "anti-Party tendencies," especially "appeals for unity with the SP [Socialist Party]." Those changes took place in April; the final issue of the paper came in late May. Lewis remained as DO for less than a year. In October 1925, once debts to the national office and operating expenses were deducted from income, only $6.71 was left for the DO's monthly wages. Lewis was blunt: "No one can give their whole time to the duties and live according to the present income of the district."[30]

In late November 1925, William Schneiderman, in Los Angeles, complained to Ruthenberg, "It is imperative that we get a D.O. who can function as a D.O., and until we get some one [*sic*] to fill Comrade Lewis' place, who is only acting in a routine capacity until his place can be filled, the district here is in a badly demoralized condition." Schneiderman asked if a special district convention could elect a new DO, but he misunderstood the relation between the district and the center. Ruthenberg replied, "The election of a D.O. is not by a District Convention," and the CEC "has recommended to the D.E.C. that Comrade Emanuel Levin be elected the D.O." The DEC balked, discussed the matter for several meetings, and then finally accepted Levin, who took over in February. Dolsen was assigned to work outside the district.[31]

Before leaving, Lewis fired off a scathing letter to Jay Lovestone in the national office, responding to Lovestone's efforts to wring money out of the district: "It is you and your methods that are turning the trick that you would like to charge to me (namely of ruining the District) You want me to forward you a check for the amount due the N.O. [national office] when their [*sic*] is no money in the treasury."[32]

Amid these problems, Ella Reeve "Mother" Bloor worked as field organizer. Born on Staten Island in 1862, daughter of a Union veteran of the Civil War, Bloor was sixty years old when she sought the appointment in California. She brought long experience in political activism—advocate for child labor laws and woman suffrage, director of the committee appointed by President Theodore Roosevelt to investigate the meatpacking industry in the aftermath of Upton Sinclair's *The Jungle*, organizer for unions, SPA officer, SPA candidate for state office in Connecticut, and founding member of the CLP. The divorced mother of six children and a tireless organizer at an age when many would have sought less demanding work, Bloor earned the honorific "Mother" in more ways than one.[33]

Bloor kept busy. In the last two weeks of November 1924, she had almost one speaking engagement each day in the Bay Area. In March 1925 she "organized an English Branch at Santa Barbara, in southern California, of 10 members" and "locals in Palo Alto, San Jose, Santa Cruz," all just south of San Francisco. She was the May Day speaker at Richmond, across the bay from San Francisco, under the auspices of "the Finnish Comrades." Later that year, she "developed unemployed and other United Front Campaigns" and "organized new Locals of Workers Party" along with "Young Workers Leagues and Junior Leagues."[34]

By 1925 William Schneiderman had emerged as an important leader in Los Angeles. Born in Russia in 1905, he came to the United States with his parents in 1908. The family first located in Chicago, where Schneiderman's father contracted tuberculosis, necessitating a move to Los Angeles in the early 1920s. Schneiderman worked during the day and took high school classes at night. At sixteen he joined the YWL. After high school he enrolled at the University of California Southern Branch (now UCLA), where, in 1924, he helped organize a Foster for President club. In 1925, at the age of twenty, he was elected secretary for the Los Angeles Workers Party local and held similar office in the local YWL.[35]

Reports from the FBI's Los Angeles field office for early 1925 suggest that Bloor and Schneiderman were among the most prominent public faces of the Communist Party in that area. On January 25 some 650 people attended a meeting in the Music Arts Hall. Schneiderman, speaking from a red-draped speakers' stand, memorialized Vladimir Lenin, Karl Liebknecht, and Rosa Luxemburg. He was followed by a Russian speaker and singing by YWL members. Communists held such memorial meetings across the country that month.[36]

Three years earlier, in 1922, many of the top leaders of the party had been arrested and indicted under Michigan's criminal syndicalism law. Ruthenberg was convicted and was appealing his conviction. Other defendants remained on bail pending the outcome of Ruthenberg's appeal. The Labor Defense Council, formed to raise defense funds, was an early effort to create a mass organization— that is, one not limited to party members. On February 22, 1925, about four hundred people, among whom the FBI estimated 25 percent were women, gathered at Music Arts Hall in Los Angeles to protest the criminal syndicalism law and raise funds for the Michigan criminal syndicalism defendants. The FBI report gibed, "The Communists always are late in starting as they take so much time to sell literature and get the money out of those present as it is for this reason that the meetings are called." Bloor was the principal speaker, announcing that "she had come to Los Angeles to make the 'White Spot' red." (The *Los Angeles Times* liked to call Los Angeles "the White Spot of America," free of Communism, crime, corruption, and unions.) The FBI report added, "[Bloor] stated that nothing on earth can stop the fall of this system of government and while the Communists do not advocate a bloody revolution they know that it is inevitable and want to be ready for it when it comes."[37]

Four weeks later, on March 18, 1925, some 190 people attended a Los Angeles meeting celebrating the anniversary of the Paris Commune. The FBI reported, "The audience was composed principally of Russian Jews, Greeks, Americans, Slavs, in fact over 85 per cent of the audience were foreigners." The meeting opened with the "Internationale," anthem of the movement, and then Schneiderman spoke on the criminal syndicalism law and explained that the purpose of the nationwide Paris Commune meetings was to raise funds for the Michigan defendants. He first asked for donations of five dollars (equivalent to $88 in 2023). When no one offered that amount, he reduced his request to one dollar, then even less. A second speaker compared the errors of the Paris Commune with the "correct" tactics of the Bolsheviks in 1917 and 1918, especially creation of the Red Army and the Cheka (the Bolsheviks' secret police, later the NKVD and still later the KGB).[38]

May Day was always a time for speeches, singing, and dancing. Schneiderman and Bloor were the lead speakers at the 1925 May Day meeting in Los Angeles. The FBI report estimated attendance at two thousand, with another fifteen hundred turned away. The hall was draped in red and decorated with portraits of Lenin, Leon Trotsky, and Karl Marx. Schneiderman introduced Bloor, who again spoke about turning the white spot red, and then introduced the party's "Junior chorus," which led the singing of the "Internationale." They were followed by the

YWL chorus, another speaker, and performances by the youth groups. A dance the next day featured everything "in red—lights, garments and music."[39]

The FBI's Los Angeles field office closely watched the local CP in the mid-1920s but significantly overestimated the number of members. A report in 1923 claimed the party had 1,800–2,000 members in Southern California, of whom about 700 were "active." Both numbers significantly exceeded the party's own count of 500 for the entire state. That FBI report credited the Trade Union Educational League (TUEL) with 250 members, of whom 25–40 percent were party members. Other party groups identified by the FBI included the YCL, 200 members; Friends of the Soviet Union, 2,000 members, of whom 500 were "active"; the Technical Aid Society, 200 members, most of whom were party members; the Labor Defense Council, thought to have about 200 members; and the Workers Party, 187 members in eight branches.[40] The last figures—about 200—most closely correspond to the party's own count of members. If the FBI's figures for the other organizations are anywhere close to accurate, it suggests that the Friends of the Soviet Union attracted ten times as many supporters as the party itself.

Like those in Los Angeles, the San Francisco comrades were busy with meetings. The schedule for March, April, and May 1925 included a "Lettish [Latvian] dance," "Esthonian [*sic*] entertainment & dance," "Jewish entertainment and dance," meetings of the English, Lithuanian, and Greek branches, a benefit for Irish relief, the annual Paris Commune meeting, a "Grand musical program," and a big May Day celebration. They also presented two films, *Beauty and the Bolshevik* and *Russia in Overalls*, followed by dancing. Other events included an evening of musical performances, a Sunday afternoon picnic along the bay with singing by the Finnish chorus from Berkeley, and a weekly class on public speaking and parliamentary procedure.[41]

By early 1927, District 13 headquarters had moved to 1212 Market Street, a three-story commercial building a few blocks from city hall. Other tenants included a business school and a dance academy. District 13's space seems to have been on the ground floor with a storefront on the street, sufficiently large to accommodate some two hundred people for a Ruthenberg memorial in May 1927. That event opened with "the Red funeral march" and concluded with the Freiheit Gesangverein (Freedom Singing Society) singing the "Internationale," which may have annoyed the business students. The district held a summer school in its front room in 1928.[42]

Outreach to Asian Americans

In the mid-1920s District 13 worked to recruit from the state's Chinese, Japanese, and South Asian communities. In January 1925 Dolsen asked the national office for literature in Chinese and Japanese, but the reply, four months later, was that there was no literature available in Chinese or Japanese and that "a great deal of the propaganda work for Communism which is being carried on in China is being done thru English literature." In June 1925 District 13 held a mass meeting in San Francisco in support of anti-imperialist activities in China, and the Los Angeles subdistrict held two "Hands Off China" mass meetings.[43]

In San Francisco, Dolsen worked with representatives of the local Kuomintang (the Chinese Nationalist Party) to prepare *Awakening of China*, a book published in 1926 by Daily Worker Publishing. Until 1927 the Chinese Communist Party had formed a united front with the Kuomintang, and the Kuomintang received aid and support from the Soviet Union. Given Dolsen's book and his diminishing support as DO, he was sent to Moscow in October 1926 to join a Comintern commission to China. He remained in China, with a visit to the Philippines, until 1931.[44]

There was another flurry of interest in recruiting Chinese Americans in early 1927. Levin, then DO, promoted *Chinese Guide in America*, a publication by Chinese students and Chinese Americans in the Bay Area. "The editor," Levin specified, "is under our direct guidance and direction." He sent copies to all U.S. branches of the Kuomintang and Chinese student organizations and had copies distributed during Chinese New Year celebrations in San Francisco. He also worked closely with the local Kuomintang, hoping to "pick out those Chinese" who could be brought into the party. Ruthenberg described this as "very valuable" and confirmed the correctness of trying to recruit "the most advanced people" among the Kuomintang. Ruthenberg died soon after, and the San Francisco memorial meeting included representatives from the local Kuomintang and the "Society for the Advance of Sun Yet Senism in America." Interest in working with the Kuomintang ended in April 1927 when Chiang Kai-shek, the Kuomintang leader in China, attacked his Communist allies.[45]

Dolsen also initiated outreach to South Asians. In January 1924 Ruthenberg wrote to Dolsen regarding "a group of Hindus in San Francisco . . . in close contact with our Party organization," hoping to connect them to the CP in India. A year later Dolsen wrote to Ruthenberg, "Several times I have written you regarding the desire of the Hindus of the state, who are mostly farmers, emigrating in mass [*sic*] to Russia." Dolsen later emphasized how useful "the Hindus" could be to Russia. Ruthenberg finally replied that "the Soviet Government" had declined because "it would be difficult under the present conditions to absorb these Hindoo workers." District 13 apparently maintained contact with South Asians, as the Ruthenberg memorial service included representatives from the Hindustan Ghadar Party, which sought an independent India.[46]

In March 1924 Dolsen organized a mass meeting at California Hall in support of Philippine independence. The meeting, with a long list of speakers, was declared a "huge success" and raised $64 (equivalent to more than $1,125 in 2023).[47] But, like Dolsen's initiatives with Asian immigrants, that issue disappeared from the party's activities after Dolsen's departure.

Reorganization and Its Problems, 1925–1928

The experiences of District 13 members in the mid-1920s took place within the larger context of Comintern-ordered organizational changes intended to strengthen the party but that significantly complicated the work of party leaders. After the Comintern forced the CPA and CLP to merge, divisions continued. Some argued to liquidate the underground organization and become completely aboveground and legal. Others insisted that governmental repression and the Russian model both pointed to the need to remain underground. At the Michigan convention that preceded the arrests in 1922, Comintern representatives tried to persuade their U.S. comrades to liquidate the underground organization but secured only a compromise. One consequence was that the party's public name became the Workers (Communist) Party.[48]

Another complication arose from the continued prominence of the foreign-language federations. In 1923 the Executive Committee of the Comintern (ECCI) called for the U.S. comrades to create an English-language newspaper no later than November of that year; the *Daily Worker* missed that deadline, making its debut in January 1924. In early 1925 the ECCI directed the U.S. party to undertake a major reorganization, replacing the language federations with shop and street (neighborhood) nuclei. The intent was to integrate and assimilate members of those federations into both the broader life of the party and political life more generally. However, reorganization produced a sharp drop in members nationwide, from 14,037 in September 1925 to 7,214 in October.[49]

In California the large majority of members belonged to language branches. As of March 1924, among 504 members in Northern California, only 60 were in the two English branches. The two Finnish branches, north of San Francisco, accounted for 240 members, 48 percent of the total. The language branches, with their regular entertainment and dancing, were as much—or more—social as political organizations, based on language and culture. California DOs dutifully worked to implement reorganization. In May 1925 in San Francisco, a membership mass meeting and branch meetings emphasized reorganization into shop and street nuclei—that is, organizations based on place of residence or place of work. In January 1926, in one of his final acts as DO, Lewis reported the results: "This district is on the road to reorganization. . . . We have not lost over ten per cent of our membership thru-out the whole district." Lewis was too optimistic. In late March 1926 the national organization department scolded Levin, DO since February, because dues-paying members from District 13 had fallen from an average of 804 in 1925 to 349 in 1926. There was slight improvement in 1927, when District 13 claimed 439 members and the YWL another 50–65. That year, there were twenty-two street nuclei accounting for 428 members and just two shop nuclei with a total of 11 members.[50]

Though Lewis had reported District 13 "on the road to reorganization" in January 1926, surviving correspondence in RGASPI tells a different story, as organized language groups continued to exist under different names, including Jewish and Hungarian groups in Los Angeles and Russian and Greek "comrades" in San Francisco. In mid-1926 Levin complained that new reporting forms were problematic for leaders of the new nuclei: "Because of their poor English they could not fill out their reports." This, Levin concluded, was "one of the first reasons why many responsible and old time party members were not taking leading parts after the reorganization. They were afraid of their English." Levin reported that he was trying to keep those comrades involved in the party.[51]

By 1928, with reorganization apparently complete, District 13 claimed 514 members, of whom 417 were in street nuclei, 11 in the lumber industry nucleus, and 34 in the district's four farm nuclei. There were 35 members at large. The remaining 17 were not accounted for. The district reported that its TUEL was functioning in the Los Angeles needle trades, which were heavily Jewish, but not anywhere else in the district.[52]

Failure of Electoral Politics, 1926–1928

Amid reorganization in April 1926, the Comintern's National Secretariat for America and Canada (predecessor of the Anglo-American Secretariat) sought information on the candidacy of Upton Sinclair for governor and on "united front action with the Socialist Party." The RGASPI files include "Suggestions for the 1926 Political Campaign in California." Of central concern was the decision by Upton Sinclair, progressive-era muckraker and novelist, to run for governor as a Socialist and opponent of the criminal syndicalism law. The "Suggestions" were that the California comrades seek a united labor ticket and avoid "open conflict with Sinclair or Socialist Party." Reasoning that Sinclair's candidacy was intended to strengthen the SPA, the "Suggestions" argued for turning the campaign into an "ideological campaign for independent working class political action" with the "ultimate aim" to "throw Sinclair into conflict with S.P." Simply stated, the California party was to propose a United Front as a ploy to disrupt the Socialists' campaign and recruit some of their members.[53]

The "Suggestions" called for having "Miss Whitney come to the front" and confer directly with Sinclair on the idea of a labor party. Whitney declined. According to Levin, "She feels that she personally has been used too much." He attributed her hesitancy to "political immaturity" and being "oversensitive about coming to the front as a person." Levin remained hopeful that he could convince her: "She must understand that she does not represent herself." Whitney continued to refuse, perhaps because she saw through the maneuvering.[54]

The District 13 Executive Committee waited until mid-July to launch their campaign for a "United Political front." In a letter to the state SPA, the DEC proposed "to issue jointly a call to all labor unions and workers Fraternal Organizations for the purpose of placing into the field a united labor ticket." The Socialists' reply is not in the files, but the DEC's five-page response, on July 21, emphasized that the CP was proposing not a joint slate of candidates but "a conference of delegates" to form a united labor front. The DEC also derided the SPA as reformist and charged them with failing to understand that "in order to abolish capitalism, and to establish Socialism, the workers must first achieve control of the governmental power as was done in Russia," and that "all history shows that a ruling, privileged class has never given up power without resorting to force to maintain its privileged position." After that lesson in Leninism, the DEC urged the SPA to send a committee to meet with their committee and with representatives of unions to plan a conference for a united front.[55]

Other letters in the exchange are missing, but the SPA's final refusal was just as testy as the DEC's earlier letter. The SPA chairman and secretary began by noting, "Your suggestions of a convention for a united front are altogether too late," since the SPA had long since nominated its own candidates. The Socialists then charged, "You split off from our organization and created the divided front." Further, the CP had "avowed . . . to destroy our organization," and the CP's own publications described "the united front as a 'Manoeuvre' [*sic*] by which you can get in touch with our members and create dissatisfaction and discord among them." Claiming that the CP was "regarded with suspicion and hostility by the whole labor movement," the SP dismissed the Communists as "an insignificant fraction of the working-class." After those insults, the SPA suggested that the CP could, on its own, call a convention and nominate candidates for those state offices for which the SPA had not nominated anyone.[56] In the end, there were no CP or "United Front" candidates on the ballot. The entire exchange, on both sides, seems intended solely to demonstrate the perfidy of the other. Sinclair took no part, apparently did not campaign for governor, and routinely refused all requests to speak until after he completed his current novel. He drew 4 percent of the vote.[57]

In 1927, for the first time, the party placed a candidate on the ballot in the nonpartisan election for supervisor in San Francisco. (Supervisors are the equivalent of city council members in San Francisco's combined city-county government;

they were then elected at large.) Among thirty-one candidates, nine were to be elected. The CP candidate placed twenty-seventh, with 6,082 votes, more than the SP's candidate but fewer than a candidate who had died several weeks before the election. That was apparently the only election in 1927 in which the California CP presented a candidate.[58] Members of the DEC subsequently claimed that this accomplishment came despite many failures by Levin, including choosing the candidate "at the last moment" and having "no real campaign."[59] Surviving minutes of the DEC include no discussion of the 1927 elections.

In the state elections of 1928, District 13 failed not only to get a place on the ballot but even to mount a significant write-in campaign. Early that year, Levin submitted a thirteen-page report on the tasks facing District 13. After a reasonably perceptive overview of state politics, he suggested the possibility of "a Labor Party sentiment" but committed the DEC only to "make a detailed program for the formation of Trade Union Committees for a Labor Party"[60]—in other words, to study the possibility of forming committees to create a party. There's no indication that any of that was done. Gitlow then came to California and directed the DEC to persuade Sinclair to commit to a united labor ticket "before Socialist Party gets agreement with him." I found no indication of any effort in District 13 either to create a united labor ticket or to reach out to Sinclair.[61]

Other files for District 13 in 1928 include nothing about the 1928 elections until after the fact, when there are three long postmortems on the multiple failures of District 13: failure to get on the ballot as a party, failure to get the party's candidates on the ballot as independents, and failure to inform party members and sympathizers how to write in the party's candidates. A ten-page summary, month by month, charts the CEC's efforts to direct and support District 13 and the failure of the District 13 leadership to act. The report noted that Whitney had agreed to be a candidate for the U.S. Senate but was not on the ballot. On October 26, 1928, W. A. Jackson of Oakland wrote to Bertram Wolfe about the failure of "the Negro candidate for Assemblyman in the 39th Assembly District" to get on the ballot, attributing that failure to "the inexcusable lack of preparations on the part of the DO. . . . From the DO down . . . they approached the entire campaign blindly and haphazardly." Jackson had similar complaints about the party's failure to get on the ballot statewide.[62]

That Jackson addressed his letter to Wolfe suggests that Wolfe may have written the five-page "Report on California: Why the Workers Party did not get on the Ballot." That report began by noting that Lovestone had asked the author to look into that question and that the author had conducted many interviews. The report explained that thirty-six thousand signatures were needed to get the party on the ballot and twelve thousand signatures were necessary to place individuals on the ballot without a party designation. The party collected only four thousand.

Levin left the district during a crucial part of the signature-gathering campaign. When that campaign failed, there was no planning to distribute instructions on writing in the party's candidates. Foster got only 112 write-in votes in California. Whitney did slightly better, with 154 votes. The report specified, "The failure to get on the ballot is only one of the symptoms of the diseased state of the district."[63]

The report also analyzed the state of the party: "There are no functioning shop nuclei in the Party in the entire state of California." The existing nuclei "were not drawn into the campaign." The fractions in the unions were not functioning, and "the election campaign was not carried into the unions." All the party's efforts had been marked by "incompetence and inefficiency." Further, "the sympathizers were not mobilized anywhere," and there was "no real effort" to reach out to the Black community in Oakland. Leading comrades, including Whitney, had not been informed that the CEC had offered money and organizers to help with the campaign and that Levin had rejected the offer.[64]

The report then turned to the "poor composition of the Party," beginning with the observation that "Our Party in California is a Workers Party in name only"; that only 40 percent of the members, at most, were workers in industry; and that in Los Angeles many of the members were "petty shop keepers" or "small employers of labor." The Los Angeles party was "overwhelmingly Jewish," and there was not a single Mexican at the membership meeting. In Oakland, home to the largest African American community in the Bay Area, there were only two Black members.[65]

The most serious charges came toward the end of the report: "There are many signs of decay and degeneration in the Party in California," including "extreme cynicism as to the whole scheme of reorganization." Many of the "most loyal, self-sacrificing and active" members "have dropped out of the Party," and others "have been driven out." "The atmosphere of the Party is one of personal gossip, rumors, scandals, investigation of private lives, family life, etc." And, even worse, "There is general cynicism concerning the CEC and the Comintern . . . the persistent commission of right errors . . . lack of self-criticism . . . conspiracy to suppress all criticism." In sum, "The district has gone ideologically from bad to worse."[66]

The report concluded with recommendations: an open letter to all California units about the deficiencies of the party and the need for reorganization, reorganization of the DEC, the Los Angeles sub-DEC, and "the District as a whole." "The District Organizer [Levin] is not competent" either in "organizational ability or ideology" and should be removed. Neither of Levin's assistants, J. G. Manus and Henry Gliksohn, "is competent to act even temporarily." The report suggested that if no one from the east were available as DO, Bloor should be appointed as acting DO. The report concluded that unless these drastic measures were taken, "the district will continue to degenerate ideologically, to lose membership, to be inactive, and to show increasing signs of internal decay."[67]

A few months later, Bloor added her criticism: in Los Angeles County, "there were 60,000 Negroes alone and 60,000 Mexicans and not one single Negro member of the Party except one. . . . They have no Negro committee in the whole district, they had no Women's Department, they had one T.U.E.L. unit." Levin was no longer DO by then, but Bloor also noted that Levin was a member of "the Opposition Group"—that is, the faction opposing Lovestone. Levin was assigned to other work: he became secretary of the Workers Ex-Servicemen's League, later helped to initiate the Veterans Bonus March on Washington in 1932, was treasurer of the Veterans National Liaison Committee, and then became circulation manager and business manager for the *Daily Worker* in New York.[68]

All of this criticism was overlaid by factionalism. Wolfe and Levin were in different factions, and Wolfe's criticism of the entire district must be read in that light. It seems highly likely that the party's organizational failures in the late 1920s were due in part—likely in major part—to intense factionalism.

"UNCEASING FACTIONAL STRUGGLE,"
1925–1930

Factionalism consumed the U.S. Communist Party from the mid-1920s until 1929–1930 and became particularly intense in District 13. At the national level, factionalism was finally resolved after intervention by the Comintern, including Stalin. Earl Browder emerged as the dominant figure nationally, and District 13 acquired yet another district organizer. Those changes coincided with the onset of the Great Depression, which moved members' attentions to economic issues in the larger society. However, District 13 party's descent into factionalism became much worse before it began to resolve.

Intensification of Factionalism, 1924–1929

Underlying District 13's electoral failures in 1926 and 1928, the many deficiencies delineated in the 1928 election analysis, the revolving door for the district organizer, and the difficulties caused by reorganization was a continuing and increasingly acrimonious factional divisiveness driven at the national level as much by personalities as by basic ideology. The mid- and late 1920s saw bitter factional struggles in both Moscow and the U.S. party. In Moscow the death of Lenin in 1924 set off a power struggle from which Stalin emerged dominant in late 1927 after the removal of Trotsky, Grigory Zinoviev, and Lev Kamenev from the Central Committee. During those struggles in Moscow, U.S. party leaders sided with one faction or another, and the U.S. factions rose or fell with their Moscow allies. In the early 1920s, one U.S. faction formed around William Z. Foster, who came from a background of union organizing and led the Trade Union Educational League, which sought to organize within AFL unions. James P. Cannon, head of the International Labor Defense (ILD), an affiliate of the Comintern's International Red Aid (MOPR), led another faction, allied first with Foster and then with Charles Ruthenberg. Ruthenberg, who had come from the language federations and the CPA, became party secretary in 1922 and died in 1927. Ruthenberg was succeeded by Jay Lovestone, who had come from the left of the SPA before joining the CPA. Foster and Cannon then became allies against Lovestone.[1]

Factional struggles extended deeply into District 13. In 1925, during the district convention, a delegate struck Emanuel Levin in response to one of his parliamentary rulings. A San Francisco party member complained to Ruthenberg about that convention: "Minority was not given any consideration whatsoever. . . . Convention was conducted to intensifie [sic] Factional Fight." The extended discussion in the District Executive Committee over approval of Levin as DO in late 1925 (see previous chapter) likely reflected such factionalism. Factionalism seemed to be especially intense in Los Angeles. In early 1926 the Workers Party committee in Los Angeles held a long discussion on the local divisions, partly revolving around personalities but including differences over several CP-related activities, notably a cooperative bakery, the party's Cooperative Center, and a party school. Tom Lewis, recently appointed as DO, concluded, "Both groups violated party decisions and discipline." In May 1926 a special convention of the Los Angeles subdistrict was scheduled to end factional fighting. It began by considering a resolution that described the former Subdistrict Executive Committee (SDEC) as "consisting of petty bourgeois and ultra-left as well as ultra-right deviations." William Schneiderman, a convention delegate, condemned the resolution as "irresponsible." The minutes recorded "considerable turmoil" before the resolution was sent back to committee. Shortly after the convention, one SDEC member asked to resign because, he said, "He is certain the Sub-Dist E.C. will not tolerate opposition and since he is in opposition" there was no reason for him to continue.[2]

Just as local factional leaders took their disputes to the state or national level, so factional leaders at the national level repeatedly took their arguments to Moscow, to the Anglo-American Secretariat and its predecessors, or to various American Commissions specially organized by the ECCI, hoping to receive the Comintern's blessing for their faction. In June 1927 the Presidium of the Comintern gave detailed and specific directions for a U.S. convention to end the factional fighting. Selection of convention delegates was hard fought. When the California state convention deadlocked, it sent two delegations, one for each faction. That national convention failed to resolve the factional conflict. Early in 1928 the AAS in Moscow heard from a number of Americans, including Earl Browder,

Sam Darcy, and Harrison George. They all denounced factionalism, and several denounced each other for factional activities.[3]

In District 13 in October 1927, shortly after the national convention that failed to end factionalism, Fred Harris tried to resign from the DEC with a long letter decrying factionalism, in which he specified, "As the result of a pernicious and systematic display of factionalism by members of the former opposition group, Comrade Manus engaged in a physical attack against Comrade Fleming." Harris concluded, "Factionalism must cease, but if you persist in it and burden the D.E.C. meetings with it to the midnight hour, to only culminate in fist fights, then I shall let you fight it out until you realize your stubborn folly, but I am not going to be a participant." The DEC denied Harris's request to resign, but he continued to ask.[4]

In 1928 Cannon announced his support for Trotsky, who had lost to Stalin in their struggle for power within the Soviet Union and had gone into internal exile. In response, the U.S. party expelled Cannon, which affected some members in District 13. Anita Whitney became suspect after she talked with a Cannon supporter. At the direction of the Central Committee, Levin wrote to Whitney and two others, assuring them that no one suspected them of supporting "the Cannon Trotsky opposition." However, since they had spoken with a Cannon supporter, they were directed to provide the DO with "all information regarding this matter," including a written statement of their "attitude towards the Cannon Trotsky danger," and to do so "at your earliest opportunity."[5] The RGASPI files did not include Whitney's response, if she ever made one.

Schneiderman was also affected. The FBI's Los Angeles field office reported that, in late 1928, Schneiderman "departed from the 'Bolshevik Line' going over to the Trotzky faction, after which on December 29th of that year orders were issued by the Communist Party of the U.S.A. to the Central Committee of District 13, reading as follows: 'To remove from all Party offices and to suspend from the Party, WILLIAM SCHNEIDERMAN, member of the California District Executive Committee and California Young Workers League District organizer, as a supporter of Trotzkyisms.[']" However, the FBI report continued, "There is supporting evidence to the effect that SCHNEIDERMAN's expulsion was a pre-arranged affair so that he could get all of the inside facts as an undercover agent of the regular Communist Party, District 13, as to the plans, membership strength, etc., of the Trotzky faction which had split away from the C.P.U.S.A. During the year 1929 nothing is recorded as to SCHNEIDERMAN's activities. He was apparently 'boring from within' the Trotzky faction and helping to 'liquidate' it." The RGASPI files tell a different, if much briefer, story. In January 1929, Lovestone wired District 13, "Unanimous Polcom decision Schneiderman be reinstated in party but censured severely for his connections with Cannon. . . . Schneiderman cannot hold any party office for one year."[6]

CHAPTER 2

Harrison George and the American Bureau
of the Pan-Pacific Trade Union Secretariat

In San Francisco in the late 1920s, Harrison George emerged as a prominent factionalist. He did so as head of the American Bureau of the Pan-Pacific Trade Union Secretariat (PPTUS). By then the party seemed less interested in recruiting among Asian immigrants in California than in using San Francisco as a base for organizing efforts in Eastern Asia by the Red International of Labor Unions (RILU, or Profintern). The Profintern sought to build Communist unions in that region through the PPTUS, which had developed from an initiative by the Labor Council of New South Wales, which produced an initial meeting in Sydney in 1926 and then the founding meeting in Hankow in 1927.[7]

The U.S. party representatives at Hankow were Earl Browder and Harrison George. Two years later, in 1929, George was appointed to head the American Bureau of the PPTUS in San Francisco. He had been among the IWW members sentenced to federal prison in 1918 and had served five years. Close to Browder, George had once been married to Browder's sister. A few historians have suggested that the PPTUS, which operated secretly in those parts of Eastern Asia where the Communist Party was illegal, may have been a training ground for covert activities. Harvey Klehr and his colleagues, in *The Secret World of American Communism*, note that in January 1929 Browder wrote of needing George for "special work" in the PPTUS, which they surmise meant underground activities.[8]

In San Francisco, George's PPTUS activities seem to have involved writing articles for CP journals and producing propaganda for China, Japan, India, and the Philippines. George and a few comrades prepared, translated, and printed that propaganda and then tried to find seamen willing to smuggle it into Japan and China. Joe Koide, who worked with George for some eighteen months, later testified that the major activity of the PPTUS was the preparation of its magazine, the *Pacific Worker*, for which George wrote a few articles each month. Koide translated them into Japanese and delivered them, and apparently other material, to Karl Yoneda for printing, an arrangement that persisted past the dissolution of the PPTUS in late 1934. This was considered "underground" work because it involved smuggling.[9]

Beyond preparation of printed material and arranging to have it smuggled into ports in Eastern Asia, the "special work" that Browder had in mind for George seems to have been primarily factional. In April 1929 Bertram Wolfe, speaking to the American Commission in Moscow, charged that Browder had arranged for George to become the editor of the PPTUS magazine specifically so that he could engage in factional work in San Francisco. Al Richmond, who worked with George in the late 1930s, noted George's "penchant for factionalism" and

24

his "resort to the most malicious personal gossip and innuendo" in his factional activities.[10]

Earlier, in the late 1920s, Sam Darcy encountered George in Moscow, where George was representing the TUEL to the Profintern and Darcy was head of the International Children's Commission, and they later butted heads in the 1930s when Darcy was DO for District 13. Darcy remembered the PPTUS as "an empty shell . . . nothing . . . ridiculous . . . badly conceived and ineffective." And, in fact, the PPTUS seems to have accomplished very little. Holger Weiss, in a 2017 study, concluded that George and his counterpart in Vladivostok "failed to establish extensive links connecting the Pacific ports, and their work among Asian sailors had been particularly weak."[11]

In San Francisco in 1929, however, George plunged into the district's most serious factional dispute, made himself a thorn in the side of the newly appointed DO, and claimed that his PPTUS status meant the local party leadership had "no jurisdiction over him."[12]

"The unfortunate and intolerable party split in California," 1929–1930

In January 1929 Lovestone's closest associate, Benjamin Gitlow, appointed John J. Ballam to go to California, "take charge," and supervise the election of delegates to the upcoming national convention. Los Angeles was again the site of the most heated contest. When the Los Angeles subdistrict convention met, the Lovestone faction claimed twenty-eight or thirty votes to thirty-eight for the opposition, and a credentials committee was elected with three of the opposition and two from the Lovestone faction. Ballam refused to accept that committee. Both factions then held separate conventions and elected separate Subdistrict Executive Committees. Levin refused to recognize Ballam's authority, but Gitlow insisted: "Ballams [*sic*] decisions are CEC decisions." In both Los Angeles and San Francisco, the opposition refused to accept Ballam's decisions.[13]

On February 8, Lovestone wired Ballam that only committees approved by Ballam were to be recognized; Levin was suspended as DO for being a "right wing opportunist"; J. G. Manus, Henry Gliksohn, and Frank Spector were subject to disciplinary action by the upcoming national convention; and an emergency committee was to take authority in the district. Open revolt continued. Mother Bloor wrote to William Z. Foster on February 12 and withdrew from his faction, stating, "Out here, the Opposition is called the 'Foster group,' and things are done in your name that would make you gasp for breath to behold." In Los Angeles the anti-Lovestone (Foster) faction occupied party headquarters, and Spector claimed to be the elected subdistrict organizer. In San Francisco, Gliksohn and

Manus occupied district headquarters at 1212 Market Street and claimed to head the legitimate district committee. On February 16, M. Martin, secretary of the District Emergency Committee, wrote to Lovestone to request suspension of Gliksohn, Manus, and eleven others. In late March, Louis Feinstein wrote a long, plaintive letter to Gitlow, concluding, "Is there an end in sight for the unfortunate and intolerable party split in California?"[14]

Though reflecting long-standing divisions, the immediate cause of the extreme disarray in California was the approach of the party's sixth convention, scheduled for March 1–9, and efforts by Lovestone and his supporters to secure a large convention majority. At issue in that convention was continuation of Lovestone's leadership. In early February the Comintern sent the U.S. party an open letter that criticized both major factions, one led by Lovestone, the other by Foster and Alexander Bittelman, for underestimating the "radicalization" of the working class and for perpetuating factionalism "not based on principle." The letter bluntly ordered that factionalism "be unconditionally stopped." The letter also proposed that Lovestone and Bittelman come to Moscow to be assigned to other work—in other words, that both be removed from leadership in the U.S. party. The convention opened with Lovestone's faction claiming 95 of the 104 delegates. Nonetheless, the convention was tumultuous. Delegates sometimes came to blows. Comintern representatives advised that Foster be elected secretary, but the convention chose a secretariat of three supposed equals: Gitlow as executive secretary, Max Bedacht in charge of agitprop, and Foster to lead trade union work. Thus, the Lovestone faction, in the person of Gitlow, held the helm of the party organization.[15]

Resolution came from Moscow. In late March, Stalin himself bluntly said, "ECCI can no longer tolerate unceasing factional struggle," and ordered Lovestone and Bittelman to come to Moscow. The ECCI convened a special American Commission to hear both sides. Lovestone headed a delegation of twelve, ten from his faction plus Foster and Bittelman. During the meetings of the American Commission, U.S. party members then in Moscow joined the official delegation in denouncing each other. Bloor deplored the leadership of Levin in California. Wolfe harshly criticized Harrison George, supposedly sent to California to head the American Bureau of the PPTUS but, Wolfe charged, actually to engage in opposition work.[16]

Lovestone and Gitlow left Robert Minor and Jack Stachel in charge of CP headquarters in New York and secretly made plans that if the ECCI decided against their faction, Minor and Stachel were to transfer ownership of all party assets to a new organization that Lovestone would head—that is, Lovestone was preparing to break ties with the Comintern. After weeks of American Commission hearings, Stalin blasted both sides for "unprincipled factionalism," "rotten diplomacy," and "diplomatic intrigue." He demanded a reorganization of the U.S. secretariat, an end to factionalism, and assignment of Lovestone outside the United States. On May 15, Minor and Stachel received Lovestone's cable directing them to implement their plan. Instead, they revealed it. In Moscow all of Lovestone's delegation except Gitlow and Wolfe abandoned him. Disobeying an order to remain in Moscow, Lovestone secretly left on June 11. The ECCI cabled instructions to the CPUSA on June 22: "POLITSECRETARIAT ECCI CALLS UPON ALL MEMBERS AND ORGANISATIONS CPUSA TO CONDEMN THESE METHODS OF INTRIGUE, FALSE-HOOD AND DISRUPTIVE ACTIVITIES.... POLITSECRETARIAT ECCI DEMANDS ALL FORMER ADHERENTS LOVESTONE PUBLICLY DISASSOCIATE THEMSELVES FROM HIM." The U.S. Central Committee expelled Lovestone, Gitlow, and Wolfe. All became strongly anti-Communist.[17]

The *New York Times* described those events, and the six years of bickering that preceded them, as a "tale of intrigue, charges of deception, trickery and political manoeuvering" that read "like a combination of Macchiaveli's [sic] 'Prince,' [and] an involved detective yarn with a dash of Baron Munchausen and bits of Mark Twain thrown in."[18] The same could have been said about events in San Francisco and Los Angeles, but more as farce. RGASPI files are incomplete, but those files present the only known record of events in District 13 in early 1929. The key figures were Henry Gliksohn and Morris Rappaport in San Francisco and Frank Spector and Frank Waldron in Los Angeles.

Gliksohn, an ironworker, born in San Francisco to Russian Jewish parents, was physically small but talked tough, with a San Francisco Mission District accent. In early March 1925 the DEC had appointed Gliksohn as district industrial organizer. He reported to the DEC that TUEL was not functioning properly. Nonetheless, Gliksohn soon became head of the Industrial Department and a member of the agitprop committee. In May 1928 he joined the DEC.[19] By late 1928 Gliksohn and Manus were the chief assistants to DO Levin.

Frank Spector, born in Odessa in 1895, and a house painter by trade, had emigrated to the United States in 1913 and was prominent in the Los Angeles party by the mid-1920s. Levin considered him "a real go-getter." Spector joined Schneiderman in attacking factionalism in the 1926 city convention, albeit from a factional perspective. In 1928 the Subdistrict Executive Committee elected him as organizer. Later that year he was denied permission to go to the Soviet Union. In early 1929 the anti-Lovestone subdistrict convention elected Spector as subdistrict organizer.[20]

Frank Waldron was born in Seattle in 1905. His father, of Irish descent but not Catholic, worked as a real estate broker and later in import-export; his mother was an immigrant from Norway. His parents divorced in 1913, and young Frank then lived with his father. He joined the Communist Party in 1926 and came to

Los Angeles in 1927 as educational director for Southern California. He met Reggie Karasick in 1928 when he was on the instructional staff of the Pacific Coast Marxist Summer School and she was one of the students. After the school, they became partners.[21]

Morris Rappaport (sometimes spelled Rapport or Raport) left much less of a record of his activity before the late 1920s. He was in his mid-thirties, married, with at least one son. His sister and his parents lived in Petaluma, California, as part of a community of Jewish chicken farmers.[22]

Following the national convention, District 13 continued with dueling DECs and SDECs. Californians in the Lovestone faction corresponded with Gitlow, Minor, and Stachel, seeking official support for their DEC and SDEC. Louis Feinstein, whom Ballam had recognized as secretary of the Los Angeles subdistrict, wrote to Gitlow on March 28, 1929: "The actions of Spector, Waldron are in our opinion absolutely impermissible" and "a direct result of the vacillating policy on the part of the new CEC [in] dealing with California situation." Feinstein continued his letter, saying, "Slanderous remarks on the convention and the new CEC are being spread openly by Spector Glickson," and he concluded, "Chaos is prevalent throughout the Party." On March 30, Martin Gottfried wired Gitlow and Stachel: "YOUR SILENCE DISASTROUS TO PARTY. DISTRICT COMMITTEE DEMANDS IMMEDIATE ACTION GLICKSON [*sic*] FRISCO SPECTOR LOS ANGELES OPENLY MOBILIZING MEMBERSHIP DENOUNCING CONVENTION AND CEC," and concluded, "STOP THE SILENCE."[23]

The CEC finally appointed Emil Gardos as the new DO. Gardos, a chemical engineer born in Hungary, arrived in San Francisco on April 8, just as the hearings were beginning in Moscow. He immediately went to 1212 Market, where Gliksohn, Manus, and others were occupying party headquarters. Gardos then reported to Minor, "After seeing comrade Glickson [*sic*], I was told categorically that no decision whatsoever is recognized and that they will continue to act, as they did in the past, as the only District Committee. . . . There are many indications showing that the decisions of the CEC, the cables of the C.I. are simply ignored and that the comrades around Glickson are ready to go as far as to precipitate a split."[24]

Harrison George openly supported the Gliksohn and Spector dissidents and may have been their major source of information. Gardos reported that George was scheduled to lecture at 1212 Market "under the auspices of the TUEL," but, Gardos continued, there was no TUEL other than an organizing committee for the needle trades. Gardos asked the CEC to investigate George, "because it is a very peculiar thing that neither the District (recognized by the CEC) nor the TUEL know anything about com. George's coming down." Gardos also reported that George was being advertised in Los Angeles as the speaker at "the 'dual' May-day meeting called by Spector."[25]

Earl Browder had been on assignment in China until January 1929, when he returned to New York and was placed on the CEC. He opposed Lovestone, had good relations with Foster, but tried to avoid the factional battles. In mid-April he composed a telegram to Gliksohn, urging him to submit to the CEC decisions, adding, "I advise this even though I voted against decisions and consider them most unwise," but noted that it was important to preserve the authority of the CEC "even when it is wrong." Not surprisingly, Browder's proposed telegram was rejected by the secretariat.[26] The relationship between George and Browder makes it highly likely that Browder, via George, was a source—even *the* source—of information to the Gliksohn and Spector groups.

On May 4, as events in Moscow were moving toward dénouement, George sent a letter to the secretariat about the situation in California, but the letter has not survived. Gardos composed a long response on May 7. He specified that George had not carried out requests from the emergency committee and was treating "the expelled splitters" as "the 'de facto' DEC-s." Gardos accused George of false statements and misrepresentations and asked the CEC to order George to "carry out the instructions of the CEC for the unification of our Party in our District." That was apparently done, as Gardos later noted, "The CEC instructions to George [are] that he shall disconnect himself from 1212 Market Street and work with the DEC."[27] Nonetheless, George continued to pursue whatever factional goals he and Browder had hatched.

On May 15, the same day of Lovestone's secret cable to implement his plan, Gardos was optimistic that things in Los Angeles were moving toward resolution. The plan was to draw all party members into meaningful party work rather than factional activities. In a letter to Waldron, Gardos urged, "Take part in the work, get rid of your notion of one so-called group having the only good elements, do not use your being on the SDEC for the continuation of the factional fight from within, do not present necessarily a counter-motion to every motion made by the others, stop sending in appeals after appeals." Gardos's letter to Waldron apparently crossed in the mail with a letter from Waldron to Minor, in which Waldron did exactly what Gardos cautioned him against: Waldron protested against the composition and actions of the reconstituted SDEC, which, he claimed, "clearly exposes their factional motives," especially their refusal "to accept our nominees," including Spector. "Instead the SDEC has kept capable comrades out of activity and appointed inactive and incapable comrades to represent the former national minority comrades on a so-called unity basis."[28]

The Comintern's directive to the U.S. party regarding Lovestone first became generally known through an article in the *New York Times* on May 18 and then by a series of publications in the *Daily Worker*. That information generated intense discussion within the party throughout District 13 and increased the internal conflict. Levin, Gliksohn, and their followers in San Francisco; Spector, Waldron, and their group in Los Angeles; and Harrison George all wrote to the new secretariat. Those letters are not in the RGASPI files, but on June 14 Gardos characterized them as interpreting the address of the Comintern to the U.S. party as "a factional victory for 1212 Market Street" and as making Gliksohn, Spector, and their supporters "more unified and more open in fighting the Party." Gardos's long letter also explained, "There are rumors already, spread openly by them, that the entire District situation will be reconsidered, functionaries changed, etc. . . . They expect the Party being turned over to them." He especially blasted George for his continuing assistance to the 1212 Market group and the Spector-Waldron faction in Los Angeles.[29]

For Gardos, the expulsion of Lovestone, Gitlow, and Wolfe was especially troublesome. Gardos wrote to Bedacht, now acting secretary, that he could not "function as a D.O. when I disagree with the line of the CEC." He submitted his resignation "with the request that it be accepted without delay." He was not replaced, however, and in early October wrote to CEC that after "the Enlightenment Campaign" by the CEC's representative, Abram Jakira, "the entire party here, with few exceptions, supports the CEC. Today there are only a handful of comrades who support Lovestone or have a concealed opposition to the Party leadership."[30]

Gardos also reported how the DEC had tried to draw the "splitters" back into the work of the party. Gliksohn, formerly an ironworker, had been put on the marine committee and was running for supervisor in the municipal election. Levin was directing the election committee and given other responsibilities. Rappaport was on the industrial committee. Manus was on the election committee. "Incompetent functionaries were removed and others elected on the basis of qualifications only." As a result, Gardos wrote, "The majority of the comrades are working harmoniously together," but, he added, Gliksohn, Rappaport, Levin, and Waldron had reverted to their factional tendencies.[31]

Gardos's last letter from California was on November 1. It was a letter of complaint about his treatment as DO and about some of the former opposition leaders, especially Waldron, "who is using his very little activities in the Marine Workers League to slander the IFC right and left" and George, who, Gardos claimed, "misinformed the CEC, while I could not defend myself."[32]

Among the CP's few accomplishments in 1929 was placing Louise Todd and Henry Gliksohn on the San Francisco ballot in the nonpartisan, at-large election for city supervisor. Todd recalled, "I was selected because . . . I was one of the few who could qualify for the ballot, having been born in the city, and having lived in the city for the required number of years." Gliksohn was similarly qualified. Nine were to be elected from a list of 49. Todd placed twenty-fourth, with 6,112 votes and 5.8 percent, and Gliksohn got 2,095 votes and 2 percent.[33]

A New Direction, 1930

Gardos complained in November 1929 that part of his shortcomings as DO had been that he "did not understand the Third period and the tasks of our party."[34] During the Sixth Comintern Congress, in Moscow in July–September 1928, Stalin had presented an analysis depicting a "Third Period" in the post–World War I development of capitalism, characterized by the imminent collapse of capitalism and likelihood of war by all capitalist nations against the Soviet Union. The CPUSA (the official name of the U.S. party after 1929) therefore needed to prepare for that struggle. Socialists and social democrats were especially scourged as the major prop of the bourgeoisie in that they were distracting the proletariat from the CP. Thus, the Third Period line viewed every non-CP group on the left as significant dangers and condemned them "social fascists" if not outright "fascists." The leading slogan, "class against class," stressed refusal to compromise across class lines and hostility toward socialists and trade union leaders who collaborated with the bourgeoisie. When the CPUSA now spoke of the "United Front," it meant the "united front from below": recruiting members of other left organizations to depose their "reformist" leaders and bring those organizations to the CP, thus making the party the sole leader of a unified proletariat. Given the labeling of AFL union leaders as social fascists, the former tactic of "boring from within"—forming fractions (the CP used the term "fractions" to describe their organization within existing unions) within AFL unions, the approach emphasized by William Z. Foster—was no longer appropriate. In 1929, in response to directives from Moscow, Foster led the CPUSA to transform the TUEL into the Trade Union Unity League (TUUL), a separate red union confederation, and set about organizing red unions in several industries.[35]

One component of Stalin's Third Period analysis emphasized the imminence of proletarian revolution. The CPUSA embraced Stalin's position that the U.S. proletariat was on the verge of revolution and that the CPUSA needed to seize leadership. The Tenth Plenum of the ECCI, in early July 1929, viewed current world events as "the starting point for a *new revolutionary forward surge* of the working class in all capitalist countries" and called for "mobilization of the proletariat to smash through bourgeois law and order."[36]

CPUSA militants responded with actions that incited police into forceful responses. In Oakland the party organized six demonstrations at the state employment agency during the last two weeks of February 1930. Police broke up the demonstrations and made arrests during the last two, including Archie Brown, described as the leader. Brown was charged with violating a city ordinance against street speaking in daytime, and he and others were charged with rioting.[37] It was on a similar occasion in early 1931 when Dorothy Rosenblum was taken into custody and became Dorothy Ray.

And at the same time, the U.S. economy was unraveling, just as the Third Period line had predicted. The booming stock market of the late 1920s began to crash in October 1929, setting off a reaction that produced business and bank failures, wage reductions, and growing unemployment over the next several years.

Late in 1929 William Simons came from Chicago to take over as DO. His efforts to unify the district were eased by having Manus and Gliksohn assigned to other duties. In late December, the District Buro (formerly DEC) decided "it was in the best interest of the party for Manus to leave the District." He was to take up party duties in Chicago. Gliksohn had already gone to New Orleans to organize maritime workers. The new DO's report declared, "The morale of the membership in San Francisco was splendid. The District Plenum, membership meeting, the demonstration for the defense of the Soviet Union and the Forum, convincing them that the Party seriously means unification of the Party, and that we have the correct line for reaching the American working class."[38]

The departures of Manus and Gliksohn were two of several reassignments that contributed to ending the district's factional strife. In late 1929 Frank Waldron left Los Angeles to assist George in producing the PPTUS magazine in San Francisco; he and Reggie Karasick spent every day at the public library, researching liberation movements in East and South Asia. In May 1930 Bloor went to North Dakota to become district organizer. Schneiderman became Connecticut DO in 1930 and then Minnesota DO in 1931.[39] Also in 1930, party activists marked out significant new directions, which persisted through 1933—organizing and demonstrating on behalf of the growing numbers of unemployed and assisting and organizing strikes by agricultural workers.

The Comintern first designated February 26, 1930, as International Unemployment Day, a day to protest unemployment, but then shifted the date to March 6. Demonstrations on March 6—and conflict between demonstrators and police—began in Europe. Sam Darcy organized events in New York City, for which the party claimed 110,000 demonstrators. The *New York Times* said it was only 35,000. When the crowd attempted to march to city hall without a parade permit, 1,000 police officers sought to stop them with clubs and fire hoses. The party claimed 100,000 demonstrators in Detroit, 50,000 each in Chicago and Boston, and 40,000 in Milwaukee. The press provided smaller, but still impressive, numbers: 75,000 in Detroit, 4,000 in Chicago, 1,500 in Milwaukee. In many cities, as in New York, police sought to stop the marchers.[40]

The San Francisco demonstration was the most impressive up to that time anywhere in California. It began on Howard Street between Third and Fourth Streets, an area with many employment agencies, low-rent housing, and large numbers of unemployed or seasonally employed single men. At 11 a.m., Harry Harvey, a TUUL organizer, mounted a truck bed and called a meeting in the name

Top: Harry Harvey in the background addressing the crowd gathered before the march began on March 6, 1930. Bottom: Harvey carries a placard as he walks on Market Street with Police Chief William Quinn. Photos courtesy of San Francisco History Center, San Francisco Public Library.

of the CP. Police obligingly stopped traffic in that block. When a crowd formed, Harvey led them to Civic Center Plaza, in front of city hall, carrying large banners with the party's slogans of the day: "Work or Wages" (the leading slogan), "Don't Starve! Fight!" "Defend the Soviet Union," and "Join the Communist Party." The press estimated there were between six hundred and two thousand marchers. The police offered no resistance and followed the marchers with a mounted escort. Police Chief William Quinn even briefly walked and chatted with Harvey at the head of the parade.[41]

At city hall the crowd swelled to between eight thousand and ten thousand people. The city provided a speaking platform decked with American flags, and Mayor James Rolph greeted Simons and the marchers. Simons spoke first. According to the *San Franciso Chronicle* (not a sympathetic source), Simons "confined himself to a long dissertation on the excellence of the soviet government and the 'iniquity' of capitalism, with which he included the Socialist party and the American Federation of Labor and all governments, national, State and city." In concluding, Simons insisted that the mayor "call a meeting of the Board of Supervisors at once to relieve unemployment, to give us work or wages." Rolph then promised, "I will read carefully the demands made by the speaker, Simons, and will take them up with the Board of Supervisors." Rolph started to leave, and city workers began to dismantle the platform, but not before Simons demanded to know when Rolph would bring their demands to the supervisors. Rolph replied that it would be the following Monday and that all unemployed men and women could attend. Part of the crowd then went to a nearby hall where a long list of speakers held forth. Police made only one arrest, for distributing handbills without a permit. "It was all," the *Chronicle* concluded, "quite chummy between the police and the demonstrators." A demonstration of a thousand people in Oakland was similarly uneventful.[42]

Louise Todd, then membership secretary in San Francisco, recalled that "hundreds of people joined the Communist Party as a result of the appeal that was made there [the civic center rally] even though they could not be absorbed by the organization which was still these small groups of foreign born members."[43]

Things were very different in Los Angeles. There, over the previous few months, party members had not only engaged in repeated battles with the city police but had also been arrested and charged with blocking sidewalks, disturbing a public meeting, disturbing the peace, or inciting a riot. On February 26, 1930, the day originally designed as International Unemployment Day, the Los Angeles comrades decided to carry out their original plans. Three hundred police officers used clubs and tear gas to break up the demonstration by some three thousand party members and sympathizers. Spector, Waldron, and Schneiderman's brother Lou were among those arrested. An effort to march to city hall on March 6 ended similarly when a thousand police with blackjacks and clubs blocked the demonstrators and arrested twenty-six of them. Twenty-one, including Waldron, were booked on suspicion of criminal syndicalism.[44]

Lillian Dinkin, then fifteen years old, recalled events:

> It was arranged that a speaker would get up on one corner and figure on a minute or less to talk before being knocked down, then another speaker would try across the street, and so on. One speaker after another was clubbed down: head cracked, blood all over, tear gas, horses, arrests. We were dispersed in all directions. Our crowd was chased down 5th Street and constantly assaulted. Miriam [Lillian's sister], all of eleven and a half years old, saw a friend being beaten, so she picked up something and hit the cop. She was clubbed in return. I got my butt mashed a bit. That was March 6, 1930.[45]

Though women and young people were not numerically prominent in the party, they sometimes received prominent press coverage in these demonstrations. In 1930 the arch-conservative and anti-Communist *Los Angeles Times* provided this description: "One 'Bolshe-vixen' . . . became so filled with the radical spirit and the fear that she would not be arrested that she screamed hysterically, threw a lot of handbills in the air and leaped on the back of an unsuspecting officer." Several other women were also among those arrested that day, including two ages fourteen and fifteen.[46]

On March 24 the San Francisco comrades finally provoked a similar police response. That day twenty-five members of the Unemployed Council attended the supervisors' regular meeting and interrupted the official agenda with demands to speak. Mayor Rolph, the board's presiding officer, informed them that they would have to follow the rules to get permission to speak. When the demonstrators continued their tirade, police moved in, carried out the four leaders, arrested them, and charged them with disturbing the peace and vagrancy. The vagrancy charge was a special version of that law, originally aimed at prostitutes and requiring bail of one thousand dollars to be paid. The "$1,000 vag" charge was used increasingly against Communist activists.[47]

The large turnout on March 6 seems to have reinforced party leaders' embrace of Stalin's insistence that the proletariat was close to revolution. In an article in the May 1930 issue of *The Communist*, M. J. Olgin declared, "The demonstrations of March 6th against unemployment were of tremendous political importance. May Day this year must represent a higher political stage in the development of the class struggle in America. . . . May Day this year must witness a mass political strike in behalf of the major class issues of the American workers." In the same issue, Clarence Hathaway predicted, "The masses are ready to respond to our slogans and fight for their demands in the streets on May First."[48]

However, on May 1 in San Francisco, only 21 marchers walked to the civic center, where 160 people rallied. Police did not interfere. In Oakland the party was denied a parade permit, and police broke up an attempt to parade without a permit, injuring 6 and arresting 4. Los Angeles authorities also refused a parade permit. When 1,000 protesters gathered in defiance of the denial, police attacked with nightsticks, blackjacks, and tear gas. The *Los Angeles Times* reported that the party threw hundreds of children into the melee and deployed special "defense squads" to attack police. The police officer in charge claimed that the demonstrations were poorly organized because most leading Communists were in jail and "the demonstrators are practically without leaders."[49] Contrary to expectations of party leaders, there was no widespread participation anywhere comparable to the events of March 6.

Throughout the remainder of 1930, the party continued to focus on organizing the unemployed into Unemployed Councils and mounting demonstrations on their behalf, but none came close to matching their results on March 6.

The California party's other major departure was organizing farmworkers, beginning in January 1930, when lettuce pickers spontaneously walked off the job in the Imperial Valley (extreme southeastern California) in response to wage cuts. After reading about the strike in the newspaper, CP leaders in Los Angeles sent Waldron, Harvey, and Tsuji Horiuchi to deliver food and other provisions and, if possible, gain leadership of the strike and organize the strikers into the new Agricultural Workers Industrial League, part of the equally new TUUL. None of the three spoke Spanish or Tagalog, but they managed to create a presence for the red union. All three were arrested and charged with vagrancy. Party efforts to bring food to the strikers were blocked, and the strike collapsed.[50]

Several party members then began to work in the Imperial Valley, organizing Filipino and Mexican field workers. Local authorities responded by arresting the most prominent organizers and charging them under the criminal syndicalism law. Of the eleven arrested, three were deported and one was found not guilty. The remaining seven, including Frank Spector, were sentenced to prison terms and two were deported.[51]

Those events contributed to the departure of two more factional leaders, Frank Spector and Frank Waldron. Spector was convicted of criminal syndicalism in June 1930 and imprisoned in San Quentin until his conviction was reversed on appeal in July 1931. He and others used their time in prison to conduct study groups among the prisoners and recruit CP members. After his release Spector worked for a time as an ILD organizer in New York.[52] Waldron, under indictment for criminal syndicalism, fled to New York, took the name Tim Ryan, went to Moscow, and was soon joined by Reggie Karasick and their one-year-old son, Tim.

Of the leaders of the occupation of 1212 Market and its counterpart in Los Angeles, only Rappaport remained in District 13. George also remained; he became a member of the District Control Commission but was sent to the Philippines in September 1932.[53]

Despite the departure of so many factional leaders, District 13 remained troubled. The surviving District 13 files for 1930 indicate frequent shuffling of activists and complaints about each other and about the district's inability to accomplish anything. Simons complained to the national office about the lack of help and the quality of the help. Others blamed Simons and sometimes Rappaport. In early September the national office complained that 875 membership books had been sent to the district but dues for only 323 people had been received. In mid-November, Rappaport wrote to Browder: "The membership in our District has absolutely lost faith in the leadership, (passive revolt). . . . Comrade Simons absolutely refuses to recognize mistakes." A few weeks later, a district member wrote to the national office that "Simons and Rapport" were "pursuing a policy of browbeating and terrorizing the membership."[54] Simons was assigned to other work late in 1930.

In *The House of Government*, Yuri Slezkine describes Karl Marx and Friedrich Engels as "millenarian prophets" and points to a millenarian aspect in the thinking of the Bolsheviks.[55] One sees a similar pattern among many Californians who embraced Bolshevism in the 1920s—they read the same "millenarian prophets," or they listened to party leaders who had done so and who preached the inevitable and imminent collapse of capitalism and the party's rise to power. In 1925 Bloor preached that "nothing on earth can stop the fall of this system of government[,] and while the Communists do not advocate a bloody revolution they know that it is inevitable and want to be ready for it when it comes."[56] Central to their thinking was the expectation of a spontaneous uprising of the working class, as had occurred in Petrograd in November 1917, and the belief that party members needed to take leadership of it just as Lenin had done. As Reggie Karasick recalled, "We were confident that we alone were tapped by history to fulfill its mission for humanity's liberation from exploitation and oppression. We alone had the answer as to how this could be done."[57]

In May 1930 Stalin reinforced such millenarian expectations: "The moment is not far off when a revolutionary crisis will develop in America," which would mark "the beginning of the end of world capitalism as a whole." Stalin defined the immediate task of the CPUSA: "Forge real revolutionary cadres and a real revolutionary leadership of the proletariat, capable of leading the many millions of the American working class toward the revolutionary class struggles."[58] Though Lovestone had doubts about the readiness of the American proletariat for revolution, his defeat and expulsion were followed by party leaders' embrace of Stalin's view that the proletarian revolution was inevitable and imminent.

Such millenarian expectations ran through the writings of U.S. party leaders—and likely characterized the thinking of many, if not most, party members. Confidence in the imminent and inevitable victory of the proletariat seems to have combined with the factional infighting and the party's major structural reorganization to detract most California comrades from serious efforts at organizing unorganized workers or developing cadres within existing unions. However, efforts in 1930 to assist striking farmworkers proved a more reliable harbinger of the coming transformation of the Communist Party in the 1930s than did the party's efforts in 1930 to "smash through bourgeois law and order."

CHAPTER 3

PRELUDE TO THE POPULAR FRONT, 1930–1935

This chapter and the next present major developments for Communist Party members in the Bay Area from late 1930 to late 1941. Chapter 5 looks at how various individuals participated in and responded to those events. This chapter treats the California CP during the tenure of Samuel Adams Darcy as district organizer, from December 1930 to mid-1935. Remembered by some as "brilliant" and condemned by others as a "swell-head,"[1] Darcy brought important new initiatives to District 13 as the comrades—and the nation—grappled with the worst economic contraction of the twentieth century.

Darcy Arrives

Just twenty-five years old in 1930, Darcy's wide-ranging experience belied his youth. Born Samuel Dardeck in Ukraine, Darcy arrived in the United States with his parents when he was a toddler. He joined the Young People's Socialist League (YPSL) in his early teens and moved with much of YPSL into the Young Workers' League. He became YWL national organizer at age seventeen and national secretary at eighteen. As YWL national secretary, he served on the U.S. party's Central Committee and Central Executive Committee, where he often disagreed with Jay Lovestone. Perhaps in response, Lovestone sent Darcy to Moscow in 1927. There he served on the Executive Committee of the Young Communist International (YCI) and the presidium of YCI, was one of three YCI representatives to the Comintern, and was chair of the International Children's Commission. He returned to the United States in 1929.[2]

Back in New York, Darcy served briefly as editor of the *Daily Worker* and head of the International Labor Defense, and he planned the New York demonstration against unemployment on March 6, 1929. In January 1930 he organized a massive funeral march for a worker killed by New York police. Soon after, in the PolBuro (Political Bureau, formerly the Central Executive Committee), Earl Browder described the funeral demonstration as "adventurism" on Darcy's part. Browder became the de facto head of the party a few months later, and he soon dispatched Darcy to California, the district most remote from party headquarters, an assignment many understood as an exile.[3] However, as Darcy soon understood, being the most remote from party headquarters could also be an advantage.

Darcy called the California CP a "mess" when he arrived.[4] Four district organizers over the previous five years had failed to motivate, much less unify, party members. The district's factional infighting, demoralization, loss of members, and revolving door for DOs seemed an invitation to failure, likely Browder's intent.

Shortly after Darcy's arrival, District 13 counted 409 members. Eighty-one (20 percent) were women; 285 (70 percent) were foreign-born, of whom 237 were citizens. Most were under forty years of age. The party's registration form provided occupations for 161 comrades, including 50 needle trades workers, 30 metal workers, 24 building trades workers, 15 railroad workers, 9 transport and harbor workers, 30 migratory workers, 18 small farmers, and 35 housewives. There were party fractions in only two AFL unions, the painters and the carpenters. Party members were spread over seven hundred miles, from Fort Bragg in the north to San Diego in the south, but almost 90 percent were in either the Bay Area (171 members) or Los Angeles (189 members). Only the information for Los Angeles listed ethnicity: Jewish, 95 (50 percent); "American," 23; Mexican, 11; Japanese, 7; German, 6; Russian, 6; Armenian, 5; Greek, 5; and 31 not listed.[5]

In early June 1931, Darcy wrote to Jack Stachel about his first six months in the district. Party headquarters was at 734 Harrison Street, in a neighborhood Darcy called the "skid-road" and the local press called the "skid-way"—an area of inexpensive residential hotels, cheap cafes, and numerous bars and pool rooms, home to many male waterfront and maritime workers and unemployed or underemployed single men, as well as poor families and single women. Darcy found party headquarters "in the hands of 'skid-road' elements." He explained, "While there are many good, normal workers on the skid-road, there are also very many degenerate elements, drunkards, dope fiends. . . . They completely discredited the Party." On Darcy's first day, he "had a physical fight with two of them who were among seven or eight who were lying around the Party Headquarters dead drunk." On his third day, "two Party members made a hold-up on some other Party members, and we had all we could do to prevent the police from learning of the situation." Darcy's first task was "to eliminate these elements and to get factory workers or at least unemployed workers into the Party and into Party leadership" and "drive out a considerable number of these degenerates from the Party and Unemployed Council."[6]

New Directions, 1931–1932

Darcy's arrival coincided with the deepening of the national economic crisis that began with the stock market crash and intensified when major banks failed and manufacturers cut back production and laid off workers or cut wages. In San Francisco 1,704 families, on average, received city relief each month in 1929; by 1933 that number was up to 18,076—almost 10 percent of all families, concentrated disproportionately among blue-collar wage earners. State agencies reported that peak unemployment in San Francisco was 32 percent.[7] The Depression, unemployment, and wage reductions became the constant context for CP activity in California.

During his first eighteen months, Darcy undertook a whirlwind of activity: he found a new location for party headquarters near city hall,[8] launched a new party newspaper, fielded candidates in elections, and developed new approaches to organizing unemployed and agricultural workers. William Simons had hired Louise Todd as secretary for membership and organizational work; she continued in that role with Darcy. Through the changed economic context, Darcy's initiatives, and Todd's bureaucratic acumen, party membership statewide almost doubled within sixteen months, from 409 when Darcy arrived in late 1930 to 808 in April–May 1932.[9]

Darcy inherited a demonstration planned for Sacramento on January 7, 1931. Morris Rappaport had secured a permit as district secretary of the Unemployed Councils and TUUL. Though billed as the "march of 10,000 jobless," about four hundred people actually walked through Sacramento's streets to a rally outside the capitol, where James Rolph had recently been inaugurated as governor. More than a hundred state police and highway patrol officers were on hand. The marchers carried signs from around the state and a large "Class Against Class" banner, but the previous year's slogan about defending the Soviet Union was absent. Ida Rothstein of the ILD spoke for the group. The organizers insisted that Rolph meet inside with a committee. Rolph insisted on speaking to the entire group. According to the *San Francisco Chronicle*, "One section of the paraders wanted to hear the Governor. The other wanted to prevent him from talking." And there the event ended.[10]

A "hunger march" by some three thousand in San Francisco, twelve days later, had a similar outcome. In front of city hall, Mayor Angelo Rossi was called upon to speak. He tried, but the crowd shouted him down. The demonstrators then moved to another location, where speakers denounced the mayor for "refusing to talk to the workers." Police arrested a few men for distributing handbills without a permit.[11]

Those marches and similar demonstrations were organized through the party's Unemployed Councils. Louise Todd recalled, "Members of the Communist Party were all very active in these organizations, but the leadership of these organizations moved very quickly into broader channels where non-communists became officers and leaders of the Unemployed Councils, which was absolutely imperative." She emphasized the degree of organization necessary for the various marches around the state and said that "the Unemployed Councils seemed to be constantly in a state of organizing for some sort of action." "Many, many people," she recalled, "came to the progressive movement, to the communist movement, to the trade union movement through the unemployed councils."[12]

Such demonstrations often turned violent. Battles between Communists and police raged on February 10, designated by the TUUL to demonstrate for unemployment insurance. Police in Oakland and Sacramento grappled with demonstrators. When two Sacramento police officers were severely beaten, the police wrecked the TUUL office. The San Francisco demonstration was quieter but nonetheless produced twenty-nine arrests. A demonstration in San Francisco on February 25, part of a "world demonstration against hunger and for the unemployment insurance bill," drew about two hundred people. In Oakland police arrested sixteen-year-old Dorothy Rosenblum for "selling communist newspapers and heckling the police" and arrested others for speaking in public without a permit.[13]

May Day 1931 was quiet in San Francisco. Five hundred marchers followed a musicians union band up Market Street, cheered speakers at a rally, and then repaired to an evening meeting in the civic auditorium. A "hunger march" on September 14 attracted several hundred and concluded with a battle with police. A jury convicted eleven men of rioting and sentenced them to jail terms ranging from ten days to six months.[14]

Some party leaders were concluding that demonstrations intended to "smash bourgeois law and order" were not attracting large numbers of workers. In January 1931 the PolitSecretariat of the ECCI directed the CPUSA that its "main task" was developing real organization among the unemployed, with leaders elected by the unemployed workers and functioning Unemployed Councils and with the goal of promoting unemployment insurance and immediate relief. The directive mentioned "mass demonstrations" only once.[15] When the CPUSA's Central Committee met in August 1931, its many resolutions included one on work among the unemployed, which concluded that the party had placed "too much reliance on demonstrations and similar actions" and too little on actually organizing the unemployed.[16]

In early November 1931 the San Francisco party, instead of mounting another demonstration, held two days of "Public Hearings," led by the secretary of the Unemployed Council and Elmer Hanoff, secretary of the local TUUL. Over two days, thirty-five men and women, likely recruited from the Unemployed Councils, described their unsuccessful efforts to find employment, the inadequacy of existing work relief, the effect of inadequate food on children, and similar experiences. Norma Noral (later Norma Perry) took down and typed up the testimony.[17]

While efforts to organize the unemployed continued, Darcy and the party gave increasing attention to organizing farmworkers.[18] As the economy unraveled, agricultural workers were suffering wage cuts, which sometimes set off spontaneous strikes. In mid-January 1931, one of Darcy's first actions after arriving was to write to Browder for assistance with agricultural organizing: "We have only two U.S. comrades now available for this work in addition to about 10 Filipino and Mexican workers. The Filipino and Mexican workers can get jobs on the farms [i.e., in the fields] and not in the sheds in the towns [where produce was sorted and packed, jobs reserved for white workers]." Darcy continued: "Our plan is that each of the white comrades be posted at strategic towns in Impeiral [*sic*] Valley and shall have five workers each on the farms as a corps of workers, and check them up regularly once or twice a week." Darcy also indicated that the party's only Spanish-speaker, Archie Brown, should be kept in agricultural organizing. (Brown, however, later acknowledged, "My abilities in the language were quite limited.") Instead of agricultural organizing, Brown was repeatedly arrested in the Bay Area during battles with the police and in late 1931 was sentenced to six months in jail.[19] Throughout the late 1920s, party leaders in District 13 had called for a Spanish-speaking organizer or even just printed material in Spanish, but neither was ever forthcoming.

Throughout 1931 and early 1932 the party's approach to farmworkers remained much like that in 1930—waiting for a spontaneous strike, usually because of wage cuts, and showing up to provide support and try to take leadership. Caroline Decker, centrally involved in those efforts, recalled, "Two-thirds of the strikes we learned about through the newspapers." The initiative came from the workers, she explained, because "we didn't have any forces; we didn't have any training. We didn't have any people.... Those things would have happened without us. It just so happened that we were on hand, and we wanted the Communist Party to get credit for it." Two such instances were strikes by Santa Clara Valley cannery workers in July 1931 and by pea pickers near Half Moon Bay (on the coast south of San Francisco) in early 1932. Both were failures.[20]

Amid unemployed demonstrations and agricultural organizing, Darcy mobilized District 13 for elections. In 1931, San Franciscans voted in nonpartisan elections for the board of supervisors and other local officials. Darcy ran for mayor, the first time the CP contested that office. Louise Todd again filed for supervisor, and Charles Bakst, who was later revealed as an informer, ran for sheriff. Darcy and Todd attracted some press attention, unlike the party's previous runs for elective office. Darcy got 1,408 votes, fewer than 1 percent; Bakst got 2,433, almost 2 percent; and Todd, one of two women in a field of twenty-two, got 10,815, or 7 percent.[21]

Another of Darcy's initiatives was a newspaper, the first since the demise of *Labor Unity* in 1925. Published in San Francisco, the *Western Worker* labeled itself the "Western Organ of the Communist Party of the U.S.A." Most *Western Worker* articles were written in, and many were about, the San Francisco Bay Area. Darcy was editor. The first issue, on January 1, 1932, carried a banner headline announcing the party's "hunger march." That issue also announced another of Darcy's initiatives, a new state headquarters at 1164 Market Street, away from the "skid-road" area and near city hall.[22]

Darcy also led the party to organize for the 1932 elections for president, U.S. Senate, and members of Congress. The CP did not have a place on the state ballot and had to rely on write-in voting for William Z. Foster, their candidate for president. Foster got only 1,023 votes statewide. Norman Thomas, the Socialist candidate, was on the ballot and drew 63,299 votes, almost 3 percent of the total and an increase of 200 percent for that party since 1928.[23] In the 1933 San Francisco elections, the CP offered five candidates for supervisor and a candidate for treasurer. The candidate for treasurer got 10,468 votes, over 6 percent of the total, and the supervisorial candidates averaged 5,185 votes, about 3 percent.[24]

With the party's new projects—and amid widespread unemployment—recruiting burgeoned. Between July 1931 and the end of February 1934, District 13 signed up 4,891 new members. However, the party counted only 2,532 dues-paying members at the end of those thirty-two months. Thus, the party had to recruit nearly 5,000 new members to gain an increase of some 2,000, a pattern also true of the party nationwide. By early 1934, District 13 also counted 16 full-time functionaries in mass organizations and 5 full-time functionaries in the district organization.[25]

The Cotton Strike, 1933

Unemployment nationwide probably reached its highest point in early 1933. In March, Franklin D. Roosevelt was inaugurated as president and launched his New Deal with a flurry of legislation aimed at providing relief for the unemployed, recovery for the economy, and reform of economic sectors that had contributed to the crash and the Depression. Section 7(a) of the National Industrial Recovery Act specified that workers had the right to be represented in collective bargaining by representatives of their own choosing. By the end of that year, an unprecedented wave of strikes swept across the nation as workers organized and demanded recognition. The CP's initial response echoed the Third Period line: Roosevelt's New Deal was "An Attack Upon the Toiling Masses," and "Every force of united working class resistance must be mobilized to fight against this attack."[26]

In California, Darcy instead prioritized a strategy for the 1933 growing season. He devoted late 1932 to extensive training and organizational groundwork for a major drive among farmworkers. By then the party's efforts for a TUUL union for farmworkers had evolved into the Cannery and Agricultural Workers Industrial Union (CAWIU). CAWIU organizers planned a series of strikes, moving from the harvest of one crop to the harvest of the next, just as workers migrated from one harvest to the next. Darcy recruited men from the Unemployed Councils, trained them in recruitment and strike strategy, and sent them to join the migratory farmworkers. The strike wave began in April. Some early strikes failed, but the organizers gained experience and then began to win some wage increases. By late August the average farmworker's wage had moved from 15–17 cents an hour to 25 cents, and some were earning 30 cents (equivalent to nearly $7 in 2023). September strikes were less successful, but Darcy planned for the big showdown in October in the cotton fields of the southern San Joaquin Valley.[27]

The 1933 cotton strike was the largest single strike in the history of agricultural labor up to that time. By then CAWIU organizers had gained practical experience, and they prepared carefully, holding meetings with farmworkers throughout Kern and Kings counties. They asked for one dollar per hundred pounds of cotton. The growers offered 60 cents. The strike began on October 4. Growers responded with attacks on the organizers and strikers. Local authorities looked the other way or joined in. The Kings County district attorney later admitted, "The sheriff and I told the growers not to worry much about the pickers' rights." Evicted from grower-owned housing, strikers camped wherever they could. State authorities eventually used federal relief funds to provide them with necessities. One camp near Corcoran housed some three thousand people.[28]

The CAWIU provided important leadership for the strike, but the few Communist organizers were augmented by significant numbers of leaders recruited among the strikers, notably Pat Chambers, the head of the CAWIU. By October 9 some twelve thousand cotton pickers were striking in Tulare, Kings, and Kern counties. The growers refused state and federal mediation efforts. Darcy was present in Pixley on October 10, when growers fired into a crowd of strikers and their families, killing two. Another striker was shot and killed by growers in

Boss Tricks Cannot Break Workers Ranks

Cotton strikers are unanimous! "Not an ounce for less than $1.00 per hundred pounds."

This cartoon and the inset photo of strikers from the *Western Worker* on October 23, 1933, p. 1, emphasized the interracial solidarity of the cotton strikers. Photo courtesy of Marxists International Archive.

Arvin. In both places more people were wounded. Authorities took no action against the growers, but they arrested Chambers and charged him with criminal syndicalism.[29]

The killings strengthened the resolve of the strikers. Federal authorities intervened, threatening that the growers would lose all New Deal agricultural subsidies if they continued their refusal to participate in fact-finding. The result was a hearing to establish whether farmworker families could live on 60 cents a hundredweight. Darcy sat in the front row during the hearings. When asked if that wage was enough to live on and provide for her family, one woman responded that she and her husband had not been able to afford shoes for her children since 1930. Under pressure from the Roosevelt administration, the growers finally agreed to

75 cents. The union claimed victory and had also claimed victory in most other strikes that year, although victory usually meant a small wage increase, no other gains, and never union recognition.[30]

Louise Todd recalled about recruiting efforts: "We had a very great success" because the strikers "saw the willingness and the efforts ... of the communists to be of assistance to them." Between April and the end of 1933, the California party signed up 2,345 new members, with the biggest numbers in October and November, at the height of the farm strikes.[31]

By the time of the cotton strike, John Steinbeck had become acquainted with members of the John Reed Club in Carmel. The John Reed Club was the party's organization for intellectuals, and club members were avid supporters of the CAWIU. Not limited to party members, the Carmel club included Lincoln Steffens, the Progressive Era muckraking journalist, and his wife, Ella Winter. Through the John Reed Club, Steinbeck met two organizers from the cotton strike, hiding near Carmel to avoid arrest for criminal syndicalism. Steinbeck talked with them about their experiences, and those conversations led to his description of the strike and the Communist organizer, Mack, in *In Dubious Battle*, published in 1936. Steffens sent Darcy a copy of the book and wrote that Mack was modeled on Darcy. Darcy, then in Moscow, was incensed by Steinbeck's account of Mack delivering a baby despite having no experience. Darcy recalled that he replied to Steffens, "Steinbeck is a jerk. If I'd caught an organizer doing anything like that, as adventurous an act as risking a child's life, I'd throw him the hell out."[32]

Though the 1933 strikes produced small increases in farmworkers' wages and a big increase in CP membership, they were less successful in meeting the goal specified in the Central Committee's directive in mid-June 1933 that all districts should "reach the decisive sections of the workers especially in mining, steel, waterfront, railroad, chemical, etc." Farmworkers were not on the list. Reflecting Third Period rhetoric that an attack on the Soviet Union was imminent, the directive specified that districts were to win those workers "for a real mass struggle against the imperialist war danger."[33] The CAWIU organizers had focused on wage improvements and failed to persuade farmworkers to "struggle against the imperialist war danger."

Longshore, Maritime, and General Strikes, 1934

In May 1934, longshore workers from Bellingham in northern Washington to San Diego in Southern California went on strike under the leadership of the Pacific Coast District of the International Longshoremen's Association (ILA-PCD). They were soon joined by shipboard workers, organized in several unions including the TUUL's Marine Workers Industrial Union (MWIU). The MWIU played only a small and early role in the strike. In mid-June striking longshore workers rejected a settlement negotiated by their international president, Joseph Ryan, and increasingly looked for leadership to the chair of the strike committee of the San Francisco ILA local, Harry Bridges. On July 5 a daylong battle between San Francisco police and strike supporters left two dead and more than a hundred injured. The governor sent in National Guard troops to protect the strikebreakers. The San Francisco Labor Council then led a four-day general strike to protest police violence and the use of the National Guard. The strikes ended in late July, and a federal arbitration board gave the striking longshore workers nearly everything they had sought. Those events have attracted many historians and journalists. I have written at length elsewhere on Bridges, the longshore workers, and the development of organization on the waterfront.[34] What follows is my understanding of the role of the CP in the early organization of longshore workers in San Francisco and during the strikes, especially the internal divisions within the CP over the correct response to those events.

Four party functionaries were significantly involved in some way before or during the strikes: Sam Darcy, Harrison George, Harry Hynes, and Harry Jackson. RGASPI records demonstrate their disagreements over how to accomplish the goal of reaching the workers, and, at times, how they fell into personal bickering over tactics and strategy.

In the spring of 1933, Harrison George returned from a brief stint in the Philippines to resume his place as head of the American Bureau of the PPTUS in San Francisco. He returned as well to serve as the eyes and ears of Browder in San Francisco—Darcy later called George "a stoolie of Browder's." By the time of the strikes, in mid-1934, the PPTUS was in its final months of existence, though George may not have known that.[35]

Harold "Harry" Hynes was born in India to an Irish father and English mother, who raised him in England and Australia. He went to sea in 1919 and sailed to ports around the world. When the party created the MWIU for waterfront and seagoing workers, Hynes became its first secretary. He was sent to San Francisco in early 1932 to create a local MWIU organization. Darcy recalled Hynes as "not very articulate, but highly intelligent" and "a wonderful man."[36]

Henry Gliksohn now called himself Harry Jackson. He returned to San Francisco as an organizer for the MWIU in September 1933. Though he'd never gone to sea, he had worked as an MWIU organizer in U.S. ports on the Gulf of Mexico and in New York.[37]

William Z. Foster was in San Francisco secretly, recuperating from a serious breakdown that began during the 1932 presidential campaign. Because of his weakened physical and mental state, Foster played no role in events, though Darcy kept him informed.[38]

MWIU organizing had lagged badly. In March 1931, a year after its founding, MWIU leaders could find only 188 members in good standing, nationwide, among the 1,975 "members" in their files. As of October 1931, the San Francisco MWIU had not remitted enough dues even to pay for the postage the national office used on its behalf.[39] Despite assignment of more MWIU functionaries, the situation changed very little.

As of mid-1933 the MWIU plan for organizing Pacific Coast maritime workers specified, "The anti-imperialist war campaign is the outstanding task in all our work in the present period. To carry on this campaign most effectively, the approach to the marine transport workers should be on the basis of their day to day problems and grievances, using these as well as the struggle itself to develop [sic] the political slogans and demands, the outstanding of which must be against imperialist war, for the defense of the Chinese people and the Soviet Union." The California TUUL in August 1933 reported that, during the previous year, the MWIU had placed primary emphasis on the "strategic position of marine workers particularly in view of war danger" and secondarily on "wage cuts and speed up of seamen and longshoremen."[40]

Such instructions required organizers to walk a tightrope: gain workers' confidence by appealing to them on the basis of their immediate work issues and then quickly politicize them and lead them into a commitment to proletarian revolution and support for the Soviet Union. Overemphasizing the first ran the risk of veering into "right-opportunism"; too much emphasis on the second risked "left-sectarianism." The MWIU created a small cadre of seafaring revolutionaries but failed to mobilize any significant number of seamen or longshore workers. Third Period rhetoric—attacks on all "reformist" organizations as social fascists, constant efforts to engage "class against class," and the importance of immediate preparations to defend the Soviet Union against the supposed war danger—must have made recruiting difficult if not impossible.

As of March 1932 in all of California there were only five CP members in the marine industry—all of them, apparently, MWIU functionaries. In his memoirs, Darcy recalled that in early 1932, District 13 leaders met for several days, examined the San Francisco waterfront, studied a failed longshore strike in 1919, and laid plans to develop an organization. On March 15, 1932, the district secretariat adopted an organizational plan that included "immediately to begin to issue the West Coast Bulletin for the marine workers." Other parts of the plan included attendance by Darcy and three others, including James Branch and Emmet Kirby, at the morning shape-up, where longshore workers sought work for the day, and recruiting of longshore workers through public speaking and individual discussions. Branch and Kirby, like Darcy, were not longshore workers. Branch was managing editor of the *Western Worker*, and Kirby was the paper's artist.[41]

About the time Darcy and his committee were making their plans, Hynes arrived in San Francisco. He soon complained to party headquarters that Darcy and the district leadership knew nothing about the waterfront. Darcy responded to party headquarters that he had held "several meetings with the comrades of the Marine Workers Union" "and that "there is absolute chaos in their methods of work. At the present time there is a Shore Organizational Committee here consisting of five comrades, all of them depending upon support for a livelihood on the union. These five comrades constitute the top fraction, the leadership of the union, and with the exception of two or three, the rank and file of the union. They are unable even to raise money for rent or any of their small expenses."[42]

At the District 13 convention in July 1932, a critique appeared in one of the resolutions, likely reflecting Darcy's views: TUUL organizers had little contact with workers, but when they did, they often employed "bombastic talk" likely to lead to "adventurism"—and alienate would-be recruits. In an open letter to all members of District 13 in October 1932, again likely drafted by Darcy, the district committee complained, "We express our radicalism falsely in sectarian acts and talk which few understand or which even drives large numbers of workers to an antagonistic attitude."[43] What Darcy did about such sectarianism reflects both his own approach to organizing and also the unusual degree of autonomy for the district organizer at the greatest distance from party headquarters.

Hynes's most important project in San Francisco seems to have been launching the *Waterfront Worker*, a mimeographed newsletter, part of the plan adopted in March 1932 to "immediately . . . issue the West Coast Bulletin for the marine workers." The first issue was less than immediate, perhaps one of Darcy's complaints about Hynes and his MWIU comrades. The *Waterfront Worker* finally appeared in December 1932. It announced only that it was "issued by a group of longshoremen for longshoremen." In April 1933, about the same time George returned as head of the PPTUS, a PPTUS operative code-named Eddy (perhaps one of George's many pseudonyms) claimed that the *Waterfront Worker* was being issued by "our people plus three dockers who are not members of our union [presumably the MWIU]." The "three dockers . . . not members of our union" may have been some of the party members Darcy had recruited in March 1932 to accompany him to the waterfront shape-up, especially Branch and Kirby, who had experience with publishing the *Western Worker*. Just as he had done in agricultural organizing, Darcy had recruited party members or supporters from the Unemployed Council to form a waterfront section. Among them was Elmer (Efrim) "Pop" Hanoff. Born in Russia, Hanoff had joined the CP in 1919 and held party leadership positions in California. Immigration officials ordered him deported in 1930, but the Soviet Union refused to accept him. He remained in the city, served as local TUUL secretary, and worked with the Unemployment

Councils. Bruce B. "Ben" Jones told me he had been involved; he was a party member and unemployed railroad fireman. Mitchell Slobodek, a seaman, was almost certainly involved in some capacity, since he was the party's waterfront section organizer throughout most of 1933.[44]

The second and third issues of the *Waterfront Worker*, in February and March 1933, apparently also Hynes's work, hinted at some new organization on the docks but provided no further information. The fourth issue, in April 1933, acknowledged the MWIU. The fifth issue, in May 1933, cited the MWIU as the only viable organization for longshoremen and called for a "United Front" of seamen, teamsters, and stevedores. The same issue carried a letter from Roy Hudson, head of the MWIU, and a long article on the refusal of Seattle longshoremen to load military supplies in 1919 for U.S. troops in Siberia, concluding, "The longshoremen hold a strategic position in the struggle." The June issue was highly critical of the newly chartered local of the International Longshoremen's Association, AFL, and pushed the MWIU as an alternative.[45]

RGASPI files contain a curious letter, unsigned and addressed to "Jack," almost certainly Jack Stachel, and dated March 10, 1933, between the second and third issues of the *Waterfront Worker*. The author was either Harrison George, who returned from the Philippines around then, or Eddy (if Eddy was not one of George's pseudonyms). Whether George or Eddy, the letter writer misspelled Hynes's name, suggesting he was not close to Hynes, despite claiming, "I have been working quite close with him." The very long letter—typical of George's letters—states that Hynes had reported, "The immediate objective is not to organize dock groups," and that the letter writer had told Hynes he was wrong. The letter continues, "On my arrive [*sic*] here, I found a badly demoralized group of marine comrades whose little work consisted in visiting a few ships and paying no attention whatsoever to work among longshoremen." This agrees with Darcy's description of the MWIU functionaries. The letter continues: "In our Bureau [PPTUS] it was immediately proposed that to get a maximum of results in our special work [smuggling propaganda into Japan and China], we would have to do everything possible to help build up the work among the American marine workers." In investigating the status of the MWIU on the San Francisco waterfront, the author learned, "our Union did not have the best standing among the longshoremen" and that "the longshoremen feared to have anything to do with us."

The letter writer's efforts on behalf of the MWIU were initially unavailing, "due to the weakness of the forces here as well as lack of proper attention on the part of the Party in this work." Further, the TUUL, "almost non-existent here," could provide no help. The letter continues: "After a long time, we succeeded in getting the Party to do something about this most important work, especially for such an important port as SF, with the result that they established a waterfront section, the units of which are to concentrate on the waterfront especially on several important docks." This may refer to the decision of the district secretariat in mid-March 1932 and Darcy's work in creating a waterfront section. However, the letter continues, "Hines [*sic*] and I drafted a plan of work for this section which the Party approved. We conceived the idea of a bulletin to be issued in the name of a group of longshoremen as a means of approach to the longshoremen." Thus, the letter contradicts both Darcy's account and the district secretariat minutes regarding the origin of the organizational plan for the waterfront and the origin and control of the *Waterfront Worker*. The letter then complained that the *Waterfront Worker* was "hiding the face of the Union," a concern George often raised later about Darcy and others.[46]

Likely in response to that letter, the national office wrote to Darcy in April to complain of the lack of support for Hynes and the MWIU, adding, "We wish to emphasize the importance of building the MARINE WORKERS INDUSTRIAL UNION, particularly on the Pacific Coast, where large shipments of war materials to the Far East is [*sic*] already taking place and which becomes of increasing importance daily with the rapidly developing war situation."[47] This exchange is typical of later relations between George and Browder, on the one hand, and between Browder and Darcy, on the other—George complained at length to Browder about Darcy, Browder admonished Darcy, and Darcy responded to Browder.

Darcy, however, assumed that it was Hynes who was complaining, and he wrote, "The reports that you have received from Comrade Hynes are obviously false in regards to a number of points." Darcy pointed to considerable success:

Since Comrade Hynes has come and with his help we have succeeded in organizing a waterfront Section of the Party. This consists in [a] great majority not of actual workers on the waterfront, but of unemployed workers, and also a considerable number who are not seamen or longshoremen at all. Our chief struggle with Comrade Hynes, and even the other Union comrades, is to make him use these comrades. He insists that they are unqualified for the work, that only seamen and longshoremen can approach seamen and longshoremen, etc. When we made a decision that the Section Organizer of that Section must be on the top fraction of that Union in order to coordinate the work, Comrade Hynes resisted and in fact, to this date, has failed to carry out the decision to notify the S.O. of the meetings regularly.

The section organizer (SO) was Mitchell Slobodek. Darcy described the waterfront section in mid-May 1933 as including "about 50 comrades of which about 25 are seamen and longshoremen," but, "Not more than five of these are involved in the work." He explained, "The reason the comrades are not involved, is largely due to the contemptuous and highly professional attitude [of] the two or three functionaries of the Union" who were given to "snotty remarks about the other comrades" and to "indecisiveness." B. B. Jones confirmed Darcy's account; he said in early 1935, "Before Jackson came here [August 1933] we were without any leadership whatsoever." Darcy continued: "Comrade Hynes has really not moved with events. . . . We decided that since Comrade Hynes had been asking to be taken out from this territory for a long time, that we grant his request and have him replaced."[48]

Darcy and Hynes apparently disagreed from the beginning and at a basic level over the proper way to organize waterfront workers. Hynes, committed to the revolutionary mission of the MWIU, was contemptuous of the ragtag group of unemployed comrades whom Darcy organized into a waterfront section. Darcy concluded that the MWIU had little appeal because it persisted in "serious sectarian errors." Hynes was gone by late July 1933, if not earlier. He was replaced as MWIU organizer by Harry Jackson (Henry Gliksohn), whose transfer from New York to San Francisco was dated August 11, 1933.[49]

In July, Darcy encouraged radicals among the longshoremen to join the newly chartered local of the International Longshoremen's Association and to form a militant, but not exclusively CP, caucus there. The caucus included Harry Bridges, Henry Schmidt, and other militants who were neither CP members nor sympathizers. They met at Equality Hall on Albion Street and called themselves Albion Hall. In September the district secretariat approved a "line" for its "opposition group" within the ILA: "To create distinct TUUL group as soon as possible, which group to issue the 'Waterfront Worker.'" The Albion Hall caucus was too politically diverse to be considered a "distinct TUUL group," and it never advocated for the MWIU, but some members of it, including Bridges, took responsibility for the *Waterfront Worker*, which now stated that it was issued by "a rank and file group in the ILA." When the Albion Hall group presented a slate in the local elections that month, they called themselves the "Committee of 500 Bona Fide Longshoremen Now Working on the S.F. Waterfront."[50]

Bridges, Schmidt, and another Albion Hall militant won election to the local's executive committee. In March 1934, as ILA locals all up and down the Pacific Coast moved toward a coastwise strike, the San Francisco local elected a large strike committee that then elected Bridges as chair. On May 9 ten thousand to fifteen thousand longshoremen walked out from northern Washington to Southern California, demanding a coastwise contract, union hiring halls, a six-hour day, and better wages, demands established by the ILA district leaders in July 1933. Greeted by picket lines upon entering Pacific Coast ports, ships' crews and officers quickly went on strike with issues of their own, adding more than six thousand seamen, marine firemen, marine cooks and stewards, marine engineers, and masters, mates, and pilots to the number on strike. Most teamsters refused to move cargoes unloaded by strikebreakers. Bridges, chairman of the strike committee for the largest ILA local, rapidly emerged as de facto leader of the local and, increasingly, for the entire coastwise strike.[51]

The Young Communist League called a meeting on the waterfront for noon, Memorial Day, May 30, to demonstrate against war and fascism and support the strikers. The YCL distributed leaflets widely, but the police refused a permit for the demonstration. Party officials tried to call off the meeting, but 250–300 young people gathered, milling in confusion when no speakers appeared. One version of events was that a YCL leader was hoisted to another's shoulders to explain that the meeting had been canceled. When he spoke, police attacked the crowd with nightsticks and blackjacks. The police version was that they were pelted with rocks before they attacked the crowd. A committee representing twenty-two organizations, headed by a Presbyterian minister, interviewed witnesses before calling it a "riot planned in advance by the police," one of the first usages of the concept of a police riot.[52]

Disputes within the local CP leadership escalated during the longshore and maritime strikes. Hynes was gone, but Harrison George remained to defend ideological orthodoxy against Darcy's more flexible approach. George, under various pseudonyms, wrote long letters to Browder complaining about Darcy. On May 26, seventeen days after the strike began, George sent a four-page, single-spaced, typed letter criticizing Darcy's conduct:

> Now, if half what I hear is true, the strike—from a Party viewpoint—is in such condition that although I'm busy as hell I simply must say something to you, since I cannot say anything to swell-head [Darcy].... 1. The Party face has been hidden, much to the injury of the Party and equally to the injury of the strike. 2.-A policy of "Tailism" is being carried out, and Economism; with almost no politicalization of the strike. If the role of the State is even mentioned, I have not heard of it.

"Hiding the face of the party" meant concealing the role of the party and keeping secret the party affiliations of those in the union. "Tailism" meant that the party was following the workers rather than leading them. "Economism," related to tailism, referred to focusing on economic issues such as wages and hours. George concluded by urging the national office to order the district committee "to bring the Party into the picture in its rightful place, and to politicalize the strike."[53] "Politicalization"—i.e., politicization—meant turning the workers from concern with immediate economic issues toward recognizing the repressive role of the state, accepting the leadership of the party, and committing to the defense of the

Soviet Union. Ten days later, George again wrote to Browder: "Exceptionalism of the rankest sort is expressed by both the comrades on the Strike Committee, (which we might understand) and by the comrades around the Dist Office. . . . An opportunist and syndicalist line is followed."[54] "Exceptionalism" referred to the argument, associated with Jay Lovestone and rejected by the party and the Comintern, that the United States was an exception to Marxist-Leninist theories of economic development.[55]

Similar concerns for the ideological quality of the strike efforts came from Seattle, CP District 12, where Morris Rappaport, an old opponent of Darcy, was now district organizer. Rappaport wrote to the New York office in mid-June: "District #12 and #13 . . . are pursuing two different policies in the strike. Our main attack [is] towards fascist and social-fascist leadership, who are our main danger in the strike. . . . In San Francisco it seems to me that their main attack is against the shipowners. . . . It is obviously clear that there is either something wrong with our policy or California's policy."[56] Following prevailing Third Period policy, Rappaport was defining the party's major obligation as "exposing" and denouncing the leaders of the striking AFL unions. Darcy, however, was focusing on the employers.

In response, Browder wired Darcy with pointed questions. The minutes of the District 13 Buro (executive committee) meeting of June 22, 1934, a time when the strike itself was moving toward its most crucial phase, reveal the Buro focused on ideological issues rather than strike tactics. The Buro resolved "that we call to Comrade H.G.'s attention that his activity, particularly in the strike, is a complete failure." Darcy wrote a long letter to Browder the same day: "How shall we judge our policy? By its academic corresponding to some formula, or by the results which our policy achieves in advancing the militant mass movement?" Darcy described Rappaport's critique as "evidence that the [District 12] comrades are outside the strike looking in, and not on the inside of the strike movement." Darcy went on to "vigorously protest against the direct mis-representation which has been made to you, and which you unfortunately accepted without verification" and specified that the District Buro was aware that George had been providing the New York office with a running criticism of their efforts.[57]

On July 5—known on the waterfront ever after as "Bloody Thursday"—police killed two unionists, Howard Sperry, a longshoreman, and Nicholas Bordoise (George Counderakis), a party member and member of the cooks' union who was volunteering in the union's soup kitchen. A hundred more were injured during a violent, daylong battle over efforts to reopen the port using strikebreakers. The governor then sent in the National Guard and the port reopened, using strikebreakers. On July 9 Darcy helped organize a funeral march by thousands of silent strikers and strike supporters from the waterfront up Market Street, filling that great thoroughfare as they followed flatbed trucks carrying the caskets of the two men killed on July 5. The police reluctantly agreed to stay away from the route of the funeral procession but specified that there were to be no Communists involved. The ILA funeral arrangements committee instead placed Darcy in one of the lead cars next to Julia Bordoise, widow of Nicholas Bordoise. Bordoise was taken to Cypress Lawn Cemetery, just south of the city, where Darcy delivered a stirring funeral address.[58]

The July 9 funeral procession for the two men killed on July 5 filled Market Street, stretching for a mile and taking an hour to pass any point. The San Francisco *News* estimated 7,000 marchers; the *Chronicle* thought it was closer to 15,000. Thousands more lined the sidewalks. Photo is from 1934 International Longshoremen's Association and General Strikes of San Francisco Collection.

On July 16–19 the San Francisco Labor Council coordinated a general strike, shutting down much of the city in support of the striking maritime workers and in opposition to police tactics and the presence of the National Guard. The Labor Council completely controlled the general strike and also took control over many aspects of the longshore and maritime strikes.[59]

On July 17, second day of the general strike, George composed yet another lengthy letter to Browder, not describing any of the momentous events then unfolding but instead citing various party resolutions in support of his accusation that Darcy was following a "wrong line" and an "opportunist line" rather than just making a few mistakes in following a correct line. He enumerated Darcy's errors:

> a) Hiding the face of the Party. . . . b) An opportunist [right deviation] distortion of the United Front. A failure to take the aggressive [*sic*] against the trade union bureaucrats, and a resignation of independent leadership. . . . d) A reliance on spontaneity. . . . Indeed, a syndicalist attitude. e) Failure to politicize the strike, particularly in reference to the war danger and to the slogan of Soviet Power. An uncritical acceptance not only of all demands, but of crassly reformist interpretation of demands, such as "spreading of work," namely, the "stagger system." f) Failure to emphasize, amounting to a concealment, of the

The trucks carrying the coffins of the two men, first that of Howard Sperry, a veteran of World War I, followed by that of Nicholas Bordoise (George Counderakis). Photo by C. B. Peterson from the Fang Family, *San Francisco Examiner* Photograph Archive. Both photos courtesy of Bancroft Library, University of California, Berkeley.

revolutionary trade union, the Marine Workers Industrial Union, and a liquida-
tory attitude toward the organization of the revolutionary opposition within
the reformist trade unions. g) Bureaucratic handling of the strike; both within
the Party where discussion was not allowed on policy; and in the trade unions,
where decisions of the trade union leadership were ignored or over-ridden.[60]

Though condemning the "stagger system"—efforts to spread work through shorter
hours—the CP had endorsed a seven-hour day.[61] A key demand of the ILA-PCD
was the six-hour day, a proposal intended to spread the work, a demand that originated with the ILA district leadership. With regard to bureaucratization, George
complained, "Day-to-day strike policy [was] being made practically by conversations between Comrade Darcy and Comrade Bridges, with perhaps some other
comrades of the fraction present by chance. In short, by bureaucratic methods
an opportunist line was being carried out." In response to the claim that he had
not been helpful during the strike, George proudly proclaimed, "The PPTUS, up
to the date of your letter to me had issued five different leaflets."[62]

During the general strike, anti-Communist actions erupted across the Bay
Area. On the first day of the general strike, Oakland police raided that city's CP
office and beat and arrested those inside; 50 men attacked the party office in
Hayward, beat its occupants, and burned its furnishings; and 150 men attacked
a communist meeting in Oakland. On the next day, as George was composing
his letter about Darcy's lapses, San Francisco police backed by National Guards-
men with machine guns raided the MWIU office and arrested everyone—85
in all—in the vicinity. Anonymous vigilantes, armed with rocks and clubs and
wearing heavy leather jackets, attacked the office of the *Western Worker* and CP
headquarters at 121 Haight Street. At each place a car drove past and men hurled
bricks through the windows. Then more cars drove up, and men rushed into the
building, broke up furniture and equipment, beat up anyone inside, and quickly
departed. Next police arrived and arrested those who had just been beaten. Seven
locations were raided that way on July 17. Total arrests that day numbered 350.
More raids followed.[63]

Vigilante and police raids continued through late July, well past the end of the
general strike. The identity of the vigilantes was never definitively established.
Ella Winter claimed that many were members of the American Legion, whom
"the police employed, gave workers['] clothes and Union buttons to break up
the workers' centers in SF." Others suggested they were strikebreakers hired by
the Industrial Association (the organization of most city corporations that was
directing the employers' side of the strikes), or businessmen, or police officers
out of uniform. An FBI report in 1940 claimed, "The raids were made by vigilante
committee composed possibly of a few members of the Police Department and
several members of the Teamsters' Union." The close cooperation between the

Damage to the *Western Worker* office caused by vigilantes, July 17, 1934. Photo courtesy of San Francisco History Center, San Francisco Public Library.

vigilantes and police points to some level of official approval, perhaps reaching to the mayor's office.[64]

CP membership had grown significantly through the early 1930s, but the vigilante actions led to a sharp drop. Darcy reported that between 1932 and 1934, membership had increased to three thousand, but "about 800 dropped out during the period of the terror. . . . the majority of those who dropped out were not in the Party a year."[65] Those losses were soon made up.

The striking unions agreed to arbitration. The CP generally opposed arbitration. In the end, the arbitration board granted the ILA's major demands: the six-hour day, a wage increase (less than the union had wanted, but significant), and union control of dispatching through a jointly funded hiring hall with a union dispatcher. ILA members returned to work late in July.[66]

The party's initial decision to focus on the San Francisco waterfront reflected Third Period concerns about disrupting the transportation of war materials, but

Darcy had worked consistently to minimize Third Period rhetoric and slogans. Darcy considered the MWIU "sectarian" and largely ignored it in organizing among longshoremen. The decision to encourage CP members and sympathizers to join the ILA took the District 13 leadership further away from Third Period concerns and toward the issues defined by the ILA Pacific Coast District leadership.

The intraparty debates in 1933 and 1934 presented two differing conceptions of the role of the party. Hynes, George, Rappaport, and others were not just defending the Third Period line but also seeking to preserve the party's revolutionary identity as they understood it. Darcy and those in the ILA leadership who were close to the CP were, in fact, "hiding the face of the party," and were, in fact, engaged in "tailism," "economism." and "opportunism." They ignored the party's revolutionary objectives in favor of immediate union objectives. The outcome—the general strike and the subsequent accession to local union leadership of a few CP members and sympathizers—owed something to Darcy's leadership. But it is also clear, as I have discussed at more length elsewhere, that Darcy and the party claimed credit for many things they did little to bring about.[67] The events in San Francisco soon contributed to a shift in the party line that led to the CP's significant role in the Committee on Industrial Organization (CIO) soon after, a topic covered in the next chapter.

Harry Bridges and the CP

The relationship between Harry Bridges and the Communist Party in 1934 and after was a subject of contention at the time and has continued to be since. Within days of the beginning of the strike, Bridges was accused of being a Communist, and claims continue to appear that Bridges was a Communist or was controlled by Communists. As I indicate in *Harry Bridges: Labor Radical, Labor Legend* (2023), my reading of evidence for the period through July 1934 is that his relationship to the CP was ambiguous. Bridges consistently denied that he had ever been a party member. He often acknowledged being a Marxist and receiving support and advice from Communists. In RGASPI documents, the first appearance of Bridges's name, chronologically, comes in correspondence from Harrison George, Browder's eyes and ears.[68]

In his letter to Browder on May 26, 1934, George called himself an "outsider," stated that no one from the district or the MWIU called on him during the strike, and said he "gathered such information as was available from events, from the Party press and bourgeois press, and any comrades whom I chanced to meet and who talked about the strike." He nonetheless identified "the Chairman of the Strike Committee [Bridges], and several of its most influen[tial] members" as "new comrades . . . scared to death" that they might be revealed as party members.

George especially criticized "Comrade Bridges" for ordering a party member to leave the union hall. "Day-to-day strike policy," George claimed, was being made "practically by conversations between Comrade Darcy and Comrade Bridges," who behaved as if "the strike is their property." Roy Hudson, after visiting San Francisco, said, "Many of the criticisms made by G were incorrect and were a result of a lack of direct contact with the situation as a whole." There is no way to establish whether George was in a position to know that Bridges was a party member or whether he was accepting the claims in the press.[69]

George's reference to Bridges as "Comrade" differs from the correspondence of both Darcy and Rappaport, neither of whom ever referred to Bridges as "Comrade."[70] Roy Hudson, secretary of the MWIU, however, in a report to the TUUL Buro on May 21, 1934 (before his visit to San Francisco), stated, "On the central strike committee in San Francisco, one-third of the members are members of our group, the chairman is a member of the P[arty]," which conflicts sharply with Darcy's statement that there were only six or eight CP members among the seventy-some members of the strike committee. Hudson, who was in New York, far removed from the scene, gave no indication of the source of his information; it may have been George's letters.[71] On July 31, after Hudson had visited San Francisco, he reported that Bridges (he did not say Comrade Bridges) had not carried out a party decision.[72] Joseph Zack, a CP functionary in Cleveland in 1934 who was later expelled, told an FBI agent in 1940 that Browder talked with him in July 1934 when en route from San Francisco to New York. Zack quoted Browder about Bridges: "In substance, 'Yes, he's our Number One Man,'" and "he was a headstrong individual, not so easy to get along with, 'but we have to get along with him.'" In 1971, long after Darcy had been expelled from the CP, he said about Bridges in 1934, "There was no question of bringing him into the party. . . . There was no need for it."[73] These contradictory sources regarding Bridges's relation to the party in 1934 are what lead me to call it ambiguous as of 1934.

State Elections, 1934

In early 1934, Darcy was planning for the state elections. For the first time, the party collected sufficient signatures to place its candidates on the state ballot. For the two most important offices, governor and U.S. senator, Darcy wanted to broaden the party's appeal by supporting candidates who were sympathetic to much of the party's program but not party members. For the Senate, Darcy wanted Lincoln Steffens. Steffens was willing, telling Darcy, "I came to like the idea of running, or standing, for the U S Senate on your ticket, because it would enable me to wind up my long life of research with an overt act to show the conclusion I had come to—finally." Darcy tried to persuade the PolBuro to permit this, but Stachel wrote the denial, specifying, "We could consider the nomination of Stephens [*sic*] . . . providing he publicly joins the Communist Party." Steffens declined, because, he said, as a "lifelong liberal, with liberal instincts and habits of mind, . . . I am not to be trusted in the Party or in the front rank of the struggle that is on."[74]

Darcy also failed to convince the national leadership to permit the California party to give any support to Upton Sinclair's campaign for governor. After Sinclair entered the Democratic Party's primary for governor, Darcy suggested dividing the statewide offices: Sinclair's organization, EPIC (End Poverty in California) would contest most state offices but support Steffens for the Senate and run no candidates for controller and state supreme court against the CP candidates, Anita Whitney and Leo Gallagher. In response, Darcy recalled, "Those sons of bitches ganged up on me, led by Browder, that I'm selling out the party and all that. And I said 'What the hell is wrong with you guys? You want [Frank] Merriam [the Republican candidate] to be Governor of California?' Stachel made a motion to test my loyalty to the Party, that I'd have to run for governor."[75]

Darcy ran for governor. When he failed to mount an aggressive campaign against Sinclair, Robert Minor took charge of the state campaign and focused it against Sinclair. Browder also demanded that the state party be more critical of Sinclair. The *Daily Worker*, on October 6, carried a highly critical article on Sinclair, attributed to Darcy.[76]

Louise Todd recalled significant difficulties in persuading party members not to support Sinclair. The vote totals suggest the likelihood of efforts to carry out the trade that Darcy had originally suggested, with many party members supporting Sinclair and some Sinclair supporters choosing Whitney and Gallagher. Six CP candidates appeared on the state ballot. Darcy got 5,826 votes (0.2 percent) for governor, but CP candidates for the relatively obscure offices of secretary of state and state treasurer received 25,725 and 47,585 votes (1.2 percent and 2.3 percent), respectively—that is, Darcy did not receive most of the vote that went to other party candidates. In the two elections for which there were no Democratic candidates, Anita Whitney got 100,820 votes (4.9 percent) for controller and Leo Gallagher received 240,000 votes (17 percent) for supreme court. Years later, Darcy told me, "I sabotaged my campaign as much as I could."[77]

Trials and Imprisonment of California CP Leaders, 1934–1935

The prominence of CP leaders and members—actual and alleged—in strikes and in the successful drive to put the party on the state ballot generated legal consequences. In the aftermath of CP support for the Imperial County farm strikers in 1930, several party members had been convicted of criminal syndicalism and sentenced to prison. The much more successful strikes of 1933 brought a similar but more far-reaching response. A new organization, the Associated Farmers, with major funding from leading California corporations, promoted charges against CAWIU activists. On July 20, 1934, when vigilantes and police were raiding left organizations throughout the Bay Area, police and sheriff's deputies in Sacramento arrested several Communists and CAWIU members, including Pat Chambers and Caroline Decker. Eighteen were charged with criminal syndicalism.[78]

The criminal syndicalism defendants came to trial in Sacramento in January 1935. After almost six weeks of courtroom maneuvers, the jury spent nearly 95 hours in deliberations and took 118 ballots before finding six defendants not guilty. Eight, including Chambers and Decker, were found guilty of conspiracy to violate the criminal syndicalism act but not of criminal syndicalism itself. The eight were sentenced to indeterminate sentences of one to fourteen years. Leo Gallagher, the most prominent of the defense attorneys, was fined for contempt of court.[79]

In August, a month after the arrests in Sacramento, Louise Todd, Anita Whitney, and others were indicted for perjury in connection with collecting signatures to place the CP on the state ballot. Todd went on trial in San Francisco in February 1935. Her trial lasted just a day, and the jury deliberated for a bit over an hour before finding her guilty. She was sentenced to one to six years in prison. After her appeals failed, she was sent to the women's prison at Tehachapi. Whitney, age sixty-eight, was next brought to trial, also found guilty, and sentenced to a hundred days in jail or a fine of two hundred dollars.[80]

Sam Darcy was indicted in August 1935 for perjury on his voter registration papers and on his filing for governor. By then, however, he was in Moscow (see the next two chapters). San Francisco police officials specified that he would be arrested as soon as he returned to the United States.[81] He remained in Moscow.

By mid-1935 the CP had become much more visible in the Bay Area and in California more generally. Under Darcy's leadership, the CP issued its own newspaper, supported strikes by farmworkers and maritime workers, gained a place on the state ballot, and made a respectable showing in the 1934 elections. In doing so, Darcy and some party members had moved away from the strident Third Period rhetoric and toward the political mainstream. Those patterns reached a high point during the next four years.

THE POPULAR FRONT, 1934–1941

The West Coast strikes of 1934 came as the Executive Committee of the Comintern was moving away from the Third Period analysis and toward what in France was called the *Front populaire*, the People's Front, and was usually called the Popular Front in the United States. Georgi Dimitrov, head of the Comintern, formally announced the change of direction in mid-1935, due largely to Hitler's rise to power and his evisceration of the German CP. By then, events in California and France were already moving toward a Popular Front.

Though national party leaders had quashed Darcy's efforts in the 1934 state election, detailed analysis of the West Coast strikes led the party further away from the millenarian thinking and Third Period sectarianism of the 1920s and early 1930s and toward the mainstream of organized labor. By the mid-1930s, many CP members in California were actively involved in unions and some had been elected to union office. Instead of preparing to lead the supposedly imminent uprising of the workers, they found themselves immersed in collective bargaining and contract enforcement.

Lessons of the Strike, Dissolution of the TUUL, and Origins of the Popular Front

San Francisco came first on the agenda when the U.S. PolBuro met on July 31, 1934. Earl Browder and Roy Hudson, head of the TUUL, had recently returned from San Francisco. In his report Browder greatly exaggerated the role of the CP in the strikes, acknowledged the failure of the MWIU, and noted that the San Francisco comrades now saw the MWIU mostly as a problem. Hudson largely endorsed Darcy's view that the party "should understand things not as a formula but as a process."[1]

Probably unknown to the participants in that July 31 PolBuro meeting, the Anglo-American Secretariat in Moscow had taken up the San Francisco strike the previous week. William Schneiderman, former YCL leader in California, now CPUSA representative on the AAS (see next chapter), took the lead in drafting "Lessons of the San Francisco General Strike." A lengthy analysis, it was approved by the ECCI in late August and filed with the most important communications from the ECCI to the CPUSA. Among many other things, the report recommended that future CP participation in labor organizing draw upon the San Francisco experience and "work within the AFL." U.S. party leaders likely had their copy by October 25, when Jack Stachel informed PolBuro members, "The main task is to work in the AFL."[2]

In what may be another example of Darcy taking advantage of his distance from party headquarters, he began to dissolve the West Coast MWIU. Following the 1934 strike, leaders of the International Seamen's Union (ISU), AFL, tried to block MWIU members from getting jobs. Darcy, long critical of the MWIU, informed Stachel on November 21, "We are instructing all comrades who are threatened . . . to join the I.S.U."—that is, the MWIU was being discarded. Morris Rappaport, District 12 organizer, and Harry Jackson, MWIU organizer, strongly opposed Darcy's move. Jackson was so adamant that he was removed from his position as a party functionary.[3] These developments in San Francisco, on the Pacific Coast, and in the PolBuro came at the same time the French CP was negotiating a united front with the French Socialist Party. With encouragement from Moscow, the French CP extended this united front to petit bourgeois and peasant parties, making it no longer a united front of the left but a coalition that extended to the center—a *Front populaire.*[4]

On December 5, 1934, Browder was in Moscow, meeting with the ECCI to present an extensive report on the U.S. party. He announced, "In California, our party has grown the most rapidly of any of our districts." He significantly exaggerated the role of the CP in the events in San Francisco before presenting his conclusions: "It was necessary to shift the main emphasis to work inside the A.F.L. and to put the Red Unions into the background, or, in some cases, to merge them entirely in the A.F.L." By "merge," Browder meant what Darcy had done with the Pacific Coast MWIU: sending members of TUUL unions into their AFL counterparts. The ECCI's response contained no Third Period rhetoric about imminent war and social fascists; instead it directed the CPUSA to dissolve the TUUL and all its unions—to follow Darcy's lead—and to work to "overcome sectarian remnants in the ranks of the Party and adherents of the revolutionary trade union movement." On December 20 the PolBuro gave post facto approval to the dissolution of the West Coast MWIU and began the same process for the East Coast. The resolution acknowledged what Darcy had said years before: MWIU activists' sectarianism held no appeal to most seamen and undermined efforts to work within the AFL seamen's union.[5]

The California CP and the Unions, 1935–1938

The CAWIU was dissolved along with other TUUL unions. It had already been decapitated when several of its leaders were imprisoned after their convictions in the Sacramento criminal syndicalism trial. Now many CP and YCL members busied themselves in the burgeoning union movement that developed beginning in 1933 and, especially, during and after the 1934 strikes.

My biography of Bridges deals at length with his and his associates' relation to the Communist Party in the mid-1930s. Notably, on June 16, 1934, the District Buro appointed "Comrade Schmidt," apparently Henry Schmidt, as "Chairman of A.F.L. opposition work," but the minutes never again mention Schmidt in that position. The minutes of the district committee for August 20, 1934, record appointment of several new members to the District Buro, including "HB." Bridges once told me he had been "co-opted" onto party committees—that Darcy had arranged that Bridges could participate without being a CP member because of the dangers involved with being a member. In CP usage, however, the term "co-opted" usually referred to a party member placed on a committee without having been elected. However, no subsequent District Buro minutes mention "HB" as a member.[6]

Throughout 1935 the minutes of District 13 Buro meetings do not indicate that Bridges was a Buro member; other people were consistently identified as reporting on waterfront matters, and a few minutes refer to "HB" as being invited, requested, or agreeing to do something. In September 1935, Jack Johnstone, acting district organizer, described the "party comrades in marine" as "an excellent bunch" and "young in the party" but complained that it was "difficult to get the units to meet" and that "political discussions are infrequent and very inadequate."[7]

By then—late 1935 and early 1936—the party's membership among union members was concentrated on the waterfront. Of 264 party members in San Francisco unions, 180 were on the waterfront—that is, about 2–3 percent of the 6,000–7,000 longshoremen and maritime workers were CP members. However, as of mid-1936, party members or sympathizers were officers in several maritime unions or locals. RGASPI documents show the comrades in the Pacific Coast maritime unions providing information to the national CP and its various subsidiaries and occasionally making requests. The RGASPI files have no directives to the waterfront fractions from the national CP or from the District 13 Buro. By mid-1937 Schneiderman, by then the head of District 13, was complaining about "a tendency of our Comrades against recruiting new people into the Party," and he lodged that complaint specifically against the "longshore unit of SF."[8]

The party's influence in the maritime unions was greater than its membership. One measure of that influence came in June 1936, at the second annual convention of the Maritime Federation of the Pacific Coast (MFP), a central body for Pacific Coast maritime unions, when delegates voted on a resolution endorsing a Farmer-Labor Party, then the CP's position. The vote was 41 percent in favor, 50 percent opposed. All delegates from the two smallest unions, the American Radio Telegraphists Association (ARTA, shipboard radio operators) and Alaska Fishermen (employees of commercial fisheries), voted for the resolution, along with about half of the International Longshoremen's Association delegates (including all from San Francisco), four of the five delegates from the Marine Firemen (shipboard engine room workers), two of the four from the Marine Cooks and Stewards, and three of the eight from the Sailors Union of the Pacific (deck workers). All delegates from the licensed officers' unions (Marine Engineers; Masters, Mates, and Pilots) opposed. In San Francisco the other large union where CP members or sympathizers had a significant presence was the ILA warehouse local.[9] (The next chapter provides examples of individual CP members' activities in several of these unions.)

RGASPI files contain three documents regarding Harry Bridges's role in the CPUSA as of 1936–1938. The minutes of the meeting of the CPUSA's Ninth National Convention (1936) do not record the names of all those elected to the Central Committee, but in April 1937 Browder reported to the AAS, "The Pacific Coast Marine Workers' Federation is under a left leadership. Its chief leader is a member of our Central Committee." The reference is clearly intended to refer to the MFP and to Bridges, although Bridges was never "chief leader" of the MFP. In January 1938 in Moscow, Browder and Foster presented the AAS with a list of the twenty-four Central Committee members elected in 1936. Number 21 was "Rossi." Browder and Foster provided this biography for "Rossi":

> ROSSI (Bridges)—CP USA CC member. President of the Longshoremen's and Warehousemen's Union. A strong trade union leader and grass-roots worker but thus far has limited party expertise and experience.[10]

A third document in the AAS files, a "Note sur les candidatures au B.P. du C.C. du P.C. Etats-Unis" (Note on the candidates for the Polburo of the Central Committee of the CP of the United States), dated 8.2.36, probably indicating August 2, 1936, and marked "strictement [strictly] confidential," presents a list of proposed

PolBuro members with brief biographies, followed by several pages of notes in Darcy's handwriting. (Darcy was then CPUSA representative on the AAS.) On one page the name Bridges appears at the bottom of a list of alternative possibilities for membership. He was not approved.[11]

Though Bridges was elected to the Central Committee in 1936, that position did not change his practice of acting contrary to the party line when it came to his union. I consider it highly unlikely that Bridges ever had a party membership card or paid dues. It's also very likely that any formal party position for Bridges ended by 1938, both because as early as March 1936 the AAS was warning of the danger that non-citizen members might be deported and because Bridges and the party had become highly aware of exactly that danger by early January 1938. Thereafter, Bridges's relationship to the CP seems to have been like that described in 1972 by Joseph Starobin, an important party functionary until 1954; Starobin described Bridges as "never a Communist" but instead an "influential," who "enjoyed intimate ties with the Party, usually on his own terms" and "cooperated closely" with CP officials. Such influentials may or may not have been party members, but they were listened to, consulted with, offered advice, and asked for advice, but were not given directions and were not under Party discipline.[12]

Party leaders closely followed developments after October 1936, when the AFL suspended all unions affiliated with John L. Lewis's Committee on Industrial Organization. Two CIO unions, the Steel Workers Organizing Committee and the United Automobile Workers, soon scored successes. Other CIO unions were organizing workers throughout the mass-production sectors of the economy, where unions had been either feeble or nonexistent. By August 1937, CIO unions counted more members than all AFL affiliates.[13]

In September 1936, in Moscow, Clarence Hathaway told the AAS about the party's difficulty in balancing support for CIO organizing with its commitment to the unity of the AFL. Hathaway reported that CIO leaders "have shown a readiness to consult with us" and that Lewis had hired forty to fifty Communists as CIO organizers. In early March 1937 the AAS decided that the CP should give full support and "guidance" to the CIO but reiterated its hopes for "eventual reunification of the whole labor movement." Browder, in Moscow on April 4, 1937, assured the AAS that "with the CIO and its leadership we have the closest cooperative relations." In August 1937, Tim Ryan (Frank Waldron), then the CPUSA's representative on the AAS, concluded, "For the first time in the history of our Party we are beginning to establish our 'legal citizenship' in the labor movement on a wide scale."[14]

As CP influence in some West Coast waterfront unions became apparent, anti-Communism grew in others, and conflict between them eventually destroyed the MFP. Within the MFP, Harry Bridges led the left faction and Harry Lundeberg of the Sailors Union of the Pacific (SUP) led the right. Lundeberg was neither a conservative nor typical of most AFL anti-Communists—he was instead a committed syndicalist, opposing the CP from an ideological position much like that of the Industrial Workers of the World. At the 1937 MFP convention, Lundeberg led those opposed to affiliation with the CIO and to endorsement of the CIO's political arm, Labor's Non-Partisan League. Soon after, members of the ILA Pacific Coast District (of which Bridges was then president) voted by almost 4–1 in favor of joining the CIO; they became the International Longshoremen's and Warehousemen's Union (ILWU), with Bridges as the founding president. The Marine Cooks and Stewards broke away from the ISU and joined the CIO as the National Union of Marine Cooks and Stewards. ARTA joined as the American Communications Association. The licensed officers' unions stayed in the AFL, and the SUP and MFOW (Pacific Coast Marine Firemen, Oilers, Watertenders, and Wipers Association) tried to find a middle way, although the SUP eventually rejoined the AFL.[15]

After the CIO held its first national conference, in mid-October 1937, Ryan reported to the AAS that the party had "*decisive political influence* [his emphasis] in the national leadership and district bodies" of five unions. Among those five, three had some presence in California. The United Electrical Workers was developing a base in Southern California, the International Woodworkers had some presence in Northern California, and the United Cannery, Agricultural, Packing, and Allied Workers was active in several areas. The ILWU and the West Coast maritime unions were not on Ryan's list.[16]

California Communists' Uncertain Path to the Popular Front, 1935–1937

Throughout 1935 the *Western Worker* continued to attack Roosevelt and the New Deal, condemning the work-relief programs of the Works Progress Administration (WPA) as "a wage-cutting, anti-strike club held over the heads of every worker." The *Western Worker* also condemned "the strike-breaking activities of Roosevelt's Labor Relation Boards, and the strike-breaking, company union Wagner Labor Disputes Bill." The party also continued to decry "social fascists," especially Upton Sinclair and his EPIC organization. In April 1935 the *WW* saw the defeat of EPIC candidates in Los Angeles elections as evidence of "the fallacy of its program of 'reformism' and 'liberalism.'"[17]

At the same time, however, the California CP was following a resolution of the U.S. Central Committee in January 1935, on creating a United Front—that is, a coalition of the left. This was done at first by organizing United Front activities around particular issues. In March the CP claimed an attendance of six thousand at a United Front rally against the state criminal syndicalism law. Speakers included party stalwarts and also Assemblyman Paul Richie, a liberal Democrat from Southern California; Redfern Mason of the San Francisco Newspaper Guild; and Ben Legere of the Democratic Council, a San Francisco Democratic Party organization. Similar United Front rallies demanded freedom for Tom Mooney.[18] (The Mooney case stemmed from a bomb that exploded at a San Francisco parade in 1916, killing nine people. Mooney and Warren Billings were convicted. Although the chief witness was later proven to be a perjurer, succeeding Republican governors refused to release the two. Throughout much of the 1920s and 1930s, the CP kept that issue alive.[19]) All of these United Front activities bore a strong similarity to those of the 1920s and early 1930s: they were all on terms defined by the CP, not terms negotiated with any other organization.

In July 1935 the Seventh World Congress of the Comintern met in Moscow. Darcy had left California in late May, and the PolBuro belatedly named him as a delegate.[20] Darcy later recalled events when Georgi Dimitrov, general secretary of the Comintern, met with the U.S. delegation. Before that meeting, Darcy and Dimitrov had spoken privately, in German. Dimitrov showed Darcy a piece of paper with the statement "Franklin Roosevelt represents the fascist trends in our country." Dimitrov asked Darcy, "Is it true that that's the position of the party?" Darcy agreed. It was customary that if Dimitrov planned to criticize a national party in his address to the Congress, he first met with the delegation to indicate his concern. In addressing the U.S. delegation, Dimitrov spoke in German and Darcy translated. Dimitrov read part of his proposed report: "Only a confirmed idiot could fail to see that the forces of reaction are uniting behind [Alf] Landon and the forces of progress are uniting behind Franklin Roosevelt." Darcy recalled Browder's reaction: "He shrunk into his clothing and looked so wretched." Asked to respond, Browder just shook his head. Dimitrov then said, "Well, since there seems to be agreement, I will change the wording to say, not 'a confirmed idiot' but 'only an addict of phrase mongering could make a mistake like that.'"[21]

In October 1935, *The Communist*, the U.S. party's theoretical organ, published Dimitrov's comments, including his statement that "only a confirmed addict of the use of hackneyed schemes" would claim that Roosevelt's New Deal represented incipient fascism. Dimitrov also suggested that the United Front in the United States "might" take the form of a "Workers' and Farmers' Party." William Z. Foster quickly expanded on this to argue for a "new mass anti-fascist party," a "Labor Party."[22]

Chastened, and perhaps with some new respect for Darcy, U.S. party leaders, while still in Moscow, decided that Darcy should replace Schneiderman as the CPUSA's representative on the AAS. Given Darcy's legal jeopardy, that assignment also kept him out of court. District 13 had no district organizer from late May to early September.[23]

With no district organizer, local activists took the lead in mid-July in inviting all San Francisco unions to send delegates to form a United Labor campaign for local elections. Thirty-six organizations sent representatives; many were not CP members or supporters. The chair was Eugene Dietrich, a militant leader during the longshore strike but not a CP member. A United Labor Party was organized. The *WW* spoke glowingly of the prospects that "a united front can be built up which will be the only guarantee against the further growth of fascism in the present reactionary city political machine."[24]

By August more information had reached California party members about the Seventh World Congress and the People's Front approach. In early August the *WW* reported that the party's "major task" was now "establishment of the proletarian united front and the people's front of all toilers against Fascism and War." On September 23 the *WW* carried a full page with the headline "Main Task Is Creating People's Front."[25]

In late August the District Buro selected Redfern Mason, president of the San Francisco Newspaper Guild, as the United Labor Party's candidate for mayor. Other candidates included George Andersen, a lawyer (see next chapter), for municipal judge; Ben Legere, a Democrat, for sheriff; and William Riesener, a Democrat, for assessor. The six candidates for supervisor included one announced Communist, a leader in the longshore union, a member of the Iron Workers' Union, a member of the Carpenters' Union, a Utopian Society activist, and a leader of the unemployed. The United Labor Party claimed the endorsement of thirty-five local unions, including most waterfront unions, and support from a section of EPIC. However, the District Buro provided all direction for the United Labor Party and selected its candidates. The party's dominant role was also obvious to others.[26]

The final United Labor rally, on October 30, featured Mason, Harry Bridges, Lincoln Steffens, and John Pelletier, a Democratic assemblyman from Los Angeles. However, as the *WW* reported, "The undoubted mass support which was developed for the program of the United Labor candidates was not sufficiently reflected in the final votes counted." The United Labor slate lost badly. Mason placed third for mayor, with fewer than 8 percent of the vote. Andersen got about 27 percent in the two-way election for judge. In analyzing the results, the District Buro acknowledged that the CP was "the driving force behind the united front" and criticized party factions in key unions as derelict in mobilizing those unions.[27]

In late October 1935, toward the very end of the political campaign, District 13 welcomed Bill Schneiderman as district organizer. Less prone to challenge party authority than Darcy, Schneiderman soon elaborated on the lessons that the CPUSA leadership had learned in Moscow, closely paraphrasing some of

Dimitrov's language. "We would make . . . [a] mistake," he warned, "if we branded Roosevelt and his policies as fascist. The real fascist threat comes from the reactionary circles of the Republican Party old guard, the American Liberty League, the Hearsts and Coughlins." He went on, however, to present the PolBuro's gloss on Dimitrov's message: "This does not mean that Roosevelt and the New Deal is an obstacle to fascism; on the contrary, the New Deal served the purposes of finance-capital and helped encourage the process toward fascism."[28]

Schneiderman was delivering the new line of the CPUSA, its initial interpretation of the People's Front. Roosevelt may not be a fascist, but he was not to be trusted. Schneiderman explained that the party needed to ally with trade unions, socialists, the EPIC movement, and "the poor and middle farmers and the city middle class, the professionals, intellectuals," and to "become a broad People's Front." And, he continued, still propounding the CPUSA leadership's position, the "most important political expression of the united front" was "a Farmer-Labor Party." Such a party, explained the *WW* in December 1935, would not introduce socialism but would instead "strengthen the working calss [*sic*] so that it may become capable in due time to seize power and establish itself [as] the master of life in a Soviet America."[29]

At the national level, United Front activities became broader than before. A "new United Front Committee for Defense of the Scottsboro Boys" included not only the party's International Labor Defense but also the Methodist Federation for Social Service, the National Association for the Advancement of Colored People (NAACP), the American Civil Liberties Union (ACLU), and the League for Industrial Democracy. In early 1936 the *WW* began to carry notices for meetings of such groups as the ACLU. In San Francisco, United Front rallies against the criminal syndicalism law included prominent liberal Democrats and union leaders who were not close to the CP.[30]

Thus, by early 1936 the "People's Front" was being interpreted as a Farmer-Labor Party. The CPUSA leadership and the CP in District 13 continued to be highly critical of Roosevelt and New Deal Democrats. The *WW* bemoaned that Culbert Olson, chairman of the Democratic State Committee, had "lined up with reactionaries" to support Roosevelt's renomination. In May the *WW* proclaimed, "The Democratic and Republican Parties are but two faces to the same coin," and "Roosevelt, Farley, McAdoo and Company . . . mislead the toilers into the camp of capitalism."[31]

Darcy, in Moscow, regularly reviewed the U.S. and CP press. He became more and more disturbed by the CPUSA's emphasis on creating a third party. He recalled, "The farmer-labor party was another name for the Communist party—it wasn't much different." Furthermore, early polls suggested that Roosevelt might lose. Darcy feared that "a farmer-labor party which would take away at least 100,000 votes, maybe more, would be a disaster." He shared his concern with André Marty, head of the AAS, and they went together to Dmitry Manuilsky, deputy head of the Comintern. Manuilsky spoke with Stalin, who asked Foster and Browder to come to Moscow. Darcy met them at the airport and told them, "Your advocacy of a labor-farmer party is sabotaging the whole idea of Stalin to make friends with Roosevelt. . . . The Germans are getting ready for war."[32]

James Ryan's biography of Browder places Foster and Browder's trip to Moscow in March 1936. Browder accepted the importance of reelecting Roosevelt but argued that an outright endorsement by the CPUSA would lose Roosevelt more votes than it would gain him.[33] Instead, Browder proposed that the party would temporarily jettison efforts for the Farmer-Labor Party and that Browder would run for president as the CP candidate. In early July, Browder explained to the party's national convention, "A large Communist vote will strengthen the movement for the Farmer-Labor Party and will exert a powerful influence upon the trade unions and the Socialist Party to join actively in building of the Farmer-Labor Party—the only effective barrier to reaction and fascism in this country." Browder spoke in San Francisco on August 13. The *WW* claimed that nine thousand people attended to hear Browder proclaim, "Landon and [Frank] Knox are the main enemy, who must be defeated at all costs." The *WW* continued: "The Communist candidate warned, however, against placing any trust in President Roosevelt to defeat Fascism, to turn back the forces who would place American[s] under a bloody dictatorship as have Hitler and Mussolini in Europe."[34] Though CP leaders claimed they were working to defeat Landon, they were constantly faced with the charge that their campaign would inevitably draw votes *away* from Roosevelt and potentially cause the election of Landon.

Though CP leaders in District 13 and the *WW* faithfully followed the party line and urged support for Browder as the best means of defeating Landon, they failed to persuade many—probably most—party members of that logic. There are fewer materials in RGASPI files for 1936 than for earlier years, but one incident reported there demonstrates how even a PolBuro member failed to understand that Browder's campaign was intended to further the election of Roosevelt. Roy Hudson, a PolBuro member, was present when the California Federation of Labor state convention met in late September. Some forty of the four hundred delegates were party members, and other delegates were close to the party. Hudson's report was highly critical of those party members for failing to protest against the endorsement of Roosevelt or to fight for a resolution endorsing a Farmer-Labor Party: "In this Convention, where the left wing influence was strong, not a single voice was raised to point out that giving a blank check to Roosevelt was not the way to defeat and hold in restraint, the reactionary forces united around the Landon-Knox ticket." Hudson also noted that the failure to attack Roosevelt "undoubtedly created confusion in the minds of some."[35] If Hudson so misunderstood the purpose of Browder's campaign, it would seem that the purpose was, in fact, never made clear to most party functionaries much less rank-and-file party members.

CP members and sympathizers who had been elected as delegates to the state federation convention were not confused. They undoubtedly understood better than Hudson how bizarre it was to insist, on the one hand, that Landon should be defeated at all costs and to maintain, on the other hand, that this could best be accomplished by voting for the CP candidate. Those union leaders were far less confused than Hudson and were undoubtedly more closely in touch with the political views of their members.

Some union leaders who were close to the CP openly supported Roosevelt. In early October, Bridges urged his local, ILA Local 38-79, to "take *independent political action*; that is to organize and build the sentiment among unions to support such groups as the Labor's Non-Partisan League, which has endorsed President Roosevelt for reelection." At a membership meeting in late October, the members of Bridges's local voted both to endorse Roosevelt for reelection and to donate $750 (equivalent to $16,000 in 2023) to his campaign. The ILA Pacific Coast District newspaper reported, "The San Francisco Local of Longshoremen boldly threw overboard the policy of non-political action. . . . This election is, indeed, a choice between Democracy and Fascism."[36]

Despite constant efforts to persuade CP members and supporters to register to vote as Communists, the total number of registered Communist voters fell significantly, from 1,857 in August 1934 to 1,095 in August 1936. Browder drew nearly 11,000 votes statewide, ten times the number registered as Communists, but only 0.4 percent of the total vote, and about one-tenth of the vote cast for Anita Whitney as the CP candidate for controller in 1934. However, party membership was growing—during the presidential campaign, the party signed up 2,600 new members. Before that recruiting drive, the California party counted about 2,300 members. Six months later, about 3,300 paid monthly dues, suggesting it was still necessary to sign up two members to gain one.[37]

Though the official position of the CPUSA leadership remained that the Popular Front in the United States would be best realized through a Farmer-Labor Party, many CP members and sympathizers in the unions openly supported Roosevelt and New Deal Democrats. By mid-1937, party leaders were hurrying to catch up.

The Popular Front at High Tide, 1937–1939

Though the CPUSA moved toward the *Front populaire* slowly and uncertainly in 1935 and 1936, the party was fully committed to working with New Deal Democrats by mid-1937. During 1937–1939 the California CP moved very close to the political mainstream—partly through circumstances over which the party had no influence, partly due to the presence of party members or supporters in CIO unions, and partly because of the People's Front line of the Comintern. The closer the CP moved to embrace Roosevelt and the New Deal, the greater grew their potential to influence local and state politics. Circumstances in California came together briefly during 1937–1939 to put the CP into a position where its leaders could meet with Democratic candidates for state and legislative office to discuss campaign tactics and legislative initiatives. Issues that the party had pressed for years became part of mainstream politics, if only for a short while.

As of January 1937, however, the *WW* was still criticizing Roosevelt. The CP's "Tasks in California" in early February still included creating a Farmer-Labor Party. Early in March, however, the *WW* noted the creation of local branches of Labor's Non-Partisan League, a CIO organization that endorsed candidates and sought to mobilize union and community resources to support its candidates. In March the paper announced that the CP was withdrawing its candidate for the Los Angeles City Council in favor of the candidate endorsed by the County Labor Council and other "progressive and liberal forces."[38]

This new role for the party posed potential dangers for its endorsed candidates. In May the party urged Los Angeles voters to defeat the incumbent mayor, Frank Shaw, but also said about the liberal candidate, John Anson Ford, "Ford is NOT the candidate of the Communist Party. . . . Ford is not a Communist. . . . The Communist Party has repeatedly and publicly criticized Ford's serious mistakes and his failure to come out with a clearer program and stronger fight for the interests of labor and the people." The CP also qualified its endorsement of Al Sessions, editor of the Kern County *Labor Journal*, as a write-in candidate in a special election in the Tenth Congressional District, stating, "Al Sessions is not a Communist," and "His program is not a Communist program. We do not agree with Sessions on many questions."[39]

In San Francisco the party announced that it would field candidates for supervisor and school board in the November 1937 elections but that the CP candidates would withdraw "in the event of a labor and progressive slate being formed." In August the party presented three candidates for supervisor and two for the school board, on a good government platform. At the same time, Schneiderman called upon "progressive unions" to create a slate of candidates and a platform. After an Honest Government Committee was formed by the city's CIO Industrial Union Council (where the party had significant influence), the CP ran only Anita Whitney for supervisor but endorsed four others supported by the Honest Government Committee. Of the five, only one, a popular incumbent, won. The others received between 9,600 and 16,000 votes, far short of the 69,000 required to win. Whitney got 9,850 votes, placing fourteenth in a field of twenty-two.[40]

The party soon completed its transition from persistent and vitriolic critic of Roosevelt and the New Deal to staunch supporter. On January 1, 1938, District 13 launched a new newspaper, *People's World* (*PW*), a daily paper replacing the semiweekly *WW*. Al Richmond, the new managing editor, twenty-three years old, brought three years of experience at the *Daily Worker*. Harrison George became executive editor, his duties limited to writing editorials and a personal column. Like the party, the new paper moved toward the mainstream, featuring some news stories with little or no political commentary. The final page became a sports page, and columns dealt with movies, radio programs, art, and helpful hints for women. Typical of most daily papers at the time, photos of attractive young women in skimpy outfits appeared regularly. Saturday's paper included a magazine with articles by prominent liberals as well as CP members, a woman's page (including Comrade Kitty's tips on how to be fashionable on a budget), a page for children, and a page of comics—though the comics were definitely political. Glowing accounts about the Soviet Union and Stalin's speeches still appeared but were fewer in number. Articles by non-Communist liberals began to appear, including Upton Sinclair, no longer a fascist or social fascist. George Washington, Thomas Jefferson, Andrew Jackson, and, especially, Abraham Lincoln all received positive stories. Along with the new format came a full-blown embrace of FDR and the New Deal. On January 5, 1938, an editorial announced, "Mr. President, We're Behind You!"[41]

The 1938 elections came amid international crisis. Japan continued to war against China. The republican government of Spain, assisted by the Soviet Union, continued to resist the army of Francisco Franco, who had support from Fascist Italy and Nazi Germany. Both conflicts had received major attention from the CP before 1938, and the struggle in Spain had brought an outpouring of funds and volunteers (see next chapter). In Moscow, trials of accused traitors, labeled "Trotskyites" and "Nazi spies" continued, but important new elements grabbed international headlines in 1938. Nazi Germany absorbed Austria in April. In September, Neville Chamberlain, the British prime minister, agreed to permit Germany to dismember Czechoslovakia. Late that year, American volunteers began to return from Spain as the republican government veered toward collapse.

The AFL and CIO continued to spar, with their affiliates sometimes engaging in bruising jurisdictional fights. This split in organized labor occupied the attention of the PolBuro in March. Browder specified that the party should work to unify labor through the 1938 elections: "We must use whatever powers we have to try to induce the CIO to carry on a real unity policy in the political field. . . . We must fight for maximum labor unity in order to keep progressive unity."[42] In California, Browder's objective was accomplished more successfully than he or anyone else could possibly have imagined, though not through the efforts of the CP.

Throughout the 1938 primary and general election campaigns, *PW* gave extensive coverage to Labor's Non-Partisan League (LNPL). Estolv Ward, a party member and LNPL officer, later estimated that 90 percent of the staff of the Northern California LNPL were party members.[43] The CP stopped short of any actual endorsement, either of the LNPL or specific candidates, but a reader would have had few doubts about the position of the paper or of the CP. The party offered only two candidates in the 1938 elections: Anita Whitney for controller and Leo Gallagher, who sought both the Communist and Democratic nominations for secretary of state (possible under California's cross-filing law). It was widely assumed that Frank Jordan, a Republican and the incumbent secretary of state, would repeat his long-standing practice of seeking both the Republican and Democratic nominations and was likely to take both. The party emphasized that Gallagher was not a party member but was registered to vote as a Communist.[44]

The party's only recommendations in the primaries were for Gallagher and Whitney. *PW* complimented Culbert Olson and other liberals seeking Democratic nominations but stressed, "We have NOT endorsed Olson nor any other candidate in the primaries. We have refrained from any endorsement in the primaries because we did not wish to become a source for any further friction in the progressive camp[,] which suffers from too great a division as it is. We trust the people's judgment."[45]

In the Democratic primary for secretary of state, Gallagher placed third among the six candidates, with 125,051 votes, equivalent to 12.4 percent of the Democratic vote and 7.7 percent of the votes cast for all candidates. He got 755 votes in the Communist primary. Whitney drew 751 votes in the Communist primary for controller. Just over half of the 1,358 voters who were registered as Communists cast primary ballots. Liberal Democrats won their party's nominations for governor, lieutenant governor, U.S. senator, and several congressional and legislative seats.[46]

In the 1938 general election, a coalition of business and conservative groups tried to constrain the state's robust union movement through a ballot initiative. Proposition 1 originated with the Industrial Association of San Francisco (which a U.S. Senate investigating committee chaired by Robert La Follette Jr. had recently called "an example par excellence of . . . success in denying labor its collective-bargaining rights"), the Associated Farmers (which Carey McWilliams labeled "farm fascism" and which the La Follette Committee accused of "flagrant and violent infringement of civil liberties"), the Merchants and Manufacturers Association of Los Angeles (the state's oldest, and highly successful, advocate of the open shop; the La Follette Committee claimed it "arrogated to itself the determination of what constituted law and order"), the Los Angeles Chamber of Commerce, and Southern Californians Inc. (an arch-conservative group dedicated to "preservation of industrial freedom").[47]

Proposition 1 proposed to restrict picketing, prohibit secondary boycotts, make unions liable for damages caused by members, and more. Its supporters launched the state's most expensive campaign for a proposition up to that time. Those efforts were closely tied to leading Republican candidates, Frank Merriam, the incumbent governor who was seeking a third term, and Philip Bancroft, candidate for U.S. Senate, who had connections to the Associated Farmers.[48]

The CP concentrated on building labor-left unity to defeat Proposition 1 and elect, as governor and lieutenant governor, Culbert Olson and Ellis Patterson, Democrats who were pro–New Deal, pro-labor, and anti–Proposition 1. Patterson was close to the CP, and rumors swirled that he was a party member. On September 20 *PW* publicized a statement by Louis Goldblatt, secretary of the California Industrial Union Council, CIO, and a party member, who called for "cooperation and unity" as "absolutely necessary" to defeat Proposition 1. "This isn't just labor's fight," Goldblatt announced. "All union[s]—AFL, CIO and [Railway] Brotherhood—must unite with progressives, small farmers and small merchants, who are equally menaced by Proposition No. 1." This version of the Popular Front reflected the party's, and the state CIO's, approach throughout the fall campaign. Although the California Federation of Labor, AFL, voted not to endorse any candidates, virtually every prominent AFL leader backed Olson and Patterson. In some local elections the CP withdrew its candidates in favor of LNPL-endorsed candidates but ran their own candidates where it seemed impossible to elect a liberal Democrat. Party members or sympathizers held leadership positions in a few AFL locals, several CIO unions, state and county Industrial Union Councils, LPNL, and other organizations opposing Proposition 1 and backing the liberal Democratic ticket.[49]

Leaders of AFL unions, CIO unions, and the railway brotherhoods created the Organized Labor Democratic Committee, a joint campaign committee to support "Democratic New Deal candidates" and defeat Proposition 1, a degree of labor-left unity that the CP advocated but could never have accomplished on its own. Germain Bulcke, a leader in ILWU Local 10 (San Francisco longshore workers) and close to the CP, if not a member, served as vice chair of the new organization. When William Green, AFL national president, endorsed Merriam, apparently solely because Olson had CIO support, California AFL leaders and members indignantly repudiated Green's action.[50]

Everything seemed to come together to promote the unity of labor and the left. Even the California Grange opposed Proposition 1. After all the party's rhetoric about a Farmer-Labor Party, a broad coalition of nearly all organized labor, some small-scale farmers, EPIC, and liberals was forming inside the Democratic Party. The campaigns of Whitney and Gallagher disappeared from *PW* during the final weeks of the campaign. Instead, the paper concentrated on boosting liberal Democrats.[51]

Proposition 1 lost by 57 percent. In most places across the country, Democrats lost ground in 1938. In California, however, Olson, Patterson, and Sheridan Downey, the Democratic candidate for the U.S. Senate, all won, and Democrats maintained their majority in the assembly. A UCLA political scientist commented that the meaning of the election was "Go Left, young man; go Left!" *PW* jubilantly asked, "What's in the Cards for California's New Deal?" and then cheerfully replied, a "Sweeping Discard of Old Abuses."[52] CP leaders, however, distinguished between this victory and their own party's goals. When, on election eve, a joyous party member said to Schneiderman, "We won! We won!" Schneiderman snapped back, "We did not win, comrade. The Democratic party won."[53]

The two statewide CP candidates, Leo Gallagher and Anita Whitney, were running in races in which the incumbent Republican had secured the Democratic nomination. Gallagher garnered more than 150,000 votes and 6 percent of the total, the largest vote for any CP statewide candidate in the 1930s. Whitney received just under 100,000 and 4 percent, fewer votes and fewer percentage points than she received in 1934. Nonetheless, if those who voted for Gallagher and Whitney represented the CP's maximum influence in the electorate, they represented a significant bloc of votes.[54]

When the CP National Committee met on December 3–5, Whitney was elected chair of the first session. Browder singled out California and Washington when reviewing the elections: "Last summer, when Comrade Stachel and I made a visit to the Pacific Coast, we came back from there with the feeling that we had learned new things about America. We gave the experiences of the Pacific Coast very prolonged and detailed study. . . . All of us throughout the Party, can very profitably do the same." He acknowledged that California's great accomplishment of labor unity had come about in significant part through the political miscalculations of the state's conservative business community and in part by the hard work of leaders in both AFL and CIO unions, some of them anti-Communist and some with close ties to the CP.[55] Browder did *not* acknowledge that the coalition seemed unlikely to persist in the absence of such a significant external threat.

With the defeat of Proposition 1 and the election of Olson and other liberals, labor and the left in California experienced a few heady months. Shortly after the election, Fletcher Bowron, the reform mayor of Los Angeles, announced that he was disbanding the Los Angeles Police Department's Red Squad, which had made a career of harassing Communists and others on the left, and that he was turning over its records to the La Follette Committee. The CP had agitated for the freedom of Tom Mooney and Warren Billings for nearly two decades, sometimes as the only voice to do so. One of Olson's first acts was to free Mooney. Mooney arrived in San Francisco on January 8 and led a huge and joyous parade down Market Street. Olson, Downey, and several legislators felt comfortable meeting with Schneiderman and other party leaders to discuss the campaign before

Election Day and legislative initiatives afterward. Schneiderman later admitted, "A certain euphoria was prevalent in Party ranks."[56]

Olson acknowledged his debt to organized labor and the left through several appointments. Carey McWilliams (an outspoken and very left Southern California journalist and lawyer) became state director of Immigration and Housing, and George Kidwell, a leader of the San Francisco Labor Council, headed the State Department of Industrial Relations. Olson also nominated Bulcke to the State Harbor Commission, the state agency that owned and operated the Port of San Francisco.[57]

In the assembly, Sam Yorty of Los Angeles introduced a "Little Wagner" bill complementing the Wagner Act—that is, the National Labor Relations Act—and Olson gave his strong endorsement. The assembly and senate passed a resolution calling for unity between the CIO and AFL. Olson pledged full support to a bill backed by the LNPL for a compulsory health insurance program for all workers earning less than three thousand dollars annually (the large majority of the state's wage earners), to be financed through taxes on wages and employers. Other bills included the right to picket, restrictions on injunctions, improvements in unemployment compensation, housing for migrant workers, repeal of the criminal syndicalism law, and establishment of state minimum wages and maximum hours. The legislature also considered a raft of other liberal bills, including abolishing cross-filing, prohibiting racial discrimination in public places, reapportioning the senate on the basis of population, and creating tenure for faculty members in state colleges. Some of the proposals—notably, health insurance and civil rights—went far beyond anything that had come from the New Deal in Washington.[58]

Resistance among conservatives dashed the hopes of the liberal-labor-left coalition. In late February the newly elected attorney general, Earl Warren, refused to pardon Warren Billings. As district attorney in Alameda County, Warren had earned a reputation as conservative and antilabor, and his opposition to Billings's pardon continued twenty years of Republican opposition to freeing Mooney and Billings. The Republican-controlled state senate rejected Olson's nomination of Bulcke as a San Francisco harbor commissioner. By the end of the legislative session, the state budget had to be cut because of the previous administration's deficit, and conservatives launched an investigation into Communist influence in the Olson administration. All liberal bills fell before bipartisan conservative majorities.[59]

Collapse of the Popular Front, 1939–1941

Before the legislature adjourned, international events seized people's attention. In mid-March 1939, Germany invaded Czechoslovakia. In April, Italy invaded

Albania. By May, Germany was making demands on Poland. Negotiations between Britain and the Soviet Union, stretching from May through August, failed to reach agreement on a mutual assistance pact. In August, German foreign minister Joachim von Ribbentrop arrived in Moscow, where he and Soviet foreign minister Vyacheslav Molotov quickly negotiated a German-Soviet nonaggression pact. In September, Germany and the Soviet Union invaded Poland and divided it between them. Much of Europe and the world was soon at war.[60]

Many CP members and sympathizers were not just surprised but seriously shaken that the Soviet Union would enter into a bargain with Nazi Germany. Browder called an emergency PolBuro meeting to consider the party's reaction. Al Richmond remembered that he was personally confused, that the *PW* staff was "unprepared, knocked off balance by this abrupt turn," and that "our reflex defense of the treaty had elements of the frenetic."[61]

The CP interpreted the Molotov-Ribbentrop Pact as an entente, and variations on Third Period rhetoric returned to *PW*, with denunciations of Roosevelt for warmongering and attacks on New Deal Democrats who supported Roosevelt or favored assistance to the Allies. Following a blunt directive from Moscow, *PW* presented this analysis: "The war that has broken out in Europe is the Second Imperialist War. . . . It is a war between rival imperialisms for world domination. The workers must be against this war." And further: "The warmakers within our country are not only determined to involve the people in a bloody, imperialist war—but in a Fascist imperialist war to destroy the Soviet Union." The Soviet invasion of Poland was undertaken to liberate the people of "the Western Ukraine" and "Western White Russia"—those parts of Poland being incorporated into the Soviet Union.[62]

As the California CP was retracting its enthusiasm for Roosevelt, San Francisco was electing a mayor and supervisors. Earlier, before the Molotov-Ribbentrop Pact and the party's abrupt change of direction, there had been hopes for a continuation of the labor-left unity that had swept the state in 1938. In Oakland in April, AFL and CIO unions and the railway brotherhoods had joined with liberal community groups to endorse a slate for the city council.[63]

In the fall, the incumbent mayor of San Francisco, Angelo Rossi, sought a third term. Rossi had received considerable support from many AFL unions when he was reelected in 1935 over the weak opposition of the United Labor Party. Now he faced Franck Havenner, a New Deal congressman who commanded the loyalty of much of organized labor, including conservative AFL unions. Havenner, a strong supporter of public ownership of electrical power, planned to campaign on that issue, but Rossi unloosed an advertising barrage linking Havenner to Harry Bridges and the CP, claiming that election of Havenner would mean red control over the city's police and other agencies. Havenner lost.[64]

In the other nonpartisan municipal elections, Oleta O'Connor Yates ran for assessor as a Communist, arguing that, if elected, she would "do everything in my power to help keep America out of the imperialistic war now raging." She also campaigned against Rossi, thus indirectly supporting Havenner. Elaine Black and Archie Brown ran for supervisor. O'Connor Yates finished fourth in a field of four, with just over 9,000 votes, about 4 percent of the total. Black and Brown did somewhat better, with 14,000 and 31,000 votes, respectively, about 5 and 11 percent. Two years before, Anita Whitney had received 9,850 votes, about 6 percent, for supervisor.[65]

As the 1940 presidential election approached, many Californians focused on the wars in Europe and Asia. Germany launched its blitzkrieg on Denmark and Norway in April and then on the Netherlands, Belgium, and Luxembourg in May. In June, German troops goose-stepped into Paris, Italy declared war on Britain and France, Roosevelt began to send military supplies to Britain, and the Soviet Union invaded and occupied the Baltic republics of Latvia, Lithuania, and Estonia. The Battle of Britain—an air war, to soften up Britain for invasion—began in August and continued through October. In September, Japan allied with Germany and Italy, and Congress approved the first peacetime draft. In October, Germany occupied Romania, and Italy invaded Greece.

The labor-left unity of 1938 and early 1939 was gone. In the 1940 primary, Olson joined with former U.S. senator William McAdoo, from the conservative wing of the state Democratic Party, to present a unity slate of delegates pledged to a third term for Roosevelt. When the CP and its CIO allies assailed this slate, Lieutenant Governor Ellis Patterson withdrew from it and formed an unpledged slate, committed to "Keep America Out of War." Patterson's slate included several CP members and others close to the party.[66]

As international tensions heightened, the CP accelerated its campaign against war. On April 6 *PW* issued a special edition titled "The Yanks Are Not Coming," dedicated to keeping the United States out of the "Imperialist War." On April 11, Estolv Ward announced a special meeting of the LNPL to reconsider their stand on a third term for Roosevelt. The Alameda and San Francisco Industrial Union Councils, where CP influence was strong, voted to oppose a third term. On April 15, Patterson blasted FDR for permitting the country to drift into war. *PW* proclaimed, "Vote for FDR Is Vote for War."[67]

In April, as the *Wehrmacht* swept through Denmark and Norway, Browder announced there was no reason to favor Britain over Germany, because they were "rapidly approaching one another in practice and in ideology." Patterson attacked Roosevelt as a warmonger and condemned Olson as a "liberal traitor." In May the Patterson slate—essentially the CP slate—got only 4 percent of the vote in the Democratic primary and 6 percent in San Francisco, placing fourth in a field of four. Though the CP and its allies in the CIO enlisted the lieutenant governor

"Yanks Are Not Coming" graphic from the cover of a
flyer issued by the Maritime Federation. Ephemera
Collection, World War II, courtesy of Labor Archives and
Research Center, San Francisco State University.

and a few other prominent left liberals in their cause, large majorities of organized labor and liberal Democrats stayed with Roosevelt and the New Deal.[68]

Whitney was the party's candidate for the U.S. Senate, and the party had candidates in thirteen of the state's twenty congressional districts, including Archie Brown in San Francisco. The party platform led with a strong antiwar plank: "'Not a man, not a cent, not a gun for the imperialist war and military preparations.'" Schneiderman argued that "in this way we can best help to crystallize a movement for a third party. But we want to unite with, even to support the candidates of all genuine anti-war forces, with all who fight for civil liberties and the right of labor in a common fight against the common enemy."[69]

The CP stressed the same message throughout the campaign, as it attacked its erstwhile liberal and labor allies. However, as the election neared, the party largely ignored such liberal candidates as Havenner, now facing a continuation of the previous year's red-baiting as he sought reelection to Congress. In October, Archie Brown quietly withdrew from that contest, although his name remained on the ballot. Throughout much of October *PW* focused its attacks on Olson (who was not on the ballot), Roosevelt, and those who backed Roosevelt. Even the Browder and Whitney campaigns got little attention as Election Day approached.[70]

In October, when John L. Lewis endorsed Wendell Willkie, the Republican presidential candidate, *PW* argued that he should have endorsed the idea of a third party instead. The same editorial condemned CIO leaders who supported Roosevelt and described the Democrats as "fiercely dedicated to imperialist war and a Fascist destruction of all that organized labor holds dear." In campaigning for the U.S. Senate, Whitney condemned her opponent, the arch-isolationist Hiram Johnson, for supporting "the imperialist war program of both President Roosevelt and Wendell Willkie."[71]

In 1936 the CP position had been to vote for Browder and Ford to defeat Landon, but many CP members or supporters had supported Roosevelt. In 1940 the party tried to prevent unions from endorsing Roosevelt. In late October the California LNLP announced it would "endorse no candidate who, in our opinion, is anti-labor and pro-war. . . . The Roosevelt record prevents our endorsement of his candidacy." Three of the four largest Industrial Union Councils (IUC) (Alameda, San Diego, and San Francisco counties) voted no endorsement for president. Only the Los Angeles IUC stood by Roosevelt. The San Francisco IUC meeting included a searing and bitter denunciation of Roosevelt by Harry Bridges, the CIO state director, who claimed, "The Roosevelt administration, if elected, particularly if elected by a large vote, will start a blitzkrieg against labor immediately after the election. . . . The most foolish thing a worker can do is to go out and vote for or support Roosevelt!" However, when Bridges attacked Roosevelt in his own local, ILWU Local 10, he was booed. A reporter described his attack on Roosevelt as "out of line with the overwhelmingly pro-Roosevelt sentiment among his men." Local 10 members voted to endorse Roosevelt.[72]

Roosevelt carried California by a somewhat reduced margin than in 1936. The party crowed that Browder had increased his vote, but it was only from 10,877 to 13,580. In percentage terms, there was no change—in both 1936 and 1940 Browder received 0.4 percent of the state vote for president. Browder drew fewer votes statewide than Elaine Black had received for San Francisco supervisor in 1939.[73]

Anita Whitney, a statewide candidate in 1934, 1938, and 1940, each time in an election where the Republican incumbent had also captured the Democratic nomination, received fewer votes each time, declining from 100,820 (4.9 percent) in 1934 to 98,791 (4.2 percent) in 1938 to 97,478 (3.6 percent) in 1940. No Communist congressional candidate drew more than 5.1 percent. In San Francisco, Havenner lost his reelection campaign for Congress but not because of the votes that went to Archie Brown.[74]

Growing Anti-Communism

As the CP zigzagged between adoring Roosevelt and hating him, anti-Communism was growing nationally and in California. On August 12, 1938, the new House of Representatives Special Committee on Un-American Activities, under chairman Martin Dies, held its first hearing. The next day the committee moved to the topic that was to be its raison d'etre over the next several decades—the danger of Communism. John Frey, an AFL vice president, denounced the CIO as part of a CP conspiracy.[75] Subsequent hearings of the committee, which soon came to be known as the House Un-American Activities Committee, or HUAC, continued to trumpet the dangers of Communism.

Within the CIO some were also attacking Communist influence. In early August 1938, amid the developing labor-left unity of the state electoral campaign, the heads of five CIO unions in Southern California announced they were withdrawing from local and state Industrial Union Councils and blasted Bridges, the regional CIO director, for running a "Communist dictatorship." Lewis quashed the rebellion, likely to maintain the emerging labor-left electoral coalition. A year later, as the Molotov-Ribbentrop Pact dominated the news, Lewis reduced Bridges's authority as CIO western regional director to just California, appointed known anti-Communists as directors in Washington and Oregon, and made clear that the purpose was to reduce Communist influence.[76]

Following the Molotov-Ribbentrop Pact and the Soviet invasion of Finland, many liberal Democrats reconsidered their willingness over the previous two years to work with Communists. In 1940 a coalition of conservative Democrats and Republicans took control of the state assembly, elected the speaker, and created the Relief Investigating Committee, to investigate Communist influence in the state relief agency. It was led by Sam Yorty and Jack Tenney, Democrats initially elected as strong supporters of the New Deal and previously willing to accept support from Communists. After the Molotov-Ribbentrop Pact, and amid growing anti-Communist sentiment in 1939–1941, both became outspoken, even strident anti-Communists.[77]

In September 1940 the legislature approved a bill to eliminate the Communist Party from the state ballot. With Olson's endorsement, the bill passed with only two votes against in the assembly and one against in the senate. The bill prohibited participation in primary elections by any party that "uses or adopts as any part of its party designation the word 'communist' or any derivative," and denied primary participation to any organization in any way affiliated with the CPUSA or the Comintern. The California CP sought to have the law declared unconstitutional, but the case did not make its way to the state supreme court until early 1942 (see chapter 6).[78]

Legal Offensive against Communist Leaders

In 1939 federal and local officials ramped up their use of the courts to bring charges against CP leaders and those accused of being CP members. Local officials revived the six-year-old indictment of Sam Darcy and extradited him to California. Federal officials brought charges against Browder, Schneiderman, and Bridges. All four cases—and others—began in 1939, and all prompted the creation of defense committees and fund-raising efforts.

Robert Jackson, then the U.S. attorney general, later recalled that the Molotov-Ribbentrop Pact and subsequent behavior of the CP made President Roosevelt "very much disillusioned about the behavior of the Communists" and that he became "very anti-Communist—militantly so." For Roosevelt, Jackson, and others, "It was all too obvious that they [U.S. Communists] were Kremlin controlled."[79]

Bridges, born in Australia, had drawn the ire of business leaders when he came to public attention early in the 1934 longshore strike, and they vied with patriotic and veterans' groups in denouncing him as a Communist and demanding he be deported. Secretary of Labor Frances Perkins, responsible for the Immigration and Naturalization Service (INS) and knowing that similar charges had often been used against labor leaders in the 1920s, initially resisted. In 1939, however, she ordered an INS hearing for Bridges; she apparently considered a hearing the best way to demonstrate the weakness of the evidence. Bridges was represented by Richard Gladstein, Aubrey Grossman, and Ben Margolis (see next chapter), and Carol King, a New York attorney, close to the CP, who specialized in immigration matters. In December the hearing officer, James Landis, dean of the Harvard Law School, concluded that the government had failed to prove its case. A torrent of disapproval and outrage broke over Landis and Perkins.[80]

In June 1940 Congress approved the Alien Registration Act—the Smith Act—which defined "affiliation" with the CP, rather than CP membership, as grounds for deportation, a move intended to "reach Bridges," according to Robert Jackson. That same month, Roosevelt moved the INS from the Labor Department to Justice. Also that month, the House of Representatives voted 330–42 to deport Bridges, undoubtedly unconstitutional as a bill of attainder. In return for Senate cooperation in blocking that bill, Jackson ordered an FBI investigation of Bridges as a prelude to a new deportation hearing.[81] In November 1940 Assistant FBI Director E. J. Connelley delivered to Jackson a massive report on Bridges, more than four thousand pages. Over half the report dealt with "the illegal status of the Communist Party," material also intended for use in other cases. Connelley acknowledged that the FBI had found "no documentary evidence listing Bridges as a member of the Communist Party" and that the case hinged entirely on "former Communists" who could testify that Bridges attended CP meetings and associated with Communists. Bridges now faced a second INS hearing, beginning in March 1941. Bridges was again represented by Gladstein, Grossman, and King. The hearing officer found against Bridges, setting off a series of appeals.[82]

Renewed hostility toward Communists at the federal level was mirrored at the local level. A few days after the conclusion of Bridges's first hearing, in late September 1939, Philadelphia police arrested Sam Darcy on the old perjury charge. Darcy and his attorneys fought extradition and then tried to have the charges dismissed. He finally went to trial in San Francisco in 1941.[83]

In December 1939, federal prosecutors brought Schneiderman to trial in San Francisco seeking revocation of his citizenship on the grounds that he had denied his CP membership when he became a citizen in 1927 and that CP membership was sufficient grounds to deny or revoke citizenship. The INS had opened its investigation into Schneiderman's citizenship in late 1935 but waited until after Bridges's hearing to bring him to trial. The Schneiderman case was widely understood as a test case to establish that the CP advocated forceful overthrow of the government and was therefore illegal. Similar charges had been lodged against Bridges, but the Schneiderman case presented the opportunity to charge an open CP member. Federal prosecutors recycled some evidence and witnesses from the Bridges INS hearing. George Andersen (see next chapter) defended Schneiderman, and Robert Kenny, a state senator and Democrat, volunteered to assist. They were joined by Carol King. On the witness stand, Schneiderman denied that the CP advocated the forceful or violent overthrow of the government either currently or when he became a member, denied that the CPUSA was bound by positions taken by the Comintern, disagreed with some aspects of Marxist-Leninist dogma, blamed the charges against him on "war hysteria," and declared that the suit against him was "an intrusion on and invasion of our civil rights individually and collectively." The prosecution apparently knew nothing about Schneiderman's tenure as the CPUSA representative to the Comintern and his part in drafting directives for the U.S. party. The judge found for the prosecution and stripped Schneiderman of his citizenship in June 1940. Schneiderman's attorneys immediately began their appeals.[84]

Browder was brought into court next. In October 1939 he had carelessly admitted in a HUAC hearing that he had traveled to the Soviet Union on false passports.

Previous attorneys general had known that but had not brought charges. In the aftermath of the Molotov-Ribbentrop Pact and Browder's HUAC testimony, the Roosevelt administration was flooded with demands that Browder be prosecuted. Browder went on trial in New York in January 1940. Acting as his own lawyer, he called no witnesses. The jury quickly found him guilty. The judge sentenced him to four years in prison and a fine. His appeals, all the way to the U.S. Supreme Court, failed to overturn the verdict, and he entered the U.S. Penitentiary in Atlanta in March 1941.[85]

Darcy came to trial next, in July 1941, charged with perjury because he had registered to vote using the name Darcy and claiming to have been born in New York, when actually he had been born in Russia and his family's name was Dardeck. George Andersen represented Darcy. The prosecuting attorney, Leslie Gillen, repeatedly challenged Andersen, but the presiding judge, George Schonfeld, frequently overruled Gillen. Andersen claimed that Darcy's "error" involved no "criminal, evil or corrupt intent" and that "thousands" of affidavits contained similar errors, but he was not permitted to introduce such evidence. Andersen also insisted that the only reason for the proceeding was because Darcy was a Communist. One observer reported that throughout the trial, whenever the proceedings seemed to be going against the prosecution, Police Chief Charles Dullea "would come into the courtroom and sit for hours in the front seat, obviously a means of browbeating the judge." The jury found Darcy guilty of perjury. He could have been sentenced to fourteen years in prison (as Louise Todd had been), but Judge Schonfeld instead imposed a sentence of five years of probation. As the press reported, "Schonfeld looked only at Sam Darcy's crime, not his politics." Dullea was outraged and publicly berated Schonfeld, claiming that Darcy should have been sentenced to prison, just as Browder had been. Darcy appealed, eventually to the state supreme court, which, on a vote of 4–3, refused to accept the case.[86]

The California CP in late 1937, 1938, and early 1939 moved very close to the political mainstream. During the existence of the Popular Front, party members worked closely with non-CP progressives and embraced Roosevelt and the New Deal. By doing so they gained some influence in local and state politics. Then the moment passed, as events in Moscow dictated a shift in the party line. From advocating the widest possible unity in support of Roosevelt and the New Deal, the CP returned to its more accustomed position on the political margins but now found itself subject to legislative investigating committees, barred from the state ballot, with its leaders charged in court with seeking to overthrow the government by force and violence.

CHAPTER 5

LIFE IN THE PARTY IN THE 1930s

The previous two chapters have surveyed major developments for the Communist Party in the San Francisco Bay Area from 1930 through the beginning of World War II. This chapter looks at the experiences of individual party members during that decade, many of whom have appeared in previous chapters and will reappear in subsequent chapters. Those who belonged to the CP in the Bay Area in the 1930s experienced party life in different ways, different from one person to the next, different from the early 1930s to the Popular Front years, different between men and women, different by race. But there were also common experiences. A surprisingly large number of San Francisco Bay Area CP members later described their experiences in oral histories, memoirs, and interviews. The pages of the *Western Worker* and its successor, *People's World*, the minutes of meetings archived at RGASPI, and FBI files all contain details of daily party life. These sources present the challenge of drawing out the most significant common experiences while preserving the wide range of individual experiences. This chapter presents typical and unique experiences for some forty individuals, both leaders and rank-and-file members.

Union Support and Organizing Activities

The 1934 strikes were important catalysts for many. Edith Arnstein's family came to San Francisco during the Gold Rush and were related to several of the city's elite German Jewish families. She later described the summer of 1934: "A long and bloody strike has divided the city. In middle-class homes the family is sharply divided, so that dinner tables are barricades—mothers and children on the side of the strikers, businessmen fathers on the side of the employers." She recalled that she and a friend borrowed twenty-five dollars (equivalent to more than five hundred dollars in 2023) from her mother to contribute to the MWIU, and how, on the day of a dramatic funeral march down Market Street, she and her cousin watched from the sidewalk: "She says, 'I am going to march.' I join her. I hope our fathers are not watching. . . . We pledge our lives that Sperry and Bordoise have not laid down their lives in vain." Angela Gizzi, daughter of middle-class Italian immigrants, left work to stand in respect during the funeral procession down Market Street; she called it "the most spectacular thing I've ever seen," and said it made her "a radical."[1]

By mid-1934, most—likely the large majority of—party members were focused on the burgeoning union movement. The longshore, maritime, and general strikes of 1934 boosted union organizing and brought increased support for the CP. The PolBuro's decision in late 1934 encouraged party members to take an active part in AFL unions. Party members who were employed sought to organize their workplaces or become active in existing unions. Other party members sought to join the unions on the waterfront or those that had a reputation for being on the political left.

In the early 1930s, party members formed "fractions" within union locals, which typically met before union meetings and formulated a position that CP members were to follow when the meeting started. However, as Dorothy Ray Healey later recalled, "Some of our closest allies were unhappy about it," and as CP members became more integrated into unions as members and leaders, the party abandoned its fraction meetings. Jack Olsen recalled, of the mid- and late 1930s, "The CP set up Party clubs on an industry-by-industry basis. There were warehousemen's, seamen's, and longshoremen's clubs. Each club had its own officer and its own delegates to the CP county committee, a literature agent, and an education director. . . . We used to meet and first take up political issues like the anti-fascist cause in the Spanish Civil War, the current election campaign, or an ongoing legal defense case."[2]

For Archie Brown, party activism led to union activism. Born in Sioux City, Iowa, to Russian Jewish parents, he and his family came to California in the mid-1920s. By 1929 or 1930, he had joined the Young Communist League, tried to organize homeless young people, and joined the Unemployed Councils' demonstrations. "We always got into a big battle with the police," he recalled, and he served six months in jail for leading a riot in 1931. During the 1934 strikes, he tried to organize young maritime workers. Arrested in Los Angeles during those strikes, he served ninety days in jail. Back in San Francisco, he volunteered to work with ILA Local 38-100, ship scalers, most of them from Central America, who had some of the dirtiest, most distasteful work on the waterfront, including climbing into ship's boilers and scraping out the scale that developed there. In late 1935, after a man fell to his death from a second-story window during a tumultuous meeting of Local 38-100, Brown and three others were charged with murder. On December 20, 1935, longshore and some maritime workers declared a political strike—they extended their noon hour by thirty minutes—in support of the four accused men. The four were acquitted when evidence surfaced that the man had climbed out the window to escape the turmoil inside and then fallen. Afterward, Brown worked as a longshoreman and a member of ILA Local 38-79 (later ILWU Local 10) until his retirement.[3]

Karl Yoneda followed a similar path, from party activism to union activism. Born Goso Yoneda in 1906 to immigrant parents from Japan, he lived in Japan from 1913 to 1926, when he became interested in socialism. After returning to the United States, he joined the CP under the name Karl (for Marx) Hama. In the late 1920s and early 1930s, he participated in the violent street demonstrations in Los Angeles and sought to organize agricultural workers. In 1933 in San Francisco, he became editor of *Rodo Shimbun* (Labor News), the CP's Japanese-language newspaper. As editor he continued the press's "underground work"—printing propaganda for Japan and arranging for it to be smuggled aboard ships. Though that work had begun through the Pan-Pacific Trade Union Secretariat's activities, Yoneda knew only Joe Koide, the contact who brought him copy to be printed. The PPTUS was dissolved in late 1934, but Yoneda's "underground" printing continued until 1936, still directed by Koide. Yoneda later concluded that Koide was probably an agent of either the U.S. or Japanese government.[4]

In addition to his newspaper and underground work, Yoneda joined campaigns to organize striking Japanese agricultural workers in the central valley. During the 1934 maritime strikes, he persuaded Japanese farmers to donate fresh fruit and vegetables for the strikers' kitchen. One of the vigilante raids in July 1934 broke up *Rodo Shimbun*'s printing equipment and furniture. That fall, as Karl Hama, Yoneda was the CP candidate in one of San Francisco's state assembly districts. He placed third in a field of three, with more than a thousand votes, almost 4 percent. Yoneda advised that *Rodo Shimbun* be phased out in late 1936, after which he became a correspondent for *Doho*, the new Japanese-language party newspaper, published in Los Angeles. Earlier that year, he helped organize the Alaska Cannery Workers Union (ACWU), composed of Mexican, Filipino, Chinese, and Japanese workers who went to Alaska each summer to work in fish canneries. With support from the maritime unions, the ACWU secured a union contract. George Woolf, a party member, won election as ACWU president. Yoneda was elected as delegate to the San Francisco Labor Council, which had long banned locals that enrolled Asians; he became the first Asian to serve on that body. He also became a member of the San Francisco longshore local and remained in ILWU Local 10 until his retirement in 1972.[5]

For Brown and Yoneda, party membership led them into union activity. Angela Gizzi's experience provides a different pattern. Her interest in the left led her to union activism and then to the CP. She was born in San Francisco's North Beach, an Italian neighborhood. Her parents were middle-class Italian immigrants and nominal Catholics. She graduated from the University of California, Berkeley, (UC—Berkeley) in 1931, amid the Depression, but couldn't find a job. In 1933 she was hired by the Bank of America because of her fluent Italian and ability with Spanish and French. She'd begun to move left politically at Berkeley and after witnessing the funeral march on Market Street. In early 1936 she attended a meeting of an AFL organizing committee for white-collar workers. After speaking up in the meeting, she was invited to a party recruiting session, led by Arthur Kent. She joined. Kent, however, was an informer. He gave employers the names of those who joined the union, and they were fired. Gizzi soon met Caroline Decker, who had recently been released from prison, and they became close friends. In 1937 Gizzi was elected president of a CIO organizing committee for office workers, and she continued to work as a CIO union organizer.[6]

Estolv Ward's efforts to found a union led him to the CP, which led him to positions with CIO unions and central bodies. He was born in Los Angeles in 1899. His father was a lawyer and former Populist who became a Socialist, and his mother was a physician, Quaker, and feminist. They moved to the Bay Area shortly after Estolv's birth. After attending the University of California, Ward became a reporter and eventually assistant editor for the *Oakland Tribune*. Covering the San Francisco general strike in 1934 led him to join the Newspaper Guild, for which he was fired. He joined the CP in 1936 and held staff positions with CIO central bodies, labor publications, and Labor's Non-Partisan League. He was executive secretary of the Harry Bridges Defense Committee in 1939. He and Angela Gizzi were married in 1939.[7]

For William "Bill" Bailey, working as a seaman introduced him to the MWIU, which led him to the CP. Born to Irish immigrant parents in 1910 in Jersey City, he grew up in the tenements of Hoboken and the Hell's Kitchen neighborhood of New York City. He left school after the fifth grade, worked at various jobs, and went to sea at nineteen. He joined the MWIU and then the CP, became an MWIU organizer, and attended a party school for potential leaders. With dissolution of the MWIU, he joined the International Seamen's Union. On July 26, 1935, he was chosen by his party section in New York City to sneak aboard the German liner *Bremen* and rip the swastika flag off its bow. He succeeded but was badly beaten by crew members, arrested, and charged with felonious assault. Vito Marcantonio defended Bailey in court, and the charges were dismissed. Expelled from the ISU for being a party member, Bailey then shipped out from San Francisco through the Marine Firemen's Union.[8]

Revels Cayton's involvement with the CP led him into union activity. Born in Seattle in 1907, he was the grandson of Hiram Revels, U.S. senator from Mississippi and the first Black member of Congress. By the time Cayton graduated from high school, he considered himself a socialist. He sat in on classes at the University of Washington and was recruited into the YCL. Active in the local International Labor Defense (a party organization), especially its Scottsboro defense activities, he joined the CP, ran for elected office as a Communist in Seattle, and then became an organizer for the MWIU. When it was dissolved, he moved to San Francisco and joined the Marine Cooks and Stewards (MC&S), the ISU's West Coast affiliate for those workers on freight and passenger ships, where he rapidly moved into leadership. During the 1936–1937 Maritime Federation strike, Cayton was elected to lead the MC&S strike committee in the Bay Area. The MC&S joined the CIO in 1937 as the National Union of Marine Cooks and Stewards (NUMCS), a union sometimes described as one-third black, one-third red, and one-third queer (not mutually exclusive categories). As an officer, Cayton worked to end divisiveness by condemning efforts to "black-bait," "red-bait," "queen-bait," or "cook-bait," the last aimed at invidious distinctions within the union between cooks and stewards. He moved steadily up union ranks in the Bay Area, serving as secretary-treasurer of the Bay Area District of the Maritime Federation in 1939–1941.[9]

Pat Tobin was born to Irish Catholic parents in San Francisco in 1921. Though he earned a scholarship to St. Ignatius, the city's most selective Catholic high school, he left school at seventeen when his father insisted he go to work. He joined the NUMCS and soon found, "you couldn't sit down in the hiring hall without some member of the CP coming up and talking to you." By the time he was nineteen, he had joined the CP.[10]

Ray Thompson was born in San Francisco in 1905. His family was one of the few Black families in the city at the time, and his father was active in fighting racial discrimination. As a young man, Thompson engaged in petty crime and was in and out of jail. He stopped committing crimes in the early 1930s and married in 1936. He joined the party in 1938 or 1939 and then went to sea in 1941 as a member of the NUMCS.[11]

ILA Local 38-44, later ILWU Local 6, had a special attraction for CP members and others on the left. In 1934 warehouse workers in San Francisco resurrected Local 38-44, set out to organize facilities near the waterfront, and then expanded to other warehouses. The local quickly established a reputation for being well to the left.[12]

Louis Goldblatt was among those who joined Local 38-44. Born in 1910 in the Bronx to Lithuanian Jewish immigrant parents who read *Freiheit*, the Yiddish-language CP newspaper, he began attending City College of New York but moved with his family to Los Angeles in 1928 and continued his studies at UCLA. There he joined the YCL. He continued with YCL activities at UC-Berkeley. Edith Arnstein remembered watching a debate in 1932 between Lou Goldblatt, for the National Student League against War and Fascism (a CP organization), and Oleta O'Connor, for the League for Industrial Democracy, affiliated with the Socialist Party. Afterward, Edith joined the National Student League. In 1933 Goldblatt was a CP candidate for the Berkeley City Council. He left graduate school and took a series of blue-collar jobs. In 1935 he was working in a warehouse and joined ILA Local 38-44. He was elected local vice president in 1936 and briefly became Northern California CIO director in 1937, when the Pacific Coast ILA joined the CIO as the ILWU (and Local 38-44 became ILWU Local 6). Goldblatt was elected secretary of the California Industrial Union Council (the state central body for CIO unions) in 1938.[13]

Jack Olsen also moved from the YCL to Local 6. He was born in Russia in 1911 and came to the United States with his parents at the age of one. They lived first in the New York City area, where his father was active in union and socialist causes, and then moved to Los Angeles in 1928. Jack joined the YCL and took part in unemployed demonstrations. Though his family name was Olshansky, he called himself Olsen when he was arrested by the Los Angeles Red Squad. He moved to San Francisco and in 1932 became YCL state secretary. He was paid five dollars a week, which he had to raise himself. Like other YCL and CP activists, he worked full-time supporting the striking maritime unions during the 1934 strikes. After the strike, he recalled, "The CP encouraged people like me to get more active in the unions." He moved from the YCL to the CP in 1936 and began working in ILWU Local 6. He was elected business agent in 1939.[14]

Keith Eickman also moved from the YCL to Local 6. He was born in 1913 in Canada, of Scottish and German parentage. After his parents divorced, he came to San Francisco in 1930 to live with his father, graduated from high school, and eventually found an office job in Santa Clara, at the southern end of San Francisco Bay. In 1936 he joined the YCL, later describing it as "the most sectarian group in the world." He recalled, "We did all kinds of things that seemed very important, like going to meetings every night. . . . I thought the revolution was just around the corner." In 1940 he took an office job in San Francisco but soon learned he could make more money as a warehouseman, so he joined Local 6.[15]

Some CP members volunteered or were hired as union staff members. In 1934 Norma Perry volunteered—or, more likely, the party directed her to volunteer—as typist for the longshore strike committee's publicity subcommittee.

The sister of Alex Noral, CP district organizer for Oregon and Washington in the early 1930s, she was living in 1934 with Arthur Kent, who had not yet become an informer. Kent later told the FBI that Perry's assignment was "to see that all publicity sent out by the strike committee was in accordance with the Communist party and policies, but not to let the non-Communists know that this was being done." Kent proved himself a liar on many occasions, however, so it is impossible to know whether to credit his statement. After the strike, Perry became secretary to Harry Bridges but was expelled from the CP when she switched allegiance to Harry Lundeberg and the Sailors Union of the Pacific.[16]

Legal Defense Activities

Some CP members committed themselves to legal defense work on behalf of unions or those on the left. By the mid-1930s several San Francisco lawyers had either become CP members or had moved very close to the CP. Herbert Resner told me that in the late 1930s the CP lawyers belonged to the Haymarket Unit.[17]

George Andersen was among the first attorneys who worked with the party. Sam Darcy met Andersen soon after Darcy's arrival in San Francisco. Darcy recounted how "Little Harris," a party member, organized a protest in which some six hundred unemployed men from skid-road flophouses showed up for a "gold plate" dinner at the Palace Hotel, with invitations that Little Harris had designed and run off on the party's mimeograph machine. All were arrested and jailed; it was up to Darcy to get them out. The local CP didn't have an attorney, but Norma Perry, then working for the Mooney Defense Committee, recommended George Andersen. Darcy gathered fifty dollars (equivalent to about one thousand dollars in 2023) and went to Andersen's office. Darcy explained the situation, and Andersen said, "Okay." Darcy then said, "Now, all I have is fifty bucks. I think it turns out to be 8c a client. . . . It's all I can pay you." Andersen replied, "All right. I'll take that. If you need some of the money, it's all right." Darcy insisted, "The whole fifty bucks is yours."[18]

During the early 1930s, Andersen was the chief attorney in the Bay Area representing the CP and its affiliates, especially the International Labor Defense. Born in Denmark to American citizens, he completed high school in San Francisco, worked as a boilermaker, and then attended the San Francisco Law School, a private night school, graduating in 1927. In the mid-1930s Herbert Resner became Andersen's partner. Resner was born in Chicago and moved with his family to Southern California in 1924. He attended UC-Berkeley, earning his BA in 1932 and his law degree in 1935. While in law school, he met Aubrey Grossman, who introduced Resner to radical causes, including that of Tom Mooney. After graduating from law school, Resner joined the defense team for

Mooney and later defended Frank Conner in the King-Ramsay-Conner case (see below).[19]

A second left law firm, Gladstein and Grossman, opened in 1936. Richard Gladstein attended high school in Oakland, graduated from UC-Berkeley, and then from Boalt Law School in 1931. After practicing in Oakland, he moved to San Francisco in 1936, partnering with Aubrey Grossman. Grossman was born in San Bernardino, California, and attended UCLA, where he met Lou Goldblatt. Grossman then attended Boalt Hall and was active in left student groups. After graduating in 1935, his first law office was in San Francisco's Union Recreation Center, a project of the Maritime Federation to give their members a place to exercise, shower, play cards, and otherwise refresh—and, if need be, consult a lawyer. One of Grossman's first big cases was assisting Andersen in the defense of Earl King (see below). Grossman soon partnered with Gladstein.[20]

Andersen and Resner were often retained by the International Labor Defense in the early and mid-1930s. The ILD was affiliated with the Comintern's International Red Aid (usually known by its Russian acronym, MOPR), created in 1922. The ILD focused on legal defense, including Sacco and Vanzetti in the 1920s and the Scottsboro case in the early 1930s. In California the ILD worked for the release of Tom Mooney. By 1934 the ILD in the Bay Area was led by Elaine Black, formerly Rose Elaine Buchman (see ch. 1). Around 1929, she and her then husband, Ed Russell, had gone to the Los Angeles ILD office looking for friends during one of the CP's violent demonstrations. The Red Squad broke into the ILD office and demanded their names. She quickly replied, Elaine and Ed Black. Though rather casual about her YCL membership, she soon joined the ILD and began to work in the Los Angeles ILD office. She became district secretary and joined the CP. In 1931 she was arrested at a demonstration and gave her name as Betsy Ross. By 1932 her marriage was falling apart, due partly to her demanding ILD responsibilities and partly to her husband's drinking. They separated and were divorced in early 1934. By then Elaine had moved to San Francisco and into an apartment with Karl Yoneda, whom she had met in Los Angeles.[21]

During the 1934 longshore and maritime strikes, the San Francisco longshore local's strike committee agreed that Black could sit in on meetings of the union's defense committee (a subcommittee of the strike committee) and use the union hall for defense training. The ILD gave strikers a pocket-size card with a list of their rights and instructions on what to do if arrested. Black tried to increase the connections between the CP and the strike committee, but committee members were leery of any close connection.[22]

Black remained centrally involved with ILD activities throughout the 1930s, providing bail and arranging legal representation during many strikes and labor actions, earning the sobriquets "Red Angel" and "Tiger Girl." Her work took her throughout Northern California. She was repeatedly arrested, especially in San

Francisco, and repeatedly charged under the "$1,000 vag" law, the vagrancy law with a thousand-dollar fine. Convicted under that law in 1934 and sentenced to six months in prison, she won on appeal. When lawyers were unavailable, she sometimes provided representation herself. Concerned that their cohabitation might lead to a legal charge, she and Yoneda took the train to Washington state, where there was no anti-miscegenation law; there they were married. In 1939 Elaine gave birth to their son, Tom, named for Tom Mooney, who recently had been released from prison.[23]

Black persisted in defense work, despite threats such as one she experienced in Salinas, site of a violent encounter between striking farmworkers and vigilantes in 1936. Arriving there to speak to the Filipino Labor Union, she was met at the train station by twenty Filipino men who escorted her because, she recalled, "the vigilantes were running rampant and said they would kill any radical who arrived on the scene." Her escorts took her to an auto court, where she spent the night. Black continued: "The next morning outside the door there was a lynch rope hanging with a note saying, 'Elaine, you are next.'"[24]

Other women were also doing legal defense work. In early 1937 eighteen-year-old Miriam Dinkin, then a YCL member, was hired as secretary for the King-Ramsay-Conner Defense Committee. She was soon promoted to acting executive secretary and then to executive secretary. The case involved Earl King, Ernest Ramsay, and Frank Conner, officers of the Marine Firemen's Union. In the midst of the 1936–1937 maritime strikes, Earl Warren, district attorney in Alameda County (across the bay from San Francisco), charged the three men with the murder of George Alberts, chief engineer on the *Point Lobos*, who had been brutally bludgeoned and stabbed aboard ship. The prosecution claimed that King and Ramsay had dispatched a "goon squad" to beat up Alberts. Conner, the MFOW delegate on the *Point Lobos*, was arrested and confessed to knowledge of the attack but later repudiated his confession. A fourth man confessed and implicated the other three along with a fifth man, who had done the actual assault and was never found. Warren claimed that the murder was "a paid assassin's job, and the basis of the plot communistic." Though King, Ramsay, and Conner were not aboard ship during the assault, all were convicted of second-degree murder and sentenced to twenty years in San Quentin prison. Bay Area maritime unions claimed not only that the case was intended to discredit unions and remove effective union officials but also that it was timed to embarrass the maritime unions during a major strike. The defense committee attracted nationwide support.[25]

Andersen, Grossman, and Resner were among the six defense attorneys. Resner later suggested that manslaughter would have been the appropriate charge, not murder. He also said, "The Communist party . . . masterminded the defense of this case" and that all the defense lawyers but one were party members.[26]

Miriam Dinkin remained executive secretary of the King-Ramsey-Conner Defense Committee until it disbanded in 1942, when the men were paroled. The defendants, especially Ramsay, were initially reluctant to deal with her. Ramsay, she recalled, "had heard that I was a Red [she was a YCL member], and he was violently anti-Red." She resigned from the YCL and persuaded the three men that she "had a commitment to the men. Not to anything else—not to a union, not to a political party, not to the Communist party." Though her nominal boss was secretary of the district council of the Maritime Federation, she recalled that various CP members tried to tell her what to do, especially Walter Stack, leader of the CP fraction in the MFOW.[27]

Years later, asked about the role of the party in the defense activities, Dinkin replied, "Which part of the party? . . . Waterfront party, uptown party? . . . The case was very unimportant to the party uptown. . . . They supported it [but] had very little concern or interest." The various party groups on the waterfront, she said, were fighting among themselves, a situation that carried over into their support for the defense committee. "The situation became who owns the case, really, between the Communist Party, the MFOW, and V. J. Malone [anti-Communist head of the MFOW]," she recalled, and said she became a "football" among contesting CP factions (see below). After the election of Culbert Olsen as governor in 1938, the committee finally succeeded in its efforts to free the three men, over the strong opposition of California attorney general Earl Warren.[28]

Life in Prison

The Communists lost some of their defense cases. Caroline Decker and other criminal syndicalism defendants went to prison. Louise Todd's party work led to her incarceration. Todd was initially arrested during the vigilante and police raids in July 1934 and charged with vagrancy, the usual charge against a Communist when no other charge seemed appropriate. When a jury declared her not guilty, she was then indicted for perjury in connection with signatures on petitions to place the CP on the state ballot. When submitting petitions, each petition carrier had to swear to having personally collected each signature. At Todd's trial, three witnesses testified that their signatures on petitions submitted by Todd had been collected by men. The jury convicted her of perjury, and the judge sentenced her to one to fourteen years in prison on each of the three counts of perjury, with the terms to run concurrently. Her appeal was denied.[29]

At Tehachapi, California's first prison for women, Todd joined Caroline Decker and Nora Conklin, both convicted in the Sacramento criminal syndicalism trial. Decker was born in 1912 in Macon, Georgia, to immigrant Jewish parents from Ukraine. She grew up in Syracuse, New York, and became radicalized while in her teens through the influence of her older brother and sister. After high school, she took courses at a business college because, she recalled, she was preparing to be an organizer. Active in the YCL at age sixteen, she later worked as an organizer in Pittsburgh and in Youngstown, Ohio, and then went to California. She quickly emerged as a leader in the Cannery and Agricultural Workers Industrial Union, taking a prominent part in the strikes of 1932–1934. As CAWIU secretary she was a chief target of those who managed the Sacramento criminal syndicalism arrests and trial. She spent three years in the women's prison.

The three CP women were assigned to the "incorrigibles" section of the prison, with perpetrators of serious crimes or those who had physically attacked a prison matron. Though locked in individual cells at night, they were free to walk around their floor during the day and to mingle with other prisoners. Each floor had a kitchen and dining room, and each prisoner had assigned work. Todd washed pots, pans, and dishtowels. Conklin was a cook. Decker worked outside as a gardener; she also cultivated vegetables in a small personal garden and shared them with the other two CP women.

Party members and sympathizers deluged the three women with mail. Prison rules prohibited them from receiving CP publications, but their correspondents snuck in a few. Prison rules allowed an unlimited number of visitors but limited each visitor to once per month. Party leaders came, and so did Upton Sinclair, journalist/activist Anna Louise Strong, and Hollywood celebrities, as well as family members and friends. The three women gathered in one of their cells each afternoon to share mail, discuss prison issues, and sometimes to eat vegetables from Decker's garden. Unlike Frank Spector and other CP prisoners at San Quentin, they did not proselytize among the prisoners, although they did try to create a sense of community and succeeded in organizing a Thanksgiving dinner, during which the women were permitted to converse.

George Andersen, Todd's attorney, solicited many letters urging that she be paroled, including from Culbert Olson, then chair of the state Democratic Party, and Roger Baldwin, general counsel of the ACLU. To be eligible for parole, Todd had to demonstrate that she had a job. The ILD arranged for her to work as secretary to Andersen. Released shortly before Christmas 1936, after thirteen months in prison she worked for Andersen during her parole and then resumed her work with the state party.[30]

Caroline Decker was released on parole about the same time, and all the other criminal syndicalism defendants were released by the state court of appeals in September 1937, based on inconsistencies in their trial and in the jury's decisions. Decker found work as a legal secretary at Gladstein, Grossman, and Margolis. She and Richard Gladstein were married in 1941.[31]

Life in the Party

For some, being a party member was an absorbing, full-time experience. Caroline Decker recalled, "Our personal lives were integrated with our political lives. Our political lives came first and also our literal lives. . . . If we were prepared to lay our lives down on the line, our literal lives, then you know that we were prepared to juggle our personal lives with our political lives." For those with jobs and family responsibilities, party expectations often came first—participation as a CP member in one's union or workplace, participation in one or more of the party's mass organizations, preparing and distributing leaflets, taking part in demonstrations, and always attending meetings.[32]

Regarding her busy life in the early 1930s, Dorothy Ray Healey recalled that she was eligible for a local food stamp program in Oakland, and "on Saturday nights my great indulgence was to . . . use my food stamps to get a package of cigarettes and the *Ladies Home Journal* and . . . have the whole evening to myself, just reading, and feeling so decadent." She continued: "Years later, Louise Todd and Oleta O'Connor Yates and I were reminiscing . . . and they both said that was also their great indulgence whenever they were exhausted and were free for a rare evening. They would get the same kind of magazine—never anything serious—and sit home and read."[33]

CP and YCL members in the 1930s had numerous party-related activities and responsibilities, ranging from branch or section meetings to the many organizations that the party created for specific activities. Few who left accounts of their life in the party during the 1930s complained of boredom. More typical were accounts of lives so busy with party work that little time was left for anything else. Ray Healey recalled, "There had never been any great line of demarcation between one organization or another. In their weekly activities, Communists would float from one organization and emphasis to another, from the Trade Union Unity League [before 1934] to the International Labor Defense to the unemployed council." The party was notorious for its frequent meetings. Healey often recounted an effort to recruit Mexican farmworkers: "The response of the Mexican workers was essentially, 'Of course, we're for the revolution. When the barricades are ready, we'll be there with you, but don't bother us with meeting all the time.'"[34]

For other party members, party activities constituted only a small part of their lives. Some refused to reveal their membership or felt the need to deny their membership. In 1934 the *San Francisco Examiner* printed an article that claimed muralist Bernard Zakheim had painted Communist propaganda as part of a New Deal art project. He was then opening an exhibition of his work at a downtown gallery. When the gallery owner asked Zakheim if he was a party member, Zakheim said no. Around the same time, Zakheim invited his assistant, Shirley Staschen, to his house to meet two Communist organizers from New York.[35]

Professionals, including college or university faculty members, occupied a special place in the party, but for most, their jobs could have been in jeopardy had they announced their party membership. Victor Arnautoff joined the party in 1938, the same year he accepted an appointment to the Stanford art faculty. Though he took a prominent role in raising funds for the republican cause in Spain and later for Russian war relief, he never publicly disclosed his party membership, although neither did he deny it. As an immigrant, he also faced the possibility of deportation had he acknowledged his party membership.[36]

Haakon Chevalier was a professor of French at UC-Berkeley. According to Chevalier's later interviews, he was a member of a "closed unit" of the party, which he said also included J. Robert Oppenheimer (UC professor of physics), Thomas Addis (Stanford professor of medicine and a nationally prominent nephrologist), Arthur Brodeur (UC professor of English and Germanic philology), Paul Radin (UC professor of anthropology), Louis Goldblatt, and Robert Muir, of the State Bureau of Labor Statistics. For university faculty members and state employees such as Muir, an open declaration of party membership could have meant losing their position. Chevalier later specified that while he and some of the others "paid dues" to the party, Oppenheimer did not, although he contributed generously for particular purposes, especially support for the republican cause in Spain. Chevalier stated that unit members did not take orders from the party and weren't under party discipline. They were, he said, "consulted about certain things," spoke at party-sponsored events, and sometimes wrote for party publications. In his memoirs, he referred to the group only as a "discussion group" and said nothing of any connection to the party, only to particular issues.[37] Chevalier's description fits Joseph Starobin's description of an "influential" (see chapter 4). In 1954 Oppenheimer similarly described his relation to the party in the 1930s: he said he had been a "fellow traveler . . . one who accepts part of the public program of the CP, was willing to work with and associate with communists, but was not a member of the Party."[38]

Violet and Paul Orr were completely open about their party memberships. After returning to the Bay Area from the Soviet Union in 1930, they lived in Point Richmond, north of Oakland on the east side of the bay. They commuted throughout the Bay Area to work for the Friends of the Soviet Union and participate in other CP-related activities. On Lenin's birthday in 1932, they became party members, convinced by their experience in the Soviet Union that the CP had the solution to the Great Depression. They returned to the Soviet Union that year as leaders of a tour group. In late 1932 Violet became organizational secretary for the party in Alameda County (centered on Oakland). They did street-corner speaking, presented classes on Marxism, participated in demonstrations, and organized meetings for visiting speakers, as well as other activities. With formation of a party branch in Contra Costa County (north of Alameda County), Violet became organizational secretary in 1933. During the vigilante raids in July 1934, their home was ransacked. The Orrs had been warned and stayed away; they then moved to downtown Richmond. In 1934 Violet was the CP candidate for the state assembly in their district, winning just under 5 percent of the vote.[39]

Late in the 1934 campaign, she was arrested in Richmond for distributing leaflets without a permit. The police chief had refused a permit, so she went door-to-door, first knocking and then offering a leaflet to anyone willing to accept one. Arrested under a local antilittering ordinance that provided a fine of up to five hundred dollars and up to six months in prison, Violet was convicted in local court, fined twenty-five dollars, and given a six-month suspected sentence. George Andersen, representing her, appealed. The superior court judge reversed her conviction and declared the Richmond ordinance unconstitutional as unreasonable interference with individual rights.[40]

During 1935–1937, after moving to San Francisco, Violet Orr worked in laundries, tried to organize within the existing laundry workers union, created a shop paper, and worked on educating women laundry workers about their rights within the union. She later reflected that such efforts were "the business of Communists in any organization." In late 1937 she became advertising and circulation manager for *People's World* and remained in that position until after World War II.[41]

Oleta O'Connor was also open about her party membership. She was born in San Francisco to a California-born mother and an Irish immigrant father, who worked as a buyer for a shoe house. She graduated in 1927 from San Francisco Girls' High School, where she managed the school newspaper, then attended UC-Berkeley, where she was on the women's debate squad, manager of that squad, and president of the debating society. She graduated in 1932 with multiple honors: membership in Delta Sigma Rho (forensics honor society), Dobro Slovo (Slavic studies honor society, of which she was president), Prytanean (women's honor society), and Mortar Board (the national women's honor society). After receiving her master's degree in Slavic languages, she joined the party in 1933, quickly moved into local leadership, and became a frequent candidate for local office.[42]

Matt Crawford took a different route to the Communist Party. Born in Alabama in 1903, he grew up in Oakland, graduated from high school, and graduated from the San Francisco College of Chiropractic and Drugless Physicians in 1927. Through the late 1920s, he was also active in the local chapter of the NAACP. In 1932 he joined the group of Black Americans who went to the Soviet Union with Langston Hughes, the poet who was one of the stars of the Harlem Renaissance. Upon Crawford's return to the Bay Area, he became active in the ILD, especially its Scottsboro campaign, and joined the CP. By 1938 he was included in the presiding committee for the state CP convention.[43]

Lillian Dinkin left her family home in Los Angeles in 1932 and hitchhiked to San Francisco, where she continued her work for the YCL, joined at times by Bobby Rappaport, son of Morris Rappaport. Bobby was, Lillian later said, "like an adopted son to my mother." Bobby and Lillian did YCL recruiting in Petaluma (where Bobby had relatives), Eureka, and other parts of Northern California before she became Pioneer director (the Pioneers were the party's organization for children) in San Francisco.[44]

Lillian's parents and the rest of her family moved to San Francisco soon after Lillian arrived, and they all threw themselves into party activities. Miriam, Lillian's younger sister, recalled that the family home "became a center for young people. . . . I'd come home and not have a place to sleep because my mother would have filled the beds with unemployed young people." Her home was "a very lively place, with hundreds of people coming through and sleeping on the floor." "I was part of YCL," she recalled, "and so was everybody who came in." The 1934 strikes were "galvanizing" for her family. The first meeting of the seamen's strike committee was held at her family home. In July 1934 the family had to leave their home when they learned it had been targeted by vigilantes.[45]

As a teenager, with her father unemployed and her mother in a sanitorium for tuberculosis, Miriam became the family breadwinner. She got a WPA job, first with the Federal Writers Project and then with the Union Recreation Center. She continued until the recreation center closed in 1937 and then found the position with the King-Ramsay-Conner Defense Committee.[46]

Tillie Lerner was one of the young people who lived with the Dinkin family for a while. She was born in Omaha in 1912 to Russian Jewish immigrant parents. That year, her father was secretary of the Nebraska Socialist Party. In 1930 she left high school, joined the YCL, married, and plunged into CP organizing. Her daughter was born in 1932. The year 1933 found the family in Stockton, when some of her poetry and fiction began to be published in left publications. She threw herself into support activities for the 1934 Pacific Coast longshore and maritime strikes and helped to organize the disastrous YCL demonstration on Memorial Day. On July 22, police raided the apartment where Lerner and others were living, arrested them, and charged them with vagrancy. The next day, the *New Republic* ran a literary review that praised her as "an early genius." Lincoln Steffens and Ella Winter then paid her bail. In mid-August, Random House offered to publish her unfinished novel. However, between poor health and her family and party responsibilities, her writing lagged.[47]

Lerner left her husband, sent her daughter to her parents in Omaha, moved in with the Dinkin family, and spent her time in blue-collar work and party activities.

She met Jack Olsen at the Dinkin home. In early 1936 they moved in together and her daughter joined them. The party then sent Lerner to Los Angeles to work in organizing and writing for CP publications. Back in San Francisco in 1938, she began to write for *People's World* and gave birth to a second daughter late that year. Directed by the party to return to Los Angeles, she refused because of her family responsibilities. her organizational work then shifted to the local parent-teacher association (PTA), the ILWU Women's Auxiliary, occasional writing for the CIO's state newspaper, and participation in party committees (see chapter 7).[48]

Another occasional resident in the Dinkin household was Leo Nitzberg. Leo was born in Canada in 1919, to Russian Jewish parents who moved to Los Angeles when Leo was four. His mother was the sister of Morris Rappaport. After Leo's father died, his mother married Sol Nitzberg, who had been born in Russia, participated in the 1905 revolution, was exiled to Siberia, escaped, came to the United States, and eventually joined a colony of Jewish chicken farmers in Petaluma, forty miles north of San Francisco. Sol adopted Leo and his brother George. Sol was at the center of the tiny left community in the small town of Petaluma. Darcy's list of CP activists in 1930 included "S Nitzberg Active collecting money no orga[nization]." Leo's parents were close friends of the Dinkin family. When vigilantes targeted the Dinkin home in July 1934, the Dinkin family fled to Leo's grandmother's home. When Leo left home at the age of fifteen, after two years of high school, he went to live with the Dinkin family. In August 1935, vigilantes in Petaluma tarred and feathered Sol and another man. Sol and his family came to the Dinkin home for safety and help in removing the tar from Sol's skin. Leo joined the CP—probably the YCL since he was not yet eighteen—around that time.[49]

The Spanish Civil War

In 1937 seventeen-year-old Leo Nitzberg was recruited by Jack Olsen to go to Spain. He was among many party members and leftists from the Bay Area who went to Spain to defend the Republican government. In 1931 anti-monarchist victories in local elections in Spain had led to the king's abdication and proclamation of a republic. In early 1936 a People's Front of Socialists, Communists, and other left groups won parliamentary elections. Opponents of the new government rose in armed rebellion, led by army officers with support from large landholders, the Catholic Church, and the Falange, a fascist organization. Nazi Germany and Fascist Italy provided military aid to the rebels. The Comintern embraced the cause of the Republic and mobilized its cadres to support and fight for it. The Soviet Union and Mexico assisted the Spanish Republicans, as did volunteers from several nations, called the International Brigades. Some two hundred volunteers from the San Francisco area joined one of the two American battalions, named for George Washington and Abraham Lincoln, both parts of the 15th International Brigade. The Washington Battalion lasted only ten days—through its first engagement—before it was merged into the Lincoln Battalion.[50]

Because Leo Nitzberg lied about his age, he always thought that he was the youngest volunteer. When his superiors discovered his age, and perhaps his poor eyesight, they assigned him to drive trucks and ambulances rather than as a front-line combatant, which likely saved his life. In early February 1938, Leo was joined in Spain by his good friend, Jack Taub, and his cousin, Robert "Bobby" Rappaport. Rappaport was killed in action in mid-March in the Battle of Caspe. Taub died the next month in the Battle of Gandesa. During and between those two battles, the battalion lost 288 men, more than a third of all Americans who died in Spain. Exact figures are not available, but about 750 of some 2,800 American volunteers died in Spain—more than 25 percent. Nitzberg was one of the last to return, arriving back in the States in March 1939. Deeply affected by the loss of his cousin and friend, he later named his sons Robert and Jack.[51]

Bill Bailey arrived in Spain on June 28, 1937, became part of a machine gun company, trained with the Mackenzie-Papineau (Canadian) Battalion, and then transferred to the Lincolns as part of the Seamen's Unit. Cecil Eby, in *Comrades and Commissars: The Lincoln Battalion in the Spanish Civil War*, says, "Because the seamen, including longshoremen, were the most cohesive (and pugnacious) faction, they set themselves off as future machine gunners. . . . They soon became a kind of super-company with the best *esprit de corps* in the battalion." On September 9, 1937, Bailey captured a Royalist flag during the Battle of Belchite and sent it to the Maritime Federation office in San Francisco with his signature. Late in the fighting he was promoted to *cabo* (corporal). He returned to the United States on December 20, 1938, and resumed work as a marine fireman, shipping out from San Francisco.[52]

Not all who went were Communists. Robert Merriman, battalion commander, was a Californian, from Santa Cruz, who had earned an undergraduate degree in economics at the University of Nevada, where he completed Reserve Officers Training and was commissioned as a reserve second lieutenant. After graduation he married Marion Stone, entered the graduate program in economics at UC-Berkeley, and secured a fellowship to study in Moscow in 1935. There, Marion secured a job with Anna Louise Strong's *Moscow Daily News*, the city's English-language newspaper. Robert went to Spain in January 1937. Given his ROTC training, he knew more about strategy and tactics than other volunteers, so he was made captain and battalion commander. The Lincolns' first action came in late February. Of some 400 battalion members, 127 were killed and nearly 200 were wounded, including Merriman. While recovering, he took charge of training

Bill Bailey, in Spain. Courtesy of the
Abraham Lincoln Brigade Archive.

"Captured machine gun, taken by us in night attack from fascists" (as described by,
apparently, Slivon Boleslaw). Boleslaw identified the person on the far left as "a sailor,"
Bailey is next, then Boleslaw in the helmet, and "Pedro [scratched out] old volunteer."
Photo from the Lisette and Sam Kutnick Abraham Lincoln Brigade collection, box 2, file
4, courtesy of Labor Archives and Research Center, San Francisco State University.

of the Mackenzie-Papineau Battalion and then became brigade chief of staff. In early April he was captured and executed.[53]

Archie Brown wanted to go to Spain but was repeatedly refused a passport. He finally stowed away on a ship and arrived in Spain on May 29, 1938. An accomplished soapbox orator, he was soon making stirring speeches to the men of his company on the theme of "You can't kill the working class." During the Battle of Gandesa, Brown rallied his comrades by leading them in singing the "Internationale." Offered a promotion to company commissar, Brown first protested that he'd had insufficient military experience. "You'll learn," he was told, and he accepted. Much of Brown's duties were carried out during the bloody retreat that began soon after his promotion.[54]

The position of commissar was patterned directly on the political commissars of the Red Army of the Soviet Union. Each unit had a commissar who held parallel rank with the unit's military commander. André Marty was commissar for all the international brigades. A prominent French Communist, Marty had headed the Comintern's Anglo-American Secretariat before being assigned to Spain. He later stated that as commissar, "I ordered to be executed not more than 500—all authentic criminals masking as defenders of liberty," among which he included Trotskyists and anarchists. Paul White, an acquaintance of Bailey and member of the same company, had deserted but then tried to return to his unit. He was nonetheless executed for desertion, after a court-martial by a tribunal consisting of commissars and party cadres. Bailey, not a part of the tribunal that sentenced White, found that trial and execution to be reprehensible, and others in the battalion reacted similarly. The order to execute deserters was discontinued the next day. For Brown and other commissars, their primary responsibilities were to maintain morale and provide political education, or as Eby puts it, "political indoctrination." John Gates, a high-ranking commissar, explained, "It would be difficult to explain how poorly armed men could fight a much more powerful army for so long and so well, if it were not for their political convictions." But political convictions could sustain the poorly trained and sometimes poorly equipped Lincoln Battalion for only so long in the face of their well-trained and well-armed opponents. Brown later reflected, "One of the most difficult duties I had to perform as a Commisar [sic] was the task of informing loved ones of the death of a brother, father or husband."[55]

People's World carried extensive information about the war. Nearly every issue included news and often featured local participants, either those in Spain or those raising funds. Fund-raising for the volunteers and for the Spanish Republic was often organized by party members but attracted many who were not members. Marion Merriman went to Spain when her husband was first wounded, became a corporal, worked behind the front lines at the brigade headquarters, and then went to the United States on a fund-raising tour. After her husband's death, she became executive secretary for the San Francisco branch of the American Medical Bureau to Save Spanish Democracy, raising funds for medical supplies and recruiting medical personnel to go to Spain. San Francisco party members also worked at fund-raising. Victor Arnautoff, a prominent artist, helped organize an art auction, with works donated by leading artists, which raised some nine hundred dollars (equivalent to more than seventeen thousand dollars in 2023). He later said that his decision to join the CP was due to the 1934 strikes and the Spanish Civil War.[56]

In July and September 1937, Dr. Leo Eloesser chaired fund-raising sessions at the St. Francis Yacht Club. A faculty member at Stanford Medical School (then located in San Francisco), Eloesser was born to wealthy German-immigrant parents in San Francisco and studied medicine at Heidelberg University in Germany. After serving at Letterman Army Hospital, in the Presidio of San Francisco, during World War I, he devised a treatment for tuberculosis that bears his name. He traveled to Moscow in 1934 to install a thoracic surgery ward there. Though not a party member, he was clearly on the left.[57]

In September 1937 Eloesser began to raise funds for an ambulance and hospital unit and announced that he planned to go himself. By late October he had raised the funds and recruited another surgeon and three nurses as part of his West Coast Hospital Unit. Eloesser and his colleagues arrived in Spain in November, and more members of his group arrived in January. Given Eloesser's social and academic status in San Francisco, the *Chronicle* carried his monthly reports from the front, in which he discussed the bravery of the Republican forces, performing surgeries by candlelight, and the desperate need for medical supplies. In February he wrote that he had just experienced "the greatest two weeks of my life!" but by May he was describing the situation as "the edge of chaos." He returned to the United States in July, after the disastrous spring campaign.[58]

With the Republic collapsing, the Lincoln Battalion and the other international battalions were demobilized in September 1938. Survivors made their way to France, where they could find a ship to return home. As the American volunteers were withdrawing from Spain, the Friends of the Abraham Lincoln Brigade, another CP organization, set out to raise $150,000 to bring them back.[59]

Life in Moscow

In the late 1920s and early 1930s, several Californians were removed from the state's factional battles by being assigned to other work. "Assigned to other work" became something of a euphemism for such moves. Several ended up in Moscow at some point in the 1930s, and a few moved into positions of some prominence before returning to assignments in the United States.

James Dolsen was the first Californian to be assigned to other work in response to criticism of his work as district organizer. He spent five years in China in the late 1920s and then went to Moscow in 1930 when the mission in China was closed. He remained in Moscow until 1934, working as a *referent*, or researcher, for MOPR. His most dangerous mission during those years was to deliver documents and funds to the German Communist Party, at the time fighting for its life against the Nazi government. In 1934 he was assigned to ILD work in Pittsburgh. He remained in Pennsylvania and continued as a party functionary.[60]

Three Californians in succession—William Schneiderman, Sam Darcy, and Frank Waldron—served as the CPUSA's representative on the Anglo-American Secretariat, the intermediary body between the English-speaking affiliates of the Comintern and the Executive Committee of the Comintern. Each representative was responsible for briefing other AAS members on major events in his (they were all males) country and leading discussions on the response of the AAS and the ECCI to those events. The U.S. representative on the AAS was the major conduit between the ECCI and the CPUSA and was potentially in a sensitive position, between and among CPUSA members in the Soviet Union, CPUSA leaders, the leaders of the Comintern, and the leaders of the Soviet Union. He received dozens of publications from the United States, which he was expected to review in order to provide analyses of major events. When Sam Darcy was CPUSA representative on the AAS, he received forty to fifty newspapers a day. The CPUSA representative had responsibility for liaison with the International Lenin School and other schools where CPUSA members were studying. A report in January 1936, in Russian, described the work this way:

> There are 3 Party Representatives in the Secretariat (from the USA, Canada, Great Britain). . . . CPUSA Representative deals with CPUSA problems. He makes reviews of USA press, examines the materials received from CPUSA, arranges the correspondence with the [U.S.] Party. He also helps CPUSA members as well as other Americans who live now in the USSR. He works in the M-L-School [Lenin School] American Section (helps to organize the program, to teach, to lead the Section). He also has contacts with the Profintern [Red International of Labor Unions] and MOPR representatives [from the U.S.].

The minutes of the AAS meetings indicate that the CPUSA representative sometimes dealt with such matters as finding appropriate medical care for a U.S. party member in Moscow or with securing appropriate credentials for American reporters.[61]

Schneiderman was the first Californian to serve in that role. He left California to be district organizer in New England in 1930 and a year later went to Minnesota as district organizer. He ran as CP candidate for governor of Minnesota in 1932, polling less than 1 percent of the vote. While there, he met Leah Schneider, who had been born in Poland in 1912 and came to the United States with her parents in 1921. Leah had joined the YCL at the age of thirteen and met Schneiderman when he came to the University of Minnesota to promote William Z. Foster for president in 1932.[62]

Schneiderman left Minnesota in April 1934 to become CPUSA representative on the AAS, under the name of Sherman. He was also elected to the National Committee in 1934. Leah joined Bill in Moscow in October 1934, and they were married. She later liked to explain that she had added a "man" to her name and a man to her life. During the Smith Act trial in 1952, Bill characterized his work in Moscow as acting "as sort of consultant," providing "data, statistics clippings from US newspapers, magazines, on pol.econ. trends in U.S.," but he was clearly minimizing his responsibilities.[63]

The Schneidermans returned to the United States in late September 1935 when Bill became district organizer for California. Leah, however, remained in Minneapolis, where she was assigned to be an organizer for the International Ladies Garment Workers Union. She wanted to go to San Francisco with her husband, but the local CP organizer in Minneapolis told her, "You are going to stay here and take the job." She did so until March 1937.[64]

Sam Darcy succeeded Schneiderman as the CPUSA representative on the AAS in September 1935. During his time on the AAS, Darcy usually used the name Randolph. The head of the AAS then was André Marty, who left in late 1936 to take charge in Spain.

Darcy recounted an event that illustrates some of the complexities of his position with the AAS. He taught American history at the Lenin School and had general responsibility for the Americans and Canadians there. He recalled that one Canadian student was brought up on charges of being a counterrevolutionary because he had written and distributed satirical poems about the food. Knowing the student, Darcy thought the charge was ridiculous. He vigorously defended the student and, in the process, mocked the woman who was head of the school. The charge was dropped. The next day, Darcy was summoned to see Dmitry Manuilsky, deputy head of the Comintern and a high-ranking member of the Soviet CP. Manuilsky reprimanded Darcy for his language toward the head of the school, reminded Darcy that the woman's husband was a member of the Russian Central Committee, and told Darcy to be more respectful toward leaders of the Russian CP. Darcy recalled, "He spoke for about three minutes, then he says, 'OK, you're done.' I turned and wondered whether I should answer or should I blow my brains out, or what should I do? I opened the door, and he says, 'One more thing. If you act any differently, I'll never talk to you again.'"[65]

The AAS had some responsibility for Americans in the Soviet Union, both the sizeable number of CPUSA members and those who were not party members;

the AAS also evaluated some requests to come to the Soviet Union. For example, in February 1935 the AAS, then including Schneiderman, denied such a request to come to the Lenin School.[66]

Some such decisions could have life-and-death implications. The AAS files include minutes of a meeting on August 25, 1935, when the CPUSA delegation to the Seventh Comintern Congress was still in Moscow. Those present included Browder, Darcy, and Schneiderman from the U.S. party, Ivan Mingulin, who was an AAS staff member, and "Gerhardt," apparently Gerhard Eisler, a German and the former Comintern representative to the CPUSA. The group considered "reported efforts of Lovett [Fort-]Whiteman to mislead some of the Negro comrades" and decided "that Comrades [William] Patterson and [James] Ford take the initiative in holding a meeting with all the Negro comrades to discuss the question."[67] Patterson was born in San Francisco, graduated from Hastings College of the Law in 1919, and then left California; he joined the CP in New York City in 1926 or 1927, traveled and studied in the Soviet Union, became a party functionary, and then national secretary of the ILD, responsible for the party's handling of the Scottsboro case.[68]

At issue was, in fact, the future of Lovett Fort-Whiteman, one of a half-dozen Black CPUSA members living in Moscow. He had first come to Moscow in 1925 as a delegate to the Fifth Comintern Congress and then returned in 1928 for the Sixth congress. He remained in Moscow, married, and began teaching at an English-language school. He requested to return to the United States in October 1933, but an unidentified AAS official denied his request. Fort-Whiteman attracted the attention of party leaders by meeting with Black CPUSA members in Moscow and arguing that the party needed to emphasize the central significance of racism, in addition to class, in its analysis of the situation of Black Americans, a position contrary to the party line. In 1935, as directed, Patterson investigated and reported that Fort-Whiteman had turned against the party. The next year, in 1936, Fort-Whiteman was called before the NKVD (the feared secret police) and sent into internal exile in Kazakhstan. In 1938 he was sentenced to five years in a prison labor camp in Siberia, where he died in 1939.[69] He was apparently the only Black American to die in the gulag. There is no indication that the AAS or CPUSA officials were involved in events after Patterson's report in 1935.

Darcy left the AAS in May 1937 and returned to the United States, where he held various positions within the party until 1939, when he became head of the Eastern Pennsylvania district, the fourth largest. Darcy's successor as CPUSA representative on the AAS was Frank Waldron. Calling himself Tim Ryan, he first came to Moscow in late 1930. Soon after, his partner, Regina Karasick, arrived with their toddler, Tim. Both were soon deeply involved in Comintern operations. Ryan traveled to the Philippines, South Africa, and China on Comintern missions, organizing in the Philippines and helping to resolve factional fight-ing in South Africa. Reggie became a Comintern courier, delivering material in Berlin, Paris, and throughout Europe. During their travels, they placed their son in the Comintern's International Children's Home, outside Moscow. In 1935, now named Eugene and Peggy Dennis, they went to Wisconsin, where Gene became state secretary (the position previously called district organizer). Their son, Tim, was left behind on orders from Manuilsky, who decided that a five-year-old child in Wisconsin speaking only Russian would raise too many questions.[70]

In spring 1937 Gene and Peggy decided to join the fight in Spain. They got as far as Paris, where they were directed to go to Moscow. In Moscow they were forbidden to go to Spain, because too many leading cadres had died there. (Darcy had a similar experience; Manuilsky told him he was not allowed to go to Spain because he was "too old." Darcy was thirty.) Dennis then became the U.S. repre-sentative of the AAS, again as "T. Ryan." After an absence of some two years, Gene and Peggy found distinct changes in Moscow. Several friends and colleagues had vanished and others avoided them. The Great Terror, Stalin's campaign to purge all "anti-Soviet elements," was under way, eventually sweeping up most of the original Bolshevik leaders, many military officers, and large numbers of ordinary citizens. When Gene and Peggy were assigned to living quarters, they learned that the previous occupant had been Ivan Mingulin, longtime deputy head of the AAS, whom they had known and worked with. He had been taken away in the middle of the night. Peggy Dennis said later, "We cannot claim we did not know what was happening. We knew that the Comintern had been decimated." Among their comrades in Moscow, no one spoke of the trials of Stalin's opponents and the disappearances of people they knew. She continued: "It was as though we each knew we could not trust ourselves to open that Pandora's box." In January 1938 they were sent back to the States, again without Tim. Gene's new assignment, as defined by Manuilsky and Georgi Dimitrov, head of the Comintern, was to serve as a "balance" between Browder and Foster at CPUSA headquarters in New York. Gene and Peggy's separation from their son became permanent. Tim grew up with other Comintern orphans and, as Timur Timofeev, became a Soviet trade union official.[71]

Although the expectation was that the U.S. representative to the AAS would serve for two years, none of the three Californians served the full two years. As of 1939, with all three back in the United States, Dennis and Schneiderman were members of the National Committee, and Darcy was a candidate member. Other Californians then on the National Committee included Harrison George and Anita Whitney. Morris Rappaport, then DO for Washington and Oregon, and Pettis Perry of Los Angeles joined Darcy as candidate members.[72]

Life on Campus

Several prominent party members had attended UC-Berkeley in the early 1930s. Lou Goldblatt began studying at City College of New York, where he joined the YCL, graduated from UCLA in 1931, and then spent two years at Berkeley, first in law, then in economics. Goldblatt later recalled that he and other student radicals had spent a good deal of time with the Social Problems Club. Other students, he later quipped, thought it was the club members who were the social problems.[73] Aubrey Grossman later told a party committee that he "began to work with the Party as [a] student in 1932 and until 1934 [his] main activity was in [the] student movement."[74]

Edith Arnstein was active in party activities at UC-Berkeley in the mid-1930s. She graduated from Girls High School in San Francisco, where she was associate editor of the school newspaper. During her freshman year in college, she was active in Crop and Saddle, the student riding club, reflecting her privileged upbringing. She soon moved to more political activities and recalled of her final two years: "We organized against fascism. We demonstrated for free speech. We called student strikes. Studying was spasmotic [*sic*] and incidental." In March 1935 she was among five women arrested for distributing antiwar leaflets. That same spring, she was at a protest meeting over the expulsion of a Communist student when the meeting was broken up by the football players. She was among a group of UC-Berkeley students sent to speak at San Mateo Junior College, but the meeting turned into a riot and police escorted the speakers away. On such occasions, she recalled, "Only one member of the faculty . . . gave shelter and moral support" to the students: Haakon Chevalier.[75]

Arnstein graduated in 1935 and then continued for another three semesters, including some time in the law school. In 1936, while in law school, she became section organizer for the party's professional section. She later recalled "everything was so secretive" that she didn't even know who was in the professional section. Membership lists were kept secret, and everyone used a code name. The code name she chose was Mary Wollstonecraft, the eighteenth-century advocate for women's rights. Having a membership card was "too dangerous," so no one had one. She remembered the professional section as composed of several units of about eight people each; each unit met every week or two at a member's house. Concluding that she should be a member of the working class, she quit law school, went to a business school, gave up learning to type, and got a job as a cashier at a department store in San Francisco.[76]

During her sophomore year, Edith Arnstein had lived in a flat upstairs from a young associate professor whom she soon knew as "Oppie"—J. Robert Oppenheimer. Edith was also a close friend of Jean Tatlock, who became Oppenheimer's girlfriend in 1935. Tatlock was a party member, although, as she said at the time, "I find it impossible to be an ardent Communist."[77] Arnstein later recalled a conversation with Oppie that she dated to "the period of the 1937 Moscow trials," while she was still at UC-Berkeley. Oppenheimer sought her out for a conversation, she recalled, because "he knew I would not be shaken in my political loyalties." He had just learned of the arrest of Soviet physicists, and "he was reluctant to believe the report, but he could not dismiss it." At the time, she was scornful of what she saw as Oppenheimer's gullibility. Writing some fifty years later and thirty years after leaving the party, she speculated, "Those arrests sowed the seeds of [Oppenheimer's] disillusionment with the USSR and, eventually, the American Left."[78]

The Strains of Party Life

Others also admitted to doubts about the party or the Soviet Union, but party discipline was designed to be strict. The party's dues book, as of 1932, carried this message: "The strictest Party discipline is the most solemn duty of all Party members and all Party organizations. The decisions of the CI [Communist International] and the Party Convention, of the CC [Central Committee] and of all leading committees of the Party, must be promptly carried out. Discussion of questions over which there have been differences must not continue after the decision has been made."[79] However, not everyone was subject to party discipline in the same way.

Observers then and later have disagreed regarding the degree to which the CP succeeded in its ambition to be a tightly disciplined organization. Even membership could be ambiguous. Caroline Decker recalled, "I never carried a book, I never paid dues.... As far as I was concerned, I was a member; I was prepared to give my life and I gave an awful lot of it. But . . . no evaluation papers or applications, and not even membership books. Not even dues. Where was I going to get money to pay dues?" Dorothy Ray Healey similarly recalled, "I never regularly paid dues until 1946. When you moved around a great deal, the way I did, the bookkeeping never kept up with you." But, like Decker, she specified that "you could still be a Communist accepted by others as a Communist, whether you paid dues or not." She added, "There is this myth that the Party ran like some kind of well-oiled machine, but it was never that well organized internally.... The FBI did a much better job of keeping track of our members than we did, unfortunately."[80]

In the 1930s the party used control commissions to maintain discipline. The American branch had a good reputation, according to Arvid Brigadier, a Latvian immigrant to the United States, who joined the predecessor of the CPUSA and then emigrated to the Soviet Union, where he worked for the AAS and later for the Comintern's Cadres Department. Brigadier said in 1936, "The CCC [Central Control Commission] in the U.S. works better than any Control Commission outside the USSR," but he provided no reasons for that assessment. During the Great Terror in the Soviet Union, the CPUSA aimed to root out all "anti-Soviet elements" just like the Soviet party was doing. Charles Dirba reported to the plenary session of the National Committee in 1938 on the need to emulate the Soviet purges and advised his comrades not just to ferret out individual "Trotsky-ites and Lovestoneites" but also to familiarize themselves with the Moscow trials of "Trotskyite and Bukharinite groups of German fascist spies" and to be alert to similar conspiracies both inside and outside the party.[81]

A major instrument for maintaining party discipline was the local control commission. Those brought before the control commission and found guilty could be disciplined, typically by suspension or expulsion. In 1935 District 13 had more than its proportionate share of expulsions and other disciplinary actions. A report of the Central Control Commission in 1935 indicated, "The greatest number of expelled functionaries falls on District 13 (San Francisco): 9 unit functionaries, 6 section functionaries and 2 in mass organizations, a total of 17. . . . 33 functionaries were disciplined in District 2 (New York), 19 in District 13 (San Francisco)." No other district had more than four such disciplinary actions.

Coming before the local control commission could be a frightening experience. Dorothy Ray was called for disciplinary action several times when she was in the YCL. When she was fifteen years old, she was sitting with a bundle of leaflets in the back of a truck on the way to an event. She fell asleep and the bundle fell off the truck. Called before the control commission on a charge of irresponsibility, she recalled, "I was absolutely terrified. I felt like I was approaching the guillotine." Instead, she said, the control commission members "were all amused by having this fifteen-year-old child appearing before them, clearly scared to death. They just gently told me to stay awake in the future." Another time she was brought up for having hitchhiked to Los Angeles without getting permission from the YCL. "The most important thing you learned" from such experiences, she later said, "was to be able to do things you really didn't like to do."[82]

Others had a much more troubling experience. Miriam Dinkin Johnson was outraged by her treatment by the San Francisco Control Commission. "The Communist party sent a person to my home at midnight one night . . . asking me to appear at seven o'clock at a control commission meeting at 121 Haight Street [CP headquarters]. No one told me why. I was scared to death." She had resigned from the YCL and never joined the CP, although her parents, sister, and husband were all CP members and her work on the King-Ramsay-Conner Defense Committee put her into frequent contact with party members. She went to the meeting. "It was very secretive. . . . There were six charges against me. One of them was that

I had love affairs with eight men or six men, three of whom I had never met. . . . I hadn't had love affairs with *any* of them. . . . That was the standard anti-female charge about anybody who was around men." Another charge was that she had misused funds, another frequent charge used by the party. She denied all charges, denied ever meeting some of the men, and pointed to the regular audits of defense committee funds. She was vindicated, either through her own protestations or because of the intervention of Henry Schmidt and Harry Bridges, who led her to understand that the whole affair was really an effort by some party members to smear Schmidt, Bridges, and others. She realized that she was just a convenient tool for that purpose. Though she never understood all that happened, she recalled, "I knew my job depended on my going to that meeting," since, if the control commission had found against her, party members in the Maritime Federation District Council would have tried to remove her from the defense committee. She never joined the CP.[83]

Elaine and Karl Yoneda made the decision to have a child. For a woman in a leadership position, having a child was a party decision, not a personal matter. Dorothy Ray Healey recalled, "Before I got pregnant, I met with Louise Todd, who was the CP's state secretary, and Oleta O'Connor Yates, who was the county organizer in San Francisco. I told them . . . I thought it was time I had a child. They said, 'Sure, of course'—but I'm sure that if they said otherwise, I would have heeded party discipline and foregone the pregnancy." Peggy Dennis had two abortions, a legal and safe one in the Soviet Union and an illegal and dangerous one in Wisconsin. At her insistence, she and her husband finally had a son in late 1942. Oleta O'Connor Yates never had a child. Louise Todd later recalled that she and her husband, Carl Rude Lambert, decided that having a child was not compatible with Louise's "primary activity as a communist." As state organizational secretary and member of the state executive committee, she later said, "My personal life became subordinate to the greater needs of the radical movement. Many of my decisions in regard to my personal life were secondary, you might say, to the needs of the party." She continued: "Women who rose to leadership . . . were prepared to make sacrifices of a different kind, sacrifices of not having children, of not having what you might call a well-rounded marriage relationship." The decision not to have children, she later concluded, "was an unnecessary, possibly even a tragic, sacrifice."[84]

Todd also had misgivings in the late 1930s: "The Party's advocacy of socialism was based on the Soviet example to the point where we spoke of the objective of a 'Soviet America.' I felt that our advocacy of socialism should be based on American realities." But she did not speak of those misgivings. "You didn't ask questions," she recalled, "if there were people who disagreed and who disagreed violently, pretty soon there would be some action taken. They were either removed from their position or they were expelled from the party." She later said of the Molotov-Ribbentrop Pact, "We muffled our anti-fascist position. We practically set a moratorium on all our anti-fascist criticism."[85]

Caroline Decker was also troubled by events in the Soviet Union in the late 1930s. She later said that when she came out of prison, "I had many questions in my mind. . . . What was happening in the Soviet Union . . . , the disposition of people like Karl Radek [an important Soviet leader sent to a penal labor camp in 1937]. . . . All of a sudden we're told that they're enemies of the people and were eradicated. I was real shook up." That was, she later said, "when I began to think about . . . where is the democratic part of the Democratic Centralism?" The Molotov-Ribbentrop Pact was, she said, "when my own association with the Communist Party went pow."[86]

Decker was not the only one to question the Molotov-Ribbentrop Pact. Todd later acknowledged, "We lost great credibility and confidence among our membership and followers. . . . We lost members and hundreds of sympathizers." Voter registration never came close to the party's count of dues-paying members, but the number of voters registered as Communists fell from 1,358 in August 1938 to 678 in November 1940, a drop of more than 50 percent. The party did not release membership numbers between January 1939 and December 1943. District 13 had 6,243 members in January 1939 and 6,152 in December 1943, two years into the Popular Front of World War II, suggesting that the party had still not recovered from its losses due to the Molotov-Ribbentrop Pact and, perhaps, the anti-Communist efforts of 1938–1941.[87]

World War II proved a time when the party not only recovered from the membership losses of 1939 but gained more members than it had ever had before. It also regained at least some, if not most, of the stature it had achieved during the Popular Front years of the late 1930s.

CHAPTER 6

THE WARTIME POPULAR FRONT, 1941–1945

The German invasion of the Soviet Union in June 1941 brought a quick return of the Popular Front. Four years later, as the Axis neared defeat, national party secretary Earl Browder led the CP into an extreme version of the Popular Front, transforming the party into a political association tied to New Deal Democrats.

Return of the Popular Front

Following its poor showing in the 1940 elections, the CPUSA continued to treat the Molotov-Ribbentrop Pact as a de facto entente and opposed any U.S. involvement in the "Second Imperialist War." In March 1941, Congress approved the Lend-Lease Act to support Britain and its dominions, then alone in opposing Nazi Germany. The CP histrionically called it the "War-Powers-Dictatorship Bill," claiming it "would lead to a war dictatorship . . . akin to fascism." The CP National Committee issued a manifesto that echoed Third Period rhetoric in denouncing AFL and CIO leaders and Socialists and charged the Roosevelt administration with wanting to "chain the workers to the war-chariot of Wall Street."[1]

The *Wehrmacht* invasion of the Soviet Union on June 22, 1941, stunned party leaders. Suddenly uncertain how to view Britain or the Roosevelt administration, they waited for instructions. The CPUSA had withdrawn from the Comintern in 1940, amid the surge of anti-Communism that followed the Molotov-Ribbentrop Pact and Soviet invasion of Poland, but party leaders did not sever connections with Moscow. Georgi Dimitrov, head of the Comintern, maintained a direct line to

CP headquarters in New York City at least through 1941. On June 26 he explained that the war was now "neither a class war nor a war for socialist revolution" but a "just war of defense," and that anticapitalist and anti-imperialist rhetoric was no longer relevant. He directed that "the Communists and the working-class in America . . . with all forces and all means, must resolutely raise struggle against German fascism. Secondly, they must demand from the American government all aid to the Soviet people."[2]

Two days later the CPUSA National Committee presented "The People's Program of Struggle for the Defeat of Hitler and Hitlerism!" which labeled Germany a menace to "the people of the world" and demanded *"full aid to the Soviet Union, Great Britain and all nations who fight against Hitler!"* The party immediately stopped its attacks on the Roosevelt administration and instead called for "the broadest united front and People's Front activities."[3] Fascism was again the enemy, the Popular Front was back, and the CPUSA was in full-throated support of U.S. aid to those fighting Germany, especially the Soviet Union.

By the time the party announced its new line, Roosevelt had already pledged all possible aid to the Soviet Union. In mid-August, Roosevelt and British prime minister Winston Churchill met in the mid-Atlantic, issued the Atlantic Charter, and assured Stalin that "the very maximum of supplies" was already on the way and more would leave soon.[4] When the United States entered the war in December, the CP gave its strongest support to the armed forces and the war effort, pushing members to enlist or to maximize war production.

Support for the Soviet Union

In addition to demanding that the United States send supplies to the Soviet Union, the CP insisted on an immediate second front—an Allied landing in Europe to divert German troops from Russia. U.S. and British strategists knew their forces were not ready for that, but the CP and its allies in the CIO ignored such realities and equated any delay with appeasement. Soviet officials contributed to such efforts, for example, through the speaking tour by Lyudmila Pavlichenko, described in *People's World* as a "Soviet Girl Sniper" with a record number of kills. She arrived in San Francisco in October 1942 and was given an official reception at city hall and separate receptions by CP-related organizations. At city hall she said, "We thank America for what aid she has given so far. But—we still want to know when you are going to open that second front." The invasion of North Africa in late 1942 wasn't enough. In March 1943 *PW* bluntly demanded, "Invade Europe Now!"[5]

Russian War Relief (RWR), a national organization, attracted broad support. San Francisco party members labored at fund-raising. In the first eight months,

RWR raised $35,000 in Northern California. A rally marking the second anniversary of the German invasion brought in $1,300. A "Victory Ball" in March 1943 netted about $4,000. An event in March 1944 garnered nearly $2,000.[6] ($1.00 in mid-1943 had equivalent purchasing power to more than $17.00 in 2023.)

CP members joined, or led, such efforts. Within a week of the German invasion, Victor and Lydia Arnautoff had organized the Russian American Society to Aid the USSR and Great Britain, later simply the Russian American Society. Within a year, they had raised twenty thousand dollars. They also plunged into RWR efforts and Victor joined its executive committee. They spoke at fund-raising events, and Lydia used her linguistic and typing skills in the Soviet Purchasing Commission's office. Once a month she and other women from the Russian American Society volunteered in the city's United Service Organizations (USO) club. She admitted in mid-1943, "I still have not been able to organize my time so that I could feed my family food—so they get cans mostly."[7]

The Soviet consulate in San Francisco bolstered such efforts. The consulate opened after Roosevelt opened diplomatic relations with the Soviet Union in 1933. Yakov Mironovich Lomakin, the consul general; his wife, Lorissa; and other Soviet consular officials joined local party members in programs to support the war or assist the Soviet Union. In June 1942 Lomakin was an honored guest at a tea hosted by the American Russian Institute and later spoke to the Russian American Society. On the second anniversary of the German invasion, he joined a rally organized by a wide spectrum of groups including the Veterans of Foreign Wars. In November 1943 he participated in the Russian American Society's celebration of the anniversary of the October Revolution. The Lomakins returned to the Soviet Union in 1944.[8]

The American Russian Institute was prominent in many such activities. It dated to 1926, when the *Vsesojuznoe obschestvo kul'turnykh svyzei s zagranitseior* (All-Union Society for Cultural Relations with Foreign Countries, or VOKS), part of the Soviet government, designated the American Society for Cultural Relations with Russia as its U.S. affiliate. Jean-François Fayet, in his study of VOKS, noted that Soviet authorities hoped to influence members of the intelligentsia and artistic communities in Western nations through VOKS activities. Such cultural diplomacy, he specified, was always directed by the Soviet state and party, and "the extremely complex links between culture, propaganda, and networks of influence were an essential aspect of Soviet foreign policy." The U.S. affiliate became the American Russian Institute in 1930 and opened its San Francisco branch in 1931. In 1943 Rose Isaak, longtime secretary of that branch, claimed that its library on the Soviet Union was the most comprehensive in the West, including many items sent by VOKS.[9]

Anti-Communists sometimes tried to block fund-raising for the Soviet war effort. Anti-Communists of Russian descent refused to have anything to do with either the American Russian Institute or the Russian American Society. In late 1942, Louise Bransten, working with the American Council on Soviet Relations in New York, a CP-dominated organization, sought to hold a "Salute to Our Russian Ally" rally at the San Francisco Opera House. Pressured by the American Legion, the opera house board refused. Bransten then mobilized several prominent San Franciscans to urge the mayor and opera house board to reverse the denial. "The whole struggle with the Opera House authorities," Bransten wrote, shows "how strong the Fascist elements here are." In the end, her group filled only half the opera house and amassed a huge deficit.[10]

Bransten had inherited significant wealth in 1929 at the death of her father, Abraham Rosenberg. She married Richard Bransten, scion of another prominent German Jewish family that dated to the Gold Rush, and they traveled in the Soviet Union in 1933. Using the pen name Bruce Minton, Richard Bransten wrote and edited several CP-related publications beginning in the mid-1930s. He and Louise divorced in 1937. When vigilantes smashed the press for the *Western Worker* in 1934, Louise contributed funds to secure a new one, and she made a major loan to *People's World* in 1944. She was one of fifteen directors of the Rosenberg Foundation, created by her uncle's will. Most directors came from San Francisco's civic elite, but Bransten was the only Rosenberg. In 1944 the Rosenberg Foundation gave $6,000 (equivalent to $102,000 in 2023) to the American Russian Institute to prepare material on the Soviet Union for use in elementary schools.[11]

The FBI labeled the American Russian Institute, the Russian American Society, and Russian War Relief as Communist fronts. Soviet authorities constantly worked to influence them. In late March 1943, Grigori M. Kheifets, the San Francisco vice-consul and NKVD *resident* (Soviet intelligence agency station chief[12]), informed Vladimir Kemenov, head of VOKS in Moscow, "We have carried through our influence at the Institute via Rose Isaak, Arnautoff and recently Bransten." Kheifets also informed Kemenov and Vasily Zarubin, "At present we manage to exercise our influence in RWR in San Francisco, Seattle, Portland and Los Angeles through Betty Gordon." Zarubin was the second secretary of the Soviet embassy in Washington and the head NKVD resident in the United States. Kheifets also cultivated San Franciscans involved in these pro-Soviet organizations. In August 1943 he asked the head of the Anglo-American section of VOKS to send "3–4 boxes with Soviet theme painting"—Palenkh boxes—"for some of the most active members of ARI Board." In November 1943 Kheifets requested $250–$300 for "Christmas presents," presumably for such friends of the Soviet Union.[13]

Internment of Japanese Americans

Karl Yoneda recalled that shortly after the attack on Pearl Harbor, William Schneiderman called for party members who were Nisei (born in the United States of Japanese parentage) to meet at the Yonedas' apartment. There Schneiderman announced that the party "was suspending all members of Japanese ancestry and their non-Japanese spouses for the duration of the war." Party leaders justified that suspension on the grounds that the best place for a Japanese fifth columnist to hide was in the CP.[14]

Soon after, on February 19, 1942, Roosevelt signed Executive Order (E.O.) 9066, authorizing the U.S. Army to establish military areas "from which any and all persons may be excluded." Two days later Congressman John Tolan's subcommittee began local hearings regarding implementation of E.O. 9066, hearings that quickly focused on those of Japanese ancestry. Prominent public figures, including California attorney general Earl Warren, supported the "relocation" of all persons of Japanese ancestry, regardless of citizenship. CIO leaders chose Louis Goldblatt, secretary of the state CIO Industrial Union Council, to address Tolan's committee and oppose Japanese relocation and any other actions based on ancestry. Goldblatt scathingly denounced "the forces of hysteria and vigilantism" that were advocating relocation and accurately predicted, "This entire episode of hysteria . . . will form a dark page of American history." Goldblatt's position—that of the ILWU and the California CIO—was directly contrary to that of most other unions and also contrary to the position of the CPUSA, which accepted Japanese relocation as "a necessary war measure." In practice, for the large majority of Japanese Americans in the Pacific Coast states, relocation meant being confined in government camps.[15]

David Jenkins remembered that some party members criticized Goldblatt's statement. Louise Todd Lambert, on the other hand, recalled, "I was very upset [regarding internment] and very critical, and Oleta [O'Connor Yates] was very critical. We discussed it between ourselves, and I think Oleta even raised it at one meeting, and the approach was sort of—let's not do anything that will rock the boat."[16]

Karl Yoneda did not rock the boat. He gave Tolan's committee a letter promising, on behalf of the Bay Area readers of *Doho*, "We will cooperate with the U.S. government to our fullest extent." He soon volunteered as a construction laborer for the internment camp at Manzanar. Three-year-old Tommy Yoneda was covered by the relocation order, and Elaine accompanied him to the camp. Yoneda tried to enlist immediately after the attack on Pearl Harbor but was not accepted until late 1942; he was then sent to the Military Intelligence Service language school in Minnesota. By then the rules had been modified to permit non-Japanese women to leave the camps with their children. Elaine and Tommy joined Elaine's parents in Los Angeles.[17]

Joining the Army

Yoneda's proficiency in written as well as spoken Japanese made him a valuable asset for the army, which had established its Japanese language program at the Presidio of San Francisco well before Pearl Harbor and had moved it to Minnesota with the implementation of Japanese internment. Those chosen to participate—mostly Nisei—received extensive training in Japanese language, culture, and military terminology. After training, Yoneda was promoted to sergeant and sent to the China-India-Burma theater, where U.S. and British forces were reopening the Burma Road into southern China to supply Chinese forces fighting the Japanese. Yoneda drafted leaflets calling upon Japanese troops to surrender and broadcast similar messages. He was among the U.S. troops who pursued the retreating Japanese from northern Burma into China.[18]

Other CP members also volunteered. Henry Gliksohn (Harry Jackson), forty-two years old, enlisted in September 1942 but was discharged in May 1943. Leo Nitzberg tried to enlist when the United States entered the war but was rejected for his poor eyesight—and perhaps his participation in the Abraham Lincoln Battalion. He persisted, was accepted into the army in November 1942, and discharged in February 1946. He was never sent out of the country but did become a citizen. Keith Eickman enlisted in May 1943 and was discharged in January 1946. Jack Olsen, an officer in ILWU Local 6, declined his deferment in April 1944 and served until December 1945.[19]

Isaac Zafrani had an unusual wartime experience. Born in 1906 in what is now Syria, he went to sea, declared his intention to become a U.S. citizen, and joined the Marine Workers Industrial Union and the CP. Active in the 1934 strike in San Francisco, he then became a longshoreman. When Harry Bridges promoted the formation of army port battalions made up of longshore workers from the ILWU, Zafrani enlisted. Though choosing to remain a private first-class, he managed the building and operation of the army's ammunition dock in Antwerp, Belgium, involving supervision of fifteen hundred civilian employees and an army engineering company.[20]

Archie Brown wanted to enlist but first asked local party leaders for permission. The party didn't want him to go, citing his family responsibilities, work in ILWU Local 10, and party activity. He recalled, "I kept on renewing my request. . . . I was turned down several times." He tried to volunteer for the longshoring unit but was turned down. He then volunteered for the draft and finally, he later said, "snuck into the army." He went to Europe as part of the 76th Infantry, arrived in England in December 1944, and took part in the invasion of Germany. He was discharged in early 1946.[21]

Shortly after the war, Carl Rude Lambert, head of the Control Commission, specified, "We had a rigid rule that . . . no Communist should avoid the draft by shipping out or using any other way to evade it."[22] Nonetheless, some CP members secured draft deferments by working in essential occupations, especially in seafaring unions. Pat Tobin joined the National Maritime Union (NMU), worked as a merchant seaman throughout the war—potentially very dangerous—and was elected delegate, equivalent to a shop steward, because, he later said, "I was a good trade unionist, not because I was a member of the CP." Shortly before the United States entered the war, party leaders directed Bill Bailey to run for Marine Firemen's Union port agent in New York, and he was elected. With the coming of the war, he recalled, "I began to feel more and more that everybody was making sacrifices in the war except me." He returned to San Francisco, passed the examination to become an assistant engineer, and shipped out on cargo ships crossing the Pacific. Revels Cayton was secretary-treasurer of the Bay Area District of the Maritime Federation in 1939–1941 but was accused by another CP member, Walter Stack of the MFOW, of malfeasance in his union office, which shook some of his faith in the party. Cayton briefly resumed shipping out through the National Union of Marine Cooks and Stewards, but spent much of the war in Los Angeles, as a CIO organizer and national representative.[23]

Dave Jenkins arrived in the Bay Area in 1939. Born in 1914 in the South Bronx to Jewish immigrant parents, both Socialists, he left school after the eighth grade, worked in factories in the New York City area, joined the CP about 1932, became part of a bohemian-left collective in Greenwich Village, and attended a CP school. He met Constance Dixon, daughter of the artist Maynard Dixon, and they had a daughter. In the late 1930s he became educational director for the NMU and then an organizer for the CIO Maritime Committee. When he came to San Francisco in 1939 to be with Constance and his daughter, he first worked with several CIO unions before the party assigned him to head the local Yanks Are Not Coming Committee. He and Constance married but soon divorced. Edith Arnstein Geist, also recently divorced, married Jenkins in 1942 when he was about to ship out with the NUMCS. Between trips to sea, Jenkins held positions with various CIO affiliates before the party appointed him as director of the Tom Mooney Labor School in 1944.[24]

Some CP members accepted draft deferments based on service as union officers. In May 1943 Eugene Paton, ILWU secretary-treasurer, waived deferment. To replace Paton, the ILWU executive board chose Louis Goldblatt, then secretary-treasurer of the state CIO council. He left the party around that time and later explained: "There's no question in my mind that while their [CP leaders'] intentions might have been good, in many respects they did not have as accurate or as careful an appraisal of the membership as its [the union's] leaders did. . . . With some of the party people the position they followed was so doctrinaire you couldn't get anywhere; it did not make any sense." He maintained what he called "cordial" relations with party leaders, which he explained, meant "we sat and chewed the fat once in a while," a status much like that of Harry Bridges.[25]

Fighting Racial Discrimination

During the war the Bay Area became the largest shipbuilding site in the world. New shipyards and expansions of existing ones constructed some fourteen hundred ships, averaging more than one a day. This rapid expansion of shipbuilding produced a huge demand for workers. Some new workers were local, including many women. Others were recruited across the country, including significant numbers from the South, both white and Black. One consequence was the expansion or development of Black communities in San Francisco, Oakland, Richmond, and Marin County.[26]

Most shipyards had contracts with the International Brotherhood of Boilermakers, AFL, which limited membership to whites. The 1937 Boilermakers' national convention had created a special status for locals considered subject to "subversive forces," that is, the CP: the national officers took direct control of such locals. Local 513, for Kaiser Shipyard workers at Richmond, was controlled that way throughout the war, with no elections or meetings. Workers at Marinship, in Marin County just north of the Golden Gate Bridge, were represented by Boilermakers Local 6, a long-established local in San Francisco. Faced with many Black workers in the Bay Area shipyards, the Boilermakers required them to pay dues to an auxiliary but denied them participation in elections or meetings.[27] CP members on opposite sides of the bay took different approaches to fight this racial discrimination.

Ray Thompson, a party member since the late 1930s, found a job at Moore Drydock, in Oakland. He recalled that he "got mad as hell" about the Boilermakers' policies. After talking with local CP leaders, Thompson led in forming the East Bay Shipyard Workers Committee against Discrimination, was elected chairman, and began to fight the Boilermakers' policy. He later claimed that his committee had more than five thousand members. They first planned to operate within the auxiliaries, win elections there, and seek to change the union's policy from inside. Then the Boilermakers' national office suspended elections.[28]

Across the bay, at Marinship, Joseph James, a member of the NAACP and not a CP member, pursued a more confrontational strategy. He led the San Francisco Committee Against Discrimination and Segregation and sought advice from C.

L. Dellums, president of the Sleeping Car Porters' union. James's organization voted unanimously not to join the auxiliaries. In response, the union withdrew their job clearances. When they lost their jobs, their attorneys, George Andersen and Herbert Resner, secured a temporary restraining order against the layoffs. The national NAACP sent its chief counsel, Thurgood Marshall, to join Andersen and Resner. The East Bay group, having failed to work within the Boilermakers, adopted the same strategy of refusing to join the auxiliary, were fired, and went to court. In 1944 the California Supreme Court decided unanimously for the shipyard workers. By then, however, the shipyards were beginning to close down.[29]

Civil Rights Activities during the Wartime Popular Front

James v. Marinship was not the only example of close cooperation by CP members with liberal civil rights organizations. Matt Crawford was involved in employment issues during World War II, as the director of the Northern California Minorities Committee of the state CIO.[30]

The influx of many Black families to San Francisco during the war brought new attention to civil rights. Party members worked with liberals in the Bay Area Council Against Discrimination, formed by prominent Jewish and Catholic civic leaders in 1942, which became the Council for Civic Unity (CCU) in 1944. Walter Stack served on the advisory committee of the former organization, Oleta O'Connor Yates served on the CCU board, and Matt Crawford was assistant director in 1946. Aubrey Grossman was on the executive committee of the former and a sponsor for the CCU; he considered his work in those organizations as his "concentration points."[31]

In 1944 San Francisco mayor Roger Lapham, created the Mayor's Civic Unity Committee, which operated alongside the CCU; among those Lapham appointed to his committee was Oleta O'Connor Yates. In March 1945 Lapham strongly endorsed a mass meeting sponsored by the CCU at which Paul Robeson was featured as a singer and speaker. Other endorsers included the CIO council, Harry Bridges, and O'Connor Yates. *People's World* ran a laudatory article about Joseph James, then head of the local NAACP, in January, and a few months later James and Crawford shared a platform to argue for better housing for Black people and other minorities.[32]

CUAC and Anti-Communist State Legislation

Though muted, anti-Communism did not disappear. In 1941 the legislature created the Joint Fact-Finding Committee on Un-American Activities, chaired by Jack Tenney. Tenney hired Richard Combs as chief counsel and investigator. That committee, its 1940 predecessor, and its successor are generally referred to as CUAC. California was not the only state to have a "little HUAC," but CUAC stood out. M. J. Heale, in his study of such state committees, noted, "Most operated in ways which offended civil libertarians, but the palm for outrageous behaviour was won by the Tenney committee." During World War II, Tenney and his committee cast a wide net, investigating Nazi-related organizations, fascism in Italian communities, and Japanese nationalism in Japanese communities, but the CP was always prominent on CUAC agendas. In 1944, after claiming that the state CIO-PAC, the political arm of the CIO (and the first-ever political action committee in the United States), was controlled by Communists, Tenney switched his party registration from Democrat to Republican.[33]

Legislation in 1940 had banned the CP from primary elections and therefore from having party candidates in the general election. Pettis Perry (of Los Angeles), chair of the state party, and Anita Whitney and Oleta O'Connor Yates, as individuals seeking to participate in the primary as Communists, brought suit. Their case reached the state supreme court in mid-1942. George Andersen, Herbert Resner, and Leo Gallagher represented the CP and the individual plaintiffs, and several organizations filed amicus briefs. On July 11, 1942, the state supreme court unanimously ruled the law unconstitutional as an unreasonable restriction of "the fundamental right of suffrage." The party offered a few candidates in the 1942 state elections, but the 1943 session of the legislature barred from the primary ballot all parties with fewer than 0.1 percent of registered voters, thus effectively removing not only the CP but all other small parties as well.[34]

Wartime Elections

In mid-1942 William Schneiderman, CP state secretary, wrote in *The Communist* that the California primary was "an important preliminary test between the antifascist and pro-defeatist forces in the state." The party called anyone reluctant to open an immediate second front a "defeatist." Schneiderman so labeled Earl Warren, the California attorney general and leading candidate for the Republican nomination for governor. Schneiderman noted discontent in organized labor over the "lack of energetic leadership" by Governor Culbert Olson, who had been unable to mobilize a legislative majority behind his programs. Some left CIO leaders had encouraged state senator Robert Kenny to seek the Democratic nomination for governor. However, CIO and AFL leaders came together to support Olson for governor and Kenny for attorney general. A referendum on legislation, passed over Olson's veto, to ban "hot cargo" boycotts offered a potential source for AFL and CIO unity similar to the way Proposition 1, in 1938, had unified organized labor and helped elect Olson and other Democrats.

There was no repetition in 1942. Voters approved the law prohibiting boycotts. Olson lost badly. Lieutenant Governor Ellis Patterson lost narrowly. Kenny won as attorney general.[35]

In the 1942 election the party ran candidates only where there was no Democratic candidate. In statewide elections Anita Whitney received 4.6 percent for controller, and the other two CP candidates got 1.8 and 4.2 percent. Walter Lambert, brother-in-law of Louise Todd, running for one of San Francisco's congressional seats, got 7.3 percent of the vote, the highest of any CP candidate in the state.[36]

Barred from the state ballot after 1943, party candidates continued to run in nonpartisan local elections. From 1938 onward the party's candidates in San Francisco were often Oleta O'Connor Yates and Archie Brown. In 1941 Brown scored 12 percent of the vote for supervisor. In 1943 O'Connor Yates, head of the city party organization, ran a well-organized campaign for supervisor. The daily press reported her endorsements by the city's left unions. On Election Day she got just under forty thousand votes, about 18 percent, the high point for any CP candidate in city elections.[37]

Oleta O'Connor Yates, in the center, is filing to run for supervisor, surrounded by supporters. Anita Whitney is on the far right. From the *People's World* photo collection, box 36, file 3, courtesy of Labor Archives and Research Center, San Francisco State University.

In 1944 the party gave the fullest possible support to the reelection of Roosevelt and to liberal Democrats running for the state legislature, and it devoted special attention to Democratic candidates for Congress, including Franck Havenner and George Miller. A few Democratic candidates, including Havenner and Miller, took out ads in *People's World*. The party also mobilized its cadres to get out the vote on Election Day. The election brought a large turnout and victories for Roosevelt and the Democrats.[38]

Trials and Defense Campaigns

When Earl Browder went to prison in 1941, the CP mobilized a nationwide protest and was joined by the ACLU and other individuals and organizations. They argued that Browder's prison term was excessive by any comparative measure and that he was being imprisoned for his politics. Wendell Willkie, the 1940 Republican candidate for president, was among those speaking out. In mid-May 1942, prior to a visit from Soviet foreign minister Molotov, Roosevelt commuted Browder's sentence.[39]

Though the Darcy case was concluded in 1942, the case against Schneiderman continued, leading the CP to invest a significant amount of energy and funds in legal defense activities throughout the war years. Before the conclusion of the Darcy case, the party had formed a Schneiderman-Darcy Defense Committee, centered in California but drawing support nationwide. The FBI noted everyone whose name appeared in support of Schneiderman and investigated some of them.[40]

After Schneiderman was stripped of his citizenship in June 1940, the FBI initiated proceedings to place him in custodial detention in the event of a national emergency. At the same time, Schneiderman's attorneys appealed, ultimately to the U.S. Supreme Court. In late 1941, in a surprise that reverberated nationwide, Wendell Willkie joined Schneiderman's defense team pro bono and agreed to argue the case before the Supreme Court. Carol King, the New York attorney specializing in immigration issues, who was also representing Harry Bridges, had initiated the appeal. In her brief she argued that no law made CP membership grounds for deportation or exclusion from citizenship and that Schneiderman had committed no fraud because the 1927 naturalization forms did not ask about CP membership. Willkie saw a broader issue: the Schneiderman case had the potential to affect every naturalized citizen.[41]

In March 1942 the FBI burglarized King's New York office, copied more than a hundred documents, and carried out at least one subsequent burglary of King's office. Those burglaries were not the FBI's first such "black-bag job," but they seem to have been the first directed at a lawyer with cases pending before federal courts. Apparently the FBI also tapped King's phone, as Schneidman's FBI file includes transcripts or summaries of some of her telephone calls.[42]

In late 1939, when Schneiderman was charged, and in April 1941, when the Ninth Circuit Court upheld his conviction, the CP was condemning the Roosevelt administration for supporting Britain against Germany. By the time *Schneiderman v. U.S.* reached the Supreme Court, the Soviet Union had become an ally. The case was scheduled for February 1942, but federal attorneys, apparently acting for the State Department, suggested a delay, presumably to save the administration from embarrassment with its new ally. The case was put off until the autumn.[43]

The Supreme Court heard *Schneiderman v. U.S.* in November 1942 but was deeply divided. Justice Robert Jackson, attorney general when the case was initially tried, recused himself. Justice Frank Murphy, attorney general when the case was initiated, did not. One seat became vacant. With the appointment of Wiley Rutledge to the vacant seat, the court asked that the case be reargued; the *New York Times* interpreted this as suggesting that the court had previously been evenly divided.[44]

During rearguments on March 12, 1943, Willkie specified that there was "not one word . . . never any overt act" that could demonstrate that Schneiderman was ever in conflict with the Constitution and that it was "preposterous" to convict him based solely on Communist literature. The government argued that Schneiderman's membership in the CP showed that he accepted the views expressed in Communist documents and that those views were in conflict with the Constitution.[45]

The decision, on June 21, 1943, was for Schneiderman, by a vote of 5–3. Justices Murphy, Rutledge, Hugo Black, William O. Douglas, and Stanley Reed formed the majority; Chief Justice Harlan Fiske Stone and Justices Felix Frankfurter and Owen Roberts dissented. Murphy's opinion found that the government had failed to prove that Schneiderman was not attached to the principles of the Constitution, specified that the naturalization laws should not be construed so as to circumscribe liberty of thought, and further specified that attachment to the Constitution was not incompatible with a desire to have it amended. The heart of Murphy's decision was that the government had failed to show by an exacting standard of proof that the Communist Party was committed to overthrowing the government by force and violence, and that the views of Communist theoreticians or leaders could not be imputed to Schneiderman without specific evidence.[46]

Frankfurter was convinced that "the present war conditions—political considerations—are the driving force behind the result in this case," but the authors of both the decision and the dissent went out of their way to claim, "Our relations with Russia . . . are immaterial to . . . this case." However, as Jeffrey Liss concluded in his 1976 analysis of the case, "No one was fooled."[47]

Liss also concluded that the *Schneiderman* decision "established that clear, unequivocal, and convincing evidence of lack of attachment [to the Constitution] must be proved in order to set aside a naturalization decree," and that "this strict standard of evidence has had the effect of reducing the volume of denaturaliza-tion prosecutions in general." Furthermore, he said, "The case has come to stand for the general proposition that the unlawful purposes of an organization do not warrant deprivation of its members' rights absent a showing of the members' knowledge of those purposes and specific intent to further them." The decision has been cited in thousands of cases, especially its evocation of the need for "clear, unequivocal, and convincing evidence."[48] Sanford Levinson has also pointed to the significance of the decision's "strong version of the 'clear and present danger test,'" in that "the majority distinguished between 'agitation and exhortation call-ing for present violent action' and 'mere doctrinal justification' of violence 'under hypothetical conditions at some indefinite future time.'"[49]

By the time *Schneiderman v. U.S.* was heard by the Supreme Court, Harry Bridges was also appealing the result of his second INS hearing and the subse-quent decision of the attorney general that he should be deported. In late June 1942 Bridges and his attorneys learned that Wendell Willkie was "willing at the appropriate time to help out," but Willkie died before the Bridges case reached the Supreme Court. An important addition to the Bridges legal support group was Robert Kenny, by then the California attorney general. Roger Baldwin of the ACLU sometimes advised the Bridges defense team.[50]

When the Bridges case finally came to the Supreme Court in April 1945, Bridges was represented by Richard Gladstein, Carol King, and Lee Pressman, chief counsel for the CIO. Jackson recused himself, given his early role in the case. In the decision, on June 18, the justices divided 5–3. Douglas wrote a nar-row decision, likely to maintain his thin majority, concluding that Bridges had "been ordered deported under a misconstruction of the term 'affiliation' . . . and by reason of an unfair hearing" and that therefore "his detention . . . is unlawful." Murphy concurred but filed a separate opinion that went far beyond Douglas's narrow reasoning, stating, "The record in this case will stand forever as a monu-ment to man's inhumanity to man. Seldom if ever in the history of this nation has there been such a concentrated and relentless crusade to deport an individual because he dared to exercise the freedom that belongs to him as a human being and that is guaranteed to him in the Constitution." Murphy also concluded that the Smith Act was unconstitutional as punishing guilt by association.[51]

Schneiderman and Bridges were not the only ones to have their right to remain in the United States challenged. By the end of 1942 some two thousand denatural-ization cases were under investigation, mostly of Italian and German immigrants suspected of fascist leanings. Communists were also targeted. In May 1941, before the German invasion of the Soviet Union, Irving F. Wixon, district INS director in San Francisco, announced that "undesirable aliens" would not be permitted to "remain at large" and pointed specifically to Elmer Hanoff, who had recently been picked up. George Andersen, representing Hanoff, blamed "war hysteria" for the renewed effort to deport his client and stated that Hanoff was no longer a party member, because the CP had discouraged aliens from membership since the late 1930s. A new deportation order, in 1941, met the same fate as the previous one.[52]

Life in the Party during World War II

Party life during World War II was not all about support for the war, the Soviet Union, and the various defense committees. Beginning in the mid- and late 1930s and continuing into the early 1950s, party members worked to create and staff several labor-left cultural institutions. In 1942 the San Francisco CP opened the Tom Mooney Labor School, similar to other CP labor schools in New York, Philadelphia, and elsewhere. The goal was to extend participation beyond party members.[53] Opening festivities emphasized support from AFL and CIO unions and congratulations by celebrities. Classes included "The Struggle for National Independence," taught by Al Richmond; "Marxism Course 1 (elementary)," by Jack Olsen; and "History of the Negro People," by Dave Jenkins and Matt Crawford. Henry Lanz, a Stanford faculty member, offered lectures on Soviet literature and culture. Holland Roberts lectured on Soviet education; he was then associate professor of education at Stanford and former president of the National Council of Teachers of English. When Jenkins became director in 1944, the school became the California Labor School (CLS). Classes in 1944 ranged from "Recreational Dance" to "Economic Theory," from "Unions and the War" to "Furniture Construction." By early 1945 the CLS had a branch in Oakland.[54] It was the wartime Popular Front at high tide.

In March 1945 the CLS jumped on the civic unity bandwagon, announcing courses on civic unity and a "better understanding of the problems of both management and labor." The lecturers included representatives of both management and labor. Other courses focused on the forthcoming San Francisco conference to organize the United Nations, including a course titled "From Teheran to San Francisco."[55] The curriculum was fully in keeping with Browder's "Teheran" vision of the postwar cooperation between the United States and the Soviet Union (see below).

Peoples' World was another of city's labor-left cultural institutions, presenting not only the party's version of current politics but also covering the arts and sports. Between 1943 and 1945, Paul Ryan, a CP member and journalist who used the pen name Mike Quin, had a regular news program on station KYA and wrote articles for *PW* and *Daily Worker*. Al Richmond, *PW* editor, called Ryan/Quin "the most talented writer" ever associated with that paper. Oleta O'Connor Yates offered occasional radio broadcasts. In 1943 she presented "The Bill of Rights: America's Most Prized Possession" on station KGO. In late 1944, by which time her title was president of the local Communist Political Association, she spoke on station KYA on "Democracy and the Crisis in Greece."[56]

O'Connor Yates's address on the Bill of Rights was introduced by John Pittman, then managing editor of *PW* and perhaps the most prominent Black party member in the city. Born in Atlanta, Pittman graduated from Morehouse College and received his MA in economics from UC-Berkeley in 1930. In 1931 he founded and edited the *San Francisco Spokesman*, a weekly newspaper for the Bay Area Black community. In 1934, when vigilantes smashed the press of the *Western Worker*, Pittman lent his printing press to the party. When vigilantes destroyed his press, Pittman joined the staff of the *Western Worker* and continued on the editorial staff of *PW*.[57]

Several newcomers to the Bay Area during the war made their own contributions to the developing labor-left culture. Robert "Bob" Treuhaft was born to immigrant, Hungarian Jewish parents in New York City in 1912, graduated from Harvard in 1934, and from Harvard Law School in 1937. He worked in a law firm that represented unions and then went to Washington to work in the Office of Price Administration in 1941. There he met Jessica "Decca" Mitford, born in England in 1917. Her father, David Freeman-Mitford, the second Baron Redesdale, came from a family of landed gentry. Her parents and two of her sisters were admirers and occasional guests of Hitler; one sister married Oswald Mosley, the British fascist leader. Decca rejected much of her family, especially their fascist sympathies, and was attracted to Communism as a teenager. At the age of nineteen, she went to Spain with Esmond Romilly, her second cousin. Decca's parents mobilized the British diplomatic corps to get them out. They married in 1937 and came to the United States in 1939. With the outbreak of war in Europe, Esmond enlisted in the Royal Canadian Air Force. Decca gave birth to their daughter a few months before Esmond was killed in action. She found a job with the Office of Price Administration (OPA), where she met Treuhaft. They came to California in 1943, where Decca continued working with the OPA and Bob took a position with the War Labor Board. They were married that same year.[58]

Bob and Jessica discussed joining the CP soon after they met, but the party was, Decca recalled, "deep underground" where they worked, so they contented themselves with supporting party activities. Upon arriving in San Francisco, they cast about for a way to join the party until Doris Brin, a coworker of Decca's and later Bob's law partner, recruited them in late 1943; Decca's response was, "I thought you'd never ask." Brin, born in Texas, had joined the party while an undergraduate at UCLA in the late 1930s and graduated from Boalt Law School in 1942. However, the party did not permit Decca to join until she became a citizen, in 1944. They were soon busy with club meetings and party assignments. Decca became county financial director, charged with balancing the books. In describing their party activities, Treuhaft later said, "We didn't do anything terribly subversive."[59]

Soviet Espionage and the Bay Area CP

The large majority of party members also did not do "anything terribly subversive," but a few—at least seven—provided knowing assistance to Soviet consular officers involved with espionage. Soviet espionage in the Bay Area was directed by Grigori Kheifets, the vice-consul and NKVD rezident from 1941 to 1944, and Peter Ivanov, the consulate's third secretary. Kheifets and Ivanov were part of an extensive Soviet effort to spy on its wartime ally. In response, the FBI mounted two major investigations of espionage in the Bay Area: COMRAP (*Com*munist *Ap*paratus) sought to identify the CP organizational structure that was involved with espionage; CINRAD (Communist *In*filtration of the *Rad*iation Laboratory) overlapped significantly with COMRAP. Coded Soviet radio messages, including those from the Soviet consulate in San Francisco, were intercepted and partially deciphered by the Venona Project, a U.S. counterintelligence operation. In the 1990s Alexander Vassiliev, a former KGB (Komitet gosudarstvennoy bezopasnosti, successor to the NKVD) officer, reviewed and made notes on a significant number of NKVD/KGB files in Moscow; his notebooks provide additional information about espionage efforts conducted from the Soviet consulate in San Francisco.[60] Of most interest to Soviet officials in the Bay Area was the atomic bomb research at UC-Berkeley. Gregg Herken, in *Brotherhood of the Bomb*, has provided a detailed study of those events, as have recent biographers of J. Robert Oppenheimer.[61]

Steve Nelson was the party member most central in those efforts. Born in Croatia in 1903, he came to the United States with his family after World War I and settled in Philadelphia. After joining the YWL in 1923 he worked as a carpenter and in CP organizing. From 1931 to 1933 he attended the Lenin School in Moscow and, like other students there, served briefly as a Comintern courier. After several years as a CP organizer in western Pennsylvania, he went to Spain, eventually became political commissar for the Lincoln Battalion with the rank of lieutenant colonel, and was wounded in battle. After returning to the United States, he served on the National Committee and in party positions in New York. The party sent Nelson and his wife, Margaret, to Southern California in 1939. Soon after arriving there, he went to the Bay Area to attend a public program about the Spanish Civil War; there he met J. Robert Oppenheimer and learned that Oppenheimer had recently married a friend of the Nelsons, Kitty Harris, who was a party member. Soon after that meeting, the Nelsons moved to San Francisco, where he was promptly made county chair.[62] Given the evidence of Nelson's later involvement in espionage, it seems highly likely that he was sent to the Bay Area for that purpose. Nelson's quick assignment to leadership positions previously held by Californians also points to outside intervention in local party decisions.

The Nelsons first rented a San Francisco flat above that of Jack and Tillie Olsen. Nelson recalled that, in early 1942, the party (specific source not identified) sent him to Oakland as Alameda County chair, again a position usually held by a local party member, and another suggestion of outside intervention. He remained there until 1945, when he was called back to New York. Nelson cites other reasons in his autobiography and in his interview with Martin Sherwin, but his move across the bay seems to have been designed to place him near UC-Berkeley and its research facilities (Oakland and Berkeley share a common border and constitute a single urban area). The FBI tapped Nelson's phone, wired his phone to transmit nearby conversations, and quoted Margaret Nelson as saying that what he "appears to be doing isn't what he is here to do chiefly." Nelson himself was recorded saying he had been recruited by Moscow.[63]

Nelson cultivated relations with members of the Federation of Architects, Engineers, Chemists, and Technicians (FAECT), a CIO affiliate that included UC-Berkeley employees. J. Robert Oppenheimer had offered his home for an early organizing meeting of FAECT; he then took no further role in the organization. The FBI concluded that several officers of FAECT at Berkeley were party members "dominated" by Nelson and that they likely acquainted Nelson "with individuals at the DSM [atomic bomb] Project in Berkeley who could be approached for information."[64]

George Eltenton, an Oxford-educated physicist employed by Shell Oil Company, was one of those at the FAECT organizing meeting in Oppenheimer's home. Eltenton's wife, Dolly, worked at the American Russian Institute in San Francisco. In late 1942 or early 1943, Peter Ivanov approached Eltenton about the work of the radiation laboratory at UCB and asked if he knew Oppenheimer, Ernest Lawrence (head of the project), or another scientist. Eltenton could provide no information but offered to ask Haakon Chevalier to talk with Oppenheimer about providing information to the Soviets. There are considerably more versions of the subsequent conversation between Chevalier and Oppenheimer than there were participants, but most versions agree that Chevalier made the request and Oppenheimer refused.[65]

On March 29, 1943, the FBI recorded a conversation between Nelson and Joseph Weinberg, during which Nelson "impressed JOE with the fact that he was looking for a Comrade who was absolutely trustworthy and informed." Nelson asked Weinberg about "'the Project' at the University of California on which JOE was employed." "The Project" was the atomic bomb, and Weinberg gave Nelson considerable information. Nelson told Weinberg "that he had already spoken to BILL (SCHNEIDERMAN) concerning the status of the Project employees in the Communist Party," and that they were to turn in their dues books and not have obvious meetings with other party members. The FBI report also states, "During the course of the conversation, NELSON made known that he was acquainted with J. ROBERT OPPENHEIMER, one of the principal physicists employed on the Project; that he had previously approached OPPENHEIMER for the purpose of securing information concerning the Project but OPPENHEIMER refused him the information." After Weinberg left, Nelson tried several times unsuccessfully to call Ivanov, finally reaching him on April 6 and setting up a brief and secluded meeting that evening.[66]

Four days later, on April 10, 1943, Vassili Zubilin (Vasily Zarubin), chief NKVD rezident in the United States, came to Nelson's home in Oakland. The FBI summary of their conversation includes the statement: "Nelson advised Zubilin that his work on behalf of the Apparatus had been predicated upon a note from Moscow which had been brought to him by a courier." Nelson also assured Zubilin that Browder "was fully cognizant" of Nelson's "secret work for the Soviet Union." Nelson explained that Schneiderman, however, was "alarmed by the fact the Soviet representatives were wont to approach Party members in California and give them specific assignments . . . instructing them to say nothing to their superiors in the Communist Party concerning the assignments given them by Soviet representatives." Nelson complained to Zubilin about the "efficiency" of two party members, Getzel Hochberg and Morris Rappaport. Soon afterward, the FBI reported, both Hochberg and Rappaport were assigned to other duties. Nelson also said that he had a new recruit, a woman named Bernstein—almost certainly Louise Bransten. Zubilin paid Nelson "a sum of money," either ten bills or ten bundles of bills.[67]

The FBI report on Nelson's conversations quickly reached President Roosevelt, setting in motion extensive investigations by the FBI and army. At Roosevelt's request, CIO president Phil Murray dissolved FAECT. Weinberg and several others involved with the bomb project were terminated without explanation; most assumed it was because of their involvement with FAECT or party activities.[68]

In March 1943 Oppenheimer left California and took charge of the final development and testing of the atomic bomb at Los Alamos, New Mexico. His brother, Frank Oppenheimer, was also one of the key personnel at Los Alamos. Both had come under suspicion because of their support for left causes and association with individuals on the left, but the FBI and army investigations produced no clear evidence of their wrongdoing. Herken concludes that by mid-1944 the army's intelligence operations in the Bay Area had "reached the point of diminishing returns." The information that Weinberg passed to Nelson may have been the most significant accomplishment for Soviet espionage in the Bay Area.[69]

The Vassiliev notebooks add a great deal of information about relations between consulate officials, especially the NKVD rezident, and local party members. Isaac "Pop" Folkoff, who had the NKVD code name Uncle, seems to have been the leading NKVD contact with the local CP. A report in 1945 by one of Kheifets's successors described Uncle as a "leader of the local fellowcountrymen [*sic*]," the code for CPUSA members, and said he had been recruited by Kheifets in 1935, at a time when Kheifets was undercover in the United States. Another report in July 1945 refers to Folkoff as a "probationer," the term for sources and agents who knowingly worked on behalf of the NKVD. As of July 1943 Folkoff was Kheifets's "legal contact"; Kheifets paid Folkoff ten dollars that month. A report in September 1944 described Folkoff as having been "used mostly on leads. Through him we have checked people and gathered background data." However, the report also noted, "Uncle's capabilities are extremely limited, considering his advanced age and illness."[70]

Folkoff appears frequently in FBI and Venona records. The FBI called him the local party's "financial adviser." Venona records indicate that Folkoff may have been the most frequent contact of the local NKVD rezident. Steve Nelson described Folkoff as "a self-educated philosopher who had read all the Marxist works" and as "responsible for raising a good deal of money." Nelson also said that people who wanted to contribute money to the party or for some party activity "would come to Pop and pass the money through him." Nelson indicated that Frank Oppenheimer was among the "professionals" from whom Folkoff collected contributions. Venona files record frequent meetings between Folkoff and Kheifets. On February 8, 1944, for example, Kheifets reported on Folkoff in connection with "500 dollars." The same message and another the following month suggest that Folkoff introduced Kheifets to an engineer working for Standard Oil.[71]

The Vassiliev notebooks attribute Folkoff with finding a "lead" for the "cultivation" of Frank Oppenheimer, and with the information that both Oppenheimer brothers "were associated with the fellowcountrymen, but due to their special military work, the connection with them was suspended"; however, the notebooks do not indicate who suspended the connection. Folkoff gave a positive recommendation for Holland Roberts, who received the code name Lion. Roberts was described in September 1944 as a "securely covert, secret fellowcountryman." That report also noted that Roberts had "a personal friendship" with several professors "of significant interest to us," including the Oppenheimers. Another report specified that Kheifets used Roberts "as a talent-spotter, background-checker and recruiter among the scient. circles of Stanford Univ." Kheifets reported in September 1944 that Roberts had tried to set up a meeting for Kheifets with Robert Oppenheimer, but the meeting "fell through." By then, Oppenheimer was in Los Alamos, not Berkeley.[72]

Louise Bransten was also the subject of extensive investigation and surveillance. The FBI planted bugs in her home, and conversations there indicated that she was intimate with Kheifets, something frequently mentioned in FBI reports. In 1944 an FBI report described her "almost as the hub of a wheel, the spokes thereof representing the many facets of her pro-Soviet activities, running from mere membership in the Communist Party and its successor, the Communist Political Association, to military and industrial espionage and political and propaganda activities." However, FBI reports indicate only that Bransten was a staff member at the American Russian Institute and that she often hosted or appeared at social gatherings that included Soviet officials, CP members, CP sympathizers, liberal Democrats, and at least one prominent Republican. Among her many social contacts were Kheifets and Nelson.[73]

The Vassiliev notebooks make clear that Bransten was the person identified in the Venona materials as "MAP" and that she was, like Folkoff, a "probationer." She was recruited by Kheifets in 1943, based on a lead from Folkoff, and was considered a valuable source because of her "extensive connections" in "political and financial circles." Kheifets reported in September 1944 that Bransten's "contacts" included Roberts, "Marshak," Martin Kamen, and George Eltenton. Marshak and Kamen were UC-Berkeley faculty members involved in research led by Ernest Lawrence. However, a report in 1944, summarizing Kheifets's work in San Francisco, noted that Bransten "has not given us anything of value."[74]

FBI reports and Venona records make clear that James Miller was directly involved in passing information—not related to the atomic bomb project—to NKVD operatives. Miller had used various names previously, including Sirkin Milawsky and Victor Milo; under the latter name he had been a party member in Los Angeles in the 1930s. In August 1942 he began working in the San Francisco post office for the Office of Postal Censorship as a clerk and translator from Russian to English. As such, he reviewed a range of mail, especially items in Russian. Venona files, though fragmentary, record that Miller passed information to Kheifets on at least four occasions. He was discharged from the post office in 1944 and later did translations for *PW* and the American Russian Institute.[75]

Kheifets returned to the Soviet Union in 1944 after a highly negative report on his work. The report specified that Kheifets "has failed to organize himself and the station's operative to carry out the tasks set for them." He "spread himself thin and didn't complete things that he started. He became carried away with the quantity to the detriment of quality." Further, during his entire time in San Francisco, he "has sent to the center only one report that more or less deserves attention." His most serious failings were with regard to the "large number of facilities that interest us, such as companies, plants, laboratories, universities and institutes engaged in research in various fields of science and technology"—perhaps, especially, the atomic bomb project. Kheifets "has not only been unable to recruit new agents for this work but has failed to secure the proper result in work even from the small number of available agents." He had also failed in recruiting agents: Kheifets "has recruited only the two agents 'Map'... and 'Park.'" "Park," apparently a code name, was a pharmacology instructor at the University of California medical school in San Francisco. When Kheifets left, four agents were transferred to a new handler.[76]

Kheifets's replacement as rezident was Grigori Kasparov, but he seems to have been no more successful than Kheifets. One report indicates that, since Kheifets

This surveillance photograph, c. 1944, includes Grigori Kheifets, the NKGB *rezident* in San Francisco from 1941 to July 1944, on the right. On the left is his successor, Grigori Kasparov. In the middle is Martin Kamen, a chemist at the University of California, Berkeley's Radiation Laboratory. Kamen was dismissed in 1944 as a suspected security risk. Photo from Wikimedia Commons, courtesy of the National Security Agency.

left, "no work on XY [scientific and technical espionage] has been done in the Western US." Kasparov may have been sent to San Francisco primarily to be present during the United Nations conference. He was soon replaced by Stepan Apresyan, who remained until the consulate closed in 1948. He was apparently not well briefed by his predecessor. One of Apresyan's first messages to Moscow Center, on April 2, 1945, noted that he was looking forward to resuming contact with Uncle and MAP and requested the name of the local party leader. The next day, he asked for Folkoff's "identifying features" because there was no photograph and a misunderstanding regarding the password. Apresyan also asked for the name of MAP. He had established official contact with "her institution" but needed to "resume liaison." When Apresyan did establish contact with Folkoff, then seventy-five years old, Folkoff had difficulty remembering the password and conditions for meeting, but he soon resumed making regular reports.[77]

William Schneiderman, Louise Todd Lambert, Oleta O'Connor Yates, Archie Brown, Al Richmond, and others in party leadership do not appear in the Venona files. Harrison George and Carl Rude Lambert each appear once.

Harrison George appears in a message by Kheifets about James Miller on November 9, 1943. The partially decrypted and translated message reads: "Liaison [or contact] with 'SMUTNYJ' [1 group unrecovered] the editor of 'People's World, Harrison [45 groups unrecoverable]." (The Venone project was unable to decrypt all of the code, and undecrypted words are described as "unrecovered groups.") SMUTNYJ was the code name for Miller. The message also refers to MAP (Bransten), notes suspicions that Miller was connected with U.S. counterintelligence, but specifies "FELLOWCOUNTRYMEN categorically rule out such an assumption." John Haynes and Harvey Klehr, in *Venona: Decoding Soviet Espionage in America*, interpret this message this way: "Miller was soon passing information to the KGB through an old friend at the *People's World*, Harrison George." I found no basis for such a conclusion. Like other probationers, Miller had his own code name in all Venona messages where he appears. George did not have a code name, appears just this once, and therefore seems unlikely as a regular contact. Nothing in the Venona messages or Vassiliev notebooks suggests that George was a courier for Miller's messages to Kheifets. Further, other Venona messages and FBI reports make clear that Miller usually met directly with Kheifets. A less speculative reading of that message would be that George or Bransten had vouched for Miller.[78]

George also seems an unlikely candidate for espionage. He had been replaced in the state party leadership and was being eased out of his position at *PW*. He complained, in one of his typically lengthy letters, that he'd been replaced on the state bureau by John Pittman and that Schneiderman and Pittman had denied him any significant role at the newspaper: "My authority as Editor in Chief was merely formal. . . . I became regarded as a person of no importance."[79] He was never restored to either position despite his repeated efforts, suggesting that, unlike Nelson, he had no call on higher authority to come to his defense.

The other prominent San Francisco party member to appear in a Venona message is Carl Rude Lambert, husband of Louise Todd Lambert. Born in 1896 in Michigan to Swedish immigrant parents, he joined the army shortly after his high school graduation, saw action in major battles during World War I, was promoted to sergeant, and left the war a pacifist. He and his brother Walter joined the CP in 1932. Like his wife, he held important, full-time positions in the state party, especially as head of the local Control Commission.[80] Lambert is mentioned in one Venona message, from "Vavilov" (probably Mikhail Sergeevich Vavilov, a Soviet diplomat and NKVD co-optee), on November 13, 1945. The message reads, "A trustworthy dock worker CALLAHAN [KALLOGAN] has advised that his friend, the communist Rudolph LAMBERT [43 groups unrecoverable] Nevada, Utah, and Arizona. Concerning uranium deposits [4 groups unrecovered] before the publication of the communication [on?] [48 groups unrecoverable] [to?] us." Vavilov was clearly not familiar with Lambert and assumed that his name was Rudolph. Haynes and Klehr interpret this message this way: "Jerome Callahan, a ship's clerk judged 'trustworthy,' had advised the KGB regarding something from (or about) Rudolph Lambert. . . . It appears that Callahan and Lambert were the sources of information about uranium deposits."[81] Haynes and Klehr's appendix lists Callahan as James. I was not able to find a Callahan, either Jerome or James, in the COMRAP and CINRAD reports; several James or Jerome Callaghans/Callahans appear in the 1944 and 1945–1946 city directories, but none are identified as a ship clerk or dockworker. Lambert did not have a code name and thus seems unlikely as a regular source of information to Soviet operatives. That is not to say George and Lambert were unwilling, only that there is no evidence that they were asked.

Schneiderman's phone was tapped by the FBI, and he was also under almost constant surveillance, either by FBI agents or by as many as seven informants on any given day, but the COMRAP and CINRAD reports include no mention of any involvement by him in Nelson's operations, other than Nelson's indication that any party members working on the atomic bomb project were to turn in their party books. Schneiderman likely had some understanding of Nelson's and Folkoff's work but apparently maintained some distance from it. Schneiderman's FBI file does describe a December 1940 meeting attended by Schneiderman and Folkoff at Chevalier's home at which Oppenheimer was present, but nothing else regarding Oppenheimer or the atomic bomb project. Schneiderman's FBI file does indicate that Schneiderman met regularly with Folkoff, whom the FBI described as "undercover financial connection of the Party," and that Bill and Leah Schneiderman sometimes had dinner with the Folkoff family.[82]

The "Mental Comintern," Teheran,
and the Communist Political Association

The Comintern had always been the most important channel for information from Moscow to New York, both through written material and, more importantly, through regular visits by top CPUSA leaders to Moscow for in-person discussions. Those channels were seriously interrupted from 1939 onward, as wars in Europe and Eastern Asia prevented U.S. party leaders from traveling to Moscow. The Comintern itself was dissolved in 1943. However, as Joseph Starobin has suggested, the leaders of the CPUSA carried in their heads a "mental Comintern," an understanding that the party line in the United States should follow and accurately reflect the position of the Soviet party. Starobin was foreign editor of the *Daily Worker* from 1945 to 1954, in charge of the party's peace activities, and a participant in many of the party's high-level meetings; he resigned from the party in 1956 and later earned a PhD in political science from Columbia University. Here is his description of the way that party leaders after the 1940s sought to discern the intent of their Soviet leaders:

> They lived in what can only be called "a mental Comintern," imagining themselves part of something which did not exist. Seen in the best light, they were a species of self-proclaimed guerillas, operating in what they believed to be a world battle, but having no significant contact with any "main force" and without a perception of the battle plan. They resorted essentially to zodiac signs for guidance.[83]

With the return of the party's commitment to a Popular Front in mid-1941, the CP heaped praise on Roosevelt's foreign policy and confidently anticipated future U.S.–Soviet cooperation. The Tehran (then commonly spelled Teheran) meeting of Stalin, Roosevelt, and Churchill in late 1943 figured largely in a shift in CPUSA policy. In February 1944, for example, *PW* cited the need to "fulfill Teheran" in supporting a fourth term for Roosevelt. Teheran shaped Earl Browder's understanding of Soviet postwar intentions: "Capitalism and Socialism have begun to find their way to peaceful coexistence and collaboration in the same world." At the party's national convention in May 1944, Browder announced that Communists should "renounce all aims of partisan advancement for ourselves in the interest of national unity," "participate in political life as independents," engage in politics through cooperation with New Deal Democrats, cease to run their own candidates for office, and change their name to the Communist Political Association (CPA). The national convention ratified those changes. Browder's vision of postwar cooperation was published in June 1944 as *Teheran: Our Path in War and Peace*. Not all CP leaders agreed. William Z. Foster and Sam Darcy wrote a strong dissent from Browder's "Teheran line." Foster recanted and was elected vice president of the CPA. Darcy, head of the CP's Philadelphia district, did not and was expelled.[84]

Not all who disagreed were expelled. The San Francisco County membership director was later asked for party members who disagreed with the Teheran line but remained members and paid their dues; she listed three, including Archie Brown. "Archie had long discussions with a series of comrades," she said, "and when he went into the army he was still not convinced. . . . He convinced ten other people in the club." However, Brown and the others were excluded from leadership because of their disagreement with the Teheran line.[85]

An extreme version of Browder's Teheran line came in May 1944 when ILWU Local 6 adopted a proposal with three main points: "A pledge on the part of the union that there shall be no strikes for the duration and beyond. A guarantee on the part of the employer that basic union security will be respected for the duration and beyond. Agreement . . . to settle disputes peaceably through arbitration and other means." The leadership of Local 6 included a significant proportion of CP members, including the president, Richard Lynden. Their version of the Teheran line went well beyond what the CP national leadership was discussing. The proposal drew immediate criticism from most non-CP leaders of organized labor. Harry Bridges defended the Local 6 proposal even as he qualified it; he also tied the pledge to Browder's Teheran line: "An employer-ILWU agreement not to engage in economic struggles would be similar to the Teheran, Moscow and Cairo agreements."[86]

The United Nations Founding Conference

Between April 25 to June 26, 1945, the Bay Area welcomed the founding conference of the United Nations. Before the conference opened, Secretary of State Edward Stettinius named the California Labor School as official host for labor delegates to the conference. *PW* gave front-page coverage to President Harry Truman's opening address, labeling it "Unity Key to World Peace." In addition to formal meetings to determine the organizational structure of the United Nations, the Bay Area hosted numerous social events and receptions for the various delegations.[87]

Vyacheslav Molotov, the Soviet foreign minister and one of the few old Bolsheviks to survive Stalin's purges, was in demand for receptions. On May 7 he met with Russian War Relief representatives at the Soviet consulate, thanked them for their assistance to the Soviet people, and proclaimed, "The friendship between the American and the Soviet people is gaining strength despite the obstacles that exist." Later that day, the American Russian Institute hosted a reception for Molotov at the St. Francis Hotel, where Molotov's message of future Soviet-American friendship was repeated with minor variations by other Soviet delegates to the conference.[88]

Molotov's optimistic message of future Soviet-American friendship was being challenged even as he spoke—party leaders in Moscow had already approved a message to the CPUSA that Browder's Teheran line was a serious mistake. Changes in party leadership and the party line quickly followed. At the same time, domestic anti-Communism, only somewhat stifled during the war, reappeared more vigorously than before as patriotic organizations and politicians vied in denouncing the Communist threat to America.

CHAPTER 7

THE PARTY IN CRISIS, 1945–1950

Joseph Stalin's determination to expand Soviet control throughout Eastern and Central Europe and Harry Truman's refusal to accept that, along with revelations of Soviet espionage during World War II, quickly ended the wartime Grand Alliance and began the Cold War. The Truman administration's criticism of the Soviet Union fueled a robust revival of domestic anti-Communism, which had been only somewhat stifled during the war. Patriotic organizations and politicians in both parties vied in denouncing the Communist threat. In 1945 the House of Representatives made the Committee on Un-American Activities a standing committee. It soon began to hold dramatic committee meetings in Washington and subcommittee meetings across the country. The media avidly covered those hearings, in which committee investigators and witnesses branded individuals and organizations as part of "the Communist conspiracy" and then grilled those so named. HUAC's California counterpart, CUAC, followed suit. In response, the party expelled or dropped members thought to be potential informants. All of this developed as the CPUSA responded to instructions from Moscow that it had taken a wrong turn and needed to reorganize.

The Duclos Article

In April 1945 Jacques Duclos, a French Communist official, initiated a crisis in the U.S. party when he put his name on an article that called Browder's transformation of the CP into a political association "a notorious revision of Marxism." The article quoted from William Z. Foster and Sam Darcy's dissent from Browder's move to change the CP to the CPA, a letter known until then only to small numbers of top CPUSA leaders and Soviet leaders. Duclos's article came from the Soviet leadership. It was first published, unsigned, in January 1945 in a secret journal for leading Soviet officials; then it was translated into French for the French party's theoretical journal.[1]

The Communist Political Association's leaders immediately recognized that Moscow was reprimanding them. Long meetings by the CPA's leaders followed. On May 24 the *Daily Worker* carried the full Duclos article. Two days later *People's World* presented a front-page discussion of the Duclos article and the ongoing reconsideration of current policies; that discussion was then distributed to all California CPA members. On June 7 *PW* presented the long resolution approved by the CPA National Board by 11–1 on June 2. Browder cast the sole negative vote; Schneiderman voted with the majority. The resolution announced that the party had drawn "erroneous conclusions" from the Tehran meeting, that Browder's Teheran line represented "opportunist deviations" and "opportunist errors," and that the situation required reestablishing "the independent Marxist party of the working class." The resolution acknowledged that Browder's "revision of Marxist-Leninist theory" had not affected membership, which had grown significantly, but claimed—without evidence—that it had "undoubtedly retarded" support among industrial workers. An emergency national convention followed in July. That body proclaimed, "Life itself . . . has fully confirmed the validity of Comrade Duclos' criticism." Stipulating that "the growth of revision was helped by bureaucracy"—that is, top-down, undemocratic decision making—the convention directed the party to "undertake an ideological organizational struggle to root out all vestiges of bureaucracy" and "make a thorough and self-critical examination of all policies and leadership."[2]

The special national convention reconstituted the Communist Party and replaced Browder and several of his supporters. Eugene Dennis became general secretary, and William Z. Foster became chairman. Browder was soon expelled. During the three months of crisis, organizing and recruiting had languished, dues were not collected, and the party lost members.[3]

At state and local levels, special party committees reviewed the leadership to eradicate "revisionism" and "root out all vestiges of bureaucracy." Dave Jenkins chaired the Northern California Committee on Leadership. The committee individually interviewed all members of the State Executive Board and asked them to criticize their own work, the board's work, and other board members' work.[4]

In early August 1945 the San Francisco County Personnel Committee began its meetings, similarly charged to review the existing county leadership and recommend new members. The committee consisted of one member elected from each county club, fifteen in all, not all of whom attended every meeting. The members included Tillie Olsen and Edith Arnstein Jenkins. The committee's criteria stipulated, "Primary consideration given to those who had a fundamentally sound opposition to the revisionist policies of the past period, the specific application of these policies, or to manifestations of burocracy [sic]." The committee also specified, "We aren't holding people responsible for Teheran, but for the way in which they carried it out." The committee met weekly and sometimes daily for a month, interviewed the county's full-time functionaries and many others, including members of the Executive Board, the county committee, and representatives of clubs. They also received criticism and complaints from rank-and-file members.[5]

At their first meeting, Oleta O'Connor Yates summarized the existing county leadership: she was the full-time president, Carl Rude Lambert was the full-time vice president, and there were two other full-time staff members. Those four met weekly, the County Executive Board met twice monthly, and the county committee met quarterly. The Executive Board was "the policy-making body," consisting of fifteen members elected by the county convention. The county committee, thirty-four people, "did not do a great deal more than hear reports from other county leaders and the Executive Board." The county council, an advisory body consisting of county and club leaders and some elected club delegates, met monthly.[6]

During her interview, O'Connor Yates responded to criticism the committee had received that she was aloof; she explained, "It is very difficult for a woman to be the top functionary in the Party on a full-time basis. There still exists a high degree of resentment against having a woman in this position," and women "have to fight to establish their leadership as a man does not." She added, "This may have tended to develop some of my own sharpness as a defensive mechanism against this resentment." Regarding bureaucratic decision making, she said, "As far as I can remember, there have been practices in the Party which would certainly be termed burocratic [sic]. The undemocratic practices in regard to political questions had been intensified in the recent period of time because the very nature of our political policies caused us to develop top dealings." She concluded: "One of the fundamental lessons to be drawn from the past period is not to accept anything before thinking it through for yourself."[7] However, neither she nor anyone else suggested that such problems were inherent in democratic centralism.

Carl Rude Lambert was interviewed next. Acknowledging "a certain amount of male chauvinism in the Party," he offered considerable self-criticism regarding bureaucratic methods, explaining that he had joined the party in 1932, was elected to the state committee in 1933, and to the state bureau (executive committee) in 1939. He added, "I have been known for years as a sort of watch-dog of the movement. I was responsible for the unearthing of hundreds of stool-pigeons during the difficult days." "During the days of the Communist Party and the Control Commission [i.e., before the CPA]," he reflected, "we had a more disciplined organization." He was critical of his own shortcomings regarding theory as well as bureaucracy and offered to leave the leadership: "I don't want to give the impression that I am one of the perennial pie-cards. . . . The best way I can answer it now is to step out."[8]

O'Connor Yates, Lambert, the two other full-time staff members, several other interviewees, and many of the clubs offered names of potential candidates for county leadership, many of whom were also interviewed. When interviewed, Angela Gizzi Ward explained her reaction to the Teheran line: "I accepted it and went along without any reservations." She added, "Don't think I am sufficiently an independent thinker for fulltime work at present." Walter Stack acknowledged that he had also "adopted [the] Teheran line unreservedly" and that his "greatest weakness is being too aggressive and domineering which leads to burocratic [sic] method of work." Tillie Olsen admitted she had "never questioned the theoretical part of it [the Teheran line]" and acknowledged having "done my share trying to convince people of its correctness." She listed among her "weaknesses" that "I felt I didn't want to belong to the Party any more a few months ago" and that, "within the movement, I have never had a consistent or reliable record, although in my mass work I have had."[9]

In the end, the committee found the work of the full-time staff to be "good" and that of the Executive Board to be "very good" even though "noticeably uncritical of its own deficiencies." The committee was especially positive regarding O'Connor Yates: "She has brilliantly brought forth the face of the Party in the community." But the committee criticized her for "political detachment from the membership." The committee was also positive regarding Lambert, "official Party disciplinarian as head of the Control Commission." He showed "sound working class instinct and feeling for high Communist Standards" and should be kept on the county committee.[10]

The committee recommended O'Connor Yates for county chair and ten individuals, in addition to Lambert, for the county committee, including Aubrey Grossman, Bill Bailey, Violet Orr (also recommended for county press director), Angela Gizzi Ward ("hard-working, energetic, devoted and sincere . . . taking the first steps towards independent thought . . . talent for working with people"), Dave Jenkins (praised for "ability to do mass work, and adept at handling organizational problems" but criticized because "it took him some time to react completely to the Duclos article"), Jack Olsen (described as "in army, and decorated for heroism . . . tremendous feeling for people"), and Tillie Olsen (who has "given much and original attention to women's work, in field of child care, and community work"). The committee suggested Archie Brown for honorary county chair and as an honorary (presumably not voting) member of the county committee.[11]

Life in the Party, Late 1940s

During reorganization of the state leadership, Loretta Starvus became organizational secretary, replacing Louise Todd Lambert, who, except for her prison term and time on parole, had been doing that work since the late 1920s. Todd Lambert later recalled that she was replaced "to make it possible to promote . . . a person with closer ties to the working class and more direct trade union experience," one of the changes promoted during the reorganization. Starvus had not sought that position and was reluctant to accept it—she was afraid she'd have to learn to type—but she was made to feel that she was failing in her duty to the party if she did not accept. She recalled that her major duties were to sit in on meetings, most of which involved things that she didn't know much about, such as party lines into waterfront unions and the Democratic Party. She dutifully attended meetings of several sorts but felt she was unable to contribute because she was so uninformed. She also recalled that her suggestions were uniformly ignored.[12]

Starvus's recent experience had been with union organizing. She was born in Connecticut to Polish Catholic immigrant parents, went to work in a silk weaving mill as a teenager, took part in a TUUL-sponsored strike in 1930, joined the YCL, and worked as an organizer. In 1932 she was the youngest in her class at the Lenin School in Moscow. Among her fellow students were her then-husband, Irving Kreichmar (Irving Keith), Walter Stack, and Al Lannon. She remembered the classes as mostly large doses of Marxist-Leninist theory and history. When the lectures didn't make sense to her, she recalled, she kept her mouth shut. Classes in self-defense and physical fitness included marksmanship with a rifle. She later claimed that she was a "crack shot." Part of her training included a trip to Germany as a Comintern courier. After returning to the United States in 1934, she worked at YCL organizing in New York and reporting for the *Daily Worker*. Her husband died in Spain. During World War II, she worked in Los Angeles as an organizer for the United Electrical Workers, the first woman to hold that position with that union. She remarried but soon divorced.[13]

Starvus remained as organizational secretary for only a few years. She found the work unrewarding and could not spend enough time with her son, Joe. As a union organizer, she had taken Joe to union meetings, where people had cared for him, but that was not possible for party meetings. In 1948 she remarried, to Walter Stack, whose own marriage had broken up shortly before. Stack was intensely ideological, a member of county and state committees, and a former officer of the Marine Firemen's Union who had been expelled for being a CP member. With the birth of their daughter, Starvus left the position of organizational secretary because, she later said, she had "had it up to here." Louise Todd Lambert returned to that position. Starvus purposefully choose a job working the late shift so that she was unavailable for evening meetings. Even so, she received party assignments.[14]

Adam and Eva Lapin were also newcomers to San Francisco. Adam was born in 1914 to Russian Jewish parents in Chile, grew up in New York City, attended City College for three years, and then became fully involved with party activities in the National Student League and YCL. In 1936 he met Eva Sonenshine, who was born in 1918 in Ukraine. Her father was killed in a pogrom when she was six months old, but in dying he saved his infant daughter. The remaining family came to New York in 1921. Her mother had belonged to the Jewish Socialist Labor Bund in Ukraine, and she joined the ILGWU in New York. After high school, Eva attended City College, joined the YCL, and then took a secretarial job with the National Student League, where she met Adam. They were married in 1936.[15]

The next year, Adam became a staff reporter for the *Daily Worker*, assigned to Pittsburgh and then Washington. Eva became a freelance reporter and in 1943 the Washington correspondent for the ILWU's newspaper, *The Dispatcher*. They returned to New York, now with two children, in early 1945. Soon after, Adam became associate editor of *People's World*. They moved to San Francisco, where Eva worked briefly for *PW* but stopped for lack of child care. She became active in her neighborhood CP club and in the usual party activities—fund-raising for *PW*, mimeographing flyers, attending meetings. "We were always at meetings," she recalled, "and asking people to sign petitions." Eva became a section leader, responsible for meeting quotas in fund-raising, recruiting, and participation in activities.[16]

Don Watson joined the party around the time he turned eighteen, in 1947 or 1948. His father, Morris Watson, a journalist in New York City and founding member of the Newspaper Guild, was fired for union activism, became an organizer for the Newspaper Guild, was active in the American Labor Party, and ran unsuccessfully for Congress. He joined the CP in the mid-1930s. In 1942, soon after Morris became founding editor of the ILWU's newspaper, *The Dispatcher*, Don, his mother, and his sister moved to San Francisco. After Don graduated from Lowell High School, the city's college preparatory high school, in 1947, he followed his father's suggestion and went to sea instead of college. He became a member of the National Union of Marine Cooks and Stewards, took classes at the California Labor School, including labor history and public speaking, was active in the Wallace campaign and in support of the ILWU-NUMCS strike, both in 1948, and joined the CP. In 1950 the CIO was purging the NUMCS at the same time the Coast Guard was screening CP members from working on U.S.-flagged ships. Don was screened, became secretary of the Committee Against Waterfront Screening, and sometimes found work through the ILWU dispatch hall. He was drafted in 1951, refused to sign the loyalty oath, and was discharged. In 1955 he became a member of ILWU Local 34, Ship Clerks.[17]

Between 1946 and 1950, Victor Arnautoff belonged to the New Era Club, for teachers, medical doctors, nurses, and other professionals, and he served at times as educational director and chair. The club was divided in early 1949, and Arnautoff became head of the teachers' group.[18]

Robert Treuhaft emphasized that much of what his club did in the years after World War II was fund-raising for *PW* and other party activities. He later described a typical party meeting around 1945–1950: "It would usually start off with an 'educational,' where somebody had been assigned . . . to report on either a theoretical work or on a practical matter of interest to Communists. And you'd have to be well prepared for that. . . . Those who weren't giving the educational were expected to have done the reading." One woman left the party, characterizing her club's educationals as "like a book club where nobody really understood the books." It was such meetings that Dorothy Ray Healey had in mind when she recalled, "Most of the meetings I sat in on were very boring."[19]

The Heyday of San Francisco's Postwar Labor-Left Culture

San Francisco's labor-left culture was not very boring. It continued to thrive into the late 1940s and early 1950s, with the California Labor School at its center.[20] The CLS long resisted the rising tensions of the Cold War, domestic anti-Communism, and the increasing isolation of the CP. The school may have been unique among the party's schools in major cities in the extent to which Dave Jenkins, the director, and the faculty maintained a diverse curriculum that attracted thousands of non-Communist students. Jenkins later said the party had allowed him a "pretty free hand" with the school but retained a veto over the curriculum and faculty. To be certain, the curriculum always presented a Marxist-Leninist approach to the social sciences. As Holland Roberts put it later, "We were explicitly and implicitly but not obtrusively or wholly Marxist."[21]

Jenkins excelled at schmoozing. By 1945 he had collected endorsements and financial support from a wide range of unions—AFL, CIO, and the railway brotherhoods—and other organizations, including Black organizations. During the heyday of the Teheran line, Jenkins even secured support and funds from the business community. The president of the San Francisco Chamber of Commerce, in late 1944, complimented Jenkins for having created "something unique" by seeking to bring "industry and labor together in a spirit of unity of purpose and friendly understanding." In 1945 the Rosenberg Foundation granted the CLS sixteen thousand dollars (equivalent to about $250,000 in 2023) to develop a program in industrial relations. In 1946 contributions and grants accounted for almost half the school's total income. The San Francisco school system granted teachers credit for some CLS classes, and CLS proudly proclaimed itself "the only progressive labor school in the U.S. where veterans can study under GI Bill benefits."[22]

Classes ranged from a Marxist-Leninist analysis of the political economy to a survey of labor relations that included presentations by an attorney for major corporations and a corporate vice president. Instructors included Paul Radin, a leading anthropologist and UC-Berkeley faculty member; Thomas Addis, a nationally prominent nephrology researcher and faculty member at the Stanford School of Medicine; and Holland Roberts, who had lost his position at Stanford because of his party activities. Enrollments in humanities and arts classes, many with little ideological content, often outnumbered those in the social sciences, which were typically Marxist. Classes and lectures on psychology and psycho-analysis were popular, despite the party's disapproval of consulting a psychiatrist.[23]

Pele De Lappe, staff artist for *People's World*, created this drawing of the faculty and staff of the California Labor School, c. 1948. Dave Jenkins is in the lower left corner. Over his shoulder, with the necktie and glasses, is Holland Roberts. Hazel Grossman is left of Roberts. Leo Nitzberg is in the upper left, with a camera. Victor Arnautoff is top center, with a palette. From the California Labor School collection, box 4, file 6, courtesy of Labor Archives and Research Center, San Francisco State University,

More than half the courses were in the humanities and arts, including art, music, dance, drama, and literature along with language classes in English, Russian, and Spanish. In 1946 the art department produced the largest enrollments in the school and featured prominent local artists as instructors, including Victor Arnautoff, Giacomo Patri, Anton Refregier, and Ralph Stackpole (recently a member of the U.S. Commission on Fine Arts). Jenkins recalled that there was practically no CP influence in the art and drama programs, even though the very size and popularity of those programs occasioned some debate within the CP leadership.[24]

The CLS provided so many lectures, presentations, exhibitions, and social activities that one could spend nearly every evening and weekend there. Lecture topics ranged from "How to Read Music" to "How to Combat Discrimination." Guest lecturers, exhibitors, and performers included W.E.B. Du Bois, Paul Robeson, Pete Seeger, Imogene Cunningham, and Edward Weston, whose photography exhibition came to the CLS directly from the New York Museum of Modern Art. The CLS also offered a wide array of social activities, including a flamboyant annual artists' carnival. In 1947 the school made a down payment on its own building, at 240 Golden Gate Avenue, where the school could offer more classes, operate a coffee shop and snack bar, and hold conferences in its own auditorium.[25]

Nearly all leading local CP members and many of the rank and file participated in the CLS in some way. Leo Nitzberg taught photography, Jack Olsen presented labor-related classes, Oleta O'Connor Yates offered a class on U.S. history, and John Pittman taught a class on China and India. Aubrey Grossman, Al Richmond, Walter Stack, and Angela Gizzi Ward were among those who spoke on current issues. Pat Tobin did fund-raising. Keith Eickman and Don Watson enrolled in classes.[26]

Carol Cuénod started taking classes at CLS in early 1948 when she was nineteen. She and her mother had moved to San Francisco in 1946, coming from Southern California, where her mother had worked in Leo Gallagher's law office. In San Francisco her mother worked for the Gladstein law firm. Carol joined the popular CLS chorus, which rehearsed once a week and regularly gave performances around the area, and she volunteered for clerical work—cranking the mimeograph, cutting stencils, staffing the switchboard. "Once I walked into the School," she later recalled, "I didn't leave until they locked it up." She also said, "My classes in Political Economy at the Labor School convinced me that capitalism was not the way to go. It led to unemployment and increasing division between workers and the rich people." She also recalled, "I felt I definitely would join the Party when I felt I could match brains with other Party members. Somewhere along the line some of the young people got to me and said, 'you don't have to wait until that happens, join now.'" And she did. Jenkins later claimed to have signed up forty new members during one recruiting drive at the school.[27]

David Jenkins later claimed the party exerted very little control over him and the CLS, but an intraparty investigation in 1950 (see next chapter) suggested both that Jenkins had maneuvered to avoid such control and that the absence of party control had become a serious problem. The draft report of the investigation specified that the county organization should have maintained the party line in school activities, but Jenkins's position on the state board had complicated that situation. As the draft report put it, "When Dave [was] on [state] Bd.—[he] disregarded the county. 'Played both ends against the middle.'" As a result, the draft report asked, "Does school represent a last outpost of revisionist outlook in movement?"[28] Whether or not the school itself represented a "revisionist outlook," its activities unquestionably represented a continuation of the broadly based approach of the wartime Popular Front. Jenkins was the least doctrinaire member of the six-member state bureau and had been slow to accept the Duclos article. He later told me that he had "more or less" given up on the party around 1950—the time of the investigation of the CLS—but did not leave.[29]

Other institutions joined the CLS in contributing to San Francisco's postwar labor-left culture. *People's World* continued to present reviews of art, music, literature, and film as well as sports and the party's perspective on the news. Subscribers far outnumbered party members. In parts of San Francisco, *PW* had carriers making home deliveries, just like the mainstream dailies. Sidney Roger presented radio broadcasts of news from a left perspective on station KGO. He was a UC-Berkeley graduate who had studied anthropology and drama and worked in the WPA Federal Theater Project. Roger never joined the CP but described himself as "very close to the Left." He had a few CIO unions as sponsors but also set up the Sidney Roger Radio Fund, creating an early form of listener-sponsored radio. His broadcasts came to an end in 1950 when KGO canceled his contract.[30]

Elections, 1945–1947

When William Z. Foster became national chairman of the CP in mid-1945, he presented a long analysis of what had gone wrong under Browder but warned of "the pitfalls of 'Left' sectarianism." Writing in *Political Affairs*, John Williamson agreed, warning against the "breaking of alliances and close working relations with other democratic forces." The emergency national convention affirmed the need "*to weld together and consolidate the broadest coalition of all anti-fascist and democratic forces.*"[31]

In deciding how the reconstituted party would relate to other "anti-fascist and democratic forces," local party members were immediately faced by decisions regarding local elections. In the 1945 local elections, *PW* did not noticeably change its approach from previous city elections. The paper promoted the supervisorial campaign of Herbert Nugent, a party member, describing him as a union member, veteran, and former organizer for the International Labor Defense; his campaign focused on ensuring jobs and a decent standard of living. In mid-October the San Francisco Voters League, in a meeting chaired by party member Benjamin Dreyfus, endorsed Nugent and four others, not party members, including three incumbents. Late in the campaign, *PW* gave significant coverage to both Nugent and Frederick Douglass Haynes, a prominent Black pastor, director of the local NAACP, member of the Council for Civic Unity, and candidate for supervisor. The local NAACP endorsed Nugent, Haynes, and three others. As in recent elections, *PW* carried paid advertising for several candidates who were not CP members. The paper also presented the slate card of the AFL Labor Council and railway brotherhoods. Among the twenty-seven candidates, Nugent ranked nineteenth, with some fifteen thousand votes, about 8 percent of the total.[32]

The 1946 elections marked the first opportunity for the reorganized party to participate in state politics. What they did differed only slightly from what they'd done since the late 1930s (except during 1939–1941). During the Democratic primary, the state CIO, where the party had significant influence, gave strong support to Robert Kenny for governor, John Shelley for lieutenant governor, and Edmund "Pat" Brown for attorney general. *PW* did much the same, focusing especially on Kenny. Shortly before the primary election, *PW* provided all CIO endorsements. Schneiderman, state party chair, took to the radio the day before the primary to attack Earl Warren, the incumbent Republican governor, and William Knowland, the incumbent Republican U.S. senator. Both Warren and Kenny had cross-filed in the Democratic primary. Warren won both the Republican and Democratic nominations for governor, beating Kenny in the Democratic primary even in San Francisco. *PW* had supported Ellis Patterson, the former lieutenant governor, for the U.S. Senate, but Patterson lost the Democratic nomination to Will Rogers Jr. Shelley and Brown did win the Democratic nominations for lieutenant governor and attorney general.[33]

After the primary, Schneiderman announced that the party would run Archie Brown as a write-in candidate for governor. *PW*, late in the campaign, endorsed Rogers, Shelley, and the city's two incumbent members of Congress, Franck Havenner, a liberal Democrat, and R. J. Welch, a Republican, who was unopposed and who usually supported labor. The paper also listed all the CIO endorsements and provided detailed instructions on writing in Archie Brown for governor. Brown received 22,606 votes, just under 1 percent. Republicans swept all the statewide elections, but Havenner and other liberal Democrats held on to their congressional seats.[34]

In the 1947 San Francisco local elections, the party's approach was also much as it had been since the late 1930s. O'Connor Yates was again a candidate for supervisor, and Grossman managed her campaign. She made prominent use of her appointment to Mayor Lapham's Committee on Civic Unity. The only woman in a field of twenty-seven, she argued that a woman's voice was needed on the all-male board of supervisors. Her platform could have come from any New Deal Democrat: support for more federal housing, a Market Street subway, a city fair-employment practices ordinance, and a city public works program. She was photographed wielding a broom to symbolize her intent to "sweep big business out of city hall." *PW* prominently covered the candidacy of several non-CP liberals, especially Haynes, who was again running for supervisor, and Havenner, again running for mayor. The paper also publicized AFL support for various candidates. The weekend before Election Day, *PW* prominently featured several liberal, non-CP candidates, including Havenner, Haynes, and Edmund Brown, the incumbent district attorney. Only Brown won. O'Connor Yates ranked eleventh with some thirty-seven thousand votes, 13 percent of the total, but slightly below her showing in 1943. *PW* read the results as showing the need to build on the labor, Black, and progressive coalition that had supported Havenner and Haynes, and for "the labor movement to strengthen its coalition."[35] As of 1947 the party's participation in state and local elections had not changed from its practice during the Popular Front.

Factions and Expulsions

After Duclos the party's support of liberal Democrats generated intraparty conflict. In *Political Affairs* in November 1946, O'Connor Yates explained the approach of the San Francisco party to that year's elections: "Welding together of all anti-fascist, anti-monopoly, and democratic forces into a broad coalition" that would eventually lead to a "third party." However, she said, a "handful of people" in San Francisco were "constantly in opposition to the Party's policies." Some challenged the entire policy and others sharply criticized specific decisions. She labeled as right-opportunists those who opposed running independent candidates. The "'Left' opposition," she explained, opposed the "concept of an anti-fascist, anti-monopoly coalition" and dismissed the party's demands as a "'reformist' program." In fact, the left opposition had sometimes described the party's current political activities as simply Browderism without Browder. In September 1946, shortly before the election, the state committee expelled several left sectarians, including Walter Lambert, the brother of Carl Rude Lambert, and Vernon Smith, a founding member of the party and part of the *PW* editorial staff. In her *Political Affairs* article, O'Connor Yates added, "Many Clubs and individual members, worn out by months of disruption, consider the expulsions long past due."[36]

The expulsions had come after extended investigations that began with a letter from the National Board, signed by Foster, directing the county leadership to end local left sectarianism immediately. In response, the county committee and its Security Commission undertook a thorough investigation "to safeguard the unity of the Party." An internal report defined the problem: "Left sectarianism consists in advancing a line which covers itself up with revolutionary phrases but which entirely disregards the objective conditions and relationship of forces existing at a given period of time, and therefore cannot provide a correct leadership for the masses of workers." The report cited Lenin and Stalin as warning of such errors, and stigmatized the position of the left sectarians as "we cannot have anything to do with any coalition or alignment of forces which does not understand the role of the state—or, to put it in another way, which is not already anti-capitalist."

The internal report emphasized that the party's approach to recent local elections had been fully in line with "objective conditions": "Communists advance election programs under capitalism which flow from the burning issues of the day, and the needs of the masses—and we propose measures to solve those issues which can be achieved under capitalism. . . . This immediate program is the basis upon which we establish our place in the coalition which will certainly have an anti-fascist, anti-monopoly program, but equally certainly it will not have a socialist program." By mid-August 1946 twenty members had been expelled and four more had resigned.[37]

A year later, in August 1947, Harrison George was expelled for left sectarianism. He accused the state party of tailism and blamed his expulsion on right opportunism. In keeping with his behavior in the factional fights of the late 1920s and in 1934, he composed a long defense and critique of the leadership, filled with extensively footnoted references to Marx, Engels, Lenin, Comintern Congress resolutions, and more. It was published as a book, *The Crisis in the CPUSA*, in December 1947, and a supplement, not quite as long, followed in July 1948.[38]

Left sectarianism was not the only basis for expulsions. In 1948 the party's State Review Commission drafted a report on its work over the three years since the reorganization. Noting that its most important work had been "smashing" the left sectarian faction, the committee's draft also reported on other investigations and expulsions: "In the course of the past three years, we conducted 300 hearings, expelling 70 members for 'left-sectarianism', and 10 'Right Opportunists'[*sic*] 2 stoolpigeons, 5 ~~homo-sexuals~~" [cross-out in draft, with "morally corrupt" written in with pencil]." The draft report noted that the California party had expelled some four hundred individuals over the previous fifteen years, the largest number of whom were "swindlers, thieves and financially irresponsible people," followed by "Trotskyites and other 'political' revisers of Marxism" along with "paid informers and stool-pigeons." The draft added, "In every one of the groupings, we find that the majority were guilty of [white] chauvinism or anti-semitism," and concluded that this experience emphasized the continuing "necessity for struggle" against "rotten liberalism" (tolerance inside the party of those who disagreed with the official party line) and "such fascist ideas as chauvinism and anti-semitism." The report singled out Harrison George: "Can Harrison George deny seeking to obtain documents from Union offices by theft? . . . Can Harrison George deny that he connived and planned to seize the People's World through members of the Board of Directors?"[39]

Surviving records from the late 1940s indicate three categories of former party members: those who left the party on their own, those who were "dropped," and those who were expelled. A key difference between being dropped and being expelled was that party members were prohibited from associating with someone who had been expelled but not with those who were dropped or who left on their own.

With the party under attack on all sides, and given harsh penalties under state law for homosexual behavior and smoking marijuana, the party feared that anyone charged under such laws might turn informer. One draft report noted, "Due to laws recently enacted in California re. homosexuals . . . (20 years in prison on act or failure to report and register as homo if practicing) . . . they have become greatest liability in and around the Party." All known lesbian and gay party members were expelled or dropped. One internal draft report noted, "Certainly there are comrades who, and justifiably so, feel sorry for these comrades when they are asked to leave our movement, but we must always keep in mind the methods the bourgeoise [sic] uses to exploit these people."[40]

A report in 1950 noted the importance of dropping "people who must visit psychiatrists." The report continued: "We drop them—*gently*, but *firmly*. We merely approach this problem at present from the point of view of security. . . . Two cases of this month have revealed two who have given information to the FBI through the doctors. . . . We separate the above category from others dropped or expelled because we don't regard them as enemies. . . . 50 dropped."[41]

That report also listed the numbers and reasons for recent expulsions for all parts of the state except Los Angeles—that is, the largest number of these would have been from the Bay Area. Of the total of 113, 31 were expelled for ideological reasons, including 16 for left sectarianism and 3 for "anti-Party rumor mongering against leadership." Twenty were "homosexuals and lesbians." Fifteen were guilty of white chauvinism. Twenty-three were expelled for drunkenness, promiscuity, or using "pornographic films, marihuana, and benzedrine." Thirteen were considered actual or potential informers. The report continued: "On some of the cases of white chauvinism, we found right opportunism—and left sectarianism—promiscuity—drunkenness—bad financial records. . . . In cases of lesbians and homos, we found the works—personal and political degeneracy, drug addicts, perverts, subject to every bohemian idea extant. Associations with police agents, Trotskyites, expelled members."[42]

A list of those who were dropped or expelled in late 1948 and early 1949 suggests some of the difference between being dropped and being expelled. The reasons for eight drops were "chauvinism, male superiority and conduct unbecoming"; "accused leadership of dishonesty in raffle"; "sexual looseness, drinking, dangerous associations"; "disagreement with cp policy"; "operating Jim Crow shop[,] conduct detrimental to working class and cp"; "drinking and direlection [sic] of duty during strike"; "psychiatry"; and "failure to carry cp politics and activities detrimental to cp." The reasons for four expulsions were "disagreement with cp policies," "Informant," "associating with expelled members and refusing to sever associations," and "financial irresponsibility."[43]

Some resigned. One woman did so because she had gotten married and her husband made leaving the party a condition of their marriage. Another woman left because, she said, "I have had doubts about some of the excuses made by American Progressives for some of the actions taken by the Soviet Union. . . . As a Party member, I was expected to have a loyalty much greater than that to this country. . . . I cannot resolve this conflict other than by leaving the Party."[44]

The White Chauvinism Campaign

In the late 1940s, coincident with a Soviet campaign against national chauvinism in Eastern Europe, the U.S. party launched a campaign against white chauvinism, which it described as the key underlying feature of American capitalism's success in keeping the working class divided.[45] The campaign quickly degenerated. Dorothy Ray Healey, then a CP leader in Los Angeles, reflected, "A legitimate concern turned into an obsession" and became "a ritual act of self-purification that did nothing to strengthen the Party in its fight against racism and was manipulated by some Communist leaders for ends which had nothing to do with the ostensible purpose of the whole campaign." She added, "Once an accusation of white chauvinism was thrown against a white Communist, there was no defense." In Los Angeles, Healey estimated, the party expelled or dropped two hundred people, "usually on the most trivial of pretexts." Healey's description was as accurate for San Francisco as for Los Angeles. CP members who ran afoul of prominent party members were called before the Security Commission, charged with white chauvinism, and expelled or dropped.[46]

After the war Leo Nitzberg had joined ILWU Local 6, and in 1951 he married Judith Fried. Judy had grown up in Chicago and attended the University of Illinois in the mid-1940s, where she and her cousin joined the CP, being careful to keep that secret from her parents. She left the university and came to San Francisco in the late 1940s, where she met Leo. She later recalled that before leaving Chicago, she was given half a torn playing card, to be matched with the other half when she reached her contact in San Francisco. She and Leo took part in California Labor School activities, and Leo offered workshops on photography. Judy recalled that she and Leo were expelled—although it is more likely they were dropped, since they continued to associate with party members—for white chauvinism. As Judy explained, they had gone to Los Angeles to see friends, and, immediately upon their arrival, their friend said that they should accompany her to a political meeting at a Black church. Judy protested that she was wearing slacks, but her friend insisted that they come anyway. Judy and Leo were expelled or dropped because wearing slacks in a Black church showed a lack of proper respect.[47]

After his discharge from the army, Keith Eickman returned to Local 6, moved from the YCL to the CP, and attended CLS classes. He was expelled or dropped from the CP in 1953, during the white chauvinism campaign, which he later called "a hysteria within the CP." The charge against him was that in a meeting of union stewards he had disagreed with a Black steward who, Eickman later said, was and remained a close friend. Regarding the white chauvinism campaign, Eickman later said, it "was useful . . . to some people who wanted to get rid of some of the others." He added, "They probably did me a favor. . . . It would have been difficult for me to voluntarily separate myself from the CP."[48]

Dorothy Ray Healey added, "One of the great ironies of the white chauvinism campaign is that we lost a large number of Black members. . . . They were just contemptuous of the whole thing because it had so little to do with fighting racism in the real world."[49]

Thus, under severe external attack, the CP fell to consuming itself. The expulsions of the late 1940s and early 1950s came as the party itself was abandoning its practice of supporting liberal Democrats in state and local elections. Instead, beginning in 1948 the party threw its cadres into quixotic third-party campaigns that had the effect of further isolating the party from the political mainstream and expelling its closest CIO allies from the CIO.

CHAPTER 8

THE CRISIS DEEPENS, 1948–1956

Beginning in 1948 the CPUSA's crisis significantly deepened. As relations between the United States and the Soviet Union grew more tense, and as domestic anti-Communism surged, party leaders interpreted events abroad as signals that the party should be more confrontational. Doing so sent its allies in the Congress of Industrial Organizations into a self-destructive clash with CIO leaders over foreign policy and led the party to embrace a third party, further separating themselves from liberal Democrats they had once supported.

"Misplaced Militancy": The Wallace Campaign and Its Consequences

The decision to support the 1948 campaign of Henry Wallace seems to have originated in the party's mental Comintern, its efforts to adapt Soviet rhetoric to U.S. politics. When Secretary of State George Marshall announced the European Recovery Program (Marshall Plan), to rebuild the war-ravaged nations of Europe, including the Soviet Union and the Soviet-occupied nations of Central and Eastern Europe, Joseph Stalin rejected it as an American imperialist attempt to expand capitalism. Stalin instead organized the Cominform (Information Bureau of the Communist and Workers' Parties), consisting of the Soviet Union, its satellites in Eastern and Central Europe, and the CPs of France and Italy. At the Cominform's founding meeting, in October 1947, Stalin's emissary, Andrei Zhdanov, announced that the world was split into two hostile camps and denounced the "expansionist" aims of the United States. Taking Zhdanov's speech as their cue, CPUSA leaders echoed his language and attacked the Marshall Plan. When the CP pushed its allies in the CIO to oppose the Marshall Plan, CIO leaders on the right lined up to support it and Truman's foreign policy more generally.[1]

Party leaders faced a difficult decision regarding the upcoming presidential election: continue to back liberal Democrats, as the party had been doing in San Francisco, or back a third party. On May Day 1947, before Zhdanov's speech, the CP National Board had endorsed "a broad democratic coalition for independent political action as an alternative to both major parties" but without any specific timeline or process. In California, party members Hugh Bryson, head of the National Union of Marine Cooks and Stewards, and Richard Lynden, a leader in ILWU Local 6, led the effort to put the Independent Progressive Party (IPP) on the state ballot. In May 1947 the NUMCS adopted a resolution calling on labor and "other progressive forces" to create "a third party, a people's party."[2]

At the same time, Robert Kenny, former California attorney general and national leader of the Progressive Citizens of America, and other California Democrats were promoting Henry Wallace within the Democratic Party. *People's World* gave Wallace extensive positive coverage throughout 1947 and by September was also encouraging its readers to register to vote as members of the IPP. In September 1947, in *Political Affairs,* Jack Stachel approved both efforts—those to make Henry Wallace the Democratic presidential nominee and those by California party members to form a third party. Stachel stressed, however, that it was wrong to assume that a third party would nominate its own presidential candidate; he pointed instead to the American Labor Party in New York, a third party that had supported Roosevelt for president but had elected Vito Marcantonio to the House of Representatives.[3] Nonetheless, in December 1947, after Wallace decided to run as an independent, national CP leaders backed Wallace as a third-party presidential candidate.[4]

By April 1948 some implications of the third-party move became clear when the California CIO council—under left control—issued primary-election endorsements, and the only Democrats they endorsed had cross-filed in both the Democratic and IPP primaries. Democrats were under significant pressure *not* to cross-file because major AFL unions were refusing to support anyone who did so. Missing from the CIO Council's endorsements, therefore, were several staunch supporters of labor, including Franck Havenner. IPP candidates filed against all of them. The third-party movement had quickly become an instrument for denying CIO endorsements to Democrats who had perfect or near-perfect voting records on CIO issues. By late August, the national Wallace campaign was denying any intent of defeating those candidates, but the IPP candidates remained on the ballot. *PW* tried to straddle: it gave full and daily support to the

Wallace campaign but ignored local and state IPP candidates except those running where there was no Democratic candidate. The weekend before Election Day, *PW* endorsed Havenner and a few other liberal Democrats who had not sought the IPP nomination.[5]

In February, Wallace polled at 11 percent in California, but he finished with 4.7 percent.[6] Truman eked out a narrow victory in the state. IPP candidates did not draw enough votes to defeat any progressive Democrat, but the CP's inept venture into third-party politics drove a wedge between the left (the CP and its allies in CIO unions) and liberal Democrats. Robert Kenny, in 1953, wrote, "From a purely California standpoint, . . . the third party movement was just part of the misplaced militancy that developed in the left after the Duclos letter." He called it "utter folly." Sam Darcy, in 1964, may have been thinking of Kenny when he added that the Wallace campaign "destroyed some leaders and candidates of real progressive character who held great promise." In early 1956 Eugene Dennis came to a similar conclusion when he called the Wallace campaign "erroneous and harmful" because it "widened the cleavage in the CIO and weakened the ties between the Left Wing and the mainstream of the labor movement."[7]

Dennis was referring to the split in the CIO produced by the CP's efforts to persuade its supporters in CIO unions to oppose the Marshall Plan and support Wallace. Relations between left CIO unions (those close to the CP) and the right CIO unions (the others) had long been strained, but the Marshall Plan and the Wallace campaign catalyzed several purges. Some unions, notably the National Maritime Union and the Marine Firemen, purged their left officers and members. The United Electrical Workers Union walked out of the CIO before it could be expelled, and the national CIO leadership expelled all other left unions. The NUMCS collapsed, and the ILWU failed in an effort to represent that jurisdiction. AFL and right CIO unions launched raids on the expelled unions. Only the UE and ILWU survived.[8]

In California the IPP continued a tenuous existence, widely understood as simply the electoral face of the CP. In 1949 in San Francisco, the IPP backed Charles Garry in a special election to succeed a member of Congress who had died. John Shelley, previously endorsed by the CP, was the candidate of the Democratic establishment, and he won. Angela Gizzi Ward, then IPP county chair, later described the Garry campaign as "stupid." In 1950 the IPP mounted campaigns for two statewide candidates, both for offices where there was no Democratic candidate; the IPP's best showing was 9.2 percent. The IPP also had nine candidates in legislative districts, all but one of them in districts with no Democratic candidate; the exception ran against Sam Yorty, Democratic candidate in the Fourteenth District. The best showing for any IPP legislative candidate was just under 17 percent.[9]

In 1952 the IPP nominated Vincent Hallinan for president of the United States. A prominent criminal defense attorney in the Bay Area, Hallinan had not associated with the left until the Wallace campaign, when Vivian Hallinan, his wife, pushed him to attend a Wallace rally and make a major contribution. In late 1949, when Harry Bridges again came to trial, his usual lead attorney, Richard Gladstein, was in prison for contempt of court during the New York Smith Act trial (see below). Bridges choose Hallinan, hoping his reputation would provide immunity to the treatment being meted out to left lawyers. Hallinan later pointed to that trial as radicalizing him. He was found in contempt of court at the end of the trial and sentenced to six months in prison. During Hallinan's and Bridges's appeals, Hallinan spoke around the country to raise funds for their defenses, sometimes accompanied by Dave Jenkins. By early 1952, lacking other viable choices, the national leaders of the IPP settled on Hallinan as the best choice for president and chose Charlotta Bass, the former publisher of the *California Eagle*, for vice president. She was the first Black woman to be nominated for the American vice presidency.[10]

The Hallinan-Bass campaign attracted little attention outside CP circles. Dave Jenkins, active in that campaign, later reflected, "It was only Hallinan's energy and the fact that he had some money that made that not totally a charade." Hallinan got 0.2 percent of the vote nationwide and 0.5 percent in California. Reuben Borough, a longtime activist for reform and progressive causes in Los Angeles, was the IPP candidate for U.S. Senate. He got 12 percent against William Knowland, the Republican who had won the Democratic nomination through cross-filing. The IPP ran eleven candidates for Congress, seven against Democrats, but none drew enough votes to affect the outcome. In 1954 George Andersen, running for Congress in San Francisco against both a Republican and a Democrat, got 2 percent of the vote, not enough to affect the outcome. Andersen's vote was the highest of any IPP candidate that year.[11]

The IPP was listed as a "subversive" organization by the Senate Internal Security Committee in 1955 and was dissolved that same year, just as CP leaders were beginning to question the party's decision to support Wallace.

Demise of San Francisco's Labor-Left Culture

At the same time the CP was engaged in its fruitless and debilitating support for the IPP, the Bay Area's liberal-left cultural institutions came under increased attack. CUAC, now officially the California Senate Fact-Finding Committee on Un-American Activities, carried out an investigation of the California Labor School and published its long report in 1947. The report claimed a direct line from a CP school in San Francisco in 1932 to the CLS, although the party schools of the early 1930s differed greatly from the CLS. Part of CUAC's evidence came from the evaluation by the State Federation of Labor that had led it to require AFL local unions to withdraw from the CLS. The CUAC report included a person-by-person analysis of prominent staff and faculty to demonstrate their connection to the CP. CUAC, not surprisingly, concluded that the CLS was a Communist front.[12]

In 1947 President Harry Truman, seeking to undercut arguments that Democrats were "soft on Communism," directed the attorney general to draw up a list of "subversive organizations." The CLS was soon added to the attorney general's list and lost its nonprofit status. The Treasury Department then billed it for back taxes during the time it had held nonprofit status. The school also lost the ability to offer benefits under the GI Bill and to offer credit for San Francisco teachers. By the winter term of 1949, the school was no longer issuing a catalog, only a one-page list of courses. With left unions facing raiding and raising funds for legal defense campaigns, contributions from unions to the CLS significantly declined.[13]

With the CLS under attack by anti-Communists, the party launched its own investigation of the school in 1950. The surviving evidence is limited—a draft report and a briefer final report. Internal and external evidence point to the source as a subcommittee of the party's Security Commission, successor to the Control Commission. The subcommittee was charged "to investigate personel [personnel] practices and problems in the s. [CLS] To determine character of the situation, collective and individual, and to make recommendations."[14]

The draft report specified, "In s. itself, s. leadership responsible for [cross-out in original] promotion of unreliable and anti-Party element into various positions of responsibility and leadership, including bohemian elements, drunkards, homos., lesbians, chauvinists, and possible agents operating within this grouping. These elements are in some cases non-Party; in many cases they carry Party books." The draft identified individuals who fit these various categories and also "male sup. [superiority]." The report continued:

> Around these elements a larger circle including vol. wkrs. in various capacities, and stds. [students] who are to be found in various groupings, carrying on life of a bohemian, including heavy drinking, loose moral conduct, smoking of m. [marijuana] in some cases. This carried on in private homes and in bars . . . with participation of various of the individuals listed and in some cases others in full-time leadership. This a sort of "extra-cur" activity, after affairs. However, sharply exemplified each year in AB [the annual Artists Ball or Artists Carnival]—at which numbers of lesbians and homos gather.[15]

In seeking to identify those responsible, the draft report concluded that Jenkins had been too preoccupied with fund-raising to pay attention to these problems and that his behavior "represented capitulation to narrow 'practicalism' with disastrous results in personal [probably personnel] and political field. DJ [Jenkins] played an imp. role [written in by hand: "opport," i.e., opportunism] in this policy—though not his sole resp. since P. [Party] leadership permitted it to continue far too long." The draft continued: "Rotten liberalism and opportunist tolerance of anti-Party and degenerate elements, shown on part of s. [school] leadership." The final section of the draft recommended many changes:

> Changes in school personel [personnel] are required. . . . Must be replaced by strong political force . . .
> Serious crisis exists in finance and in enrollment. . . . Quick action needed to save the school . . .
> Should discontinue Artists Ball . . .
> Political line of school is involved. Does school represent a last outpost of revisionist outlook in movement. Need for complete readjustment of political line to new situation.
> Relation of Party with the school—unsatisfactory for a long period of time.
> Opportunism arises in part from the problem of maintaining the financial load. Must close Bldg.[16]

As early as 1945, a special county committee had concluded that Jenkins was "deeply involved in carrying out Teheran policies through his work at Labor School" and that "it took him some time to react completely to the Duclos article."[17]

The final report on the school was shorter and less detailed but nonetheless clear:

> The orientation in *all* fields of L.S. [Labor School] work must be to reach and meet the needs of the working class and the Negro people, from whom the great bulk of the student body must be drawn. . . . The role of the L.S. must be two fold: 1. To provide explicit Marxist education for the P. and for a broader circle who can be drawn into such classes. . . . 2. to develop broader type classes and programs wherever possible in the labor and progressive movement, striving to the extent possible to maintain the features of *labor* school, of a broad type, but *in a new way*, based on the new situation. . . . Only those aspects of cultural work which will most directly aid in carrying out the above orientation, and which can be realistically supported in terms of sharply reduced finances and personel [personnel], can be maintained.[18]

Jenkins had left the CLS before the investigation—possibly, the draft report suggests, assigned to other work as a way to remove him from the school. In September 1949 Holland Roberts became director. His academic credentials were impressive, but he faced a very difficult situation, due both to external attacks and to such directives from the party. The school gave up its building in 1951 and relocated to smaller, rented quarters. Classes became fewer and shorter. On May 3, 1957, federal marshals ordered everyone out of the building, padlocked the doors, and seized the school's property to satisfy a tax lien. The marshals only slightly shortened the school's life, as Roberts had already announced that the school would close due to financial constraints.[19]

KGO refused to continue Sidney Roger's radio broadcasts in 1950. *People's World* lost subscribers, from more than 15,000 in 1947 to 6,000 by the late 1950s. It shrank to a tabloid and in 1957 became a weekly.[20]

Art, too, came under attack. In the late 1930s the Roosevelt administration had authorized a new post office, the Rincon Annex, in downtown San Francisco. In the largest commission issued to a single artist under any New Deal art project, Anton Refregier, a New York artist, was chosen to create murals in the lobby. World War II interrupted construction, and Refregier returned and completed the murals in 1948.[21] Refregier's work drew complaints at the time he was working. A major controversy erupted over his mural on the 1934 strikes, depicting an evil-looking figure hiring longshore workers, a union organizer in the center, and the maritime unions' annual memorial service for those killed during the 1934 strikes. In the end, he made some small changes, but most of the mural remained intact. Other murals were also modified, including removal of a portrait of President Roosevelt. Five years later, in 1953, with anti-Communists raging both nationally and in the state, Representative Hubert Scudder, a Republican from north of San Francisco, introduced a joint congressional resolution to remove Refregier's "anti-American" murals. Patriotic and veterans' organizations joined in the attack, claiming that several murals were "communist propaganda . . . intended to promote racial hatred and class warfare." Unlike most targets of anti-Communist crusaders, Refregier's art drew broad support. Both of San Francisco's U.S. House members—now including John Shelley—spoke against the resolution, as did the directors of the city's art museums, many prominent San Franciscans, and a long list of artists, museum directors, and citizens all across the country. Scudder's bill died in committee.[22] It was one of the few victories for the left.

CUAC and HUAC

In 1950 Congress passed the Internal Security Act over a veto by President Harry Truman. That act required the party to register and submit information regarding its members, finances, and activities and also required individual members of the party to register. It defined a "Communist-action organization" as endeavoring "to carry out the objectives of the world Communist movement by bringing about the overthrow of existing governments by any available means, including force if necessary, and setting up Communist totalitarian dictatorships which will be subservient to the most powerful existing Communist totalitarian dictatorship." That is, if one registered as a party member, one was admitting to criminal behavior.[23]

HUAC held highly publicized hearings in 1947, including accusations that Hollywood celebrities were Communists or Communist dupes, and more in 1948 and 1949, including dramatic accusations of espionage. HUAC also staged subcommittee hearings outside Washington, for which the usual agenda was that one or more witnesses, often former party members, provided a long list of local people who, the witness claimed, were now or had previously been party members. The list was known to the HUAC staff in advance, as those on the list all received subpoenas to testify. For party members or former party members so identified and subpoenaed, the subcommittee demanded to know if the person was now or ever had been a member of "the Communist conspiracy" and, if so, to reveal the names of anyone the witness had ever encountered in a CP context. Refusal to comply with either the first or second question could result in a contempt of Congress citation. Citing the Fifth Amendment was the only choice for a witness who refused to "name names." By doing so, the witness became labeled as a "Fifth Amendment Communist." HUAC members insisted that such hearings had some legislative purpose, but it was clear to all that the point of nearly all such hearings was to label a person as a "Red" in a way that would make local headlines and might cause the person to lose their job.[24]

California was a popular place for HUAC subcommittee investigations. The subcommittee that came to San Francisco in 1953 was chaired by Harold Velde, chair of the full committee and a former FBI agent once assigned to the San Francisco field office. A hundred subpoenas were issued in advance of the hearing. On the first day, two witnesses named a long list of local people as party members, including Lou Goldblatt (who had left the party a decade before) and Hugh Bryson, then under indictment for perjury. The subcommittee called nine witnesses on its second day, beginning with an FBI informant who reeled off a long list of East Bay residents who, he claimed, were party members, although he also stated that all he knew about them was that they had attended meetings and took part in "educational work." The other eight witnesses declined to answer questions. One who declined to answer, John Mass, a teacher at San Francisco City College, was accompanied by an ACLU lawyer. By refusing to name names, he and all those present knew he was sacrificing his job, because a new state law prohibited state employees from invoking the Fifth Amendment before a legislative committee; Mass was relieved of his duties immediately after he finished his testimony.[25]

On the third day of the hearing, a former *PW* reporter claimed that Congressman Robert Condon, who represented an East Bay district, had attended a "closed" meeting of the CP Political Affairs Committee. Condon, a former member of the law firm that included Robert Treuhaft, immediately issued a denial. The next day, the subcommittee heard from one former Communist who gave them much the same list of names they had previously received, and twelve witnesses who refused to cooperate, including Doris Brin Walker, described by the *Chronicle* as the "most belligerent witness." She gave the subcommittee an extended lecture on the first three articles of the Constitution and the First, Fourth, Fifth, Sixth, Ninth, and Tenth Amendments. That same day, Velde spoke to the Commonwealth Club, a group of business and civic leaders, and claimed that former president Harry Truman was largely to blame for the Communist conspiracy. In the end, the subcommittee heard thirty-six witnesses, only five of whom were "friendly." The subcommittee concluded that there was "widespread Communist infiltration into almost every activity in the Bay Area." Velde projected CP membership in the Bay Area at "several thousand." The FBI's San Francisco field office, however, estimated total Northern California membership at 969.[26] Afterward, CUAC and other state agencies continued their own investigations, hearings, and loyalty programs.

A HUAC subcommittee returned to San Francisco in December 1956. The subcommittee consisted of Velde; Clyde Doyle, a Democrat from Southern California; and Gordon Scherer, a Republican from Ohio. Richard Arens, of the committee's staff, led the questioning of Holland Roberts, whom Arens described as "an agent of the international Communist conspiracy," "a nerve center for transmission of foreign, Communist propaganda," and "part and parcel of an international, godless, atheistic conspiracy controlled by Moscow." Roberts repeatedly cited the Fifth Amendment. The next day, Louis Goldblatt was ejected from the hearing after he referred to Arens as a "little phony counsel . . . using sarcasm . . . [to] make an impression on the press." Victor Arnautoff, Aubrey Grossman, and other subpoenaed witnesses cited the Fifth Amendment in refusing to respond to the committee's questions. Norman Leonard represented Arnautoff and a few others, and local ACLU attorneys represented the rest.[27]

Leaving the Party, Early 1950s

In 1944 the party had counted 63,064 members nationwide, and District 13 claimed 6,897 (11 percent of the total). By late 1947 national membership had reached 75,388, and District 13 claimed 9,817 (13 percent). Then, attacked by government agencies and civic organizations and wracked by internal disputes following the Duclos article and the "misplaced militancy" of 1948, the party began to shed members. In San Francisco, Bjorne Halling, a member of the Albion Hall group in 1934 and later a leader in the ILWU, and Paul Heide, an officer

in ILWU Local 6, both left in 1948. By 1950 half the national party membership disappeared and only 37,751 remained. District 13 did not suffer so large a
proportionate loss but was down to 5,208 (14 percent of the total). In the early
1950s, in reregistering all members, the party dropped about a third and kept
only 16,000–17,000.[28] If the same proportions between district and nation had
persisted after reregistration, District 13 would have had about 2,300 members.
If earlier proportions had continued, nearly half—about 1,150—would have
been in the northern part of the state. That calculation coincides closely with the
estimate in late 1952 by the FBI's San Francisco field office, which claimed there
were 969 members in its area.[29]

Revels Cayton left the party in the early 1950s. He returned to San Francisco
at the end of the war; he and his wife soon divorced, and he moved to New York
to become executive secretary of the National Negro Congress (NNC), a CP-
front organization. When that organization came under attack for its ties to the
CP, its major source of financial support, CIO unions, began to dry up. Cayton
ignored the party's prohibition, entered psychoanalysis, and remarried. The party
dissolved the NNC in 1947. Cayton then held menial jobs before becoming a
retail clerk and then a union organizer. By the early 1950s he was at odds with CP
leaders, who criticized his influence on Paul Robeson and opposed his argument
that Black union members should form separate caucuses. By 1952 he had stopped
attending party meetings. He later reflected, "I did not leave the Communist
Party because I was disillusioned. . . . It was through the Communist Party that I
first found my way to contribute to the struggle of working peoples everywhere.
. . . I drifted out of the Party. I didn't have any quarrel with them. . . . I no longer
belonged."

Lincoln Fairley received a PhD from Harvard in economics and labor relations
in 1931, joined the research department of the Works Progress Administration in
Washington, D.C., went to the Board of Economic Warfare during World War II,
became a staff member for a congressional committee, and then worked in the
UAW's Washington office. He joined the CP during the war. In 1946 he was hired
by the ILWU as research director. Upon arriving in San Francisco, Fairley joined a
CP club of ILWU Local 10 members. He later described them as "strident" and the
club as "a complete farce" with "little influence." He was even more dissatisfied with
the CP's publications, especially *Political Affairs*. He found its economic writing to
be "very, very poor, and the analysis worse." Not quite willing to call the economic
articles "illiterate," he settled on saying they were "always wrong." He dropped out
of the party around 1950, although he continued to be active in the CLS.[30]

After Jack Olsen was discharged from the army, he became the full-time director
of Local 6's education and publicity committee and taught labor-related classes at
the CLS. With the expulsion of the ILWU from the CIO, the Teamsters launched

a raid on Local 6 that included extensive red-baiting. Olsen was a major target, and he was pressured to resign from his union office. Upon being dispatched to a warehouse job, he found he was always fired soon after, which he attributed to the FBI. He left the CP about the same time he left Local 6, in 1951 or 1952. He later said, "I felt the Party had lost its viability as an American working-class force. . . . It was unable to react properly to events or to provide leadership."[31]

While Jack was in the army, Tillie Olsen had taken a job as Northern California director of the CIO War Relief Committee and was active in her own party club. As early as 1945, she was thinking about leaving the party, but she served on that year's special county committee on reorganization and was recommended for membership on the county committee. After the war she wrote a few columns for *PW*, but her time for party work was limited by family responsibilities, including the birth of a fourth daughter in 1947. She was active in the PTA, participated in the CLS, and worked in the Wallace campaign. Like Starvus, she learned that children were not welcome at party meetings. She was also criticized once for bringing her ironing to party meetings. Charges that she was using the PTA to spread Communist propaganda led to her removal from the city's PTA board. Tillie left the party about the same time as Jack.[32]

Richard Gladstein and the First Smith Act Trial

The Alien Registration Act of 1940, the Smith Act, made it illegal to advocate the violent overthrow of the U.S. government. Beginning in 1949, Attorney General Tom Clark charged CP leaders with violating the Smith Act. The first trial, in New York City, was of eleven top national leaders, including Eugene Dennis. In an award-winning legal history, Stanley Kutler called the trial "the most blatant political trial in American history, a trial of the Party's purposes, ideology, and organization, as well as of its leaders."[33]

The trial, before Judge Harold Medina in the Foley Square Courthouse in New York City, proved one of the longest in U.S. history. Prosecutors presented an immense compilation of documentary evidence and testimony by professional witnesses to argue that the CP was and always had been committed to the violent overthrow of the government and that party membership was therefore illegal under the Smith Act. This was the approach used against Schneiderman in 1939 and against Bridges in 1939 and 1941. By the time of the Foley Square trial, the FBI had accumulated an enormous collection of publications on Marxism, Leninism, and the CP. Federal attorneys also had a sizeable stable of professional witnesses, especially former party members, all willing to testify to the party's commitment to violent overthrow of the government and to identify individuals as party members. The defense emphasized that the CP was a political party that sought to achieve socialism through education, not revolution, and that the entire proceeding was biased against the defendants. The defense also followed a strategy of challenging and disparaging virtually everything and everyone, including the prosecution and Judge Medina. In the end, the jury found all eleven guilty; they were all sentenced to prison. After appeals the verdict was upheld by the Supreme Court in *Dennis v. U.S.* (1951). That decision immediately set in motion further Smith Act trials, of lower-level CP leaders.[34]

Richard Gladstein was among the attorneys who represented the Foley Square defendants. Judge Medina found all five attorneys guilty of contempt of court and sentenced them to short prison terms. Gladstein spent six months in federal prison. Upon his return to San Francisco, some members of the state bar tried to have him disbarred. However, 10 of the city's trial lawyers filed depositions in support of Gladstein, and 164 lawyers in the Bay Area filed an amicus brief on his behalf. Not until 1956 did the Board of Governors of the California State Bar finally acknowledge receiving the material on Gladstein. They simply ordered it filed and did nothing more.[35]

By the time the California bar decided to ignore the charges against Gladstein, his firm had undergone several changes. During World War II, Ben Margolis left the firm and went to Los Angeles, where he set up his own firm, with the ILWU and other left unions as his major clients. From 1943 to 1947, Bert Edises had been part of the firm, but he left to set up his own firm in the East Bay, one that included Robert Treuhaft. In 1946 George Andersen and Herbert Resner merged with the Gladstein firm; Resner soon left and was also expelled by the CP.[36]

Norman Leonard joined the firm in 1938 and became a partner after World War II. He was born in New York City, the son of Russian and Polish immigrants. His father was a garment worker. The family moved to Los Angeles, where Norm entered UCLA, majored in political science, met Aubrey Grossman, and moved to the left politically. He received a scholarship to Columbia University, where he earned his masters and law degrees. He came to the Gladstein firm shortly before World War II, served in the navy during the war, and then returned to the Gladstein firm. He most often focused on legal research and writing briefs rather than making courtroom presentations. However, he soon found himself defending Smith Act defendants in Los Angeles.[37]

Some Party Leaders Go Underground

During the appeals of the New York Smith Act convictions, William Schneiderman went to New York, where he was being groomed to replace Eugene Dennis if Dennis went to prison. There Schneiderman participated in intense discussions about the party's direction. A majority of the National Board, he recalled, believed it was "five minutes to midnight"—that fascism loomed, war against the Soviet

Union was imminent, and party leaders must go underground. Schneiderman disagreed, but the national office directed district leaders to disappear, close offices, and reduce the size and visibility of clubs. Schneiderman later reflected, "These measures were carried to extremes in many places," and the results were "devastating." When Dennis directed Schneiderman to go underground, he refused. He, William Z. Foster, and Elizabeth Gurley Flynn became what Schneiderman called "a make-shift Secretariat" with Schneiderman as acting national secretary. On July 26, 1951, still in New York, Schneiderman was arrested at the same time as other California party leaders (see below).[38]

The party had created a "reserve" underground leadership. Dorothy Ray Healey later described the plan: "The idea was that we would have both an open aboveground leadership and an 'unavailable but operative' underground leadership. The real decisions would be made underground and conveyed to the open leaders," who might find themselves subject to arrest. She also recounted how the party "bought dozens of mimeograph machines and thousands of reams of paper and cached them in people's houses"—and sometimes forgot where the machines had been hidden.[39]

Louise Todd Lambert was chosen for the reserve National Committee. She didn't want to do it, but she did as she was told. She went to New York City to prepare, was sent to another location with a new identity, was permitted no communication with anyone on the outside, traveled a good deal, and did not return to California until 1955, although she requested several times to be released. She and her husband were separated for more than five years, which adversely affected their relationship.[40]

Archie Brown, a member of the CPUSA National Committee, went underground immediately after the Foley Square trial. He stayed underground until mid-1955, mostly in California, moving from place to place. Like Todd Lambert, he received funds, a false driver's license, a social security card, and "whatever I needed." He later said that he spent most of his time studying. Esther Brown, his wife, took their four children and dog to live with her father in Southern California, where the FBI kept them under constant surveillance.[41]

Adam Lapin was associate editor of *PW*. In 1951 he was sent underground when Al Richmond, the editor, was arrested. Eva Lapin and the children took the train to New York to be with family. Adam remained underground for more than three years, on the move but submitting his material to *PW* via party couriers. Given the party's emphasis on the fate of Ethel and Julius Rosenberg, such children as the Lapins' feared that their parents would be arrested. Nora Lapin recalled her anxiety about her mother: "When she didn't come home by the time she had promised . . . I would worry that she had been arrested." They returned to San Francisco in 1954, and Eva became the party's education director, first for the city and then for the state.[42]

After leaving the CLS, Dave Jenkins helped lead the state Wallace campaign in 1948 and headed the Bridges Defense Committee from 1949 to 1952. Told to go underground, he later recalled, "I even started to leave town, and I thought what bullshit this is." Some party members criticized him for "stepping outside the discipline of the Party," and Archie Brown sought to expel him for "denigrating the face of the party." Jenkins continued: "Schneiderman apparently told him [Brown] it was nonsense, but Brown was a persistent and relentless opponent."[43]

Bill Bailey refused even to consider going underground. He was blunt in his memoirs: "I thought the whole idea stunk. . . . No, I said, I will not partake in the disappearing act. I will hold my ground, and the nuts in the Party who made the decision can go to hell."[44]

Those who went underground were often negatively affected by the experience. Separated from families and friends, they were cut off from many of their usual sources of affirmation for their commitment to the party. Joseph Starobin later reflected, "The self-imposed isolation almost immediately caused profound soul searching, and in most cases, a political re-evaluation. . . . Members of this underground began to have the most profound doubts about the whole course of American Communism." According to Starobin, one discouraging aspect of going underground was the revelation that the FBI often knew where they were the whole time: "It was unnerving to a good cadre to be confronted by an F.B.I. man who asked what those maneuvers were all about. The fact that government agents seemed to know all about it utterly undermined its credibility." And, Starobin noted, many who went underground left the party in 1956 and 1957.[45]

The California Smith Act arrests and simultaneous undergrounding hollowed out the party's leadership in the Bay Area—Schneiderman, O'Connor Yates, Richmond, Rude Lambert, and Starvus were all detained in Los Angeles, and Todd Lambert, Brown, and Adam Lapin were underground. Club members suffered from the absence of party leaders. Because "the old, trained leaders are gone, some to jail and some underground," a subsection leader explained in 1955, "the rank and file comrades do not get sufficient leadership." Attendance fell at local CP club meetings. Victor and Lydia Arnautoff had become members of a club composed entirely of Russians, with four or five members. As a security measure, they sometimes met in the Arnautoffs' car parked at the beach. One of the members was an FBI informant.[46]

The California Smith Act Trial

At 8 a.m. in California (11 a.m. in New York), the morning of July 26, 1951, FBI agents arrested 10 California party leaders in addition to Schneiderman, including Carl Rude Lambert; Albert "Mickey" Lima; Al Richmond; Loretta Starvus Stack; Oleta O'Connor Yates; two others in the Bay Area; Dorothy Ray Healey;

her husband, Philip "Slim" Connelly; and two others in Southern California. Three others were subsequently arrested. The Californians were among 126 state and local party leaders arrested after the Supreme Court's *Dennis* decision. Ernest Tolin, U.S. attorney for the Southern District of California, made clear that the California arrests were intended "to destroy the Communist Party in the West." The *Los Angeles Times* reported that the grand jury was told that "the defendants, beginning in April, 1945, engaged in a series of meetings during which they advocated overthrow of the United States government." The grand jury indicted all 15 five days after they were arrested. The indictment listed fifteen overt acts, times when the defendants and others, including some of the *Dennis* defendants, had engaged in meetings with one another "to further the conspiracy."[47]

The Smith Act defendants were handcuffed together when they moved from one location to another, although there was no real risk of escape. On the left, Al Richmond (carrying bag), Ernest Fox, Oleta O'Connor Yates, Loretta Starvus Stack; on the right, Mickey Lima, Carl Rude Lambert (handcuffed to Richmond); others not identified. From the *People's World* photo collection, box 3, file 21, courtesy of Labor Archives and Research Center, San Francisco State University.

Federal attorneys apparently brought the indictments in Los Angeles so that the trial would be held there rather than San Francisco. The defendants were represented by a panel of lawyers led by Ben Margolis. Other defense attorneys included Norman Leonard; A. L. Wirin, the longtime lead attorney for the ACLU in Southern California; Leo Branton, a young Black attorney from Los Angeles who had just argued his first case; and Alex Shulman, attorney for the Los Angeles AFL Labor Council, which promptly discharged him because he was representing Smith Act defendants. Al Richmond later identified Margolis and Leonard as the team's "Left attorneys." Each lawyer had primary responsibility for a few defendants, but they all took part in strategy discussions. The defense team had four more lawyers doing research and analysis, including two from the Bay Area, Benjamin Dreyfus and Doris Brin Walker, both party members. To save money, Margolis organized a team of volunteer stenographers and typists, who took down each day's proceedings, typed them, and mimeographed them for use by the defendants and their attorneys.[48]

Five defendants were members of the state board: Schneiderman, Richmond, O'Connor Yates, Ray Healey, and Lima. They and their attorneys determined defense strategy. They began by reviewing the current party line and the party's approach to the Smith Act prosecutions. They quickly and unanimously agreed that both the "five minutes to midnight" line and the party's approach to the Foley Square trial were mistakes. They agreed on a two-pronged approach, emphasizing civil liberty issues and denying the prosecution's equation of Marxism-Leninism with force and violence. As Richmond later put it, they focused on "defense of our right to advocate as we did and defense of what we advocated." Ray Healey recalled that they wrote a letter to national leaders explaining how the current party line was mistaken and encouraging the party to come aboveground. The response, she said, was a message "essentially telling us to mind our own business." Some underground party leaders criticized the defendants for having "bourgeois legalistic illusions," for being too "enamored" of their lawyers, and for offering a legal defense instead of a political defense. Schneiderman and Ray Healey had permission, during Memorial Day recess, to go to New York, where they discussed the trial with Foster. Foster discouraged them from cross-examining the prosecution witnesses and criticized their decision that only one defendant would take the witness stand. In the first trial all the defendants had done so, and all were relentlessly badgered to provide the names of other party members. Foster equated the Californians' decision that only one would provide testimony as misplaced faith in "bourgeois legalism" and personal cowardice.[49] The Californians continued on their own course.

Loretta Starvus held no party office, so she was curious why she was charged. She concluded that it was because the prosecution wanted to present testimony from Leonard Patterson, previously a witness in several cases in the east. He testified that Starvus and her first husband, Irving Kreichmar, had attended the Lenin School in Moscow from 1932 to 1934, that he had talked with them upon their return, and that Starvus had "won prizes on the rifle range." He said he had attended the previous session of the Lenin School and described the curriculum as including training in weapons, building barricades, and overturning vehicles. Starvus later described Patterson's testimony as mostly false, since the curriculum had consisted mostly of lectures on theory and history, but she acknowledged that he knew the specific dates of her attendance and her medal for marksmanship. She was among Norman Leonard's defendants; he urged her take the stand to refute Patterson's testimony. She refused because she couldn't deny having been at the Lenin School and having received a medal for marksmanship.[50]

The centerpiece of the defense, not only for herself but for all the defendants, was testimony by Oleta O'Connor Yates. A champion debater in college, she was more familiar with Marxist-Leninist theory than anyone in the prosecution, and her debating experience prepared her well for exchanges with the prosecuting attorneys, who sometimes displayed a surprising ignorance of the voluminous documents they had presented as evidence. She spent nine and a half days on the witness stand. As in other Smith Act cases, the prosecution repeatedly asked her for names or asked her about individuals not on trial. Each time she declined to answer, she was found in contempt of court. By the end of the trial, she had eleven citations for criminal contempt and was sentenced to eleven years in prison. Appeals of her contempt citations reached the U.S. Supreme Court twice, in 1957 and 1958. The first time, the Court reduced the eleven citations to one and directed that the case be returned for resentencing; the second time, the Court reduced her sentence to time served.[51]

The trial lasted six months. The jury took four days to reach a verdict of guilty. Their appeals reached the Ninth Circuit Court in July 1954. In keeping with the *Dennis* decision, that court affirmed the trial court decisions in March 1955.[52]

Next appeals were directed to the U.S. Supreme Court. Both the context and the Court itself had changed significantly since the *Dennis* decision in 1951. The war in Korea ended in 1953. Stalin died the same year. His successor, Nikita Khrushchev, initiated a thaw in the Cold War. In 1954 the Senate censured McCarthy. By 1956, when the California Smith Act case, *Yates v. U.S.*, finally reached the Court, four of the six justices in the *Dennis* majority were no longer on the Court. In 1953 Earl Warren became chief justice. Robert Jackson, Stanley Reed, and Sherman Minton were replaced by John Marshall Harlan, William Brennan, and Charles Whittaker. However, the timing of Brennan's and Whittaker's appointments was such that neither took part in the *Yates* case.

In earlier cases Justices Hugo Black and William O. Douglas had taken an "absolutist" position on First Amendment issues, arguing that the language "Congress shall make no law" was to be understood literally, and they had made separate dissents in the *Dennis* case. Though Douglas and Black had often been the lone dissenters in such cases in the early 1950s, Douglas later wrote that "Warren made part of the difference" when the Court began "to protect the rights of the people by limiting the thrust of the anti-subversive program."[53]

Warren had sometimes engaged in red-baiting as district attorney, California attorney general, and governor, but by 1955 he was emphasizing the need to resist "the temptation to imitate totalitarian security methods." Harlan was more outspoken in 1955, condemning recent "excesses of thought, utterance, and action," an unmistakable reference to McCarthy and his imitators. Harlan also identified as dangerous the notion that "in order to preserve our free society some of the liberties of the individual must be curtailed."[54]

It was somewhat by chance that the *Yates* case reached the Supreme Court ahead of other Smith Act cases. In October 1955 the Court accepted appeals for both the California and Pittsburgh cases, but circumstances removed the Pittsburgh case, so only the California case was heard in early 1956. Several briefs were filed: one by Robert Kenny, who had been California attorney general during Warren's first term as governor, on behalf of Schneiderman, arguing that the same issues had already been decided in 1943; one by Augustin Donovan, an Oakland attorney, a Catholic and Republican who had regularly played handball with Warren when both were living in Oakland, on behalf of Richmond and Connelly, arguing that their actions as journalists were protected by the First Amendment; and one by Leonard, Margolis, Shulman, and Wirin, on behalf of all the defendants. Instead of explicitly arguing that the *Dennis* decision should be overturned, Leonard and his colleagues claimed that the *Yates* case should be differentiated from it, an argument that several justices seemed to be looking for.[55]

When the *Yates* case was argued in October 1956, some justices posed tough questions to the government lawyers. Douglas asked what specific acts the defendants had carried out to overthrow the government. Reed wanted to know if membership in the CP by itself constituted an overt act. Harlan pressed for explicit links between the defendants and "the conspiracy." The government's reply was that the conspiracy was of such a magnitude that it was not necessary for the government to prove that the specific defendants had urged violence "with their own lips."[56]

When the justices met in conference to discuss the case, Warren suggested that the government had not established "that the Communist Party is force and violence" and that "the government has not made clear proof of the purpose of the Party." Black agreed that there was not sufficient evidence to convict, as did Douglas. Of the remaining justices, Reed, Minton, Harold Burton, and Tom Clark wanted to affirm the convictions, but Felix Frankfurter and Harlan were undecided. Warren held the case over. Minton retired. Frankfurter and Harlan agreed that the convictions should be reversed on the narrow ground that instructions to the jury were inadequate. So the vote was then 5–3 to reverse. Warren assigned the decision to Harlan. By the time Harlan completed writing and the case was again discussed, Reed had retired, and Burton had joined the majority, making the vote 6–1 with two vacancies. Clark was the lone dissenter.[57]

Warren and Frankfurter joined Harlan's decision, based on an interpretation of the word "organize" in the Smith Act and on the instructions given to the jury. Harlan specified that the judge had failed to instruct the jury to determine whether the actions of the defendants would have incited others to undertake violent overthrow of the government. Harlan also specified that the Smith Act had to be interpreted as prohibiting advocacy of action, not advocacy of ideas. "The essential distinction," Harlan said, "is that those to whom the advocacy is addressed must be urged to do something, now or in the future, rather than merely to believe in something." The decision was for the acquittal of five defendants for lack of evidence and retrial of the others. Burton concurred separately, agreeing with everything but Harlan's treatment of "organize."[58]

Black and Douglas concurred in Harlan's opinion but went far beyond it. In a decision by Black joined by Douglas, they argued for the acquittal of all defendants on the grounds that the Smith Act abridged "freedom of speech, press, and assembly in violation of the First Amendment," an echo of Murphy's opinion in the 1945 *Bridges* case. Black disparaged the introduction of "massive collections of books, tracts, pamphlets, newspapers, and manifestoes," which he described as "turgid, diffuse, abstruse, and just plain dull," and which "no juror can or is expected to plow his way through." Black continued: "Guilt or innocence may turn on what Marx or Engels or someone else wrote or advocated as much as a hundred or more years ago," and also specified that "prejudice" against "obnoxious or unorthodox views . . . makes conviction inevitable." The decision was announced in June 1957.[59]

Given the Court's narrow interpretation of the word "organize" and its new standard of evidence, there was no retrial of the defendants. Federal attorneys admitted that they could not satisfy the evidentiary requirements set by the Supreme Court. The Smith Act, though not declared unconstitutional, became a legal dead letter. The remaining Smith Act cases, in various stages of appeal, were dismissed.[60]

The California defendants' reliance on "bourgeois legalism" created a different set of circumstances than *Dennis*, and the specific jury instructions in their case provided an opening for the Supreme Court to accept their case. However, the larger political context was also important in both pushing and permitting the justices to find for the defendants. If McCarthy's tactics had pushed some of the justices to take the case, the end to the Korean War, the death of Stalin, the thaw in the Cold War, and the censure of McCarthy may have permitted the civil libertarians on the Court more latitude than was possible in 1951.

Soon after, in what seemed a case of sour grapes over the *Yates* decision, the Department of Justice renewed an effort to strip Al Richmond of his citizenship on much the same basis as the unsuccessful efforts against Schneiderman and Bridges. Richmond had been born in London to refugee parents from Russia. He was nine years old in 1922 when his parents brought him to the United States. He became a citizen in 1943, while serving in the army. The form he signed to apply for citizenship asked only if he was an anarchist or wanted to overthrow the government by force and if he was attached to the principles of the Constitution. He answered "no" to the first, "yes" to the second. Thus, in almost every way, the case was a repetition of the Schneiderman case *except* that before Richmond had applied for citizenship, he had filed at least three official federal forms in which he had explicitly indicated that he was a CP member. The charges had been brought in 1952 and then put on hold until the *Yates* case was resolved.[61]

George Andersen represented Richmond. The case was heard by Judge Louis Goodman in 1959. Goodman had dismissed a similar case against Bridges in 1956 for lack of evidence. Goodman lectured the federal attorneys for bringing the Richmond case: "The Government knew Richmond was a Communist when he was naturalized. . . . I see no fraud here and no concealment." He dismissed the charges. Andersen told another attorney soon after, "I got the impression that there was a sort of revulsion at the bad faith of the Government, which probably motivated Goodman to a great extent."[62]

Most party members took little time to celebrate the *Yates* or *Richmond* decisions. By the time of those decisions, the party—nationally and in the Bay Area—was even deeper into crisis, one so profound that it never recovered.

THE CRISIS OF 1956–1958, THE COLLAPSE OF THE OLD LEFT, AND AFTER

In 1956, before the Supreme Court decision in the *Yates* case, the U.S. Communist Party was shaken to its core. Soviet premier Nikita Khrushchev's secret speech in February 1956 detailing Stalin's crimes became known to U.S. party members a few months later, setting off extensive intraparty discussions that often went to the party's very nature. Then, in late 1956, came the Soviet army's brutal invasion of Hungary. Party members, including important leaders, began to leave, either through formal resignation or by simply dropping out. A national convention in 1957 failed to heal the wounds, much less chart a new direction. By late 1958 many local leaders and rank-and-file members in the Bay Area had left. More left in the 1960s. For all practical purposes, the party that had come into existence in San Francisco and Los Angeles in 1919 had collapsed by late 1958. The California CP after the mid-1960s was under new leadership and took new directions, but it never came close to the prominence it had during its Popular Front periods. Then it, too, experienced a mass of resignations in the early 1990s.

The Party in Crisis, 1956

Khrushchev's secret speech was delivered to the Twentieth Congress of the CP of the Soviet Union. Even before that speech became available in the United States, the public positions of the Twentieth Congress, including some contrary to current CPUSA positions, generated extensive intraparty discussions. In early April, for example, Schneiderman spoke to party meetings in San Francisco and

Los Angeles to address questions raised by the Soviet Congress's actions. Three hundred attended the San Francisco meeting, at which Schneiderman emphasized that the Soviet Union now posed a "peaceful challenge" for "economic competition."[1]

The party, national and local, began a detailed and searching self-examination, stimulated by both the actions of the Twentieth Congress and the return of top leaders from prison or underground. As Joseph Starobin has indicated, many of those party leaders had spent their time in prison or underground in study and contemplation of the party. In April 1956 the party prepared for its first National Committee meeting since the events of 1951, including not only National Committee members but also other local and state leaders. Eugene Dennis, the general secretary, prepared a lengthy report focused on the party's recent failures. He described the CP's insistence that its allies in the CIO oppose the Marshall Plan as "very harmful, untenable and sectarian," and he called the Wallace campaign "erroneous and harmful." Dennis accepted some responsibility for those failures, especially the Wallace campaign, but put more blame on "left-sectarianism," which many understood as criticism of William Z. Foster, CPUSA president.[2]

Before the National Committee meeting, in response to the news about the Twentieth Congress, rumors about Khrushchev's secret speech, and Dennis's report to the National Committee, John Gates and Al Richmond, editors of the *Daily Worker* and *People's World*, the party's two daily newspapers, opened their columns to a wide range of views, something never done before. On April 19, for example, *PW* reprinted a *Daily Worker* article by Dennis in which he argued that the extent of Soviet anti-Semitism that had been recently confirmed was being addressed, that "the Soviet government is already beginning to restore various institutions of Jewish life and culture." *PW* then printed letters from readers questioning or criticizing that article. The newspaper also began to publish articles reevaluating Stalin and letters to the editor either attacking or supporting those articles. One of those articles was by Anna Louise Strong; within the previous decade, four Bay Area party members had been expelled for being "supporters of Anna Louise Strong."[3]

Schneiderman later described the expanded National Committee meeting: "After reviewing the party's experiences, the National Committee was in a mood to be self-critical about its wrong political estimate, as well as about a number of sectarian errors." However, Schneiderman continued, "The lines began to form as to how much of this should be admitted. While Dennis was inclined to be self-critical, Foster and others minimized the harmful effects of our recent policy and contended that the persecutions and objective historical factors were the main reasons for our setbacks."[4] That division persisted through the following months.

Perhaps most importantly, those attending that National Committee meeting were read a translated summary of Khrushchev's February speech, supplied by the Soviet consulate. Dorothy Ray Healey remembered her reaction: "I was convulsed in tears. It was unbearable. Just this voice going on, piling facts upon facts, horrible facts about what had happened in the Soviet Union during the years of Stalin's leadership. . . . Suddenly all the pieces fell into place; all those doubts . . . over the past few years were not only confirmed but magnified a thousand times." Al Richmond said, "Such disclosures posed questions about the Soviet regime and, to the extent that your fundamental beliefs were intertwined with this regime, these, too, were placed in question."[5] And for nearly all party members, their "fundamental" political views were "intertwined" with the "Soviet regime."

On June 4 the State Department released a fifty-eight-page, thirty-thousand-word version of Khrushchev's speech, probably the same version that had been read to the National Committee meeting. The next day, the *New York Times* printed it in full, with extended analyses. Other major newspapers also carried it. Acknowledging "monstrous injustices and terrorism under Stalin's regime," *PW* printed it all on June 11, 12, and 13. Edith Arnstein Jenkins later wrote about those revelations: "We who had linked years of humanist struggle to our belief in the USSR were shocked past understanding. We swung between anger at those who had deceived us and at ourselves for our own part in our deception." Dave Jenkins was more explicit: "It was like a rape, a mental and emotional rape because we were involved with hundreds of non-Party people to whom we had denied the possibility of these 'slave labor' camps, the murder of honorable and fine people."[6]

Jessica Mitford was less shocked because, she later wrote, "I had never been as thoroughly convinced as most comrades of Soviet infallibility." She saw the speech as a hopeful sign that the Soviet Union was setting out on a course of fundamental change, the beginning of political and intellectual freedom. She and Bob Treuhaft participated fully in the intraparty discussions that followed. In mid-1956 Mitford, assisted by a few friends, all party members, produced the funniest critique of the party ever published by a party member: *Lifeitselfmanship or How to Become a Precisely-Because Man: An Investigation into Current L (or Left-Wing) Usage*, twelve pages, printed on a mimeograph, and assembled and stapled on the Treuhafts' kitchen table. Inspired by her sister, Nancy, the author of *Noblesse Oblige*, a book that described British U (upper-class) and non-U language, Mitford described "L" (left, that is, CP) and "non-L" language; for example:

Non-L: Time will tell whether that plan was O.K.
L: The correctness of that policy will be tested in life itself (alt., in the crucible of struggle).
Non-L: Suggesting a bum plan.
L: Projecting an incorrect perspective.

Mitford had previously been brought up on charges for making jokes in party meetings, and she now provided hilarious questions and answers to test one's understanding of "L" along with examples of "L" drawn from *Political Affairs*. She also acknowledged the editors of and contributors to *Political Affairs*, "without whose inspiration this book would never have been written." In conclusion, she acknowledged, "We are quite certain that many readers will now wish to criticize the author," so she provided a checklist of "appropriate criticisms": "Anti-leadership, Anti-theoretical, Rotten Liberalism, Fails to Chart a Perspective, Right-opportunism, Left-sectarianism, Philistinism, Petty Bourgeois Cynicism." The initial five hundred copies were quickly snapped up and another two thousand as well. All income (there were no expenses, since the paper and stencils had been filched), a total of $1,250, went to *PW*.[7]

Such levity evaporated in late October, when student demonstrations in Hungary sparked widespread, and often violent, opposition to the Communist regime and brought the appointment of Imre Nagy, a reformer, as prime minister. When Nagy withdrew from the Warsaw Pact (the Soviet Union's counterpart to the North Atlantic Treaty Organization, or NATO) and proposed that Hungary become neutral, Khrushchev sent Soviet troops into Hungary; they overthrew Nagy's government, killed thousands of Hungarians who fought the invaders, and initiated a reign of terror. On November 6 *PW* presented a statement by the National Committee, concluding that the Soviet invasion "violated the essence of the Leninist concept of national self-determination" and also a criticism of that statement by Eugene Dennis. Once again *PW* carried a variety of perspectives, including a full-page debate between Sidney Roger, identified as "liberal, pro-labor," and John Pittman. Pittman had been a European correspondent for *PW*, the *Daily Worker*, and the *Chicago Defender* beginning in 1947 and then stayed in New York until 1955, when he returned to the editorial staff of *PW*. Roger condemned the Soviet invasion as "dreadful," immoral, and cynical, stating, "You can't impose socialism by shooting people." Pittman opposed "any condemnation of the Soviets for some fancied violation of 'morality,'" used most of his column for "whataboutism" regarding the recent British and French seizure of the Suez Canal, but acknowledged that the invasion of Hungary had "confused and divided the left."[8]

Bill Bailey was not confused. For him, the invasion of Hungary was "the straw that broke the camel's back." He remembered thinking, "You stupid bastards. Is this socialism at work?" He informed Walter Stack later that day, "I've had enough of the Party's stupidity and bungling." For Angela Gizzi Ward, Hungary was also the tipping point. Estolv Ward recalled that he "had been convinced for several years that the Party was not going to get anywhere in this country" but that he "had to wait for Angela" before leaving. Angela later said, "It took a long time for me to raise questions," but she pointed to the Duclos article as the starting point of her questioning.[9]

By late 1956 party membership nationwide had fallen by two-thirds. The losses seemed greater to some of those leaving—Dave Jenkins estimated that the party lost 80 percent of its members in San Francisco, likely reflecting the situation among those he knew. Some who left simply stopped attending meetings, but others submitted a formal resignation. When Dave and Edith Jenkins resigned, Bill Schneiderman came to their home to dissuade Dave but ignored Edith though she was in the same room. Angela and Estolv Ward met with members of Angela's club and Oleta O'Connor Yates to announce their decision, and two club members joined them in resigning. Angela later recalled that one of those present informed the FBI about the resignations. Bill Bailey was visited by the FBI three days after his resignation and invited to talk. He told them to "get the hell away."[10]

The Failure of Reform: The 17th CPUSA National Convention

Amid controversy and desertion, the 17th National Convention of the CPUSA met in New York in February 1957. The national leadership was deeply divided, with Gates calling for major changes, Foster standing pat, and Dennis somewhere in between. The Khrushchev revelations and the invasion of Hungary were discussed, but the deepest divisions were over the future of the party itself. Bay Area participants provided differing accounts of those events.

Al Richmond later said, "I was associated with the heterogeneous mix for renovation. Some people in it . . . had one foot out [of] the party ideologically." He may have been thinking of Gates. Richmond defined three goals for the Bay Area delegates: "a sharp break with bureaucratic patterns, an effective exercise of autonomy in a fraternal relationship with the world movement, and an independent confrontation with American reality in the spirit of Marx and Lenin." That is, they wanted a more democratic organization, affiliation with a world movement but not subject to dictation from abroad, and a party that was both Marxist-Leninist and American. The last, he specified, was the most difficult. And, he concluded, his group "was decisively defeated." However, Richmond himself was elected to the National Committee and continued to edit *People's World*.[11]

Schneiderman took a more theoretical perspective: "In over-simplified terms, it was a debate between the role of objective factors versus subjective factors. . . . A large number of delegates, perhaps the majority, recognized both factors . . . but were up in arms against the leadership, and felt that changes were needed in its whole political approach and its methods of work." The convention, he concluded, failed to resolve anything.[12] He left party leadership.

Others were more blunt. Eva Lapin described the two sides this way: "The 'Young Turks' criticized the Party for blindly following the Soviet line and insisted we had to think for ourselves and focus on American realities. The *Daily Worker* and *PW* staffs supported this position. The other group, the 'Old Guard' were less critical . . . and stood by international ties."[13]

Jessica Mitford was also a delegate. Like Richmond, she described her side as advocating a "sharp turn": more internal democracy, more autonomy vis-à-vis foreign Communist parties, and an independent road to socialism compatible with U.S. politics. "The sharp-turn advocates," she said, "included our California delegation, led by Oleta." Mitford saw the opposition as "the hidebound, orthodox leadership of past decades" who "flocked to the banner of William Z. Foster." Noting that old habits remained on both sides, she described a two-hour debate over whether to substitute "reject" for "oppose" and a four-hour debate over whether to "interpret" or "creatively apply" Marxism-Leninism. She concluded that the meeting was dominated by the "sharp-turn" advocates, but the "hidebound, orthodox" leaders remained in power and refused to change. She agreed that the convention was a failure.[14]

Leaving the Party

Gates led a departure from the party over the results of the convention. Eva Lapin recalled that she and Adam "sat down one evening with a bottle of *PW* brandy to come to our decision. We became nostalgic thinking of the idealistic young Communists we had been." But, she added, "The passion and drama had just about vanished by that night." They decided it was time to leave.[15]

Those leaving included five of the defendants in the California Smith Act trial. Loretta Starvus found the invasion of Hungary "shocking," considered the party's leadership—nationally and locally—to be "bankrupt" and the party itself stagnant and paralyzed. Bill Sennett, after some twenty-five years as a party functionary in Illinois and several years underground, became so disaffected after the national convention that he moved to California, intending to become a nonparticipating party member. Instead, he put his name first on the group resignation letter drafted by O'Connor Yates. O'Connor Yates, Starvus, Sennett, and Todd (the latter two of whom had also been delegates to the national convention) were among twenty-six Californians, mostly local or state leaders, who resigned en masse in March 1958, citing the party's "deeply rooted dogmatism" and "total isolation" from emerging social movements and the failure of the convention to change the leadership. Their resignation letter expressed no regrets. They described the party as "the great radical movement of our generation" and explained:

> Had we to choose again, we would identify ourselves with it for the same reasons that caused us to do so then: these include the Party's important role in the unemployed movement, its contributions to organizing workers in basic industry, its effective participation in the fight for Negro rights, its pioneering

efforts in the struggle against war and fascism, its solidarity with the socialist sector of the world, its aspirations for a socialist America, and its study of scientific socialism, Marxism-Leninism.[16]

When Oleta O'Connor Yates died six years later, at the age of fifty-two, her husband, Allan Yates, attributed their resignations to the Khrushchev revelations, which, he said, "caused us and other hard-core Marxists to reevaluate our positions." But, he added, "We came to reject the absolutism of communism ... [its] pat answers for everything—party line answers." In 1945, in the wake of the Duclos article, O'Connor Yates had said, "One of the fundamental lessons to be drawn from the past period is not to accept anything before thinking it through for yourself." Louise Todd Lambert later cited her own disillusionment with both the Soviet Union and the party's leadership, adding, "the party had become totally irrelevant in the political life of the country" and "so isolated and sectarian nothing could be accomplished by remaining as members." She did not say so explicitly, but her description of isolation and sectarianism must surely have been intended to point to the effects of the Duclos article.[17]

When Carol Cuénod decided to leave the party, she could find no one to receive her resignation:

> I was trying to find someone to talk to ... I called Oleta saying, "Oleta, I have to talk to someone." My recollection is that we set up a time and place and before that meeting took place, Oleta left the Party. I remember doing the same thing with Loretta Stack, and the same thing happened. It became almost a comedy. I didn't know who else to turn to.... So, by default, I left the Party.[18]

Though deeply disappointed by the results of the convention, Decca Mitford and Bob Treuhaft briefly continued their local party membership. However, Mitford recalled, it had become "dull work, rendered duller by the growing suspicion that the locomotive of history had roared on without us." One evening, two longtime friends sounded them out about leaving the party. The four met with the county chairperson to announce their decisions.[19]

For most, the resignations came after years of disappointment and frustration with life in the party. The sharp, sectarian turn in the party line in response to the Duclos article had disturbed many who had participated in Popular Front activities. Jack Olsen's departure in the early 1950s was made because he "felt the Party had lost its viability as an American working-class force." Estolv Ward, who had headed Labor's Non-Partisan League in the heady Popular Front campaign in 1938, became deeply dissatisfied with the post-Duclos party.[20]

Others had chafed over the extent to which party assignments came before family responsibilities. Carl Rude Lambert chaired the committee that expelled his brother Walter, an experience Lambert's wife described as "very traumatic" for both brothers, who didn't speak to each other for ten years. When told to do party organizing in Los Angeles, Tillie Olsen left her partner and young daughter. Todd recalled that when the party was organizing its underground leadership in the early 1950s, one woman was told, "You are to do this, but you must forget that you have a son. You must forget that you have a husband. You must forget that you have a family." The woman refused. Todd, Adam Lapin, and Sennett did go underground, leaving their families for as long as five years. Lapin and Sennett left small children.[21]

For some activists, the party even took precedence over having a family. "I had the feeling that people who were dedicated to making a better world had no business having children," Gizzi Ward recalled. In the late 1930s and 1940s, according to Todd, "The atmosphere in the party was that, if you held a position of leadership, you were trying to get out of work if you wanted a child." Todd noted that for women in the party with children, "there were great difficulties," especially "with their children for reasons of neglect, leading children to feelings of great resentment toward their parents." Both Starvus and Tillie Olsen described how children were not welcome at party meetings; for Olsen, that exemplified the sexism that led her to leave the party.[22]

Todd recalled "many manifestations" of "male supremacy" within the party leadership. Starvus was also critical of the male chauvinism of party leaders, which led to women being "shoved" into clerical and secretarial positions and discouraged from speaking out. Gizzi Ward said that for women, "One's qualifications were not the determining factors governing promotions, job opportunities, etc.," but she also noted an exception: "Women were always elected to be dues collectors," which she described as "a thankless task."[23]

A few studies have suggested that Soviet anti-Semitism led some Jewish party members to leave.[24] However, none of the San Francisco Bay Area party members for whom I found records pointed to that as a cause for their leaving. I asked Nora Lapin whether it had been a factor for her parents, and she told me, "Anti-Semitism was not the reason that my parents and their friends left the CP although they might have been upset by rumors about Jewish doctors being killed. They left primarily because of the Hungarian revolution and the horrible way the Soviets responded."[25]

Keith Eickman later observed, "The discipline of the party was great because of the fact that after you had been in the party for many years, your whole social life developed around the party.... You were almost afraid of being thrown out into the wilderness." For Eva and Adam Lapin, leaving "was a momentous decision," both political and "deeply personal and emotional," but was easier because so many of their comrades were leaving, which meant they would not be shunned by longtime friends. Those observations help to explain why so many party veterans decided to leave at about the same time, and why, like the Wards, the Treuhafts, and the signatories of the mass-resignation letter, they did so in the company of comrades.[26]

Once resignations started, it was as if a dam had burst, releasing years of pent-up frustration with the party. By mid-1958 an informant told an FBI agent that Harry Bridges "was of the opinion that the CP should cease to function as it was a dead issue and no longer served any purpose."[27] CUAC gleefully reported in 1959: "There was very little Party activity conducted openly in California. . . . [The CP] was unable to attract new recruits and suffered from a dire lack of financial support. . . . Front organizations shriveled, dried up and withered away from lack of interest and finances."[28] This proclamation was premature. Though the Bay Area party had been devastated, it did not completely disappear. A core of loyalists remained, even as the party continued to shed members and leaders throughout the 1960s.

The Last HUAC Hearing in the Bay Area: The City Hall "Swim," 1960

CUAC may have considered the California CP virtually defunct, but HUAC was not about to admit that its traveling subcommittee hearings no longer served any purpose. HUAC had last held subcommittee hearings in San Francisco in mid-June 1957. For the first time, those hearings were televised. Prior to the opening of the hearing, William Sherwood, a Stanford researcher who had been subpoenaed, committed suicide and left a statement explaining that he refused to be "assassinated by publicity." Not only did Sherwood's suicide hang over the hearing, but so did a recent resolution of censure from the California Bar Association. During the hearings the *Chronicle* published an editorial calling the committee "arrogant" and "contemptuous of the Constitution and the courts." That same week, Chief Justice Earl Warren noted in a decision, "There is no congressional power to expose for the sake of exposure."[29] Though HUAC continued as before, opposition in the Bay Area grew and expanded in new directions.

In 1959 HUAC subpoenaed forty Bay Area public school teachers for a subcommittee hearing in San Francisco. Local opposition mobilized, including the American Civil Liberties Union, teacher organizations, religious organizations, labor organizations, and the *Chronicle*. HUAC twice rescheduled and then canceled. The head of the California Democratic Council, a liberal organization within the Democratic Party, exulted, "McCarthyism is dead in California."[30]

That obituary was premature. The resistance in 1959 apparently stiffened HUAC members' resolve to hold hearings in San Francisco and identify San Franciscans as part of "the Communist Conspiracy." HUAC announced subcommittee hearings for May 12–14, 1960, in the supervisors' chamber of city hall. The announcement brought a renewal of opposition. Though the hearings were announced as open to the public, HUAC issued enough passes to patriotic organizations to fill nearly all the seats. A HUAC representative explained, "There were about 150 passes. I issued them to individuals—to keep the Commies from stacking the meeting. We wanted some decent people here." The passes could admit more than one person, and the total seating capacity of the room was about 225. Those with passes were admitted first, largely filling the room. Critics of HUAC mobilized, recruiting significant numbers of students, most from San Francisco State College and UC-Berkeley. Several San Francisco State faculty members were centrally involved in planning the resistance.[31]

On May 12, the first day of the hearings, anti-HUAC activists held a protest meeting downtown at 11 a.m. A thousand people, mostly students, heard from California Assembly members and an Episcopal clergyman. They then marched to city hall, where they were told there was no room for them in the supervisors' chambers. That day, the first witness described a deluge of Communist propaganda entering the country, and another witness recounted Communist methods of operation. In between, Archie Brown was ejected from the room for his denunciations of the committee and its methods. Then Brown was called as the third witness. George Andersen, Brown's attorney, explained that Brown could not testify because he had been ejected from the room. Brown was admitted and again ejected. Three other witnesses, all charged with being CP members, did testify.[32]

The next day, May 13, began similarly, with HUAC's chosen audience admitted first and throngs of students left outside. The sheriff, responsible for security in city hall, told students that some would be admitted after the noon recess. When they were not, they began singing and shouting to be admitted. Told to disperse, they practiced the nonviolent resistance that civil rights demonstrators were using in the South. Shortly after 1 p.m., police turned a firehose on the demonstrators, soaking them and creating a cascade of water down the wide marble steps from outside the supervisors' chamber to the main floor. Helmeted police clubbed nonresisting demonstrators and dragged them down the water-slickened steps, outside, and into waiting paddy wagons. Sixty-four were arrested, including Becky Jenkins, daughter of Dave Jenkins. Margy Jenkins, Nora Lapin, and Danny Grossman were also there, cutting high school classes, but they avoided being arrested.[33]

Harry Bridges was having lunch with a few ILWU officials when they heard what was happening. They went to city hall and arrived as the water was being mopped up. Bridges went inside to make inquiries but soon left and was filmed leaving. On May 14, the third day of hearings, the committee asked Police

Inspector Michael Maguire if he knew Bridges "came to town" (he lived and worked in San Francisco) and took part in creating the "riot." Maguire answered no. The subcommittee chair, Edmund Willis (D-LA), nonetheless denounced Bridges as "one of the agitators." Eventually all charges against the students were dismissed, and Mayor George Christopher announced that HUAC was no longer allowed to use city buildings.[34]

Soon after, HUAC released a film and printed report, *Operation Abolition*, that claimed the "riots" were created by Communist agitators, continuing a HUAC

The doors at the top of the stairs are to the supervisors' chamber at San Francisco City Hall, where the HUAC subcommittee was meeting. When the anti-HUAC demonstrators, mostly students, were refused entrance, many of them sat down and sang or chanted. The photo shows the police dragging some of the demonstrators down the water-slickened steps to the waiting paddy wagon. Photo courtesy of San Francisco History Center, San Francisco Public Library.

campaign from 1957 that labeled opposition to HUAC as part of the Communists' "Operation Abolition."[35] The film was filled with distortions and falsehoods; for example, over film of Bridges leaving the building, the narrator claimed, "Among the Communist leaders who had an active part in the San Francisco 'abolition' campaign and the protest demonstrations was Harry Bridges, whom you see here being escorted out of the building by police officials moments before the rioting broke out." Archie Brown's diatribe in the film had come during the committee members' lunch break, when they left the room but kept their camera rolling and Brown obligingly declaimed loudly and at length to the empty chairs. The film, however, made it appear that his invective was directed to the committee while in session.[36]

Those were a few of the distortions and outright falsehoods in the film that was shown across the country to prop up HUAC and keep Americans concerned about the CP, which by then had shrunk to just a tiny fraction of its former size. In response, the Northern California ACLU (NCACLU) created *Operation Correction*, a film narrated by NCACLU head, Ernest Besig, who went through the HUAC film scene by scene, explaining the falsehoods, distortions, and scenes taken out of chronological sequence.[37] *Operation Abolition* drew harsh criticism from the *Washington Post, San Francisco Chronicle,* and the National Council of Churches. The events at city hall and the HUAC film led to renewed calls to abolish HUAC. HUAC held no more subcommittee meetings in the San Francisco Bay Area. For Bay Area college and university campuses, the mobilization of college and university students and faculty against HUAC marked the beginning of the tumultuous 1960s.[38]

The *Archie Brown* and *Roscoe Proctor* Cases

A year after those turbulent HUAC hearings, Archie Brown was charged under the Landrum-Griffin Act. During the 1950s Congress held extended hearings on unions, focused on corruption, racketeering, and lack of internal democracy. The Landrum-Griffin Act, one result of those hearings, included new regulations on unions. Section 504 prohibited Communists from serving as union officers and required unions to submit to the Labor Department a list of officers who were party members. Harry Bridges promptly announced that the ILWU could not comply with §504 because the law did not require him to investigate his union's officers, and he was therefore unable to submit any such list.[39]

Senator John F. Kennedy had contributed to the act's language. During the 1960 presidential campaign, Kennedy announced, "An effective Attorney General with the present laws" could remove Harry Bridges from union leadership.[40] However, in 1961, with John Kennedy in the White House and his brother Robert as attorney general, the administration made no effort to remove Bridges. Instead, Attorney General Kennedy moved against a seemingly easier target: Archie Brown, an increasingly lonely but still very loud voice for the CP, who had been elected to ILWU Local 10's Executive Board in 1959.

Norman Leonard recalled that the Justice Department sent a letter to Bridges, notifying him that Brown's election was in violation of §504 and that Bridges should "do something about it." By then Bridges had long since run out of patience with what was left of the local CP. Years before, in 1957, Herb Caen reported that Bridges said of CP members in Local 10—Brown was the most prominent—"I want you Commies to stay out of my hair!" However, Leonard described Bridges's response to the Justice Department's demand about Brown: "The members of Local 10 had the right to elect anybody they damn-well pleased," and "He didn't have the authority or the power, and if he had it, he wouldn't exercise it anyway, to upset a democratic election by the members of Local 10."[41]

In May 1961 Robert Kennedy had Brown arrested and charged with violating §504. Kennedy held a press conference to announce the arrest, stated that Brown was the first to be charged under §504, and implied that Brown was a test case. Bridges denounced the arrest and indictment as "a national disgrace" and "a direct attack against the ILWU and other American trade unions which insist upon the rights of its members to elect anyone to office they wish." Local 10's Executive Board and the ILWU Executive Board supported Brown but made clear that they were supporting "the right of the membership to adopt a union constitution . . . guaranteeing the right to be nominated for and be elected to any office" and not supporting Brown's political views or the Communist Party.[42]

The case went to trial in April 1962. Gladstein and Leonard defended Brown, admitted he was in violation of §504, and argued that §504 was unconstitutional. The jury found Brown guilty. His attorneys immediately appealed. The local ACLU joined with an amicus brief. In June 1964 the full Ninth Circuit Court of Appeals, by a vote of 5–3, decided that §504 violated the First and Fifth Amendments. Federal attorneys appealed to the Supreme Court. In June 1965 the Supreme Court, by a vote of 5–4 and with the decision by Chief Justice Earl Warren, agreed that §504 violated the First and Fifth Amendments. Warren also presented a long discussion of the Constitution's ban on bills of attainder, concluding that §504 was a bill of attainder and was also unconstitutional on that ground.[43] The Court's voiding of that part of §504 was not the only result of the *Brown* case. Warren's long discussion of bills of attainder has been of long-term significance, cited in some two thousand cases since then.

Brown was not alone in continuing to uphold the standard of the much smaller party. After 1960 Albert "Mickey" Lima became the head of the CP for the recently created Northern California District. Lima had joined the CP in 1937 and had become an East Bay party functionary by the 1940s. He served on the state committee, was among the defendants in the Smith Act case, and became head of the party in the Northern California District after the state was divided. Dorothy Ray Healey later characterized Lima as "one of the most rigid defenders of ideological orthodoxy."[44]

In May 1962 Lima was among ten people identified by Attorney General Robert Kennedy as CP members required to register under the Internal Security Act of 1950. Another of the ten was Roscoe Quincy Proctor, a Black resident of Berkeley, member of the CP since 1941, and a National Committee member since 1959. That act required the Communist Party to register and submit information regarding its members, finances, and activities and also required individual party members to register. The party never registered, nor did individual members. Robert Kennedy undertook to enforce that law. He indicted the party for not registering in December 1961, and in March 1962 he indicted the party's two top leaders, Gus Hall and Benjamin Davis.[45]

When the Subversive Activities Control Board (SACB) separately directed Proctor and William Albertson, a New York party member, to fill out registration forms, they declined, asserted their Fifth Amendment right not to incriminate themselves, and denied that the CP was a Communist-action organization as defined by the 1950 statute. The two men sued the SACB and argued that the SACB directive violated their Fifth Amendment right to avoid self-incrimination.[46]

The District of Columbia Court of Appeals upheld the SACB directive. On further appeal, the Supreme Court had to decide if the registration procedures of the 1950 act violated the Fifth Amendment right to avoid self-incrimination. By the time the case reached the Supreme Court, some forty individuals had also been directed to file statements. In an 8–0 decision written by Justice William Brennan, the Court agreed that the registration provision of the law was unconstitutional. Justice Byron White concurred in a separate opinion that recounted his advice as attorney general that the act itself likely violated both the First and Fifth Amendments.[47]

The Continuing Collapse of the Old Left

In September 1956, amid the discussions of the Twentieth Soviet Congress and the Khrushchev speech and before Hungary, Bill Schneiderman made the decision to withdraw from party leadership, telling the state convention, "I have served too long as Party Chairman. I have been your State Chairman in California for 21 years, and that is too long for anybody." In her memoirs, Dorothy Ray Healey recounted another reason for Schneiderman's decision. Boris Ponomarev, a member of the Soviet Central Committee, writing in a Soviet CP theoretical journal, had derided Schneiderman for articles in which Schneiderman had criticized the absence of genuine democratic centralism in the CP. Ray Healey characterized Ponomarev's article as using "the vilest language" to attack Schneiderman. "California Party leaders were outraged," she said, and demanded that Dennis publicly defend Schneiderman. Dennis did nothing.[48]

After declining to continue as state chair, Schneiderman also declined to run for the National Committee in 1957, but he was elected as a delegate to the national convention that year. Thereafter, he continued to refuse leadership positions other than the district committee. He returned to college, completed a degree in accounting—he earned As in economics, contracts, speech, and history—and took a job as a bookkeeper. He resigned from the district board in 1963, but he never left the party.[49]

In 1958, amid the many resignations, Al Richmond was interviewed and asked if he thought his previous twenty years of work on *PW* was worth it. He replied, "Yes. . . . We helped break down prejudices. Like fighting McCarthyism before it became fashionable. I believe our paper is vital and necessary. I believe it is a service to the democratic climate." In 1969, however, Richmond resigned as editor after the Soviet invasion of Czechoslovakia, citing "serious differences" with "the national party leadership." He and Dorothy Ray Healey resigned from the party in mid-1973, and both were expelled later that year. Peggy Dennis, the widow of Eugene Dennis, had worked on *PW* for several years after her husband's death in 1961; she left the party in 1976.[50]

Aubrey and Hazel Grossman left no clear record of their subsequent connection to the party, but most of their later work was not obviously related to it. In the late 1950s he served as legal counsel for those arrested during sit-ins demanding equal treatment for Black applicants for employment at San Francisco businesses. During the Vietnam War, he defended draft evaders. In 1969 he was one of two attorneys representing the American Indians who occupied Alcatraz. In the 1970s he represented the Pomo and Pit River people in legal contests over land that had once been theirs. There was an effort to disbar him in 1974 in connection with his work for the Indian tribes, but his defense included former governor Edmund Brown, who wrote, "Grossman and I did not agree on too many things, but his ethical standards, courage and intelligence were of the highest degree." Grossman was not disbarred, in part because of what the board called his "representation of unpopular political causes." Although he closed his law office in 1977, he represented Gus Hall and Angela Davis in 1980 in their unsuccessful effort to get on the California election ballot. Grossman had married Hazel McKannay, of Irish ancestry, in 1938; they had been student activists together at Berkeley. She, too, had a lifetime of activism, teaching in the California Labor School, working in the Wallace campaign, and working in various peace movements from the 1950s through the 1980s, especially the Women's International League for Peace and Freedom.[51] Others who had been prominent in the 1930s and 1940s continued as party members, including Morris Rappaport, Doris Brin Walker, Walter Stack, Archie Brown, and Karl and Elaine Yoneda.

The activism of the 1960s brought some new, mostly young, members to the California CP, and, by the late 1960s and early 1970s the California party had new leaders, notably Angela Davis and Kendra Harris Alexander.[52] But the party remained very small and far from the political mainstream. Their presidential candidate received 260 write-in votes in California in 1968 and 373 in 1972. The party's best showing in these years came in 1976, when Gus Hall, the party's perennial presidential candidate, apparently benefited from widespread disenchantment with the Democratic candidate, Jimmy Carter; Hall received 12,766 votes, 0.2 percent of the total. In 1980, Hall's and the CP's last campaign in California, his write-in count dropped to 847.[53]

After the Party

Some former CP members faced problems finding employment. Those who had been members of seafaring unions could not continue in that work, either because they had been expelled from their union or because they had been barred from working aboard ships. Dave Jenkins and Revels Cayton had stopped going to sea before the Coast Guard instituted its screening program, but Pat Tobin and Don Watson were screened off. Bill Bailey was expelled by the Marine Firemen. Cayton and Jessica Mitford had held salaried positions in party-front organizations, Cayton in the National Negro Congress and Mitford in the Civil Rights Congress, both of which were dissolved by the party. Before Adam Lapin resigned, he was associate editor of *PW*. When Jack Olsen was unable to remain in any warehouse job to which he was dispatched for more than a short time, apparently because the FBI talked with his employers, he left Local 6 and became an apprentice typographer in Typographical Local 21, where his brother was an officer. In 1974 he became the first director of the new labor studies program at San Francisco City College, where he remained until his retirement in 1983, after which he continued to teach classes.[54]

Harrison George's departure from *PW* ended some twenty years of his employment as a party functionary in one capacity or another. He remained bitter about his expulsion and committed to his views. In early 1949 he was quoted in the press as claiming the party leadership was bankrupt, too focused on "respectability," and too willing to cooperate with capitalism. Called before HUAC in 1953, he testified that he lived in Los Angeles and was doing "clerical work," the same occupation listed on his World War I draft card. He was represented by an ACLU attorney, not one of the left attorneys. He was registered to vote as a Democrat. He died in 1961.[55]

Sam Darcy had been expelled for his refusal to accept Browder's decision to convert the CP to the CPA. When invited back, he refused. Because he had contact with some of those expelled as left sectarians in the mid-1940s, he was condemned for associating with "renegades." He became a successful furniture merchant in Philadelphia and was active in the Democratic Party.[56]

The ILWU became a place of refuge for some former party members. Keith Eickman and Leo Nitzberg continued as members of Local 6 (warehouse), and Nitzberg later moved to Local 10 (San Francisco longshore) and then Local 34 (ship clerks). Around 1952 the party told Dave Jenkins that he should spend some time doing blue-collar work, so he first found a position in the ILWU local in Sacramento, then in Stockton, and eventually transferred to Local 10, where he continued after leaving the party. Bill Bailey started in the ILWU longshore local in Eureka and then transferred to Local 10. Tobin joined Local 10, Cayton briefly joined Local 6, and Don Watson joined Local 34 (ship clerks). Carol Cuénod found a clerical position at ILWU headquarters, where she eventually became librarian and archivist. Tobin, the Olsens, the Caytons, and Cuénod all lived in St. Francis Square, a housing development created by the ILWU.[57]

The day he left the party, Bill Bailey told a friend, "I feel that a very heavy weight has been lifted from me, . . . like I have just been handed a whole new set of freedoms." Eva Lapin reflected, "Once you left the Party, you were free to move in any direction." Allan Yates said of his and Oleta O'Connor Yates's decision to leave, "We felt truly liberated." Don Watson recalled, "I felt relieved by my decision." Others had similar reactions.[58]

Several women used their new freedom to chart new careers for themselves, and San Francisco State College provided most of them with that opportunity. Tillie Olsen participated in a summer workshop on human relations and then took a class in creative writing and continued to work with the instructor. Judy Nitzberg and Eva Lapin completed baccalaureate degrees, Nitzberg in history and Lapin in social work. Nitzberg continued for a master's degree in history, and Lapin went to UC-Berkeley for a master's in social work. Edith Jenkins earned a master's degree in English at San Francisco State, taught literature at a community college, and served on the board for SF State's poetry center. Judy Nitzberg became a high school history teacher in the San Francisco public schools. Eva Lapin (later Maas) became a social worker at Kaiser Permanente, the pioneering prepaid health program whose physicians had a reputation for challenging the then-conservative American Medical Association. While working as the ILWU archivist/librarian, Carol Cuénod was chosen for a National Endowment for the Humanities seminar with Herb Gutman at New York University, after which she completed a BA at Goddard College. She later became an archivist at San Francisco State.[59]

Loretta Starvus learned typing and bookkeeping at a commercial school, enabling her to work for a company that was not concerned about her past politics. When Revels Cayton became deputy director of the city's Public Housing Authority, he helped Starvus to get a job screening and assisting applicants for public housing. Louise Todd worked first as a legal secretary (which she had first done while on parole) and then as a medical secretary.[60]

Several former party members became published authors. After leaving *People's World*, Adam Lapin wrote travel books under a pseudonym, a career cut short by his death at the age of forty-seven. Lincoln Fairley continued as director of research at ILWU headquarters until he retired, wrote an analysis of the path-breaking Modernization and Mechanization agreements between the ILWU and the Pacific Maritime Association, and followed that with a history of Mt. Tamalpais, the dominant topographical feature of Marin County, north of San Francisco. Edith Jenkins published her poetry in journals and separate volumes as well as a memoir, *Against a Field Sinister*. Eva Lapin Maas and Bill Bailey also published memoirs. Don Watson was the author of journal or anthology articles and conference papers on the history of California farm labor.[61]

Jessica Mitford was the most prolific author. Her memoir, *Hons and Rebels*, was published in Britain in 1960 and in the United States as *Daughters and Rebels*. Other books came at a rapid pace: *The American Way of Death* (1963); *The Trial of Dr. Spock* (1969); *Kind and Usual Punishment: The Prison Business* (1973); *A Fine Old Conflict* (1977); *The Making of a Muckraker* (1979); and *The American Way of Birth* (1992). *Daughters and Rebels, A Fine Old Conflict*, and *The Making of a Muckraker* were autobiographical. Her husband, Bob Treuhaft, was extensively involved in the research and analysis of *The American Way of Death*, an exposé of the funeral industry, which made Decca's reputation as a muckraker. After Decca's death, he researched and wrote *The American Way of Death Revisited* (1998).[62]

Tillie Olsen was probably the most distinguished of the authors. Her first short story appeared in 1956 and was chosen in 1957 for an anthology of the year's best short stories. Over the next several years, she received a fellowship from the National Endowment for the Arts, a Guggenheim, and other impressive awards, appointments as artist-in-residence at prestigious locations, and nine honorary degrees. *Tell Me a Riddle*, her best-known work, appeared in 1961, and *Yonnondio: From the Thirties*, the long-delayed, never completed novel she had begun in the 1930s, was finally published in 1971. *Silences*, a nonfiction volume, appeared in 1978.[63]

Several former party members held significant union positions. Jack Olsen became a Labor Council delegate from Typographical Local 21. Keith Eickman was elected as business agent and later president of ILWU Local 6. Bill Bailey was elected vice president of ILWU Local 10. Pat Tobin held elected positions in Local 10 and then served as the ILWU's legislative representative in Washington from 1971 to 1980. Don Watson served on ILWU Local 34's Executive Board for twenty-four years, with nineteen years as chair and eleven years as secretary of the ILWU's Northern California District Council. Judy Nitzberg served for many years on the Executive Committee of the San Francisco Federation of Teachers, Local 61 of the American Federation of Teachers (AFT).[64]

Most of the group left a record of their support for the civil rights movement, the antiwar movement, and the women's movement. Don Watson became deeply involved in supporting the United Farm Workers, eventually volunteering half his working hours to building support and assisting with legal research, the origin of his interest in the history of agricultural labor. After retiring, Loretta Starvus took an active part in a tenants' organization at the housing development where she lived and advocated for better public transportation. Leo Nitzberg and Bailey belonged to the Veterans of the Abraham Lincoln Brigade, an organization of those who had fought in Spain, and both joined other veterans of that war in traveling to Spain after the fall of the Franco government.[65]

Nearly all of those who left the party became liberal Democrats. Don Watson left the CP just as party leaders were trying to advance him into leadership and instead joined the Young Democrats and the California Democratic Council (CDC), an organization of liberal Democrats.[66] Dave Jenkins was the most deeply involved in city and state Democratic politics. In 1963 he was appointed labor director for the mayoral campaign of John F. Shelley, for whom Jenkins secured endorsements from the ILWU and other unions. He then advised Shelley on appointments. Jenkins moved closer to San Francisco's political middle in 1967 when he joined the mayoral campaign of Joseph Alioto, a mainstream Democrat, rather than Jack Morrison, a more progressive Democrat. Jenkins later explained, "We had a frankly opportunistic line of staying with a guy who we thought could win." Jenkins brought Revels Cayton and two Black leaders from the ILWU to a meeting with Alioto, at which Alioto agreed to demands for Black representation in city government. In office Alioto appointed union members and African Americans to nearly every city commission and board, all with advice from Jenkins. In 1977 the *Chronicle* described Jenkins as "one of the canniest operators ever to insinuate himself into the City Hall mainstream" and as "a kind of jack-of-all-liberal trades."[67]

In 1964 Mayor John Shelley, likely with advice from Jenkins, appointed Revels Cayton to the city's new Human Rights Commission. Two years later Cayton became deputy director of the city's Public Housing Authority. After the 1967 election, Mayor Alioto appointed Cayton as deputy mayor for social programs, a position he held until 1972, when he reached the age of sixty-five, mandatory retirement age for city employees. Cayton then served in several appointed positions, including ten years on the city's Juvenile Justice Commission.[68]

Keith Eickman served on the city's Recreation and Park Commission, the board of KQED (public radio and TV), the governing board for the city zoo, and the San Francisco Bay Conservation and Development Commission (a regional agency). His son, Kent, observed, "He felt he needed to give back to society," but also "he liked going to meetings."[69]

In 1968, after mayors Shelley and Alioto had appointed several former Communists to city positions, Harry Bridges wrote in a personal letter, "No longer in this country does the accusation of being a communist ruffle anybody's feelings. . . . To be known as a communist these days is to be known as someone who is more in the line of an old-fashioned, Old Left kind of liberal, someone who may be a few degrees to the left of the policies enunciated by Franklin Roosevelt and the New Deal."[70]

Bill Sennett's post-party employment was perhaps most at variance from his erstwhile comrades. Within six years he had become a corporate vice president for the company where he had worked in Chicago, and he eventually became president of an international corporation that leased truck trailers for heavy freight. In addition to his corporate positions, he belonged to the Democratic Socialists of America and helped organize a tenants' association at the high-rise luxury apartment complex where he lived. In retirement in Tiburon, an affluent suburb north of San Francisco, he became publisher of *In These Times*, a weekly that presented left perspectives on current events and supported organizations that worked to eliminate poverty and racial discrimination.[71]

Nearly all who left the party remained politically active. Bailey later said, "Many of the people who left the Party . . . never abandoned their principles, but by various methods continued to pursue those aims."[72] Though the organizational structures of the Old Left were withering away, many of its erstwhile adherents continued to espouse, advocate, and agitate for the goals of the party's Popular Front periods—support for working people and their unions, equality, peace, civil rights, and civil liberties. Eva Lapin, for example, became involved with a militant group of social workers, marched against the war in Vietnam, counseled draft resisters, threw herself into the emerging women's movement, and prepared meals for the homeless.[73]

Maurice Isserman, in his study of the transition from the Old Left to the New Left, concludes, "It probably would not be going too far to say that the most influential adult radical group in the 1960s was this 'party' of ex-Communists."[74] Isserman's observation has resonance for the Bay Area, where former party members took active roles in the various radical causes of the 1960s. Jack Kurzweil joined the party in 1962 while a student at UC-Berkeley; he became a more public member after marrying Bettina Aptheker and was active in the United Professors of California, AFT, the union for faculty in the California State University system. Kurzweil remained in the party until 1991, when he became one of the founding members of the Committees of Correspondence for Peace, Democracy, and Socialism. He recently reflected, "My experience is that members and former members of the Party formed a dense network that was able to move and support the social and political movements of the 1960's based upon their previous participation in and leadership of movements of all sorts in the '30s, '40s, and '50s."[75]

When Treuhaft and Mitford resigned, they did so to use their time for other movements for social change. Treuhaft and his law partner, Doris Brin Walker, who remained in the CP, represented several clients on the left in the 1960s and 1970s, including Black Panthers, Free Speech Movement activists at UC-Berkeley (Treuhaft was among those arrested), Vietnam War draft resisters, and Angela Davis. Brin Walker was elected president of the National Lawyers' Guild in 1970, the first woman to hold that position, and she was the lead attorney defending Angela Davis in 1971–1972. (Hillary Rodham spent the summer of 1971 as an intern at Treuhaft and Walker but was apparently not radicalized.) Treuhaft and Walker also provided the legal paperwork to incorporate a cooperative for the United Farm Workers. Treuhaft and Mitford were active in the New Politics movement of the mid-1960s, and he ran unsuccessfully for district attorney under its auspices. He also led the left opposition on the board of the Consumers' Cooperative of Berkeley, which, at its height, was the largest consumers' co-op in North America. (The politics of the Berkeley Co-op were fought out between liberals and radicals; there were no conservatives.)[76]

Matt Crawford worked at the Berkeley Co-op after leaving his last party functionary position in 1949 and eventually became assistant manager. He seems to have left the party around 1956. In 1958 he moved to the co-op's credit union as a loan officer and later manager. After retiring as a co-op employee in 1974, he remained active as a co-op board member and advocate for the Black community and for seniors.[77]

Ray Thompson also became involved with the co-op. He left the party in 1960 because, he later said, "I got tired of the activity and I got tired of some of the people I had contact with. I had no quarrel with the CP or the principles of the CP." He also admitted, "It wasn't easy to be a Communist because the discipline was demanding. I was expected to do a lot of things that the average person is not aware of. I had meetings to attend, I had things to study, I had discussions to go into." He went back to school, taking evening classes at Berkeley High School. He was elected to the council of the Berkeley Co-op in 1962, became chairman of the council in 1964, was elected to the board of directors in 1969, and served three years as vice president. He remained on the board until 1978.[78]

Al Lannon stayed well to the left of the Democratic Party. He had moved to San Francisco shortly after the 1957 convention. The son of Italian immigrants, he was baptized as Francesco Alberto Vitere in 1907. He ran away from home at the age of fifteen, bummed around until early 1926, and then joined the U.S. Coast Guard. By then he had begun to call himself Al Lannon. Discharged from the Coast Guard for being underage, he went to sea, joined the Sailors Union of the Pacific, and later the Marine Workers Industrial Union. He became an organizer for the MWIU, joined the CP, did organizing in Baltimore, and attended the Lenin School. In New York in 1936 he helped to lead the rank-and-file strike that led to the formation of the National Maritime Union. He became a CIO organizer and then the full-time organizer for the party's Waterfront Section in New York. Among the first Smith Act defendants, he served two years in prison. At the 1957 national convention, he caucused with the left and was a major critic of the party leadership. Later that year he and his family moved to San Francisco, where he began to work as a warehouseman through ILWU Local 6. In 1958 the New York Waterfront Section disaffiliated from the CP and joined the Provisional Organizing Committee for the Reconstitution of a Marxist-Leninist Party. In San Francisco the party charged Lannon with left sectarianism and factionalism. He explained that his membership was still with the New York Waterfront Section, which was no longer part of the CP, hence he could not be brought up on charges by the San Francisco party. He had left the party. His wife, Elva, also left the party. He seems to have largely avoided politics during the ten years he worked as a member of Local 6. When he retired in 1968, he and his wife moved to Los Angeles, where he rejoined the CP. Elva did not.[79]

Some former party members turned to nonpolitical pastimes. Leo Nitzberg frequented the beatnik coffeehouses in North Beach, worked on photography, and eventually became an accomplished potter. Louise Todd renewed a youthful enthusiasm for hiking in the Sierra; after retiring she became a volunteer docent at the California Academy of Sciences and later a part-time employee. O'Connor Yates also took up wilderness hiking and became what her obituary called "a nature lover and rock hound"; she joined the San Francisco Horticultural Society and became secretary of the San Francisco Bonsai Society. Starvus took the lead in creating a community garden at her housing development. Fairley helped to organize the short-lived San Francisco New School, patterned after the New School for Social Research in New York. Bailey was featured in ten documentary films, two of them by the British Broadcasting Company, and also two feature films.[80]

While some former Communists elsewhere embraced hard-right conservatism, I found not one former Bay Area party member or leader who followed that trajectory.

Reflections on Life in the Party

In keeping with a long tradition of the party, some of those who left the party could be quite critical of what others had done while party members. In his memoir, Schneiderman specified, "We had faults; we were guilty of mistakes; hindsight makes it easy to identify misjudgments." But, he said, "Over the years the errors and shortcomings were far outweighed by the contributions made by the Communist Party." In line with the party's practice of self-criticism, Dorothy Ray Healey criticized herself for saying nothing when Archie Brown and Bill Schneiderman drove Roy Hudson out of the party after Hudson had come to San Francisco in the post-Duclos reorganization; she claimed that Brown and Schneiderman were jealous of Hudson's popularity among seamen and used his wife's ancestral ties to Hungarian royalty to force Hudson either to leave his wife or leave the party.[81]

Angela Gizzi Ward later wondered if she would join the CP if she could relive her life. She decided, "I would have preferred to be very *close* (laughing) to it, but not to have been so subservient to it. I would have preferred my thinking processes to have been better so that I would have challenged, sooner, some of the theories and some of the positions that the Party put out." She added, "I still believe in socialism."[82]

Though those who left the party could be quite critical of the party, other party members, and even themselves, few regretted the time they had given to the party. Sennett said, "My life was enriched by having been a Communist." Eva Lapin Maas reflected, "The Party had shaped our lives, given us a way of viewing the world, framed our family life, and influenced our selection of friends, books, movies, and activities." Bailey concluded his memoir by reiterating what had guided his life in the party: "To witness an injustice and do nothing—that is the biggest crime." Eickman was quite critical of the CP but did not regret his time as a member. "The Party gave me an understanding of the class relationship of society," he said. "It gave me a political attitude that made me different from any of the others in the union who didn't have that background. I don't think they understood politics to the same degree." Tobin also voiced no regrets: "I don't think anything I ever did countered the interests of the people in this country. . . . What we went out to do, was a good cause." Angela Gizzi Ward considered that her experience in the party had been "positive," that she had "learned a great deal," and that whatever success she had as a union organizer came in part "because of the support I did get from the Party in *thinking*, and in organizing my ideas." Carol Cuénod's major regret was that the Labor Youth League she led had advised high school students to work in factories rather than go to college.[83]

The resignation letter by O'Connor Yates, Sennett, Starvus, Todd, and twenty-two others emphasized that theirs was "not the action of hopeless people retiring from a fruitless cause" but instead "the beginning of an active search for what we are convinced will be a hopeful future," and they advocated efforts "by those who have left the Communist Party, to preserve and develop further what was healthy and valuable in our experience." For most, perhaps the large majority of the group, leaving the party did not mean rejecting ideals that had motivated them as party members—racial equality, an end to poverty, peace, and varying versions of socialism—but it did mean rejecting Stalinism and the Soviet version of socialism. "The Party's advocacy of socialism was based on the Soviet example," Todd reflected, adding, "I felt that our advocacy of Socialism should be based on American realities." Cuénod was more direct in 1994: "The idea of socialism I accepted, and I still do. . . . But the glorification [of the Soviet Union] we practiced was dangerous ignorance."[84]

Bailey, too, remained a socialist. He too was highly critical of the Soviet Union: "We cannot say that socialism did not work in the Soviet Union. The fact is they did not have socialism in the Soviet Union, nor did they practice it. . . . Somewhere along the rocky road bureaucracy got the better of them and the only thing the masses got was lip service and more dogma." In 1989 he was pleased when Whitey Disley, head of the Marine Firemen's Union, reinstated and apologized to Bailey and Walter Stack.[85]

Those Who Remained

Some activists from the 1930s and 1940s remained party members to the end. I interviewed Doris Brin Walker in 2007, and she had no regrets for her long-term party membership. Archie Brown continued to promote the party. Walter Stack, too, remained loyal to the party, eventually finding employment as a hod carrier and representing the hod carriers in the San Francisco Labor Council. Labor Council meetings always began with the Pledge of Allegiance, and Stack's foghorn voice always boomed "WE HOPE" after the words "with liberty and justice for all." He began running at the age of fifty-seven. Each morning, he cycled five miles, ran seventeen miles, and swam a mile in the bay before going to work carrying cement. He participated in hundreds of marathons, typically with a six-pack of beer in hand, appeared with Johnny Carson on *The Tonight Show* to discuss his running, and was featured in a Nike commercial. He remained a Communist to the end.[86]

John Pittman and his second wife, Margrit Adler, became the Moscow correspondents for the CPUSA press from 1959 to 1961. In 1968 he became cofounding editor of the *Daily World*, the merger of *People's World* and *Daily Worker*. He later became the party's representative on the editorial board of the *World Marxist Review* and lived in Prague for ten years. He remained a party member until his death in 1993.[87]

Isaac Zafrani, like Bill Sennett and Sam Darcy, had a highly successful career in business, eventually becoming president of the Harbor Lumber Company. When I interviewed him in 1987, he explained that he had remained a party member, was likely among the largest financial contributors to the party, and that his business associates, knowing his politics, would not permit him to take part in bargaining sessions with their employees.[88]

Elaine Black and Karl Yoneda remained under FBI surveillance until 1974. After they moved to a chicken farm near Petaluma in 1947, Elaine was active in party affairs in that area, including the Civil Rights Congress and the Independent Progressive Party, and she served as secretary-treasurer of the Sonoma County Communist Party organization in the 1940s and 1950s. The FBI classified her as DETCOM (*Det*ain as *Com*munist in case of national security emergency) until 1955. The Yonedas moved back to San Francisco around 1960 and eventually came to live in the St. Francis Square housing project. In 1972 Elaine was a delegate to the national convention and was apparently a member of the county committee. The FBI stopped its surveillance of them in 1974, after they had both retired.[89]

In retirement Karl authored several books: *The Heritage of Sen Katayama* (1975), published by Political Affairs; *A Brief History of U.S. Asian Labor* (1976), also by Political Affairs; and a memoir, *Ganbatte: Sixty-Year Struggle of a Kibei Worker* (1983), by the Asian American Studies Center at UCLA. He also

Karl and Elaine Yoneda, c. 1992. From the *People's World* collection, box 36, file 3, courtesy of Labor Archives and Research Center, San Francisco State University.

published books in Japan, in Japanese, including *History of Japanese Workers in the U.S.* (1967); *Another Face in America* (1978); and *A Nikkei M.I.S. Soldier's Diary, 1942–1945* (1989).

In 1983, on the fiftieth anniversary of the time Elaine and Karl moved in together, the San Francisco Board of Supervisors presented them with a certificate of honor that noted their lifetimes of effort for "Labor, Civil Rights, Peace, and Against Racism" and stated that "their example has been an inspiration to many of us." The *San Francisco Examiner* devoted an article to their lifelong commitment to the CP, noting that "their lives are almost synonymous with labor organizing, civil and racial rights causes and an unceasing commitment to involvement." When Elaine died five years later, Walter Johnson, secretary of the San Francisco Labor Council, spoke at her memorial service and observed that for many years no picket line in the city had been complete without the presence of Elaine and Karl.[90]

I first encountered Leah Schneiderman, the widow of Bill Schneiderman, in the late 1970s, after San Francisco voters adopted a charter amendment to elect the Board of Supervisors by district rather than at large. In most of the newly created districts, activists organized district Democratic clubs to serve as endorsing bodies since the positions were officially nonpartisan. I attended the meeting in District 11 to organize a Democratic club. Leah Schneiderman (I later learned who she was) was there with her party club. She argued that it should not be a Democratic club but instead a political association so that everyone could take part regardless of party. She carried the day. The District 11 Political Association proved to be as politically ineffectual as the Communist Party.

I next met Leah Schneiderman in 1987, when I interviewed her at her home in the Sunset District of San Francisco. She was wearing a necklace with a small gold hammer and sickle, and Lenin's portrait was centered on the wall of the room where we sat. I interviewed her again in 1993. She was then living in an assisted living facility in Oakland. She confided to me that most of the residents were "very conservative." The hammer-and-sickle necklace was gone, and Lenin's portrait had moved to the side. She told me that she had attended the party's national convention in 1991, roundly denounced Gus Hall, and resigned from the party. She was not alone. Jack Kurzweil told me that he also left the party that year, "along with most of the people in the Bay Area who were still in the Party."[91]

When I talked with Leah Schneiderman in 1993, she was enthusiastic about a new organization, the Committees of Correspondence for Peace, Democracy, and Socialism, that, she thought, promised to be more effective in representing working people in their struggle against capitalism. She died in 1998. She may have been the last survivor of the Old Left in the Bay Area.[92]

Legacies

By leaving the party, the large majority of San Francisco CP members freed themselves to participate in politics on their own terms. Most joined the city's political mainstream as liberal Democrats and did their own small part to push that mainstream to the left. The city's politics had begun moving left with the elections of Franck Havenner to Congress in 1936, John Shelley to the state senate in 1938, and Edmund Brown as district attorney in 1943. The CP had been supportive of those and other liberal Democrats during its Popular Front periods and sometimes after. Shelley's election as mayor in 1963, with David Jenkins's assistance, marked the first time that a liberal Democrat held that office. Jenkins, Revels Cayton, and the other former party members who supported first Shelley and then Alioto helped to end fifty-two years of Republican rule in the mayor's office. Former Communists also helped push Shelley, Alioto, and subsequent mayors a little to the left. Former party members did not create the city's volatile politics of the 1960s, 1970s, and 1980s—including opposition to HUAC, the civil rights movement, opposition to the war in Vietnam, the women's movement, the LGBTQ movements—but many of them, and sometimes their children, were involved. The presence of so many Communists and former Communists in the ILWU played some role in keeping that union securely on the left of U.S. unions, a position it still holds.

Another important long-term legacy of the Bay Area Communist Party was the interpretation of civil liberties that emerged from the Supreme Court decisions in the cases of William Schneiderman, the California Smith Act defendants, Archie Brown, and Roscoe Quincy Proctor. It is a common observation that key Supreme Court decisions regarding civil rights and civil liberties have almost always come from cases involving racial, religious, gender, or political minorities. The California Communist Party left only a very small impression on the state's political system other than in 1938, but its legal battles left a more lasting imprint on the nation's definition of civil liberties.

It is perhaps one of the ironies of this history that three of these important and precedent-setting civil rights decisions came only when the party was already in decline and that these decisions did not arrest that decline. But, then, if the experiences of these forty-some individuals are any indication, the collapse of the CPUSA was not due so much to the Smith Act, other repressive legislation, or the activities of the FBI and HUAC, as to long-term disappointment and frustration with the post-Duclos party, disquiets that were brought into sharp focus by the news from the Soviet Union in 1956 and the realization among many of them that their faith in the Soviet Union had always been seriously misplaced.

APPENDIX

BIOGRAPHICAL SUMMARIES

This appendix summarizes information for the fifty individuals who appear frequently and cites the chapters that include additional information.

Andersen, George (1901–1966): b. Denmark, parents U.S. citizens; raised SF; worked as boilermaker; grad. SF Law School (night school); lawyer; left CP ca. 1946; continued to represent unions and the left. (See chapters 4–6, 8, 9)

Arnautoff, Victor (1896–1979): b. Imperial Russia, parents Russian Orthodox; artist; joined 1938; emigrated to Soviet Union, 1963. (See chapters 5–8)

Arnstein Jenkins, Edith (1913–2005): b. SF, third-generation German Jewish; grad. UC-Berkeley; joined mid- or late 1930s; left 1956; subsequent liberal Dem; MA, SF State, community college instructor. (See chapters 5, 6, 9)

Bailey, William "Bill" (1910–1995): b. New Jersey; Irish Catholic parentage; 5th grade education; seaman; joined in early 1930s; union officer; Abraham Lincoln Battalion; left 1956; subsequent liberal Dem, longshoreman, union officer. (See chapters 5–9)

Balcomb, Violet: See Orr, Violet Balcomb

Black Yoneda, Elaine (1906–1988): b. Connecticut; Russian Jewish parentage; raised Southern California; joined c. 1930; active in ILD, other CP organizations; never left party. (See chapters 1, 4–6, 9)

Bridges, Harry (1901–1990): b. Australia; English and Irish parentage; always claimed never to have been a member; union leader. (See chapters 3, 4, 5, 6, 8, 9)

Brin Walker, Doris (1919–2009): b. Texas; joined in late 1930s; lawyer and union organizer. (See chapters 6, 8, 9)

Brown, Archie (1911–1990): b. Sioux City, IA; Russian Jewish parentage; came to SF Bay Area 1920s; joined late 1920s; agitator, early 1930s; Abraham Lincoln Battalion, commissar; candidate for office; ILWU Local 10 member; never left party. (See chapters 3–9)

Buchman, Rose Elaine: See Black Yoneda, Elaine

Cayton, Revels (1907–1995): b. Seattle; Black; HS grad., attended Univ. of Washington; joined early 1930s; union officer; left c. 1952; subsequent liberal Dem., appointed public official. (See chapters 5–9)

Crawford, Matt (1903–1996): b. Alabama; Black; grew up Oakland; chiropractic school; joined early 1930s; various positions in CP or related organizations; apparently left CP mid-1950s; active in Berkeley Co-op. (See chapters 4–7, 9)

Cuénod, Carol (1929–2015): b. SF; father Swiss, mother old-stock Protestant; HS grad.; joined 1949; left 1956; subsequent liberal Dem./socialist; earned BA, archivist. (See chapters 7, 9)

Darcy, Samuel Adams (1905–2005): b. Russia, Russian Jewish parentage; brought to U.S. as infant; HS grad.; high-level CP functionary from mid-1920s until expelled in 1945; subsequent liberal Dem. in Philadelphia. (See chapters 4–9)

Decker Gladstein, Caroline (1912–1992): b. Georgia, Russian Jewish parentage; HS grad.; joined YCL in teens; organized farmworkers in California, imprisoned for criminal syndicalism, left party 1939? (See chapters 3, 5)

Dennis, Eugene (Francis X. Waldron, Tim Ryan, 1905–1961): b. Seattle; Irish and Norwegian parentage; joined 1926; came to California, 1928; in Moscow, 1930–1935, 1937–1938; district organizer, Wisconsin; general secretary of CPUSA, 1945–1959; never left party. (See chapters 1, 2, 4–9)

Dennis, Peggy (Regina Karasick, 1909–1993): b. New York City; parents Russian Jewish; grew up Los Angeles; partner of Eugene Dennis after 1928; left party, 1976. (See chapters 1, 2, 5, 9)

Dolsen, James (1885–1988): b. SF, old-stock parentage, parents not religious; attended college and law school; CP functionary in California, China, Soviet Union, Pennsylvania; never left party. (See chapters 1, 5)

Eickman, Keith (1914–2006): b. Canada, Scots, and German/Protestant parentage; HS grad.; expelled c. 1952; subsequent liberal Dem., union officer. (See chapters 5–9)

George, Harrison (1888–1967): b. Kansas; old-stock parents; IWW member, imprisoned 1918; CP functionary, journalist; expelled 1948. (See chapters 2–7, 9)

Gizzi Ward, Angela (1910–1997): b. SF; parents Italian immigrants, nominal Catholics; UC-Berkeley grad.; joined 1936; union organizer; left 1957. (See chapters 5, 7–9)

Gladstein, Richard (1909–1981): b. New Haven, CT; parents Russian and Ukrainian Jewish; grad. UC-Berkeley, undergrad and law; attorney; party membership unclear. (See chapters 5, 6, 8, 9)

Gliksohn, Henry (1900–1973): b. SF, Russian Jewish parents; 8th grade education; active in CP mid-1920s, functionary in late 1920s–1935; warehouse worker; army in WWII. (See chapters 1–3, 6)

Goldblatt, Louis (1910–1983): b. Bronx, parents Lithuanian Jewish, educated at UCLA, UC-Berkeley; joined ca. 1930; union official; left CP ca. 1943; subsequently liberal Dem. (See chapters 4–6, 8)

Grossman, Aubrey (1911–1999): b. San Bernardino CA; parents Hungarian Jewish; grad. UCLA, UC-Berkeley law; attorney, CP functionary; subsequent lawyer for Native California tribes and other left causes. (See chapters 4–8)

Hama, Karl: See Yoneda, Karl

Jackson, Harry: See Gliksohn, Henry

Jenkins, David (1914–1993): b. New York City; parents Russian and Turkish Jewish; 8th grade education; joined late 1930s; came to SF ca. 1940; significant CP offices; director of CLS; left 1956; subsequent liberal Dem., political organizer, member of ILWU Local 10. (See chapters 6–9)

Karasick, Regina: See Dennis, Peggy

Lambert, Carl Rude (1896–1976): b. Michigan; parents Swedish immigrants; party functionary; left in 1958. (See chapters 5, 6, 8, 9)

Lapin, Adam (1914–1961): b. Chile; parents Russian Jewish; came to U.S. as child; HS grad., attended CCNY; joined ca. 1935; came to SF ca. 1940; assoc. editor of *PW*; left 1957; subsequent author. (See chapters 6–9)

Lapin, Eva: See Sonenshine, Eva

Leonard, Norman (1914–2006): b. New York City; parents Russian and Polish Jewish; grew up LA; grad. UCLA, Columbia Univ. MA and law; lawyer. (See chapters 8, 9)

Lerner Olsen, Tillie (1912–2007): b. Omaha; parents Russian Jewish; 11th grade education; joined 1930; left c. 1952; subsequent liberal Dem, attended SF State, author. (See chapters 5, 6, 8, 9)

Mitford, Jessica "Decca" (1917–1996): b. England; parents landed gentry; educated by private tutors; joined 1943–1944; local CP offices; left ca. 1957; subsequent author, 1960s radical. (See chapters 6, 7, 9)

Nitzberg, Leo (1919–1981): b. Canada; parents Russian Jewish; joined ca. 1931; Abraham Lincoln Battalion; ILWU Locals 6, 10, 34; expelled ca. 1952; subsequent liberal Dem. (See chapters 5–9)

O'Connor Yates, Oleta (1911–1964): b. SF; fourth-generation Irish Catholic; joined 1933; BA, MA UC-Berkeley; significant local CP offices, full-time functionary; left 1958. (See chapters 4–9)

Olsen, Jack (1911–1989): born Russia; parents Russian Jewish; joined ca. 1931; YCL functionary, ILWU Local 6 official; left c. 1952; subsequent liberal Dem., typographer, labor studies educator. (See chapters 5–9)

Orr, Paul (1904–1996): b. Kansas, parents old-stock; BA Stanford, MEd Columbia Teachers College; party activist, later high school teacher in Oregon; later party activity unclear.

Orr, Violet Balcomb (1904–1989): b. SF, parents old-stock, Methodist; BA Stanford, MEd Columbia Teachers College; party functionary; later grade school teacher, Oregon; later party activity unclear.

Pittman, John (1907–1993): b. Georgia; Black; MA; journalist; never left party. (See chapters 6, 7, 9)

Ray Healey, Dorothy (1914–2006): b. Denver, parents Hungarian Jewish; joined YCL ca. 1928; organizer and functionary; left 1973. (See chapters 1–6, 8, 9)

Resner, Herbert (1909–1995): b. Chicago, parents Russian Jewish; grad. UC-Berkeley law; attorney; expelled, 1950; subsequently practiced law in LA and SF. (See chapters 5, 6, 8)

Richmond, Al (1913–1987): b. England, parents Russian Jewish; came to U.S. as child; joined YCL age 15; came to SF 1937; longtime editor of *People's World*; member National Committee, 1957; left 1973. (See chapters 4–9)

Rosenblum, Dorothy: See Ray Healey, Dorothy

Schneiderman, Leah (1912–1998): born Poland; came to U.S., 1921; parents Polish Jewish; joined YCL age 13; Univ. Minn.; met Bill Schneiderman 1932, married in Moscow in mid-1930s; ILGWU organizer briefly; left party 1991.

Schneiderman, William "Bill" (1905–1985): b. Russia, parents Russian Jewish; came to U.S. as child; UCLA; joined YWL in 1922, WP ca. 1924–1925; party functionary, ca. 1930–1957, member of National Committee, 1934ff; never left party. (See chapters 1, 2, 4–9)

Sonenshine, Eva Lapin Maas (1919–2011): b. Ukraine; parents Russian Jewish; HS grad., 2 years CCNY; joined ca. 1937–1938; journalist; left 1956–1957; subsequent liberal Dem.; BA SF State, MA UCB; social worker. (See chapters 7–9)

Stack, Walter (1908–1995): b. Michigan; parents Polish Catholic immigrants; joined ca. 1930; marine fireman, union official; never left party. (See chapters 4–7, 9)

Starvus Stack, Loretta (1913–2001): b. Connecticut; parents Polish Catholic immigrants; 8th grade education; joined ca. 1930; Lenin School; organizer, functionary; Smith Act defendant; left 1958; subsequent liberal Dem. (See chapters 7–9)

Thompson, Ray (1905–?): b. SF, Black; joined ca. 1939; active in shipyard organizing, WWII; subsequent active in Berkeley Co-op. (See chapters 5, 6, 9)

Tobin, Pat (1921–1995): b. SF; father Irish Catholic; 8th grade education; joined ca. 1940; seaman; left ca. 1958; subsequent liberal Dem., peace activist, Local 10 official. (See chapters 5–7, 9)

Todd Lambert, Louise (1905–1997): b. SF, parents German immigrants, freethinkers; HS grad.; longtime local/state party functionary; Smith Act defendant; left 1958; subsequent liberal Dem. (See chapters 1–9)

Treuhaft, Robert "Bob" (1912–2001): b. NYC, parents Austrian Jewish; BA, LLB Harvard; lawyer; joined ca. 1943–1944; left ca. 1958; subsequent 1960s radical. (See chapters 6–9)

Waldron, Francis X.: See Dennis, Eugene

Ward, Estolv (1899–1993): b. LA, parents old-stock; grad. UCB; journalist, joined Newspaper Guild 1934, CP soon after; various CIO and CP positions; left ca. 1956–1957; subsequent liberal Dem., author. (See chapters 4, 5, 9)

Watson, Don (1929–2015): b. NYC; parents born Midwest; HS education; joined late 1940s; seaman, longshore worker; left 1956; subsequent liberal Dem., elected office in ILWU Local 34. (See chapters 7, 9)

Whitney, Anita (1867–1955): b. SF, parents old-stock Protestants; joined 1919; party candidate; never left party. (See chapters 1–6)

Yoneda, Karl (Goso Yoneda, Karl Hama, 1906–?): b. Glendale, CA; parents Japanese immigrants; HS grad.; journalist, longshoreman; never left party. (See chapters 5, 6, 9)

NOTES

Abbreviations

Chronicle	*San Francisco Chronicle*
CPA	Communist Party of America
CUAC	California Un-American Activities Committee, California State Archives, Sacramento
GARO	Gosudarstvenny arkhiv Rostovskoy oblasti (State Archive of the Rostov Region)
LARC	Labor Archives and Research Center, San Francisco State University
LAT	*Los Angeles Times*
LC	*Library of Congress*
News	[San Francisco] *News*
NYT	*New York Times*
PW	[San Francisco] *People's World, People's Daily World*
RGASPI	Rossiiskii gosudarstvennyi arkhiv sotsial'no-politicheskoi istorii (Russian State Archive for Social and Political History)
WW	[San Francisco] *Western Worker*

Preface

1. For Bridges, see my *Harry Bridges: Labor Radical, Labor Legend* (Urbana: University of Illinois Press, 2023), esp. chs. 8–10, 13, 14, and Vernon Pedersen, *The Communist Party*

on the American Waterfront: Revolution, Reform, and the Quest for Power* (Lanham, MD: Lexington Books, 2019). For Oppenheimer, see Gregg Herken, *Brotherhood of the Bomb: The Tangled Lives and Loyalties of Robert Oppenheimer, Ernest Lawrence, and Edward Teller* (New York: Henry Holt, 2002); Kai Bird and Martin J. Sherwin, *American Prometheus: The Triumph and Tragedy of J. Robert Oppenheimer* (New York: Alfred A. Knopf, 2005); Ray Monk, *Robert Oppenheimer: A Life Inside the Center* (New York: Doubleday, 2012).

2. Oral history interview with Angela Gizzi Ward by Sue Cobble, 1976, for the California Historical Society, 120.

3. For a somewhat similarly biographical approach to the history of the Communist Party, see Bettina Aptheker, *Communists in Closets: Queering the History, 1930s-1990s* (New York: Routledge, 2023), a work that became available only when this book was about to go into production.

4. Party Registration [mimeographed form]—1931, 515-1-2499 RGASPI.

5. See, e.g., Harvey Klehr, John Earl Haynes, and Fridrikh Igorevich Firsov, *The Secret World of American Communism* (New Haven, CT: Yale University Press, 1995); and Harvey Klehr, John Earl Haynes, and Kyrill M. Anderson, *The Soviet World of American Communism* (New Haven, CT: Yale University Press, 1998).

6. Herken, *Brotherhood of the Bomb*; Bird and Sherwin, *American Prometheus*; Monk, *Oppenheimer*; Steve Nelson, James R. Barrett, and Rob Ruck, *Steve Nelson, American Radical* (Pittsburgh: University of Pittsburgh Press, 1981), esp. ch. 8; Steve Nelson interviewed by Martin Sherwin, 1981, file 3, box 6, Sherwin Papers, Library of Congress.

7. Mark Naison, *Communists in Harlem during the Depression* (Urbana: University of Illinois Press, 1983); Robin D. G. Kelley, *Hammer and Hoe: Alabama Communists during the Great Depression* (Chapel Hill: University of North Carolina Press, 1990); Vernon L. Pedersen, *The Communist Party in Maryland, 1919–1957* (Urbana: University of Illinois Press, 2001); Randi Storch, *Red Chicago: American Communism at Its Grassroots, 1928–1935* (Urbana: University of Illinois Press, 2009); Gregory S. Taylor, *The History of the North Carolina Communist Party* (Columbia: University of South Carolina Press, 2009); Mary Stanton, *Red Black White: The Alabama Communist Party, 1930–1950* (Athens: University of Georgia Press, 2019); and Ryan S. Pettengill, *Communism and Community: Activism in Detroit's Labor Movement, 1941–1956* (Philadelphia: Temple University Press, 2020).

8. Some recent histories of the CP have centrally considered gender, notably Aptheker, *Communists in Closets*, and Kate Weigand, *Red Feminism: American Communism and the Making of Women's Liberation* (Baltimore: Johns Hopkins University Press, 2001). There are also some that have addressed gender in the California party: Lisa Jackson, "Twenty-Four-Hour Party People: A Gendered Social History of California Communism" (MA thesis, San Francisco State University, 2015); and Beth Slutsky, *Gendering Radicalism: Women and Communism in Twentieth-Century California* (Lincoln: University of Nebraska Press, 2015). Finally, there have been a few academic studies of California Communist women: Panthea Reid, *Tillie Olsen: One Woman, Many Riddles* (New Brunswick, NJ: Rutgers University Press, 2010); Lisa Rubens, "The Patrician Radical: Charlotte Anita Whitney," *California History* 65 (1986): 158–71, 226–27; and Rachel Schreiber, *Elaine Black Yoneda: Jewish Immigration, Labor Activism, and Japanese American Exclusion and Incarceration* (Philadelphia: Temple University Press, 2022).

Chapter 1. An Uncertain Beginning

1. Southern Pacific timetables for the 1920s are available online at https://wx4.org/to /foam/maps/and_timetables1.html/ (accessed Sept. 29, 2022). Given that a Ford Model-T had a maximum highway speed of 40–45 mph, and given the state of roads and the need to slow down through towns and to stop to eat and get gas, auto travel was likely slower than the train.

2. Ralph E. Shaffer, "Formation of the California Communist Labor Party, *Pacific Historical Review* 36 (1976): 59–78, esp. 59–68; "Communism in California, 1919–1924: 'Orders from Moscow' or Independent Western Radicalism," *Science & Society* 34 (1970): 412–29; "Robert Whitaker: 1919, A Crisis Year," *Southwest Economy & Society* 6 (1984): 14–27; Shaffer, "Formation," 59–68.

3. Shaffer, "Formation," 68–78; *San Francisco Chronicle* (hereafter, *Chronicle*), Nov. 15, 1919; Max Bedacht, *The Memoirs of Your Father* (bound, photocopied typed pages, no place, c. 1968), chs. 15 (the first ch. 15), 14 (follows the preceding), 15 (follows 14); James H. Dolsen, *Bucking the Ruling Class: Jim Dolsen's Story* (n.p.: n.p., 1984), 26. Dolsen was ninety-eight when he wrote his memoir.

4. *Chronicle*, Jan. 29, 1920; Dolsen, *Bucking the Ruling Class*, 26. The Jan. 29 article in the *Chronicle* notes that the German branch met at "Pivo Hall," 141 Albion Street, San Francisco; *pivo* in several Slavic languages means beer, so Pivo Hall was simply the beer hall. That address was the location of Equality Hall, 141–43 Albion Street, which, with 540a Valencia Street, made up the headquarters of the Workmen's Educational Association—the Arbeiter Bildungs Verein—a German working-class organization. For Dolsen's trials, see *Bucking the Ruling Class*, 38–43; Dolsen provided a longer account of his trials in an interview done under the direction of Paul Buhle, Oral History of the American Left, NYU Libraries, http:// digitaltamiment.hosting.nyu.edu/s/cpoh/item/3923/. For Bedacht, see his *Memoirs*, ch. 15 (second by that number). The Palmer Raids were directed by, and accordingly have been named for, Attorney General A. Mitchell Palmer.

5. Lisa Rubens, "The Patrician Radical: Charlotte Anita Whitney," *California History* 65 (1986): 158–71, 226–27; *Whitney v. California*, 274 U.S. 357 (1927); for other treatments of Whitney's life, see Al Richmond, *Native Daughter* (San Francisco: Anita Whitney 75th Anniversary Committee, 1942), and Beth Slutsky, *Gendering Radicalism: Women and Communism in Twentieth-Century California* (Lincoln: University of Nebraska Press, 2015), ch. 2.

6. *Whitney v. California*, 274 U.S. 357 (1927). The Whitney decision has attracted several legal scholars; see, e.g., Haig A. Bosmajian, *Anita Whitney, Louis Brandeis, and the First Amendment* (Madison, NJ: Fairleigh Dickinson University Press, 2010); and Philippa Strum, *Speaking Freely: Whitney v. California and American Speech Law* (Lawrence: University Press of Kansas, 2015).

7. Roger Lotchin, "John Francis Neylan: San Francisco Irish Progressive," in James P. Walsh, ed., *The San Francisco Irish* (San Francisco: Irish Literary and Historical Society, 1978), 87–112; Rubens, "Patrician Radical"; *Chronicle*, June 10, June 21, 1927; Shaffer, "Communism in California," 418; [San Francisco] *Rank and File*, July 22–Nov. 9, 1920, esp. July 22.

8. Louise Todd Lambert, interviewed by Lucy Kendall, May–August 1976, transcript at California Historical Society; hereafter, Louise Todd Lambert oral history.

9. Vivian McGuckin Raineri, *The Red Angel: The Life and Times of Elaine Black Yoneda, 1906–1988* (New York: International Publishers, 1991), chs. 1, 2. Raineri's book is based directly on interviews that Elaine Black Yoneda did with Lucy Kendall in 1976–1977; transcripts are at the California Historical Society. Rachel Schreiber, in *Elaine Black Yoneda: Jewish Immigration, Labor Activism, and Japanese American Exclusion and Incarceration* (Philadelphia: Temple University Press, 2022), refers to her as Elaine Rose (e.g., p. 22) but provides no citation. The 1915 New York State census, available through Ancestry.com, confirms that her first name was Rose. See also Schreiber's account of Elaine Black's early years, pp. 31–37.

10. Violet Orr oral history, interviews by Lucy Kendall, 1976, California Historical Society, https://californiarevealed.org/islandora/object/cavpp%3A14455/; Lisa Jackson, "Twenty-Four-Hour Party People: A Gendered Social History of California Communism," MA thesis, San Francisco State University, 2015, 25–27.

11. Peggy Dennis, *The Autobiography of an American Communist* (Westport, CT: Lawrence Hill, 1977), ch. 1; marriage information from Ancestry.com. Schneiderman, *Dissent on Trial*, has no mention of the marriage. Schneiderman filed for divorce on November 4, 1936, on the grounds of desertion, and the divorce was finalized on January 27, 1937; see report of William F. Giesen, Jan. 18, 1943, 97-26-89, p. 4, Schneiderman FBI file.

12. Dorothy Ray Healey and Maurice Isserman, *California Red: A Life in the American Communist Party* (Urbana: University of Illinois Press, 1993), chs. 1, 2.

13. Lillian Carlson, "A California Girlhood," in *Red Diapers: Growing Up in the Communist Left*, ed. Judy Kaplan and Linn Shapiro (Urbana: University of Illinois Press, 1998), 20–25.

14. Shaffer, "Communism in California," 418; *Chronicle*, Jan. 24, 1923; *Rank and File*, July 22, 1920; [San Francisco] *Labor Unity*, May 15, May 29, June 5, 1924.

15. For the Comintern decision, see Jacob A. Zumoff, *The Communist International and US Communism, 1919–1929* (2014; Chicago: Haymarket Books, 2015), 136–44; letter, Ruthenberg to W. J. McVey, April 2, 1924, 515-1-324, RGASPI. For the campaign in San Francisco, see *Labor Unity*, June 5–Nov. 13, 1924, esp. July 17, Aug. 28, Sept. 4, Oct. 23, Nov. 13; *Chronicle*, Sept. 27, 1924.

16. Letter, Schneiderman to Ruthenberg, May 7, 1925, 515-1-497, RGASPI. The *Los Angeles Times* did not report on the party candidates; see, e.g., May 6, 1925.

17. This treatment of the California Commune is drawn in part from Seth Bernstein and Robert Cherny, "Searching for the Soviet Dream: Prosperity and Disillusionment on the Soviet Seattle Agricultural Commune, 1922–1927," *Agricultural History* 88 (2014): 22–44; *Rank and File*, Dec. 1, 1920; March 9, 1921. The San Francisco commune, formed at about the same time in the same area, was not related to party activity but was instead formed by the San Francisco Molokan Church; it lasted only a brief time, and its disillusioned members returned to San Francisco.

18. *Labor Unity*, Aug. 14, 1924. Seth Bernstein researched the records of the California Commune in the State Archive of the Rostov Region (*Gosudarstvenny arkhiv Rostovskoy oblasti*; hereafter, GARO), esp. 2563-1-118 and 4340-1-333; translations are by Lara King. For requests to transfer membership from District 13 of the CPUSA to the California Commune, see, e.g., Dolsen to NO, March 11, 1925, 515-1-497 RGASPI. Other requests to move to the California Commune or elsewhere in Soviet Russia can be found in RGASPI 515-1-496, 497.

19. *Labor Unity*, March 6 and Aug. 14, 1924. Equivalent purchasing power here and throughout were calculated on the CPI Inflation Calculator website, https://data.bls.gov /cgi-bin/cpicalc.pl/.

20. *Labor Unity*, Aug. 14, 1924; Dolsen to Browder, March 12, 1925, RGASPI 515-1-497.

21. H. D. Greenberg, letter to the editor, *Daily Worker*, Feb. 20, 1926; Reports on the California Commune are in 1485-1-488-208 GARO. For sale of the commune's assets; see 2563-1-118 GARO. On the Pioneer Commune, see 2563-1-143-8 GARO.

22. Allen Nelson, *The Nelson Brothers: Finnish-American Radicals from the Mendocino Coast* (Willits, CA: Mendocino County Museum and Immigration Research History Center (IRHC), University of Minnesota, 2005), chs. 2, 8–14; Enoch Nelson to Arvid Nelson, July 9, 1924, folder 9, box 5, Nelson Letters, IRHC, University of Minnesota. See also Bernstein and Cherny, "Searching for the Soviet Dream"; and Cherny and Bernstein, *Seattle/Seiatel'*— *"The American Commune" in the Soviet Union, 1922–1939*, http://depts.washington.edu /labhist/strike/seattle_commune.shtml/. Under Stalin's direction, the NKVD (*Narodnyy komissariat vnutrennikh del*, People's Commissariat for Internal Affairs) began in 1934 to arrest, try, and execute or imprison Soviet party leaders who opposed Stalin, but the target groups rapidly expanded. In 1937 and 1938, the NKVD arrested almost 1.7 million people for "counter-revolutionary crimes" or "anti-Soviet agitation," executed 681,682 of them, and sent 634,820 to prison camps. J. Arch Getty and Oleg V. Naumov describe this horrific phase of the Terror as "simply a mass killing with numerical quotas of vaguely specified opponents" and as "a sign of failure to rule with anything but force." In Karelia the large numbers of Finnish Americans were a special target. See J. Arch Getty and Oleg V. Naumov, *The Road to Terror: Stalin and the Self-Destruction of the Bolsheviks, 1932–1939* (New Haven, CT: Yale University Press, 1999), esp. 480–81. There have been several subsequent works on the Great Terror, based, like Getty and Naumov's work, on archival research in Soviet documents.

23. Shaffer, "Communism in California," 425–26. There is almost no correspondence to or from California in RGASPI for 1921–1924, unlike the significant volume of correspondence during 1923–1924 for District 12 (Washington and Oregon); see 515-1-187, 230, 324, 325, 326, 327, 349, 384.

24. See correspondence in 515-1-230, 327; *Labor Unity*, Dec. 11, 1924, and also notices of social events in nearly every issue.

25. *Rank and File*, May 1, 1920, through Feb. 16, 1922, esp. Feb. 5, July 27, Sept. 29, Nov. 24, 1921. The last extant issue of *Rank and File* is that of February 16, 1922, although the paper seems to have survived another year. The paper was owned by a long list of left organizations.

26. *Labor Unity*, May 17, 1923, through May 14, 1925, esp. Oct. 11, 1923.

27. Letter, Dolsen to Workers Party of America, Sept. 12, 1924, 515-1-327 RGASPI; *Rank and File* and *Labor Unity* are filled with notices for such events; for examples, see *Rank and File*, Oct. 20, 1920; Aug. 17, 1921; March 13, 1924; Aug. 17, 1924.

28. *Labor Unity*, Sept 11, 1924; summary of branch reports, March 1924, 515-385; letters, Charles [illegible], Eureka English Branch, to WPA hq, April 24, 1925; Tom Lewis to National Office, May 8, 1925; Lewis to Ruthenberg, May 22, 1925; James H. Dolsen to Earl Browder, March 4, 1925, 515-1-497, RGASPI.

29. Letter, Levin to CEC of WPA, undated, 515-1-497 RGASPI. On Levin, see unidentified clippings, both April 24, 1956, file 54, carton 23, People's World Research Files Collection, Labor Archives and Research Center; hereafter, LARC.

30. Letters, Acting Secretary to Dolsen, March 25, 1925, March 28, 1925; General Secretary [Ruthenberg] to Levin, Dec, 7, 1925; all 515-1-496; Dolsen to Earl Browder, March 4, 1925; Lewis to Browder, April 20, 1925; Lewis to Ruthenberg, May 22, 1925; Lewis to Ruthenberg, Nov 2, 1925, Dec. 21, 1925, 515-1-497; Minutes of DEC, March 4, 1925; May 20, 1925; 515-1-559; all RGASPI.

31. Letter, Schneiderman to Ruthenberg, Nov. 28, 1925; General Secretary [Ruthenberg] to Schneiderman, Dec. 7, 1925, 515-1-496; Levin to Ruthenberg, Dec. 14, 1925; Lewis to Ruthenberg, Dec. 21, 1925; Lewis to CEC, Dec. 24, 1925; all 515-1-497, RGASPI; Dolsen, *Bucking the Ruling Class*, 47.

32. Letters, Lewis to Lovestone, Feb. 6; Lovestone to Lewis, Feb. 9, 1926, 515-1-760 RGASPI.

33. Kathleen A. Brown, "Ella Reeve Bloor: Suffragist, Trade-Unionist, Socialist, and Revolutionary in the Making, 1862–1919," MA thesis, San Francisco State University, 1987; and "Ella Reeve Bloor: The Politics of the Personal in the American Communist Party" (PhD dissertation, University of Washington, 1996).

34. *Labor Unity*, Nov. 13, 20, 27, 1924; letters, Lewis to Browder, April 20, 1925; Levin to CEC of WPA, undated, both 515-1-497; Minutes of DEC, Dist. 13, March 4, 1925; Minutes of DEC, Dist. 13, March 19, 1925, both 515-1-559 RGASPI.

35. William Schneiderman, *Dissent on Trial: The Story of a Political Life* (Minneapolis: MEP Publications, 1983), 15–18. Schneiderman's FBI file seems to begin in 1940, although it is clear that he was under surveillance by the Los Angeles field office much earlier and by the San Francisco field office beginning in 1936. In May 1941 a lengthy report summarized information acquired from the Los Angeles field office, the Los Angeles Police Department, and the Immigration and Naturalization Service (INS). That report cites the INS that Schneiderman was born in 1895. Pages 4–5 of the report contain a year-by-year account of his CP activities from 1925 to 1935. See report of R. C. Taylor, May 29, 1941, 97-26-27, Schneiderman FBI file.

36. Report of [name redacted], May 28, 1925, file 100-3-25-67, FBI Los Angeles Field Office files on Communist Party of America (hereafter, LA FBI CPA files), esp. pp. 100–106 (top center numbers) or 44–50 (upper right numbers).

37. Report of [name redacted], May 28, 1925, file 100-3-25-67, LA FBI CPA files pp. 90–91 (upper right).

38. Report of [name redacted], May 28, 1925, file 100-3-25-67, LA FBI CPA files, pp. 107–114 (center), 51–58 (upper right); *Labor Unity*, March 13, 1924.

39. Typed reports on Communist activities following report of [name redacted], Nov. 7, 1925, file 100-3-25-68, LA FBI CPA files; *Labor Unity*, May 1, 1924.

40. Report of [name redacted], June 8, 1922, file 100-3-25-11; report of [name redacted], March 14, 1923, file 100-3-25-33, LA FBI CPA files. The Technical Aid Society assisted the Soviet Union with funds, technical advice, and support for the creation of communes by Americans in Soviet Union.

41. Minutes of Bay District City Central Committee, March 9, 1925, 515-1-559 RGASPI; *Labor Unity*, Feb. 26–April 16, 1925.

42. Minutes of DEC, Dec. 25, 1927, 515-1-1169 RGASPI; article for *Daily Worker* on Ruthenberg memorial held March 18, 1927, 515-1-1171; Minutes of DEC, April 25, 1928, 515-1-1435, RGASPI.

43. Letters, James H. Dolsen to Ruthenberg, Jan. 8, 1925; Lewis to Ruthenberg, June 17, 1925, Schneiderman to Ruthenberg, July 25, 1925, all 515-1-497; Ex Secy to James H. Dolsen, May 8, 1925, Executive Secretary to Tom Lewis, June 22, 1925, 515-1-496 RGASPI.

44. Dolsen, *Bucking the Ruling Class*, 44–55.

45. Letters, Levin to Ruthenberg, Feb. 17; Ruthenberg to Lewis, Feb. 23; Levin to Ruthenberg, March 1; Levin to Lovestone, April 26, 1927, all 515-1-1443 RGASPI; article for *Daily Worker* on Ruthenberg memorial held March 18, 1927, 515-1-1171 RGASPI.

46. Letters, Ruthenberg to Dolsen, San Francisco, Jan 8, 1924, 515-1-327; Dolsen to Ruthenberg, Jan. 8, 1925; Dolsen to Browder, March 12, 1925, both 515-1-497; Ex Secy to Dolsen, May 8, 1925, 515-1-496; article for *Daily Worker* on Ruthenberg memorial held March 18, 1927, 515-1-1171 RGASPI.

47. *Labor Unity*, March 13, 27, 1924.

48. Jacob A. Zumoff, *The Communist International and US Communism, 1919–1929* (2014; Chicago: Haymarket Books, 2015), 65–67.

49. Zumoff, *Comintern and US Communism*, 172–83.

50. Minutes of Bay District City Central Committee, March 9, 1925, 515-1-559; letters, Lewis to Lovestone, Jan. 28, 1926; ORG DEPT (AB) to Levin, March 25, 1926; ORG DEPT to Levin, June 21, 1926; ORG DEPT to Levin, July 15, 1926, all 515-1-760 RGASPI; *The Party Organizer* 1 (April 1927, Dec. 1927).

51. Summary of branch reports by District, March 1924, 515-1-385; Minutes of the (Los Angeles) Sub-District Exec Com, Aug. 2, 1926; Minutes of Sub-District Exec Com, Nov. 16, 1926, both 515-1-890; Minutes of DEC, June 15, 1927; Minutes of DEC, Oct. 18,1927, Dec. 28, 1927, 515-1-1169; letter, Levin to Lovestone, June 11, 1926, 515-1-760, RGASPI.

52. District Questionnaire, National Organization Dept., District Number 13, handwritten date 1928, 515-1-1438 RGASPI.

53. Minutes of the National Secretariat for America and Canada, April 14 [1926], April 21, 1926, 495-72-11; unsigned, undated Suggestions for 1926 Political Campaign for California, 515-1-889, both RGASPI. I date the "Suggestions" as likely from April because of Levin's letter on May 2, cited in the next note, responding to the "Suggestions."

54. Shaffer, "Communism in California," 418; letter, Levin to Comrade Lovestone, May 2, 1926, 515-1-760 RGASPI. The various biographies of Whitney say nothing about any political activity in 1926, and the only newspaper references that year are to her ongoing appeals from her conviction.

55. Minutes of DEC Dist. 13, July 7, 1926; copy of letter, District 13 DEC to SP, July 21, 1926, 515-1-889 RGASPI.

56. Undated copy of letter, Cameron King and Lana Lorrow Lewis to Levin, both 515-1-889 RGASPI.

57. The Upton Sinclair Papers at Indiana University shed no light on the exchange between the state SPA and CP. For examples of his refusal to speak until he completed his novel, see Sinclair to Sam Weisenberg, Oct. 28; R. W. Anderson to Sinclair, Nov. 5, 1926, box 7, Sinclair Papers.

58. *Chronicle*, Nov. 10, 1927; District Questionnaire, District 13, 1928, 515-1-1438, RGASPI.

59. Letter, Dick Ettlinger et al. to Political Committee, Jan. 30, 1928, 515-1-1438 RGASPI.

60. Report District Executive Committee (submitted by E. Lewin, D.O.), Jan. 9, 1928, 515-1-1438 RGASPI.

61. Minutes of meeting of Anglo-American Secretariat, Jan. 14,19, 25, 1928, 495-72-32; Minutes of DEC, Jan. 12, 1928, 515-1-1435 RGASPI. There is nothing in the Sinclair Papers, box 9, to suggest that there was any contact from District 13.

62. Memorandum Concerning the Failure of District 13 to Place the Presidential Candidates of Our Party on the Ballot in the Present Election, unsigned, undated; letter, Jackson to Wolfe, Oct. 26, 1928, both 515-1-1438 RGASPI. Slutsky's treatment of Whitney (p. 59) notes that the party nominated her to run for the Senate but ignores the reality that she never appeared on the ballot.

63. Report on California, undated, unsigned, 515-1-1438 RGASPI.

64. Report on California, undated, unsigned, 515-1-1438 RGASPI; *Statement of Vote at General Election held on November 6, 1928* (Sacramento: California State Printing Office, 1928).

65. Unsigned Report on California, 515-1-1438 RGASPI.

66. Unsigned Report on California, 515-1-1438 RGASPI.

67. Unsigned Report on California, 515-1-1438 RGASPI.

68. Files of American Commission meetings, April 13 and 21, 1929, 495-72-62, 64 RGASPI; unidentified clipping about Levin, May 4, 1956, file 54, carton 23, People's World Research Files Collection, LARC.

Chapter 2. "Unceasing Factional Struggle"

1. See, e.g., Jacob A. Zumoff, *The Communist International and US Communism, 1919–1929* (Leiden: Brill Academic Publishers, 2014); Harvey Klehr and John Earl Haynes, *The American Communist Movement: Storming Heaven Itself* (New York: Twayne, 1992), ch. 1; Edward P. Johanningsmeier, *Forging American Communism: The Life of William Z. Foster* (Princeton, NJ: Princeton University Press, 1994), chs. 7. 8.

2. Letters, General Secretary (Ruthenberg) to Lewis, Sept. 12, 1925, 515-1-496; I. Bernhard, San Francisco, to Ruthenberg, undated, 515-1-497; Minutes of the City Committee of the Workers (Communist) Party, Local Los Angeles, Jan. 10, 1926; Proceedings of Special Sub-District Convention of District #13, held May 16, 1926; letter, Manya Airoff to the special convention, May 15, 1926; Minutes of the Sub-District Exec Com, June 6, 1926; Minutes of the Sub-District Exec Com, Aug. 31, 1926, 515-1-890, RGASPI.

3. Letter, Dick Ettlinger to Lovestone, undated, but see also Ettlinger to Bedacht, Aug. 14 [1927], both 515-1-1044; see also, e.g., Minutes of meeting of Anglo-American Secretariat, Jan. 10, 1928, Jan. 14, 1928, 495-72-32 RGASPI. The files of the AAS are filled with these factional denunciations; see 495-37-5 through 12, covering the years from 1925 through 1928. See, esp., the session of the American Commission of June 28, 1927, 495-37-13 for the specific instructions about the 1927 convention.

4. Letter of resignation from DEC, from Fred Harris to Emanuel Levin, Oct. 21, 1927, 515-1-1169; Minutes of DEC, Jan. 25, 1928, 515-1-1435, RGASPI.

5. Copy of letter, Levin to Whitney et al., Jan. 10, 1929, both 515-1-1654 RGASPI.

6. Report, R. C. Taylor, May 29, 1941, 96-26-27, p. 7, Schneiderman FBI file; telegram, Lovestone to J. J. Ballam, Jan. 10, 1929. Polcom was the National Executive Committee, later called the Political Bureau, or PolBuro.

7. Frank Farrell, *International Socialism and Australian Labor: The Left in Australia, 1919–1939* (Sydney: Hale and Iremonger, 1981), 126–43, 188–97. A briefer treatment may be found in Robin Gollan, *Revolutionaries and Reformists: Communism and the Australian Labor Movement, 1920–1955* (Sydney: George Allen & Unwin, 1975), 15–18.

8. James G. Ryan, *Earl Browder: The Failure of American Communism* (Tuscaloosa: University of Alabama Press, 1997), 31–34, 137–38; Harvey Klehr, John Earl Haynes, and Fridrikh Igorevich Firsov, *The Secret World of American Communism* (New Haven, CT: Yale University Press, 1995), 49–53. On the PPTUS and George, see Vernon L. Pedersen, "Underfunded, Understaffed, and Underground: The History of the San Francisco Bureau of the Pan-Pacific Trade Union Secretariat," *Continuity: A Journal of History* 26 (Spring 2003): 1–20; and Josephine Fowler, "From East to West and West to East: Ties of Solidarity in the Pan-Pacific Revolutionary Trade Union Movement, 1923–1934," *International Labor and Working-Class History* 66 (Fall 2004): 99–117. PPTUS activities are treated in *The Pan-Pacific Worker*, vols. 1–4 (1928–1931), which can be found in the Mitchell Library, State Library of New South Wales, Sydney; the same with the first number of volume 5 is in the State Library of Victoria, Melbourne, and at the University of Melbourne library. See, esp., Harrison George, "The Philippine Islands," [Sydney] *Pan-Pacific Worker* 2 (Aug. 1, 1929): 10–12; "The Struggle in Australia," *Pan-Pacific Worker* 3 (May 1, 1930): 137–39. Regarding "underground" work, see Karl G. Yoneda, *Ganbatte: Sixty-Year Struggle of a Kibei Worker* (Los Angeles: Asian American Studies Center, UCLA, 1983), 90–94.

9. *Hearing before the Committee on Un-American Activities, House of Representatives, 83d Congress, First Session, December 5, 1953*, 3422–27; Yoneda, *Ganbatte*, 90–92.

10. Wolfe, in Minutes of the American Commission, April 21, 29, 495-72-64; Minutes, Anglo-American Secretariat, Jan. 5, 1928, 495-72-32 RGASPI; Al Richmond, *A Long View from the Left: Memoirs of an American Revolutionary* (New York: Dell, 1972), 276–77.

11. Sam Darcy interview by Cherny, Aug. 19, 1996; Holger Weiss, ed., *International Communism and Transnational Solidarity: Radical Networks, Mass Movements and Global Politics, 1919–1939* (Leiden: Brill, 2017), 296, citing report from Albert Walter to "Werte Genossen," February 12, 1932, 534-5-231 RGASPI. Regarding the effectiveness of the PPTUS, see also Pedersen, "Underfunded, Understaffed"; Fowler, "From East to West."

12. As quoted by Gardos in letter, Gardos to Minor, April 15, 1929, 515-1-1654 RGASPI.

13. These events can be traced through the telegrams and letters in 515-1-1654 RGASPI, esp. telegrams, Ben [Gitlow] to John Ballam, Jan. 13; Ballam to Gitlow, Jan. 13; Spector and Levin to National Conventions Arrangements Committee, Jan. 15; Brooks et al. to Lovestone, Jan. 15, 1929; Ballam to Gitlow, Jan. 21; Gitlow to Ballam, Jan. 21 (two telegrams of that date); Lovestone to Ballam, Jan. 26, all 1929.

14. Telegram, Lovestone to Ballam, Feb. 8; letters, M. Martin to Lovestone, Feb. 16; Feinstein to Gitlow, March 26, all 1929, 515-1-1654 RGASPI. Bloor quoted in Theodore Draper, *American Communism and Soviet Russia: The Formative Period* (1960; New York: Vintage Books, 1986), 384–85.

15. Zumoff, *Comintern and US Communism*, 266–71; Draper, *American Communism and Soviet Russia*, 394–404. The Comintern's open letter and related materials were published by the U.S. party in mid-1929 as a small booklet with the title *On the Road to Bolshevization*, https://www.marxists.org/history/usa/parties/cpusa/anti-trotsky/On%20the%20Road%20to%20Bolshevization-038.pdf/. Agitprop, or agitation and propaganda, involved both organization and publicity.

16. Files of American Commission meetings, April 9, 1929—April 24, 1929, 495-72-59, 61, 64 RGASPI.

17. Zumoff, *Comintern and US Communism*, 266–84; Draper, *American Communism and Soviet Russia*, 399–429; copy of cablegram from Communist International (CI), Moscow, June 22, 1929, to Communist Party of America; Statement of the Central Committee of the Expulsion of Jay Lovestone from the Communist Party of the United States of America, both in 495-72-59 RGASPI. Stalin's speeches are available at https://www.marxists.org/history/usa/parties/cpusa/1931/nomonth/0000-stalin-onamericanparty.pdf/.

18. *New York Times*, July 5, 1929, 1, 7.

19. Minutes of District 13 DEC, March 4, 1925; March 19, 1925, 515-1-559; June 23, 1926, 515-1-889; Minutes of District 13 DEC, May 9, 1928, 515-1-1435 RGASPI; Darcy interview, Aug. 19, 1996.

20. Letters, Levin to Lovestone, June 11, 1926, 515-1-760; from Frank Spector, April 6, 1926, 515-1-890; Proceedings of Special Sub-District Convention of District #13, held May 16, 1926; Minutes of SDEC, May 29, Sept. 29, 1928, 515-1-1439 RGASPI; Frank Spector interview by George Ewart, 1972, Bancroft Library, https://californiarevealed.org/islandora/object/cavpp%3A11611/; further biographical information from Ancestry.com.

21. Peggy Dennis, *The Autobiography of an American Communist: A Personal View of a Political Life, 1925–1975* (Westport, CT: Lawrence Hill, 1977), 13–14; 1910 and 1920 census information from Ancestry.com; other information from "elfinn" through Ancestry.com.

22. Ancestry.com cannot find Morris Rappaport until the 1950s, by which time he was living in Petaluma. Ancestry.com searches find the 1930 census listing for Rappaport's sister, Mildred, married to Sol Nitzberg, a chicken farmer in Petaluma; Rappaport's parents, Benjamin and Bella, lived with them.

23. Letter, Feinstein to Gitlow, March 26, 1929; telegram, Gottfried to Gitlow Stachel, March 30, 1929, both 515-1-1654 RGASPI.

24. Letter, Gardos to Minor, April 9, 1929, 515-1-1654 RGASPI. For Gardos, see *NYT*, March 3, 1934.

25. Letter, Gardos to Minor, April 9, 1929, 515-1-1654 RGASPI.

26. Ryan, *Browder*, 37; handwritten text for telegram, Browder to Gliksohn, April 13, 1929, and following note, 515-1-1654 RGASPI.

27. Letter, Gardos to Minor, May 7, 1929; Gardos to Secretariat, June 14, 1929, both 515-1-1654 RGASPI.

28. Letters, Gardos to Minor, May 15, 1929; copy, Gardos to Waldron, May 15, 1929; Gardos to Shaap, May 15, 1929; Panagopoulas and Waldron, signed by Waldron, to CPUSA and DEC, May 13, 1929, all 515-1-1654 RGASPI.

29. Letter, Gardos to Secretariat, June 14, 1929, 515-1-1654.

30. Letter, Gardo to General Executive Committee, Oct. 4, 1929, 515-1-1654 RGASPI.

31. Ibid.

32. Letter, Gardos to Jakira, Nov. 1, 1929, 515-1-1654 RGASPI.

33. *Chronicle*, Oct. 6, Nov. 6, Nov. 21, 1929; Louise Todd Lambert oral history, interviews by Lucy Kendall, interviews of May 13 and 27, 1976, California Historical Society, tape 2.

34. Letter, Gardos to Jakira, Nov. 1, 1929, 515-1-1654 RGASPI.

35. For overviews of the Comintern and the CPUSA during the time of the Third Period line, see Zumoff, *Communist International and US Communism*, ch. 12; Kevin McDermott and Jeremy Agnew, *The Comintern: A History of International Communism from Lenin to Stalin* (New York: St. Martin's Press, 1997), ch. 3. For contemporary explanations of the Third Period by U.S. party leaders, see, e.g., William Z. Foster, "The Trade Union Line of Lovestone and Cannon-Muste Auxiliaries," *The Communist* 9 (Oct. 1930): 884–99, or Earl Browder, "How We Must Fight against the Demagogy of Fascists and Social Fascists," *The Communist* 10 (April 1931): 300–304.

36. "The 10th Plenum of the E.C.C.I.," *The Communist* 8 (Nov. 1929): 565, 566. Harvey Klehr and John Earl Haynes, in *The American Communist Movement: Storming Heaven Itself* (New York: Twain, 1992), 60, state, "In late 1929 for the first time the Communist party began to plan political demonstrations designed to lead to clashes with the police." What is abundantly clear is that the party was staging many more demonstrations and sometimes—or often—not seeking official approval for taking to the streets, a clear invitation to police confrontations.

37. *Chronicle*, March 1, 1930.

38. District Organizer (unidentified, likely Simons) to Bedacht, Dec. 16, 1929, 515-1-1654 RGASPI. On the change in names of various committees in early 1930, see *Party Organizer* 3 (Feb. 1930): 15–16.

39. Dennis, *Autobiography*, 39–40. Brown, "Bloor," 95; Schneiderman, *Dissent on Trial*, 29–47; Leah Schneiderman interview by Robert Cherny, April 26, 1993. Klehr et al., *Secret World*, 56, assume Waldron was being trained for underground work. I think it's more likely that Waldron's removal from Los Angeles was part of the shuffling of factional leaders that began in mid-1929. In Minnesota, one of Schneiderman's protégés, head of the Young Communist League (YCL), was Arvo Kustaa Halberg, son of Finnish immigrants, who took the name Gus Hall.

40. Harvey Klehr, *The Heyday of American Communism: The Depression Decade* (New York: Basic Books, 1984), 31–34, 50; *NYT*, March 7, 1930; *LAT*, March 6, 1930; *Washington Post*, March 7, 1930; *Chronicle*, March 7, 1930.

41. *Chronicle*, March 7, 1930.

42. *Chronicle*, March 7, 1930.

43. Louise Todd Lambert oral history, interview of May 27, 1975.

44. *LAT*, Feb. 5, 1930; Feb. 27, March 7, 1930; *NYT*, Feb. 27, 1930.

45. Lillian Dinkin Carlson, "California Girlhood," 25.

46. *LAT*, March 7, 1930.

47. *Chronicle*, March 25, 1930.

48. C. A. Hathaway, "May First 1930," *The Communist* 9 (May 1930): 400–401; Moissaye J. Olgin, "From March Sixth to May First," *The Communist* 9 (May 1930): 417.

49. *Chronicle*, May 2, 1930; *LAT*, May 2, 1930.

50. Cletus E. Daniel, *Bitter Harvest: A History of California Farmworkers, 1870–1941* (Berkeley: University of California Press, 1981), 111–16.

51. Daniel, *Bitter Harvest*, 118–24.

52. Spector interview by Ewart, 1972.

53. Dennis, *Autobiography*, 44–58; Dorothy Ray Healey and Maurice Isserman, *California Red: A Life in the American Communist Party* (Urbana: University of Illinois Press, 1991), 30; Pedersen, "Underfunded," 5.

54. See the correspondence in 515-1-1994 RGASPI, esp. secretariat to Simons, Sept. 9, 1930; Morris Raport to Browder, Nov. 30, 1930; and N. H. Allen to CPUSA, Dec. 2, 1930.

55. Yuri Slezkine, *The House of Government: A Saga of the Russian Revolution* (Princeton, NJ: Princeton University Press, 2017), 109–118, esp. 115.

56. Report of [name redacted], March 28, 1925, file 100-3-25-67, FBI Los Angeles Field Office files on Communist Party of America, pp. 90–91 (upper right).

57. Dennis, *Autobiography*, 21, 26; see also similar comments in Healey and Isserman, *California Red*, 25; Dinkin Carlson, "California Girlhood," 23.

58. Stalin, speaking during the American Commission session of May 14, 1929, https://www.marxists.org/reference/archive/stalin/works/1929/cpusa.htm/.

Chapter 3. Prelude to the Popular Front

1. Caroline Decker Gladstein oral history, interview by Sue Cobble, 1976, California Historical Society, 70; letter, "Fisher" [Harrison George] to "E" [Browder], May 26 [1934], 515-1-3613, RGASPI.

2. Interview of Sam Darcy by Richard Wormser, 1981, Oral History of the American Left, box 14, Darcy 1–3, Tamiment Library/Robert F. Wagner Labor Archives, New York University, hereafter, Darcy interview by Wormser. Darcy drafted and redrafted an autobiography that was never published; the various drafts are part of the Sam Adams Darcy Papers, Tamiment Library and Robert F. Wagner Labor Archives, New York University; hereafter, Darcy Papers. Because Darcy extensively rewrote his memoirs, I have tried to cite the version that is most legible and most recent. Darcy's arrival in San Francisco in 1929 is from Ancestry.com.

3. Darcy interview by Wormser; Darcy, taped presentation at State University of New York at Albany, early 1990s, Oral History of the American Left, box 14, Darcy 1–3, Tamiment Library/Robert F. Wagner Labor Archives, New York University, hereafter, Darcy, Albany. See also Klehr, *Heyday of American Communism*, 26, 32, 33; Ryan, *Earl Browder*, 47.

4. Darcy, draft of history of the CP in California, box 2, folder 51, Darcy Papers.

5. Party Registration [mimeographed form]—1931, 515-1-2499 RGASPI. The Bay Area included 70 party members in San Francisco; 62 across the bay in Oakland; 20 in Mountain View, a small town south of San Francisco; 10 in San Jose; and 9 in Petaluma, a small town north of San Francisco (of which, see the next chapter). In Southern California, in addition to the 189 members in Los Angeles, there were 9 in San Diego. The 42 members in the Central Valley were scattered over 175 miles: 27 in Sacramento, 10 in Stockton, 5 in Fresno. Fort Bragg, 165 miles north of San Francisco, a four-hour drive, had 10 members.

6. Letter, sd [Darcy] to Jack Stachel, June 4, 1931, 515-1-2499 RGASPI. Darcy expanded on this account at considerable length in his unpublished memoirs; see folder 33, box 3,

Darcy Papers. See also the record of photo AAK-1147, the Salvation Army's woodyard, San Francisco Public Library History Center photo collection.

7. Paul Webbink, "Unemployment in the United States, 1930–1940," Papers and Proceedings of the American Economic Association 30 (1941): 250–51; Emily H. Huntington, Unemployment Relief and the Unemployed in the San Francisco Bay Region: 1929–1934 (Berkeley: University of California Press, 1939), esp. 7, 9, 34; William H. Mullins, *The Depression and the Urban West Coast, 1929–1933: Los Angeles, San Francisco, Seattle, and Portland* (Bloomington: Indiana University Press, 1991), 36–38, 73–75, 102–104, and esp. 92, 52.

8. During the first few years of Darcy's tenure as DO, party headquarters moved three times: first to 1164 Market Street, near city hall, then to 36 Grove, also near City Hall, and finally to 121 Haight, near San Francisco State College, the former home of the Young Men's and Young Women's Hebrew Association. These moves can be tracked through city directories; Darcy was the first DO to list the party headquarters in the city directory.

9. Louise Todd Lambert oral history, tape 2; District 13 had an average of 468 dues-paying members in Oct. and Nov. 1931, signed up 599 new members in Dec. through May 14, 1932, but averaged only 808 dues-paying members for April 1–May 14, 1932, i.e., a turnover of 24 percent over six months, as compared to the national turnover rate of 35 percent. See District 13 membership data, 515-1-2723 RGASPI. In his unpublished memoirs, Darcy states that there were only 285 dues-paying members when he arrived in district in late 1930; see box 2, file 52, Darcy papers, New York University (NYU).

10. *Chronicle*, Jan. 7, 8, 1931.

11. *Chronicle*, Jan. 20, 1931.

12. Louise Todd Lambert oral history, tape 2.

13. *Chronicle*, Jan. 19, Feb. 2, Feb. 11, 19, 26, 1931.

14. *Chronicle*, May 2, Oct. 18, 1931.

15. "Directives of the Politsecretariat of the ECCI to the Communist Party of the USA relative to the decisions of the Twelfth Plenum of the CPUSA," *The Communist* 10 (May 1931): 402–404. See also Earl Browder, "'Fewer High-Falutin' Phrases, More Simple Every-Day Deeds,'—Lenin: Report of the Political Committee to the Twelfth Central Committee Plenum, CPUSA, November 22, 1930," *The Communist* 10 (Jan. 1931): 31.

16. "Resolution on Work among the Unemployed," *The Communist* 10 (Oct. 1931): 838.

17. The typed testimony of unemployed men and women is in file 25, box 2, Darcy Papers, Tamiment Library, NYU.

18. On the CP's efforts to organize farmworkers at this time, see, esp., Cletus E. Daniel, *Bitter Harvest: A History of California Farmworkers, 1970–1941* (Berkeley: University of California Press, 1981), chs. 4–6; Devra Weber, *Dark Sweat, White Gold: California Farm Workers, Cotton, and the New Deal* (Berkeley: University of California Press, 1994), chs. 3, 4. Daniel interviewed Darcy and had a chance to review his unpublished memoirs, now at NYU. See also Carey McWilliams, *Factories in the Field: The Story of Migratory Farm Labor in California* (1939; University of California Press, 1999), chs. 13, 14; Dick Meister and Anne Loftis, *A Long Time Coming: The Struggle to Unionize America's Farm Workers* (New York: Macmillan, 1977), ch. 2. The following summary of events draws largely on Daniel and Weber. George Ewart, a student of mine in the early 1970s, interviewed a number of the

CP participants and made those interviews available through the Bancroft Library, https://californiarevealed.org/islandora/object/cavpp%3A11611/.

19. Letter, Darcy to Browder, Jan. 14, 1930 (clearly an error, as Darcy did not arrive in California until late in 1930), 515-1-1930 RGASPI. Regarding Brown, see *Chronicle*, Oct. 18, 1931, 47; biographical material, Archie Brown Collection, box 1, folder 2, LARC.

20. Daniel, *Bitter Harvest*, 127–30; Caroline Decker Gladstein oral history, 70–71.

21. *Chronicle*, Sept. 30, Oct. 23, Nov. 20, 1931; Darcy, Albany; Louise Todd Lambert oral history, tape 2.

22. *Western Worker*, hereafter *WW*, Jan. 1, 1932.

23. The official tally published by the secretary of state does not record the vote for Foster. The data cited is from Join California, http://www.joincalifornia.com/.

24. *WW*, Nov. 6, 1933; *Chronicle*, Nov. 9, 1933.

25. The Darcy Papers include four charts that track such data between early 1931 and early 1934, file 7, box 1, Darcy Papers.

26. "The Roosevelt Program—An Attack upon the Toiling Masses," *The Communist* 12 (May 1933): 419–25, esp. 419, 425.

27. Daniel, *Bitter Harvest*, ch. 5; Weber, *Dark Sweat, White Gold*, ch. 3; McWilliams, *Factories in the Field*, ch. 13. Darcy wrote of the agricultural strikes of 1933 in his various unpublished autobiographical works; the final version seems to be ch. 5 of "Tales of Three Worlds," written in the early 1960s; box 3, file 15A, Darcy Papers, NYU; hereafter, Darcy memoirs.

28. Daniel, *Bitter Harvest*, ch. 5, esp. 182.

29. Daniel, *Bitter Harvest*, 252; Weber, *Dark Sweat, White Gold*, 121.

30. Daniel, *Bitter Harvest*, 201–217.

31. Louise Todd Lambert oral history, tape 2; data from the charts in box 1, file 7, Darcy Papers.

32. Darcy, Albany; Darcy interview by Robert Cherny, April 14, 1994.

33. CC to All District Committees [mimeographed letter], June 17, 1933, 515-1-3123 RGASPI.

34. I deal with longshore organizing in 1932–1934 at more length in *Harry Bridges: Labor Radical, Labor Legend* (Urbana: University of Illinois Press, 2022), chs. 2–3. Among other accounts, the one that I find the most complete and reliable is by David F. Selvin, *A Terrible Anger: The 1934 Waterfront and General Strikes in San Francisco* (Detroit: Wayne State University Press, 1996). See also Bruce Nelson, *Workers on the Waterfront: Seamen, Longshoremen, and Unionism in the 1930s* (Urbana: University of Illinois Press, 1988); Howard Kimmeldorf, *Reds or Rackets: The Making of Radical and Conservative Unions on the Waterfront* (Berkeley: University of California Press, 1988); Ottilie Markholt, *Maritime Solidarity: Pacific Coast Unionism, 1929–38* (Tacoma: Pacific Coast Maritime History Committee, 1998); Paul Eliel, *The Waterfront and General Strikes: San Francisco, 1934* (San Francisco: Hooper Printing, 1934); Mike Quin, pseud. for Paul William Ryan, *The Big Strike* (Olema: Olema Publishing, 1949); Vernon L. Pedersen, *The Communist Party on the American Waterfront: Revolution, Reform, and the Quest for Power* (Lanham, MD: Lexington Books, 2019). See also the accounts by Sam Darcy: "The Great West Coast Maritime Strike," *The Communist* 13 (July 1934): 664–86; "The San Francisco Bay Area General Strike," *The Communist* 13 (October 1934): 985–1004; "The San Francisco General Strike—1934," *Hawsepipe* 1

(Sept.–Oct. 1982): 1, 7–9; "The San Francisco General Strike—1934: Part II," *Hawsepipe* 1 (Nov.–Dec. 1982): 1–2, 4–6.

35. Darcy interview by Cherny, Aug. 19, 1996. On the PPTUS and George, see the sources noted in chapter 2.

36. Richmond, *Long View from the Left*, 206–219; Nelson, *Workers on the Waterfront*, 90; Darcy interview, Aug. 19, 1996; letter, Darcy to Robert W. Cherny, Oct. 17, 1986.

37. Richmond, *Long View from the Left*, 162–63; Pedersen, "Reform or Revolution," citing 515-1-2995 RGASPI. Jackson's transfer to San Francisco on Aug. 11, 1933, is in 515-1-3146 RGASPI.

38. Johanningsmeier, *Forging American Communism*, 266–67; Darcy interview by Cherny, Aug. 19, 1996.

39. Report of George Mink, 515-1-1864; Central Committee of the CPUSA, "RESOLU-TIONS ON PARTY WORK," undated but 1930, 515-1-2242; "Organizational Status of the T.U.U.L." [1931], 515-1-2542; Minutes of the National Bureau of the MWIU, Feb. 24, 1931, 515-1-2554; Minutes of TUUL Bureau meeting, April 4, 1932, 515-1-2979; Hudson to Wellstone and Foster, March 12, 1931, 515-1-2554; Minutes, TUUL National Executive Board, Aug. 24, 1931, 515-1-2543; Minutes, MWIU National Committee Meeting, Oct. 10–11, 1931, 515-1-2554, all RGASPI.

40. "Plan for Work among the Pacific Marine Transport Workers" [unsigned and undated, with penciled annotation in upper right, "For Earl"], 515-1-3350; Minutes, [California] State Convention of the Trade Union Unity League, Aug. 6, 1933, 515-1-3345 RGASPI.

41. District 13 membership by trade, Jan. 11–March 18, 1932, 515-1-2723 RGASPI; Darcy, "The San Francisco General Strike—1934," Hawsepipe 1, no. 6 (Sept.–Oct. 1982), 1, 7; secretariat meeting minutes, March 15, 1932, 515-1-1932 RGASPI; Darcy interview by Wormser, 1981. Darcy acknowledged that the planning meeting did not include any MWIU functionaries in the interview with Cherny on Aug. 19, 1996. For Branch and Kirby, see, e.g., *WW*, Feb. 15, 1932.

42. George Mink to Browder, July 1, 1932, 515-1-2995; letter, DO Dist. #13 [Darcy] to Org. Dept. C.C. [Central Committee], April 12, 1932, 515-1-2916 RGASPI; Darcy, "Great West Coast Maritime Strike," 665.

43. *WW*, Aug. 1, Oct. 24, 1932.

44. All known issues of the *Waterfront Worker* are online at http://archive.ilwu.org/?page_id=1854/. Darcy, "The San Francisco General Strike—1934," Hawsepipe 1, no. 6 (Sept.–Oct. 1982), 1, 7; secretariat meeting minutes, March 15, 1932, 515-1-2910 RGASPI; Eddy to Alex, April 22, 1933, 534-4-423 RGASPI, quoted in Pedersen, "Underfunded," 12, 20; Efim Hanoff, 495-261-883-1 RGASPI; Archie Green interview by Robert Cherny, Oct. 12, 1986; report on Mitchell Slobodek, part of report of [name redacted], July 30, 1941, file 39-915-1488, esp. 17–23, Bridges FBI file; B. B. Jones interview by Robert Cherny, Sept. 14, 1986. For Darcy's use of activists from the Unemployed Councils in agricultural organizing and his similar use of unemployed men to create a waterfront section, see [District 13] Secretariat [Darcy?] to Central Committee, May 17, 1933, 515-1-3295 RGASPI.

45. *Waterfront Worker*, http://archive.ilwu.org/?page_id=1854/.

46. Copy of letter, unsigned and unidentified, to Jack, March 10, 1933, 515-1-3350 RGASPI. Vernon Pedersen, in *The Communist Party on the American Waterfront* (2019),

81–82, cites the unsigned letter to claim that the PPTUS and Eddy were centrally important in creating both a group of CP members among longshoremen and *Waterfront Worker*; he also cites the letter as evidence that the "editorial board would consist of longshoremen who were secret members of the Communist Party. . . . For chair of the editorial board Darcy and Eddy chose Harry Bridges." Pedersen also cites this letter and Bruce Nelson's *Workers on the Waterfront* (1988), esp. 78–80, for his statement that "Bridges secretly joined the Communist Party." However, nowhere does the letter refer to "longshoremen who were secret members of the Communist Party," and nowhere does it mention Harry Bridges. Nor does Nelson make that claim. I have quoted at length from the letter and other sources to suggest that Darcy's account corresponds most closely with all materials in RGASPI other than the unsigned letter from early March 1932.

47. Central Committee to Darcy, April 26, 1933, 515-1-3127 RGASPI.

48. [District 13] Secretariat [Darcy?] to Central Committee, May 17, 1933, 515-1-3295 RGASPI; handwritten letter, B. B. Jones to Central Committee, Jan. 1, 1935, 515-1-3875 RGASPI.

49. Darcy, "Great West Coast Maritime Strike," 665. The last reference to Hynes in the District 13 materials is in the minutes of the District 13 Secretariat meeting, June 28, 1933, 515-1-3292; regarding Jackson's arrival, see the approval of his transfer from New York to San Francisco, Aug. 11, 1933, 515-1-3146 RGASPI.

50. Minutes, District 13 Secretariat, June 28, 1933, 515-1-3292; Minutes, District 13 Secretariat, Sept. 9, 1933, 515-1-3293 RGASPI; Darcy, "Great West Coast Maritime Strike," 666. FBI agents interviewed many of the members of the Albion Hall group; see Report of E. J. Connelley, Nov. 11, 1940 (some sections are dated as Nov. 20, 1940, and some are corrected by hand to Nov. 20, 1940), file 39-915-614, 538–689, 1588–1600. All of this is presented in more detail in Cherny, *Bridges*, ch. 3.

51. Cherny, *Bridges*, ch. 4, and also those accounts listed in note 34.

52. *San Francisco News*, May 31, 1934, 3; Henry Schmidt, *Secondary Leadership in the ILWU, 1933–1966*, interviewed by Miriam F. Stein and Estolv Ethan Ward, Regional Oral History Office, Bancroft Library, University of California, Berkeley, 1983, 85; Press Release, May 30, filed under Strike Publicity Materials and Notes; unsigned, untitled report on events of May 30, filed under Testimonies of Strike Observers, both 1933–34 Series, ILWU Library; Strike Committee minutes, May 30; New Economics Group, "Preliminary Testimony Taken by the San Francisco Committee Against Police Brutality" (mimeographed pamphlet), ILWU Library.

53. "Fisher" [Harrison George] to "E" [Browder], May 26 [1934], 515-1-3613 RGASPI. For definitions of these terms, see, e.g., McDermott and Agnew, *The Comintern*, 103.

54. "Fisher" [Harrison George] to "E" [Browder], June 2 [1934], 515-1-3613; The Strike of the Longshoremen on the Pacific Coast (Report to PolBuro, June 21, 1934)," apparently by Browder, 515-1-3613 RGASPI.

55. "F." [Harrison George] to "E." [Earl Browder], June 9, 515-1-3613 RGASPI.

56. M. Raport to Central Committee, June 15, 1934, 515-1-3605 RGASPI. "Raport" is the spelling of his name that occurs most frequently in RGASPI files, though it is also spelled occasionally as "Rapport." Because his real name was Rappaport, that is the version I have used in the text. In the footnotes, I have cited correspondence using the spelling used in

that particular document. For the earlier antagonism between Rappaport and Darcy in San Francisco, see, e.g., letter, Secretariat Dist 13 [Darcy] to Secretariat CC, July 22, 1932, 515-1-2916 RGASPI; see also Darcy interview by Cherny, Aug. 19, 1996.

57. Minutes, District [13] Buro meeting, June 22, 1934, 515-1-3613; letter, Darcy to Browder, June 22, 1934, 515-1-3613 RGASPI.

58. Cherny, *Bridges*, ch. 5; Selvin, *Terrible Anger*, 11–13; *News*, July 9, 1934; *Chronicle*, July 10, 1934; Quin, *Big Strike*, 119–130; Eliel, *Waterfront and General Strikes*, 127–28; Darcy, memoirs, 379–80.

59. Cherny *Bridges*, ch. 5; Selvin, *Terrible Anger*, ch. 15.

60. "Wallace" [Harrison George] to District Bureau, Dist. #13, July 17, 1934, sent to "Mr. E" [Browder] with penciled annotation at top: "This was not sent—as you recommended it not be—however, as the facts in it should be available to you, am sending it to you as a source of material. Press clippings, etc. follow /F", 515-1-3613 RGASPI.

61. See, e.g., "Our Tactics in Connection with AFL appeal on 30 hours week" (Anglo-American Secretariat to CPUSA), dated January 4, 1933 [in Russian, translation by Datia Lotareva]: "The tasks of communists: 1) To expose in the press that the '30 hour week' slogan is the camouflage of the stagger system, which leads to salary reduction"; 515-1-3088 RGASPI. Or see the condemnation of the "stagger" plan by Earl Browder, "How We Must Fight against the Demagogy of Fascists and Social Fascists," *The Communist* 10 (April 1931): 301–302.

62. "Wallace" [Harrison George] to "Mr. E" [Browder], July 17, 1934, 515-1-3613 RGASPI.

63. Cherny, *Bridges*, 97–98; Selvin, *Terrible Anger*, chs. 17–19; *News*, July 17, July 18, 1934; *Chronicle*, July 18, 1934; Robert Cantwell and Evelyn Seely, "War on the West Coast," *New Republic* (Aug. 1, 1934): 308–311.

64. Cherny, *Bridges*, 97–98; Selvin, *Terrible Anger*, 193–94; Eliel, *Waterfront and General Strikes*, 160; Quin, *Big Strike*, 159–62; *NYT*, July 18, 1934, 3; letter, Ella Winter to Taub and Wirin, July 30, 1934, 515-1-3613 RGASPI; *The Nation* 139 (Oct. 10, 1934): 411–13; press release from American Civil Liberties Union, Sept. 23, 1934, David P. Barrows Papers, cartoon 18, file S.F. Waterfront Strike, 1936–37, Bancroft Library, University of California, Berkeley; Report of E. J. Connelly, Jan. 20, 1940, p. 99, file 39-915-558, Bridges FBI file. I agree with Selvin that the close cooperation between the vigilantes and the San Francisco police implies official approval for at least some of the vigilante actions, approval that may have reached to the mayor's office.

65. Comments by Randolph (Darcy), Transcript of AAS discussion "Meeting on Cadre Question and Political Emigrants," Jan. 28, 1936, marked "Strictly Confidential," 495-14-10 RGASPI.

66. Cherny, *Bridges*, ch. 5.

67. Cherny, *Bridges*, ch. 8.

68. Letter, "Fisher" [Harrison George] to "E" [Browder], May 26 [1934], 515-1-3613 RGASPI; Cherny, *Bridges*, chs. 3–5, 8.

69. Letter, "Fisher" to "E," May 26 [1934], op. cit.; letter to "Mr. E." with unsent letter, "Wallace" [George] to District Bureau, Dist. #13, July 17, 1934; letter, Hudson to Earl [Browder], July 12, 1934, 515-1-3613 RGASPI.

70. Browder, in Minutes of PolBuro, July 31, 1934, 515-1-3445; letters, M. Raport [Rappaport] to Central Committee, Sept. 27, 1934; M. Raport to Comrade Stachel, Dec. 11, 1934, both in 515-1-3605 RGASPI.

71. TUUL Buro minutes, May 21, 1934, 515-1-3657 RGASPI. For press claims of CP control of the strike, see, e.g., *San Francisco Examiner*, May 21, 1934, 1, 8; *LAT*, May 21, 1934, 1, 2; *NYT*, May 21, 1934, 35.

72. Minutes of the PolBuro, July 31, 1934, 515-1-3445 RGASPI.

73. Report approved by B. K. Sackett, October 26, 1940, p. 8, file 39-915-437, Bridges FBI file; Memorandum, Gerard D. Reilly to The Secretary, Oct. 13, 1937, file Reilly, Gerard D, Oct. 1–Oct. 13, 1937, box 38, Perkins Papers, Columbia University; Darcy interview by Ron Filipelli, undated (1971?), p. 68, box 3, file 32, Darcy Papers, NYU.

74. Lincoln Steffens to Darcy, April 19, 1934, 515-1-3613; Darcy to Central Committee, April 16, 1934; Org Commission CC [Stachel] to District #13, April 28, 1934; Lincoln Steffens to Darcy, April 28, 1934; Darcy to Earl Browder, May 5, 1934; all in 515-1-3613 RGASPI.

75. Darcy interview by Cherny, Aug. 19, 1996. See also Michael Furmanovsky, "Lost Chances and New Possibilities: The EPIC Movement and the United Front, 1934–35," unpublished paper, Robert W. Cherny Research File, LARC, 12.

76. *Daily Worker*, Oct. 6, 1934; Darcy to Central Committee, Dec. 30, 1934, 515-1-3613 RGASPI; Darcy interview by Cherny, April 14, 1994; Furmanovsky, "Lost Chances," 13–20, esp. 15; report of "A. X.," Oct. 21, 1934, series 1, box 1, folder 1, and report of unidentified informant, covering events from Oct. 5 to 25, series 1, box 1, folder 11, Surveillance Papers, LARC. For a continuation of the criticism of Sinclair long after the end of the election campaign, see, e.g., *Western Worker*, March 11, 1935.

77. Louise Todd Lambert oral history, tape 3; Darcy interviews by Cherny, April 14, 1994; Aug. 19, 1996; *Statement of Vote at General Election Held on Nov. 6, 1934* (Sacramento: California State Printing Office, 1934). See also Furmanovsky, "Lost Chances," 13–20, esp. 15. Sinclair received significantly fewer votes than the Democratic candidate for lieutenant governor, suggesting that significant numbers of otherwise Democratic voters had been persuaded by the intense anti-Sinclair advertising.

78. *Chronicle*, July 21, 1934; Kathryn S. Olmsted, *Right Out of California: The 1930s and the Big Business Roots of Modern Conservatism* (New York: New Press, 2015), ch. 9; Daniel, *Bitter Harvest*, 252; McWilliams, *Factories in the Field*, 118.

79. *Chronicle*, Jan. 3, 17, April 2, 11, 1935. Olmsted, *Right Out of California*, ch. 9, provides a summary of the trial.

80. *Chronicle*, Feb. 7, 8, 10, Nov. 7, 23, 27, Dec. 3, 6, 1935; Louise Todd Lambert oral history, tape 2.

81. *Chronicle*, Aug. 1, 2, 1935.

Chapter 4. The Popular Front

1. Parts of this chapter are adapted from my "Prelude to the Popular Front: The Communist Party in California, 1931–1935," *American Communist History* 1 (2002): 5–37; "The Communist Party in California, 1935–1940: From the Political Margins to the Mainstream and Back," *American Communist History* 9 (2010): 3–3; and *Harry Bridges: Labor Radical,*

Labor Legend (Urbana: University of Illinois Press, 2022), chs. 6–9. See also minutes of PolBuro, July 31, 1934, 515-1-3445; letter, Darcy to Browder, June 22, 1934, 515-1-3613, all in RGASPI.

2. Cherny, "Prelude to the Popular Front." See also Meeting of the Bureau, July 23, 1934 495-72-257; agenda, meeting of the secretariat, Aug. 8, 1934, 495-72-255; "Lessons of the San Francisco General Strike," original in English, with translations into Russian, German, and French, dated Aug. 22, 1934, stamped Aug. 25, 1934, typed notation "Confidential," stamped "000" with notations Politkommission, 15 VIII 34 and Protokol No. 395, 515-1-3399; file is bound, with the title in German on the binder, "Protokoll No. ____ der Sitzung des Prä-sidiums des EKKI vom _____ 19 ____ [blanks not filled in] 495-20-508"; Minutes of CPUSA PolBuro, Aug. 16, 1934, 515-1-3449; PolBuro Minutes, Oct. 25, 1934, 515-1-3446, all RGASPI. Stachel's report was printed in *The Communist* 13 (Nov. 1934): 1087–1105.

3. Cherny, "Prelude to the Popular Front"; Cherny, *Bridges*, ch. 6. See also S. D. [Darcy] to Comrade Stachel, Nov. 21, 1934, 515-1-3613; M. Raport to Comrade Stachel, Dec. 11, 1934, 515-1-3605; Sam Darcy to Jack [Stachel], Dec. 17, 1934; Darcy to Central Committee, Dec. 30, 1934; both in 515-1-3613; Minutes of PolBuro meetings of Dec. 20, 1934, 515-1-3447, and Feb. 14, 1935, 515-1-3752, all RGASPI.

4. Serge Wolikow, *Le Front populaire en France* (Brussels: Éditions Complexe, 1996), 55–83; Guillaume Bourgeois, "French Communism and the Communist International," in *International Communism and the Communist International*, ed. Rees and Thorpe, 95–102; Kevin McDermott and Jeremy Agnew, *The Comintern* (New York: St. Martin's, 1997), 124–27; James G. Ryan, *Earl Browder: The Failure of American Communism* (Tuscaloosa: University of Alabama Press, 1997), 68.

5. Minutes, Meeting of the Presidium of ECCI, Dec. 5, 1934, on the American Question, 495-72-263; [Presidium of the ECCI] to "Dear Friends," described in the index as "Resolution on the immediately [*sic*] tasks of the CPUSA," dated both Dec. 5 and Dec. 20, 1934, 495-72-263; PolBuro Minutes, Dec. 20, 1934, 515-1-3447, all RGASPI; *Daily Worker*, Dec. 28, 1934, 1, 7; William L. Standard, *Merchant Seamen: A Short History of Their Struggles* (New York: International Publishers, 1947), 83–85.

6. Cherny, *Bridges*, ch. 8; Minutes of the District Buro, June 16, Aug. 20, Oct. 6, Oct. 13, 1934, 515-1-3609 RGASPI. Bridges told me about being co-opted to serve on party committees on Sept. 2, 1986. It was not in a taped interview, but I made written notes immediately afterward.

7. Minutes of District 13 Buro meetings of Aug. 5, 14, Sept. 5, 10, 24, Oct. 7, Nov. 14, Dec. 25, 1935, 515-1-3874; Jack Johnstone to Jack [Stachel], Sept. 24, 1935, 515-1-3875; unsigned report on West Coast and Denver, dated July 13, 1935, 495-14-31, both RGASPI.

8. Undated letter c. late 1935–early 1936, from [Dist 13] District Trade Union Sec. to Trade Union Commission, 495-14-22 RGASPI; table 4, *Fifteenth Census of the United States: 1930: Population: Occupations by States* (Washington, D.C.: Government Printing Office, 1933), 4:177; table 11, *Sixteenth Census of the United States: 1940: Population: The Labor Force* (Washington, D.C.: Government Printing Office, 1943), 3:227, 230; Schneiderman, report to June 1937 Plenum, 495-14-67 RGASPI.

The FBI file of J. Robert Oppenheimer contains a long report by FBI special agent Joe Craig, Washington, D.C., on June 18, 1954. The report includes an attachment from Colonel

Joseph Stearns, Military Intelligence, that includes a two-page excerpt purportedly listing members of the longshore, seamen, warehouse, and professional branches of the CP in the Bay Area. The source of the lists is not identified nor is the date. The list of longshoremen includes Archie Brown, Henry Schmidt, John Schomaker, Isaac Zafrani, George Woolf, and four others, and the list of seamen includes Walter Stack, Revels Cayton, Allan Yates, Dave Jenkins, Hugh Bryson, and four others—a total far short of the 180 the party claimed on the waterfront in 1936. The list has no date, but the inclusion of both John Schomaker and Dave Jenkins is curious, since Schomaker claimed to have left the party around 1936–1938, and Jenkins did not arrive in San Francisco until 1939 (for Schomaker, see my *Harry Bridges*, 246; for Jenkins, see ch. 5 of this book). This suggests to me that the list of members of these various branches did not come directly from party documents but was instead compiled from various sources and informants. The lists are, nonetheless, of interest; those on the lists whom I can identify were all, at one time or another, party members. Interestingly, Harry Bridges does *not* appear. A copy of Craig's report is in box 15, file 3, Sherwin Papers, Library of Congress.

9. Minutes of June 3, 1936, 2nd annual Maritime Federation of the Pacific Convention, box 2, file 1, Maritime Federation of the Pacific Records, LARC.

10. Minutes of Meeting of the Ninth National Convention of the CPUSA, New York City, June 24–28, 1936, 495-14-37; transcript of meeting, AAS, on the American Question, April 4, 1937, marked "confidential," 495-20-521; List of Members and Candidate Members of the U.S. Communist Party Central Committee, Jan. 31, 1938, 495-74-467 RGASPI. The original of this last is in Russian, compiled by an official named Belov, based on information provided on Jan. 17, 1938, by Browder, Foster, and Eugene Dennis (then known as Tim Ryan). A copy of the original and a translation was made available to me by John Haynes, to whom I owe thanks for this and many other forms of assistance in using the Russian archives. That file was closed by the time I was doing research at RGASPI, but it had been open when Haynes made his pioneering trip to RGASPI. This translation was done by Nina Bogdan and differs in minor ways from the translation done for Harvey Klehr and John Haynes.

11. NOTE SUR LES CANDIDATURES AU B.P. DU C.C. DU P.C. DES ETATS-UNIS, 8.2.36, 495-20-515 RGASPI. When Andre Marty was chair of AAS, some of the materials for that secretariat were in French. The handwritten notes are in English. This must be from either August 1936 or February 1937 (with the year mistyped); I'm guessing August 2, 1936, since it deals with the new PolBuro following the national convention. February 1936 seems unlikely, since it was before the 1936 convention.

12. I present examples of Bridges's departures from the party line in my *Bridges*, chs. 6, 7. As early as March 1936, before Bridges was elected to the Central Committee, a report of the AAS noted, "There are even several members of the CC who are not citizens. These people are in danger of expulsion if they show the slightest activity," and urged "a campaign . . . among the members of the CP so that they will do everything in their power to become citizens of the USA"; see I. Mingulin, "THE CADRE POLICY OF THE CP USA," March 10, 1936, 495-20-515 RGASPI. In 1938 the CPUSA debated whether to require that all members be or become citizens; see Roy Hudson, "The Charter of Party Democracy," *The Communist* 17 (1938): 704–710. See also *Chronicle*, May 23, 1941, 3, regarding Elmer Hanoff's termination of party membership as an alien.

13. Robert H. Zieger, *John L. Lewis: Labor Leader* (Boston: Twayne, 1988), 87–88, 92–95; Melvyn Dubofsky and Warren Van Tine, *John L. Lewis: A Biography* (New York: Quadrangle, 1977), 253–79.

14. Meeting of the AAS, Sept. 15, 1936, 495-14-16; AAS, "Memorandum on the Most Important Issues Facing the CPUSA," March 3 and March 23, 1937, 515-1-4065; Meeting of the AAS, April 4, 1937, 495-20-521; Decision of the Secretary of the ECCI on the American question, dated April 4 and 14, 1937, May 8 and 10, 1937, 495-20-509; MEMORANDUM ON THE JUNE PLENUM OF THE CPUSA AND SOME ASPECTS OF THE LATEST POLITICAL DEVELOPMENTS IN AMERICA AND THE WORK OF THE COMMUNIST PARTY, August 9, 1937, 495-20-515, all RGASPI.

15. Cherny, *Bridges*, ch. 7.

16. T. Ryan, report to AAS on "C.I.O. NATIONAL CONFERENCE, October 11–15, 1937, Atlantic City, N.J.," Nov. 15, 1937, marked "confidential," 495-20-519 RGASPI.

17. *WW*, Jan. 10, April 11, May 23, June 13, July 4, 28, 29, Aug. 8, 15, Sept. 23, Oct. 14, 1935.

18. *WW*, Feb. 25, March 11, 1935.

19. For the Mooney case, see Richard H. Frost, *The Mooney Case* (Stanford, CA: Stanford University Press, 1968). For the role of the CP in the case, see Estolv Ethan Ward, *The Gentle Dynamiter: A Biography of Tom Mooney* (Palo Alto, CA: Ramparts Press, 1983).

20. Darcy said he was initially omitted from the delegation but later learned from Manuilsky that he was added after Stalin questioned why he was absent from the list of CPUSA members seeking visas; Darcy interview by Cherny, Aug. 19, 1996.

21. Darcy interview by Cherny, Aug. 19, 1996.

22. Georgi Dimitrov, "The Threat of Fascism in the United States," and William Z. Foster, "Fascist Tendencies in the United States," *The Communist* 14 (Oct. 1935): esp. 901–903, 908.

23. Hanoff to Central Committee, Aug. 7, Jack [Johnstone] to Stachel, Sept. 4, 1935, 515-1-3875 RGASPI.

24. *WW*, July 16, 22, 1935.

25. *WW*, Aug. 8, Sept. 23, 1935.

26. Minutes of Aug. 27, Oct. 7, 14, 24, 1935, 515-1-3874 RGASPI; *WW*, Sept. 5, 1935; March 2, 1936; Ben Legere Collection, Walter Reuther Library, Wayne State University.

27. *WW*, Oct. 28, Nov. 11, 1935; *Chronicle*, Nov. 6, 1935; Draft Resolution on the [1935] Election Campaign, 515-1-3876; District Buro minutes, Dec. 5, 1935, 515-1-3874 RGASPI.

28. *WW*, Oct. 31, Nov. 18, 1935. For Schneiderman, see his *Dissent on Trial: The Story of a Political Life* (Minneapolis: MEP Publications, 1983). He does not mention the Dimitrov speech to the U.S. delegation.

29. *WW*, Nov. 21, 25, Dec. 2, 1935.

30. *WW*, Jan. 16, 30, Feb. 10, 1936.

31. *WW*, Jan. 20, Feb. 24, May 25, July 9, 1936.

32. Darcy interview by Cherny, Aug. 19, 1996.

33. Ryan, *Earl Browder*, 108–110. Johanningsmeier, *Forging American Communism*, 279, notes, "The Comintern finally weighed in with an opinion that the Party must find a way to support Roosevelt." Johanningsmeier indicates that the notion of a Farmer-Labor Party

was a favorite of Foster's and that it was dropped in favor of running a separate CP ticket in order not to draw votes away from Roosevelt.

34. *WW*, July 6, Aug. 7, 1936. The new slogan appears frequently in the *WW* as filler, e.g., on July 9, 1936.

35. *WW*, Sept. 28, 1936.

36. ILA 38-79 *Bulletin*, Oct. 5, 1936; Minutes of reconvened meeting of Local 38-79, Oct. 26, 1936, File: Local 10, ILA #38-79 Minutes, Membership Meetings, ILWU Library; John Schomaker, report from Local 38-79, [Seattle] *Pacific Coast Longshoreman*, Nov. 2, 1936, 6.

37. For examples of the repeated efforts to persuade people to register as Communists, see *WW*, April 20, May 21, June 1, 1936; for membership data, see *WW*, June 7, 1937. For registration statistics, see Frank C. Jordan, Secretary of State, comp., *Statement of Vote at Primary Election Held on August 28, 1934* (Sacramento: California State Printing Office, 1934), 4; *Statement of Vote at General Election Held on Nov. 6, 1934* (Sacramento: California State Printing Office, 1934), 4; *Statement of Vote at Presidential Primary Election Held on May 5, 1936* (Sacramento: California State Printing Office, 1936), 2–3; *Statement of Vote at Primary Election Held on August 25, 1936* (Sacramento: California State Printing Office, 1936), 3; *Statement of Vote at General Election Held on November 3, 1936* (Sacramento: California State Printing Office, 1936), 3.

38. *WW*, Feb. 1, March 4, 15, April 1, May 20, 27, 1937.

39. *WW*, May 3, 1937.

40. *WW*, Aug. 23, 27, Sept. 30, Oct. 21, 28, Nov. 1, 1937; *Chronicle*, Oct. 10, Nov. 3, 19, 1937.

41. *WW*, Nov. 18, Dec. 9, Dec. 23, 1937; *PW*, Jan. 1, Jan. 5, and throughout Jan., 1938; Al Richmond, *A Long View from the Left: Memoirs of an American Revolutionary* (New York: Dell, 1972), 265–77.

42. PolBuro minutes, March 1, 1938, 495-14-96 RGASPI.

43. Estolv Ethan Ward, *Organizing and Reporting on Labor in the East Bay, California, and the West, 1925–1987*, an interview conducted by Lisa Rubens in 1987 (Berkeley: Regional Oral History Office, Bancroft Library, University of California, 1989), 107.

44. *PW*, July 29, 1938; Frank C. Jordan, Secretary of State, comp., *Statement of Vote at General Election Held on Nov. 6, 1934* (Sacramento: California State Printing Office, 1934), 5–11; Frank C. Jordan, Secretary of State, comp., *Statement of Vote at Primary Election held on August 28, 1934* (Sacramento: California State Printing Office, 1934), 48.

45. *PW*, Aug. 18, 1938.

46. Frank C. Jordan, Secretary of State, comp., *Statement of Vote at Primary Election Held on August 30, 1938* (Sacramento: California State Printing Office, 1938), 12–13, 17. See also *PW*, Aug. 18, Sept. 19, 1938, regarding politics in Los Angeles.

47. Carey McWilliams, *Factories in the Field* (1939; reprint, University of California Press, 1999), ch. 14; U.S. Congress, Senate, 76th Congress, 3d Session, Committee on Education and Labor, *Hearings*, part 60; U.S. Congress, Senate, 77th Congress, 2d Session, *Report of the Committee on Education and Labor*, part IV; and U.S. Congress, Senate, 78th Congress, 1st Session, *Report of the Committee on Education and Labor*, part V.

48. Kevin Starr, *Endangered Dreams: The Great Depression in California* (New York: Oxford University Press, 1996), 209.

49. Klehr, *Heyday of American Communism*, 271; *PW*, Sept. 20, 23, Oct. 12. 1938.

50. *PW*, Oct. 17, 19, 20, 1938. For Bulcke, see Germain Bulcke, *Longshore Leader and ILWU-Pacific Maritime Association Arbitrator*, interview conducted by Estolv Ward in 1983 (Berkeley: Regional Oral History Office, Bancroft Library, University of California, Berkeley, 1984).

51. *PW*, Oct 31, Nov. 7, 1938.

52. Ward, *Gentle Dynamiter*, 244; *PW*, Nov. 15, 1938.

53. There are two versions of this exchange. Al Richmond's version appears in *Long View from the Left*, 274, and also in a letter to Dorothy Healey, June 30, 1971, quoted in Dorothy Ray Healey and Maurice Isserman, *California Red: A Life in the American Communist Party* (Urbana: University of Illinois Press, 1993), 59. Schneiderman's own version is in *Dissent on Trial*, 63. Richmond identifies the party member as a woman, Schneiderman as a man.

54. Frank C. Jordan, Secretary of State, comp., *Statement of Vote at General Election Held on Nov. 8, 1938* (Sacramento: California State Printing Office, 1938), 2–3, 6–7; *Chronicle*, Nov. 10, 1938.

55. Minutes, plenary session of the National Committee, Dec. 3–5, 1938 (cont.), 495-14-95 RGASPI.

56. *PW*, Nov, 21, 22, 23, 1938; Jan. 7, 9, 1939; Schneiderman, *Dissent on Trial*, 63.

57. *PW*, Dec. 22, 1938; Jan. 16, 17, 20, 24, 25, 1939.

58. *PW*, Dec. 22, 1938; Jan. 17, 20, Feb. 21, 28, March 17, 20, 23, 30, April 10, 20, 1939.

59. *PW*, Jan. 21, 24, Feb. 25, 27, March 7, 18, April 10, 20, 1939; *Chronicle*, June 25, 1939, *This World* section.

60. These events all had significant coverage in *PW*, see, e.g., March 15, 29, April 8, May 1, 12, June 8, Aug. 1, 23, 28, 1939.

61. Maurice Isserman, *Which Side Are You On? The American Communist Party during the Second World War* (Middletown, CT: Wesleyan University Press, 1982), 43; Richmond, *Long View from the Left*, 283.

62. *PW*, Sept. 25, Oct. 12, 18, 28, 1939; Ryan, *Earl Browder*, 162.

63. *PW*, April 5, 24, 26, May 22, 1939.

64. *PW*, Nov. 9, 1939; *Chronicle*, Nov. 10, 1939; Franck Roberts Havenner, *Reminiscences: Oral History*, interview by Corinne Lathrop Gilb (Berkeley: Regional Oral History Office, Bancroft Library, University of California, 1953), 96–98. The "guilt by association" campaign that defeated Havenner in 1939 and 1940 forecast tactics later used against such liberals as Jerry Voorhis and Helen Gahagan Douglas.

65. *Chronicle*, Oct. 15, 17, Nov. 1, 9, 1939; Nov. 19, 1937.

66. *PW*, March 21, 22, 23, 25, 30, April 4, 1940.

67. *PW*, April 6, 11, 15, 17, 19, 23, 1940; Bulcke interview with Estolv Ward, March 10, 1986.

68. *PW*, April 24, 29, May 2, 1940; *Chronicle*, May 8, 1940; *PW*, May 9, 1940.

69. *PW*, May 13, 1940.

70. *PW*, July 1, Sept. 27, Oct. *passim*, 1940.

71. *PW*, Oct. 28, 29, 1940.

72. *PW*, Oct. 29, Nov. 4, 1940; *Chronicle*, Jan. 25, 1940; Bridges to Rosco Craycraft, Aug. 17, 1940, Bridges correspondence, ILWU Library; John Brophy Oral History, Columbia University, 853–54; unidentified clipping, dateline Nov. 1, 1940 (AP), file: Harry Bridges, Material about, 1939–1943, ILWU History Collection, ILWU Library; *Chronicle*, Nov. 5,

1940; *Business Week*, Nov. 16, 1940; [ILWU Local 1-10] *Longshoremen's Bulletin C.I.O.*, Sept. 24, 1940, Oct. 29, 1940.

73. *Chronicle*, Nov. 4, 1940.

74. *Chronicle*, Nov. 7, 1940.

75. 75th Cong., 3d Sess., House of Representatives, Special Committee on Un-American Activities, Public Hearings, Aug. 12, 13, 1938, esp. 104, 106, 107; *NYT*, Aug. 14, 15, 17, 1938.

76. For more information, see my "Anticommunist Networks and Labor: The Pacific Coast in the 1930s," in *Labor's Cold War: Local Politics in a Global Context*, ed. by Shelton Stromquist (Champaign: University of Illinois Press, 2008), 17–48.

77. This summary based on M. J. Heale, "Red Scare Politics: California's Campaign against Un-American Activities, 1940–1970," *Journal of American Studies* 20 (1986): 5–32, esp. 6; Robert L. Pritchard, "California Un-American Activities Investigations: Subversion on the Right?" *California Historical Quarterly* 49 (1970): 309–327; and Ingrid Winther Scobie, "Jack B. Tenney and the 'Parasitic Menace': Anti-Communist Legislation in California, 1940–1949," *Pacific Historical Review* 43 (1974): 188–211. See also the Inventory of the California Un-American Activities Committees Records, California State Archives.

78. *Chronicle*, Sept. 23, 1940. See also Schneiderman, *Dissent on Trial*, 73–74. Schneiderman viewed Olson's action as a capitulation to anti-Communism, but Olson may have had a more pragmatic motive: had the CP been removed from the California ballot in 1940, some ten thousand votes may have shifted from Browder to Roosevelt.

79. Robert Houghwout, Jackson, *Reminiscences of Robert Houghwout Jackson: Oral History, 1952*, Columbia University, 304, 314.

80. Cherny, *Bridges*, ch. 11.

81. Cherny, *Bridges*, ch. 11; *Reminiscences of Robert Houghwout Jackson*, 304.

82. Cherny, *Bridges*, ch. 12. For the massive report, see E. J. Connelley, "Part I Harry Bridges' Membership in and/or Affiliation with the Communist Party of the United States of America," file 39-915-558; "Part II Communist Party of the United States of America: *Illegal Status*," file 39-915-592-595; Report approved by E. J. Connelley, Nov. 29, 1940, file 39-915-617, all Bridges FBI file, which I have deposited with LARC.

83. *Chronicle*, Sept. 20, Oct. 15, Dec. 17, 1940; Jan. 22, July 4, 1941.

84. *Chronicle*; Oct. 17, Dec. 6, 8, 9, 13, 14, 17, 1939, June 13, 1940. For Schneiderman's version of events, see his *Dissent on Trial*, chs. 6–8. For Carol King, see Ann Fagan Ginger, *Carol Weiss King: Human Rights Lawyer, 1895–1952* (Niwot: University Press of Colorado, 1993), esp. ch. 24. The FBI opened its file on Schneiderman following the trial; see especially p. 8a of the card file summarizing chronology, apparently 97-26-133 (but not individually numbered), Schneiderman FBI file.

85. Ryan, *Earl Browder*, 170–83, 192–94.

86. *Chronicle*, July 27, 30, 31, Aug. 1, 2, 7, Sept 19, 21, 1941; July 23, 1943. Untitled, unsigned report on the trial, Sept. 18, 1941, box 3, file 6, Darcy Papers.

Chapter 5. Life in the Party in the 1930s

1. Angela Gizzi Ward, oral history interview by Sue Cobble, 1976, for the California Historical Society, esp. 32; Edith A. Jenkins, *Against a Field Sinister: Memoirs and Stories* (San Francisco: City Lights Books, 1991), esp. 51, 52, 62.

2. Healey, *California Red*, 74, 98; "Jack Olsen: Activist and Educator," in Harvey Schwartz, *Solidarity Stories: An Oral History of the ILWU* (Seattle: University of Washington Press, 2009), 284; hereafter, Olsen oral history.

3. Biographical material, some in first person, Archie Brown Collection, file 1-2, box 1, LARC; Archie Brown interview by Timothy V. Johnson, undated, Abraham Lincoln Brigade Archives Oral History Collection, https://wp.nyu.edu/albaoh/archie-brown/ c. 1985 but not specifically dated; (San Francisco) *Voice of the Federation*, Dec. 5, 1935, 2; *Chronicle*, Dec. 21, 1935, 19.

4. Karl G. Yoneda, *Ganbatte: Sixty-Year Struggle of a Kibei Worker* (Los Angeles: Asian American Studies Center, UCLA, 1983), xi, xiv, chs. 1–3 and 90–94; Fowler, "From East to West and West to East," 109.

5. Yoneda, *Ganbatte*, chs. 4, 5.

6. Gizzi Ward, oral history, esp. 32–49.

7. Estolv Ethan Ward, *Organizing and Reporting on Labor in the East Bay, California, and the West, 1925–1987*, interview by Lisa Rubens, 1987, Regional Oral History Office, Bancroft Library, University of California, Berkeley.

8. Bill Bailey with Lynn Damme, *The Kid from Hoboken: An Autobiography* (San Francisco, Circus Lithographic Prepress, 1993), chs. I/1–I/2, II/7–II/19; Bill Bailey, interview by Robert Cherny, 1993. See also Peter Duffy, *The Agitator: William Bailey the First American Uprising against Nazism* (New York: Public Affairs, 2019), which mostly follows Bailey's autobiography.

9. Richard S. Hobbs, *The Cayton Legacy: An African American Family* (Pullman, WA: Washington State University Press, 2002), ch. 6.

10. Pat Tobin, interviews by Robert Cherny, Feb. 9 and 25, 1987.

11. Ray Thompson, interviews by Jesse Warr, Oct. 11, Nov. 6. 1978, San Francisco Public Library History Center.

12. Harvey Schwartz, *The March Inland: Origins of the ILUW Warehouse Division, 1934–1938* (Los Angeles: Institute of Industrial Relations, University of California, Los Angeles, 1978), presents the early history of this local.

13. *Louis Goldblatt: Working Class Leader in the ILWU, 1935–1977*, interviews by Estolv Ward, 1978–1979, Regional Oral History Office, Bancroft Library, University of California, Berkeley, 1980; hereafter, Goldblatt oral history; Jenkins, *Against a Field Sinister*, 64.

14. Olsen oral history, 280–88.

15. "Keith Eickman: Idealism and Disappointment," in Schwartz, *Solidarity Stories*, 274–80; hereafter, Eickman oral history; Keith Eickman, interview by Robert Cherny, 1993.

16. Regarding Perry, see "Brief History of Arthur James Kent," doc. 2123, Leonard Papers; affidavit of Arthur Kent, Los Angeles, Dec. 28, 1937, series 1, box 3, file 2, Surveillance Papers, LARC; Estolv E. Ward, *The Gentle Dynamiter: A Biography of Tom Mooney* (Palo Alto: Ramparts Press, 1983), 236–37; Schwartz, *Brotherhood of the Sea*, 120–21. Perry was interviewed by the FBI, which also collected information about her from other informants; see, e.g., report by [name redacted], Nov. 20, 1940, 3–5, file 39-915-571; and esp. report of E. J. Connelley, Nov. 20, 1940, 875–93, 39-915-558, Bridges FBI files.

17. Herbert Resner, interviews by Robert Cherny, Dec. 18, 1992, and Jan. 23, 1993. The term "Hay-Market Branch" also appears in Norman Leonard's FBI file, as reported in Colin

Wark and John F. Galliher, *Progressive Lawyers under Siege: Moral Panic during the McCarthy Years* (Lanham, MD: Lexington Books, 2015), 203.

18. Sam Darcy, interviewed by Ron Filipelli, 45–46, box 3, file 32, Darcy Papers, NYU; for Andersen, see Wark and Galliher, *Progressive Lawyers under Siege*, ch. 6 and appendix B. Appendix B contains excepts from Andersen's FBI file, and there is a good deal of erroneous information about Andersen's personal life—e.g., the claim that his sister was married to Alex Noral, the brother of Norma Perry. There is contrary evidence at Ancestry.com regarding both his sisters and Noral's two spouses.

19. Miriam Feingold, *The Shipboard Murder Case: Labor, Radicalism, and Earl Warren, 1936–1941*, Earl Warren Oral History Project, Regional Oral History Office, Bancroft Library, UC-Berkeley, 1976. This oral history contains interviews by Miriam Feingold with Ramsay, Grossman, Resner, Dinkin, and others (hereafter, Resner oral history), pp. i, ii, 1. Both Andersen and Resner have lengthy index cards in California Un-American Activities Committee Records, California State Archives; hereafter, CUAC.

20. Wark and Galliher, *Progressive Lawyers*, ch. 8, appendix D; Aubrey Grossman oral history, in Feingold, *Shipboard Murder Case*, 2; Aubrey Grossman, interviewed by Robert Cherny, 1993. Gladstein and Grossman have lengthy index cards in CUAC.

21. Vivian McGuckin Raineri, *The Red Angel: The Life and Times of Elaine Black Yoneda, 1906–1988* (New York: International Publishers, 1991), 21–22, 25, 29, 32–33, 36, 40, 47. See also the Elaine Black Yoneda Collection, LARC, esp. her FBI file, in file 2, box 2, which includes her arrest in 1931; and Rachel Schreiber, *Elaine Black Yoneda: Jewish Immigration, Labor Activism, and Japanese American Exclusion and Incarceration* (Philadelphia: Temple University Press, 2022), 38–56, 61–65.

22. Strike Committee Minutes, May 9, 13, 14, 30, 31, Strike Committee Minutes, 1933–34 Series, ILWU Library. Schreiber, *Elaine Black Yoneda*, 2, 78, 79, mistakenly claims that Black was the only woman to serve on the executive committee of both the longshore strike and the general strike. Only members of the longshore union were eligible to serve on the longshore strike committee, and all members of the general strike committee were members of local unions; the latter committee included a few women. Members of the general strike executive committee were elected by the Labor Council from among its members; all were male. If Black met with any of those committees, it does not appear in the minutes. Her role with the longshore strike committee's defense subcommittee is recorded in the minutes of that subcommittee. On June 22 the Labor Council overwhelmingly approved a resolution repudiating and denouncing all Communist organizations and calling upon the longshore union to do the same, which it did shortly afterward; see Cherny, *Bridges*, 77.

23. Raineri, *Red Angel*, chs. 9–19 passim, 155; Schreiber, *Elaine Black Yoneda*, part 3.

24. Raineri, *Red Angel*, chs. 9–19, esp. 132–33; Schreiber, *Elaine Black Yoneda*, 70–71.

25. Feingold, *Shipboard Murder Case*, iii–vi; see also Miriam Feingold, "The King-Ramsay-Conner Case: Labor, Radicalism, and the Law in California, 1936–1941" (PhD dissertation, University of Wisconsin, Madison, 1976).

26. Resner oral history, in Feingold, *Shipboard Murder Case*, 7, 11.

27. Feingold, *Shipboard Murder Case*, iii–vi, Dinkin Johnson oral history, 4–6.

28. Feingold, *Shipboard Murder Case*, iii–vi, Dinkin Johnson oral history, 8.

29. *Chronicle*, Aug. 15, p. 2; Aug. 18, p. 3; Feb. 10, 1935, p. 1; *People v. Todd*, 9 Cal. App. 2d 237 (Cal. Ct. App. 1935); Todd's version of the trial is quite different, see Louise Todd Lambert, interview by Lucy Kendall, May–August 1976; hereafter, Louise Todd Lambert oral history. There is a transcript at the California Historical Society, and the original tapes can be heard at https://archive.org/details/chi_00006/chi_00006_t05_a_access.mp3. Some parts of my research were in the transcript but others were in the online tapes. Her account of her trial is from the interview of June 3, online tape number 8.

30. Todd's account of her life in prison is from online tape numbers 8–11. Information on efforts to secure her parole are in the Louise Todd file, box 441, file 8, Norman Leonard Collection.

31. *Chronicle*, Sept. 29, 1937; Caroline Decker Gladstein, interview by Sue Cobble, August–November 1976, California Historical Society, 96; hereafter, Decker Gladstein oral history, 101–102; marriage information from Ancestry.com.

32. Decker Gladstein oral history, 96; Dorothy Ray Healey and Maurice Isserman, *California Red: A Life in the American Communist Party* (Urbana: University of Illinois Press, 1993), 41, 45, 101.

33. Healey and Isserman, *California Red*, 39.

34. Healey and Isserman, *California Red*, 41, 45, 101.

35. Joseph Danysh interview by Lewis Ferbrache, Dec. 3, 1964, Archives of American Art; Shirley Staschen Triest, "A Life on the First Waves of Radical Bohemianism in San Francisco: oral history transcript," 1997, Regional Oral History Office, Bancroft Library, 71–72.

36. Robert W. Cherny, *Victor Arnautoff and the Politics of Art* (Urbana: University of Illinois Press, 2017), chs. 7–10.

37. Kai Bird and Martin J. Sherwin, *American Prometheus: The Triumph and Tragedy of J. Robert Oppenheimer* (New York: Alfred A. Knopf, 2005), 138. Sherwin interviewed Chevalier in 1982, a year before Chevalier's death. Bird and Sherwin speculate that the "closed unit" Chevalier described may have been the same as the party's Professional Section that appears in the army intelligence report discussed at length in chapter 4, note 8. That report listed Gladstein, Grossman, Andersen, Resner, Chevalier, Alexander Kaun, Addis, and Oppenheimer. Kaun was professor of Slavic languages at UC-Berkeley. See my previous suggestion that this report was based on compiling information from various sources rather than on CP records. Resner told me that the lawyers had their own unit, which casts further doubt on the accuracy of the report from army intelligence. Chevalier published his memoir as *Oppenheimer: The Story of a Friendship* (New York: George Braziller, 1965); for references to the "discussion group," see chs. 1 and 2.

38. Ray Monk, *Robert Oppenheimer: A Life Inside the Center* (New York: Doubleday, 2012), 247. Muir's draft registration card, available at Ancestry.com, identifies him as a state employee. The 1954 quotation is from an Atomic Energy Commission Personal Security Boar hearing, as quoted in Katherine Oppenheimer's FBI file, report of Nov. 28, 1969, stamped Dec. 10, 1969, FBI file number 100-309633. For a recent argument that Oppenheimer was, in fact, a party member because he attended closed meetings with party members, contributed funds to party front groups, and wrote for party publications, see Harvey

Klehr and John Earl Haynes, "Oppenheimer Was a Communist," *Commentary* (Sept. 2023), https://www.commentary.org/articles/harvey-klehr/oppenheimer-was-a-communist/.

39. Violet Orr oral history, interview by Lucy Kendall, 1976, California Historical Society, https://californiarevealed.org/islandora/object/cavpp%3A14455/; hereafter, Orr oral history; see also Lisa Michelle Jackson, "Twenty-Four-Hour Party People: A Gendered Social History of California Communism," MA thesis, San Francisco State University, 2015, esp. 33–35, 38, 44.

40. Martinez *Contra Costa Gazette*, Oct. 30, 1934, Mar. 19, 1935; *Oakland Tribune*, Feb. 1, 1935; Violet Orr case, box 441, file 10, Norman Leonard Collection, LARC.

41. Orr oral history.

42. *NYT*, July 27, 1951; information on parents and high school and university activities from Ancestry.com.

43. Biographical Note, Matt N. and Evelyn Graves Crawford Papers, Rose Manuscript, Archives, and Rare Book Library, Emory University; State Convention Minutes, p. 2, as recorded in *Hearing before the Committee on Un-American Activities, House of Representatives, 83d Congress, 1st Session, Dec. 1, 1953* (Government Printing Office, 1954), 3113.

44. Lillian Dinkin Carlson, "A California Girlhood," in *Red Diapers: Growing Up in the Communist Left*, ed. by Judy Kaplan and Linn Shapiro (Urbana: University of Illinois Press, 1998), 26.

45. Miriam Dinkin Johnson interviews by Robert Cherny, Feb. 11 and March 19, 1993; Miriam Johnson interview by Timothy V. Johnson, May 3, 1986, Manny Harriman Oral History Collection, Tamiment Library/Robert Wagner Labor Archives, New York University.

46. Dinkin Johnson interview by Cherny; Dinkin Johnson interview by Johnson.

47. Panthea Reid, *Tillie Olsen: One Woman, Many Riddles* (New Brunswick, NJ: Rutgers University Press, 2010), chs. 1–5.

48. Reid, *Tillie Olson*, chs. 6, 7.

49. District 13 [list of local activists], file 1967, opis 1, fond 515, RGASPI; Judy Nitzberg interview by Robert Cherny, March 25, 2018; Judy Nitzberg interview by Timothy V. Johnson, July 9, 1985, Manny Harriman Oral History Collection, Tamiment Library/Robert Wagner Labor Archives, New York University; Jack Withington, "A Night of Tar, Feathers and Terror," http://www.jewish-american-society-for-historic-preservation.org/images/A_Night_of_Tar,_Feathers_and_Terror-1.pdf/. Kenneth L. Kann's book *Comrades and Chicken Ranchers: The Story of a California Jewish Community* (Ithaca, NY: Cornell University Press, 1993) includes stories of the Nitzberg family, but Kann disguised his narrators with different names and sometimes conflated individuals from different families. Thus, Ben Hochman's story is basically that of Sol Nitzberg, Leo's father; Joe Hochman's story is basically that of Leo.

50. On the International Brigades and the American volunteers, see esp. Cecil D. Eby, *Comrades and Commissars: The Lincoln Battalion in the Spanish Civil War* (University Park: Pennsylvania State University Press, 2007); Peter N. Carroll, *The Odyssey of the Abraham Lincoln Brigade: Americans in the Spanish Civil War* (Stanford, CA: Stanford University Press, 1994); R. Dan Richardson, *Comintern Army: The International Brigades and the Spanish Civil War* (Lexington: University Press of Kentucky, 1982). For a highly critical view of

the involvement of the Soviet Union, see Ronald Radosh et al., *Spain Betrayed: The Soviet Union in the Spanish Civil War* (New Haven, CT: Yale University Press, 2001).

51. Nitzberg interview by Cherny; Nitzberg interview by Johnson; Jack Withington, "Petaluma Young Men Went to War," *Petaluma Argus-Courier*, http://bill-hammerman .blogs.petaluma360.com/13266/petaluma-young-men-went-to-war/. For the battles of Caspe and Gandesa, see Eby, *Comrades and Commissars*, 307–340. For Taub, see https://alba -valb.org/volunteers/jack-isadore-taub/. For Rappaport, see https://alba-valb.org/volunteers /robert-raport/. For the extent of American casualties, see Eby, *Comrades and Commissars*, xi, who notes that the exact numbers are not available.

52. Interestingly, Bailey included only a stream-of-consciousness account of his first battle and nothing more about his experiences in Spain in his long autobiography, Bill Bailey with Lynn Damme, *The Kid from Hoboken*. He did comment at length about going to Spain and returning from Spain. See also the biography online as part of the Abraham Lincoln Brigade Archives, https://alba-valb.org/volunteers/william-james-bailey/, and Bailey's interview online at https://digitaltamiment.hosting.nyu.edu/s/albafilms/item/2729/. For his capture of the flag, see [San Francisco] *Voice of the Federation*, Oct. 28, 1937, 6. For Belchite, see Eby, *Comrades and Commissars*, 218–27, and Carroll, *Odyssey of the Abraham Lincoln Brigade*, 156–59. Thanks also to Peter Carroll for information from his interview with Bailey.

53. Marion Merriman with Warren Lerude, *American Commander in Spain: Robert Hale Merriman and the Abraham Lincoln Brigade* (Reno: University of Nevada Press, 1986).

54. For Brown, see Brown interview by Johnson, https://alba-valb.org/volunteers/archie -brown/; biographical material, box 1, file 2, Archie Brown Papers, LARC; Carroll, *Odyssey of the Abraham Lincoln Brigade*, 192–93, 199; and Carroll's interview with Brown. Alvah Bessie publicized the incident but had the men singing *The Star-Spangled Banner*. See also Eby, *Comrades and Commissars*, 403. Despite promotion to commissar, Brown remained *soldado* (private).

55. Carroll, *Odyssey of the Abraham Lincoln Brigade*, 95–96, 181–88; Eby, 8, 314, 386; biographical material, box 1, file 2, Archie Brown Collection, LARC. Carroll, *Odyssey of the Abraham Lincoln Brigade*, 183–88, discusses four other possible executions. Bailey did not even mention White's execution in his memoirs, but he did so in an interview with Carroll. David and Edith Jenkins told me on May 8, 1987, that Archie Brown, as commissar, had approved "executions," apparently a story common among San Francisco party leaders.

56. For examples from the *People's World*, see Feb. 9, March 16, April 7, 19, 1938; Merriman *American Commander in Spain*; Cherny, *Victor Arnautoff*, 120.

57. For Eloesser, see William Blaisdell, "Leo Eloesser: The Remarkable Story of a Medical Volunteer in Spain," *The Volunteer* (Dec. 3, 2016), https://albavolunteer.org/2016/12 /leo-eloesser-the-remarkable-story-of-a-medical-volunteer-in-spain/; *Chronicle*, July 28; Sept. 8, 9, 11, 1937. There are collections of Eloesser's papers at the Lane Medical Archives, Stanford Medical Center, and the Hoover Institution.

58. Blaisdell, "Leo Eloesser"; *Chronicle*, Oct. 21, 22, 1937; Jan. 9, 12, Feb. 13, March 13, May 8, 1938.

59. *Chronicle*, Oct. 16, 1938.

60. James H. Dolsen, *Bucking the Ruling Class: Jim Dolsen's Story* (n.p.: n.p., 1984), ch. 9.

61. "About the Parties' Representation in Marty Secretariat (Information)," marked "Top Secret," Jan. 20, 1936, 495-14-4, RGASPI, translation by Datia Lotareva; Sam Darcy interview by Richard Wormser, 1981, Oral History of the American Left, box 14, Darcy 1–3, Tamiment Library/Robert F. Wagner Labor Archives, New York University; hereafter, Darcy interview by Wormser. See also Harvey Klehr, John Earl Haynes, and Kyrill M. Anderson, *The Soviet World of American Communism* (New Haven, CT: Yale University Press, 1998), 200–202.

62. William Schneiderman, *Dissent on Trial: The Story of a Political Life* (Minneapolis: MEP Productions, 1983), chs. 2, 3; Leah Schneiderman interview by Robert Cherny, April 26, 1993; Schneiderman, handwritten biographical notes, box 2, file 13, Schneiderman Papers, LARC; Leah Schneiderman speech 1985, box 2, file 16, Schneiderman Papers, LARC; place of birth and other information on the Schneider family from 1930 census through Ancestry.com.

63. Schneiderman, *Dissent on Trial*, chs. 2, 3; Schneiderman, typed biographical notes, box 1, file 9, Schneiderman, handwritten biographical notes, box 2, file 13, Schneiderman Collection, LARC.

64. Schneiderman, *Dissent on Trial,* chs. 2, 3; Schneiderman, handwritten biographical notes, box 2, file 13, Schneiderman Papers, LARC.

65. Sam Darcy interviewed by Robert Cherny, Aug. 19, 1996; Randolph (Darcy) to Dimitrov, May 4, 1937, 495-20-81 RGASPI.

66. Minutes, Closed Bureau Meeting, AAS, Feb. 28, 1935, 495-14-1 RGASPI.

67. Minutes of Sub-Committee CPUSA Meeting on Organisational Questions—Aug 25, 1935; 495-14-1 RGASPI. That same meeting recommended to the ECCI "to replace Sherman No. 1 by Sherman No. 2 (Darcy)." Sherman No. 1 was Schneiderman.

68. Biography, Finding Aid to the William L. Patterson Papers, Howard University, https://dh.howard.edu/cgi/viewcontent.cgi?referer=https://en.wikipedia.org/&httpsre dir=1&article=1151&context=finaid_manu/.

69. Klehr et al., *Soviet World*, 218–24, 343; Joshua Yaffe, "A Black Communist's Disappearance in Stalin's Russia, *New Yorker*, Oct. 18, 2021, https://www.newyorker.com /magazine/2021/10/25/a-black-communists-disappearance-in-stalins-russia-lovett-fort -whiteman-gulag/.

70. Peggy Dennis, *The Autobiography of an American Communist* (Westport, CT: Lawrence Hill, 1977), chs. 3, 4. On Dennis's tenure in Wisconsin, see S. Ani Mukherji, "Reds among the Sewer Socialists and McCarthyites: The Communist Party in Milwaukee," *American Communist History* 16 (2017): 129–31.

71. Dennis, *Autobiography*, ch. 5, esp. pp. 115–18, 124; Darcy unpublished autobiography, ch. 21, p. 12, box 3, file 25A, Darcy Papers. On the Great Terror, see J. Arch Getty and Oleg V. Naumov, *The Road to Terror: Stalin and the Self-Destruction of the Bolsheviks, 1932–1939* (New Haven, CT: Yale University Press, 1999); William J. Chase, *Enemies within the Gates? The Comintern and the Stalinist Repression, 1934–1939* (New Haven, CT: Yale University Press, 2001); Wendy Z. Goldman, *Inventing the Enemy: Denunciation and Terror in Stalin's Russia* (New York: Cambridge University Press, 2011); Paul Hagenloh, *Stalin's Police: Public Order and Mass Repression in the USSR, 1926–1941* (Baltimore: Johns Hopkins University Press, 2009); Hiroaki Kuromiya, *The Voices of the Dead: Stalin's Great Terror in the 1930s* (New Haven, CT: Yale University Press, 2007); Barry McLoughlin and Kevin McDermott, eds., *Stalin's Terror: High Politics and Mass Repression in the Soviet Union* (Basingstoke, UK:

Palgrave MacMillan, 2003); David Shearer, *Policing Stalin's Socialism: Repression and Social Order in the Soviet Union, 1924–1953* (New Haven, CT: Yale University Press. 2009).

72. Browder supplied a list of committee members to HUAC and they were published, among other places, in *Hearing before the Committee on Un-American Activities, House of Representatives, 83d Congress, 1st Session, December 2, 1953* (Washington, D.C.: Government Printing Office, 1954), 3161.

73. Decker Gladstein oral history, 90–99, esp. 95.

74. Minutes of the San Francisco County Personnel Committee, Sept. 3, 1945, box 4, file 4, Lisette and Sam Kutnick Collection, LARC.

75. Girls High School yearbook, 1930; *Oakland Tribune*, March 20, 1935, D3; *Blue and Gold* [UC-Berkeley yearbook], 1931, 171; accessed through Ancestry.com; Edith A. Jenkins, *Against a Field Sinister* (San Francisco: City Lights Books, 1991), 25, 95.

76. Edith Arnstein Jenkins, interview by Gregg Herken, May 9, 2002, box 4, file 8, Martin Sherwin Collection, Library of Congress.

77. Bird and Sherwin, *American Prometheus*, 112–13.

78. Jenkins, *Field Sinister*, 27.

79. Membership Book No. 60 937, dated Oct. 1932, box 1, file 1, Margaret Kerr papers, Hoover Institution.

80. Decker Gladstein interview by Sherwin; Healy and Isserman, *California Red*, 71.

81. Unsigned "Report of Central Control Commission to the Central Committee Plenum," Nov. 1935, 515-1-3801; transcript of discussion, "Meeting on Cadre Question and Political Emigrants," Jan. 28, 1936, marked "Strictly Confidential," 495-14-10; Dirba, report for the Control Commission, minutes of the plenary session of the National Committee, Dec. 3–5, 1938, 495-14-04, all RGASPI. Dirba's report appears in full in Harvey Klehr, John Earl Haynes, and Fridrikh Igorevich Firsov, *The Secret World of American Communism* (New Haven, CT: Yale University Press, 1995), 133–39.

82. Healey and Isserman, *California Red*, 30.

83. Dinkin Johnson oral history, 10–11; Dinkin Johnson interview by Cherny, Feb. 11, 1993.

84. Healey and Isserman, *California Red*, 88; Dennis, *Autobiography*, 101–102, 152–53; Louise Todd Lambert oral history, transcript, 123–27.

85. Louise Todd Lambert oral history, transcript, 120–12, 143, 153.

86. Decker Gladstein interview, 91.

87. Louise Todd Lambert oral history, transcript, 153; Frank C. Jordan, Secretary of State, comp., *Statement of Vote at Primary Election Held on August 30, 1938* (Sacramento: California State Printing Office, 1938), 3–4; *Statement of Vote at General Election Held on Nov. 5, 1940* (Sacramento: California State Printing Office, 1940), 2–4, 7; Communist Party Membership by Districts, 1922–1950, Mapping American Social Movement Project, University of Washington, https://depts.washington.edu/moves/CP_map-members.shtml/.

Chapter 6. The Wartime Popular Front

1. Maurice Isserman, *Which Side Were You On? The American Communist Party during the Second World War* (Middletown, CT: Wesleyan University Press, 1982), 83–85; "Defeat Roosevelt's War-Powers Bill! Get Out and Stay Out of the War!" Statement by the National

Committee, Jan. 23, 1941, *The Communist* 20 (Feb. 1941): 115; unsigned, "What Do We Learn from the Struggle against the Lend-Lease Bill?," *The Communist* 20 (March 1941): 202–217, esp. 206; "Close Ranks on May Day/Take Our Country Out of the Bankers' War—No Convoys—No A.E.F.—Manifesto of the National Committee, Communist Party," *The Communist* 20 (May 1941) 404–409, esp. 407; *PW*, June 21, 1941.

2. Dimitrov to New York, June 26, 1941, RGASPI 495-184-3, as quoted in John Earl Haynes and Harvey Klehr, "The 'Mental Comintern' and the Self-Destructive Tactics of the CPUSA, 1944–8," *Post–Cold War Revelations and the American Communist Party: Citizens, Revolutionaries, and Spies* (London: Bloomsbury Academic, 2021), ed. Vernon L. Pedersen, James G. Ryan, and Katherine A. S. Sibley, 18, 21, 22, 24–25.

3. "The People's Program of Struggle for the Defeat of Hitler and Hitlerism!" Manifesto of the National Committee, June 28–29, 1941," *The Communist* 20 (Aug. 1941): 678–83; Isserman, *Which Side Were You On?*, 104–12, 272n15.

4. *NYT*, June 25, Aug. 16, 1941.

5. *PW*, June 8, 22, July 31, Aug. 10, Sept. 21, 26, Oct. 3, 7, 8, 1942; "Lady Sniper," *Time*, Sept. 28, 1942; *NYT*, Aug. 5, 1942, March 10, March 20; [San Francisco] *Labor Herald*, Oct. 16, 1942.

6. *PW*, Oct. 30, Dec. 3, 1941; *NYT*, Aug. 20, 1941; Lydia to Mike, March 30, June 27, 1943, Michael Arnautoff Letters, Robert W. Cherny Research Files, LARC; Arnautoff to Louise Bransten, April 6, 1944; Nan to Louise [Bransten], Dec. 3, 1945, file 3, box 1, Louise R. Berman Papers, Wisconsin Historical Society.

7. Robert W. Cherny, *Victor Arnautoff and the Politics of Art* (Urbana: University of Illinois Press, 2017), ch. 8, esp. 135.

8. *Chronicle*, April 25, May 30, 1942; *PW*, June 4, 26, 1942, June 24, Nov. 6, 8, 1943; May 6, 1944; Viktor Mikhailovich Arnautov, with Leonid Sanin, *Zhizn' zanovo* (Life Anew), 2nd ed., (Donetsk: Izdatel'stvo Donbas, 1972); trans. Lloyd Kramer, LARC, 42.

9. *Rosenberg Foundation, 1937–1946*; Jean-François Fayet, "VOKS: The Third Dimension of Soviet Foreign Policy," *Searching for a Cultural Diplomacy*, ed. Jessica C. E. Glenow-Hecht and Mark C. Donfried (New York: Berghahn Books, 2010), ch. 1 esp. 33; *PW*, Oct. 7, 1944; "The Story of a Long Friendship, 1931–1956: The First 25 Years of the American Russian Institute in San Francisco" (pamphlet, American Russian Institute of San Francisco Inc., 1956); California Legislature, *Eleventh Report of the Senate Fact-Finding Subcommitee on Un-American Activities* (1959), 118–20.

10. Louise Bransten to Friends, Nov. 14, 1942, box 1, file 8, Berman Papers.

11. There is a short biography of Bransten in the finding aid to her papers at the Wisconsin Historical Society. For her contribution for a new printing press, see my interview with David Jenkins, May 8, 1987; Richard Bransten was a cousin of Edith Arnstein Jenkins. See also House of Representatives, Committee on Un-American Activities, Hearing Regarding the Communist Infiltration of the Motion-Picture Industry, Oct. 30, 1947, 515. The contributions of the Rosenberg Foundation, 1937–1946, are listed in *Rosenberg Foundation, 1937–1946* (San Francisco: Rosenberg Foundation, 1947); the large majority show no particular political orientation, but others include the contribution to the American Russian Institute and sixteen thousand dollars to the California Labor School in 1945.

12. The official name of the Soviet intelligence during World War II was Naródnyy komis-sariát vnútrennikh del (NKVD), which became Ministerstvo gosudarstvennoy bezopasnosti (MGB) in 1946 and then Komitet gosudarstvennoy bezopasnosti (KGB) in 1954.

13. Kheifets to Kemenov, March 30, 1943, fond 5283 (VOKS), opis s.ch.-2a, delo 12, p. 126, State Archive of the Russian Federation (GARF); Kheifets to Kemenov with copy to Zarubin of NKVD, May 22, 1943, fond 129, opis 27, papka 153, delo 50, p. 2, Archive of Foreign Policy of the Russian Federation (AVP RF); Kheifets to Kislova with copies to Zarubin and Vladimir Bazykin, the VOKS representative in the embassy in Washington, Aug. 4, 1943, fond 5283 (VOKS), opis s.ch.-2a, delo 12, p. 222, State Archive of the Russian Federation. Svetlana Chervonnaya generously provided these citations and translations. For the Christmas presents, see Venona message from Kheifets to Moscow, Nov. 2, 1943.

14. Karl G. Yoneda, *Ganbatte: Sixty-Year Struggle of a Kibei Worker* (Los Angeles: Asian American Studies Center, UCLA, 1983), ch. 6. A fifth columnist is someone within a country who sides with or actively works for that country's enemies.

15. Goldblatt oral history, 286–87; *Chronicle*, Feb. 22, 1942; Isserman, *Which Side*, 144; "'As Truly American as Your Son': Voicing Opposition to Internment in Three West Coast Cities," Ellen Eisenberg, *Oregon Historical Quarterly* 104 (2003): 542–65, esp. 552–53. I am aware of the disagreements among historians regarding the words used to describe the process of relocating Japanese Americans from the Pacific Coast military districts. See, e.g., Roger Daniels, "Words Do Matter: A Note on Inappropriate Terminology and the Incar-ceration of the Japanese Americans," in *Nikkei in the Pacific Northwest*, ed. Louis Fiset and Gail M. Nomura (Seattle: University of Washington Press, 2005), 190–214; and Roger W. Lotchin, *Japanese-American Relocation in World War II: A Reconsideration* (Cambridge, UK: Cambridge University Press, 2018).

16. Jenkins oral history, 152; Louise Todd Lambert, interview by Lucy Kendall, July 22, 1976, 6th interview, first tape, California Historical Society; hereafter, Louise Todd Lambert oral history.

17. Yoneda, *Ganbatte*, chs. 6–8; Schreiber, *Elaine Black Yoneda*, 112–52.

18. Yoneda, *Ganbatte*, ch. 8.

19. Enlistment records are from Ancestry.com; see also interviews with Judy Nitzberg interview by Robert Cherny, March 25, 2018, and Judy Nitzberg interview by Timothy V. Johnson in 1985, https://vimeo.com/246813359/; Keith Eickman: Idealism and Disap-pointment," in Harvey Schwartz, *Solidarity Stories: An Oral History of the ILWU* (Seattle: University of Washington Press, 2009), 274–80; "Jack Olsen: Activist and Educator," in Schwartz, *Solidarity Stories*, 285; Panthea Reid, *Tillie Olsen: One Woman, Many Riddles* (New Brunswick, NJ: Rutgers University Press, 2010), 151–67.

20. Isaac Zafrani, interview by Robert Cherny, April 1, 1987; citizenship and enlistment records from Ancestry.com.

21. Biographical material, box 1, file 2, Archie Brown Collection, LARC; Archie Brown, interview by Timothy V. Johnson, undated but c. 1985, Abraham Lincoln Brigade Archives Oral History Collection, https://wp.nyu.edu/albaoh/archie-brown/. Brown's claim that he "snuck into" the army suggests the use of a false name. I could find no record for him other than his 1940 draft card in searching the Veterans' Administration (VA) records

using Ancestry.com. For the 76th Infantry, see https://history.army.mil/html/forcestruc/cbtchron/cc/076id.htm/.

22. Minutes of the San Francisco County Personnel Committee, Aug 28, 1945, box 4, file 4, Lisette and Samuel Kutnick Collection.

23. Pat Tobin, interviews by Robert Cherny, Feb. 9 and 25, 1987; Bill Bailey with Lynn Damme, *The Kid from Hoboken*, 338, 354, 357; Bill Bailey, interview by Robert Cherny, March 16, 1993; Richard S. Hobbs, *The Cayton Legacy: An African-American Family* (Pullman: Washington State University Press, 2002, ch. 12.

24. *The Union Movement, the California Labor School, and San Francisco Politics, 1926–1988,* interviews with David Jenkins by Lisa Rubens, 1987 and 1988, University of California, Bancroft Library, Regional Oral History Office; hereafter, Jenkins oral history; Jenkins interview by Robert Cherny, May 8, 1987.

25. *Louis Goldblatt: Working Class Leaders in the ILWU, 1935–1977,* interview conducted by Estolv Ethan Ward, 1978–1979, Regional Oral History Office, Bancroft Library, University of California, Berkeley, 419–22.

26. For a pictorial overview with maps of the major shipyards, see Wayne Bonnett, *Build Ships! Wartime Shipbuilding Photographs: San Francisco Bay: 1940–1945* (Sausalito: Windgate Press, 1999). For wartime changes in the East Bay, see Marilynn S. Johnson, *The Second Gold Rush: Oakland and the East Bay in World War II* (Berkeley: University of California Press, 1993), and Gretchen Lemke-Santangelo, *Abiding Courage: African American Migrant Women and the East Bay Community* (Chapel Hill: University of North Carolina Press, 1996); Shirley Ann Wilson Moore, *To Place Our Deeds: The African American Community in Richmond, California, 1910–1963* (Berkeley: University of California Press, 2001).

27. Johnson, *Second Gold Rush,* 70–72; Charles Wollenberg, *Marinship at War: Shipbuilding and Social Change in Wartime Sausalito* (Berkeley: Western Heritage Press, 1990), 51–55, 74–75.

28. Ray Thompson, interviews by Jesse Warr, Oct. 11, Nov. 6. 1978, SFPL History Center; Johnson, *Second Gold Rush,* 72–73.

29. Charles Wollenberg, "James v. Marinship: Trouble on the New Black Frontier," *California History* 60 (1981): 262–79; Johnson, *Second Gold Rush,* 73–75; Thompson interview by Ward, 1978; *James v. Marinship Corp.,* 25 Cal.2d 721 (1944). Resner told me of working closely with Marshall in an interview on Dec. 18, 1992.

30. Biographical note, Matt N. and Evelyn Graves Crawford Papers, Emory University.

31. William Issel, *Church and State in the City: Catholics and Politics in Twentieth-Century San Francisco* (Philadelphia: Temple University Press, 2013, 126–32; Stack, Grossman CUAC cards, State Archives; biographical note, Crawford Papers; Minutes of the SF County Personnel Committee, Sept. 3, 1945, box 4, file 4, Kutnick Collection.

32. Issel, *Church and State in the City,* 126–32; *Chronicle,* March 7, 11; Aug. 12, 1945, 10; *PW,* Jan. 6, 1945, 5. On Crawford, see clippings dated May 29, 1983 and May 30, 1993, file 159, box 18, People's World Research Files, LARC.

33. M. J. Heale, "Red Scare Politics: California's Campaign Against Un-American Activities, 1940–1970," *Journal of American Studies* 20 (1986): 5–32, esp. 6, 11–14; Robert L. Pritchard, "California Un-American Activities Investigations: Subversion on the Right?"

California Historical Quarterly 49 (1970): 309–313, 317–20; and Ingrid Winther Scobie, "Jack B. Tenney and the 'Parasitic Menace': Anti-Communist Legislation in California, 1940–1949," *Pacific Historical Review* 43 (1974): 188–211.

34. *Communist Party v. Peek*, 20 Cal. 2d 536; *Chronicle*, July 12, 1942; Winther Scobie, "Jack B. Tenney," 200.

35. William Schneiderman, "The California Elections," *The Communist* 21 (Aug. 1942): 602–609; *Chronicle*, Nov. 5, 1942.

36. All election data is from Join California, http://www.joincalifornia.com/.

37. *Chronicle*, Nov. 5, 1941; Oct. 10, 19, 25, Nov. 3, 4, 1943.

38. *PW*, Election Supplement, undated but c. Oct. 13, 1944; *PW*, Nov. 3, 4, 6, 1944.

39. James G. Ryan, *Earl Browder: The Failure of American Communism* (Tuscaloosa: University of Alabama Press, 1997), 204–205.

40. Samples of Schneiderman-Darcy Defense Committee materials are in box 3, file 3, Darcy Papers, NYU; Ryan, *Earl Browder*, 204–205; for the FBI investigations, see pp. 96-26-2 through 96-2-12, Schneiderman FBI file.

41. *Chronicle*, July 18, Nov. 29, Dec. 7, 1941; Ann Fagan Ginger, *Carol Weiss King: Human Rights Lawyer, 1895–1952* (Niwot: University Press of Colorado, 1993), ch. 24. Regarding Willkie, the standard biographies treat his role in the Schneiderman case as part of his commitment to civil liberties; see, e.g., Steve Neal, *Dark Horse: A Biography of Wendall Willkie* (New York: Doubleday, 1984), 267–70. For the FBI's initiation of custodial detention, see p. 96-14-14, Schneiderman FBI file.

42. For material copied from King's office and cover memos from Ladd of March 23, 1942, May 12, 1942, and Oct. 5, 1942, see files 39-015-1-81, 39-915-1-86, 39-915-1-94, 39-915-1-96, Bridges FBI file. For examples of transcriptions or summaries of King's phone calls, see, e.g., Dec. 30, 1942, 97-27-86; Feb. 13, 1943, 97-26-99, Schneiderman FBI file. See also Athan G. Theoharis and John Stuart Cox, *The Boss: J. Edgar Hoover and the Great American Inquisition* (Philadelphia: Temple University Press, 1988), 13–14.

43. Jeffrey F. Liss, "The Schneiderman Case: An Inside View of the Roosevelt Court," *Michigan Law Review* 74 (1976): 500–523, esp. 507–508; *Los Angeles Times*, Jan. 17, 1942, 11; *New York Times*, May 7, 1942, 12.

44. *NYT*, Feb. 16, 1943.

45. *NYT*, March 13, 1943.

46. *Schneiderman v. U.S.*, 320 U.S. 118 (1943); Liss, "Schneiderman Case"; Fagan Ginger, *Carol King*, 377–80.

47. Liss, "Schneiderman Case," 507–508.

48. Liss, "Schneiderman Case," 520 and 520n114; Google Scholar, https://scholar.google.com/scholar_case?about=53021727921919774491&q=Schneiderman+v.+United+States&hl=en&as_sdt=2006, lists all cases that have cited *Schneiderman*. The Justice Department immediately began reconsidering or dismissing existing cases that did not meet the new standard; see *Bureau Bulletin* 49, 9-29-43, 97-26-131, Schneiderman FBI file.

49. Sanford Levinson, *Constitutional Faith* (Princeton, NJ: Princeton University Press, 1988), 120.

50. Cherny, *Bridges*, ch. 12.

51. Cherny, *Bridges*, ch. 12; *Bridges v. Wixon*, 326 U.S. 135 (1945).

52. Liss, "Schneiderman Case," 500–501; Efim Hanoff, 495-261-883-1 RGASPI; *Chronicle*, May 23, 1941. Hanoff went to the Soviet Union voluntarily in 1958, at the age of sixty-five; unidentified clipping dated Sept. 13, 1958, file Hanoff, Elmer, carton 21, file 64, People's World Collection, LARC.

53. For CP-sponsored schools, see Marvin Gettleman, "The Lost World of United States Labor Education: Curricula at East and West Coast Communist Schools, 1944–1947," in *American Labor and the Cold War: Grassroots Politics and Postwar Political Culture*, ed. Robert Cherny, William Issel, and Kieran Walsh Taylor (New Brunswick, NJ: Rutgers University Press, 2004), 205–215.

54. *PW*, July 28, Aug. 4, 6, 1942; June 9, 1944; Jan. 6, 1945. On Jenkins, see Jenkins oral history, p. 153; Pele Edises, "The Solid Scholar of Lower Market Street," *PW*, Nov. 18, 1944. On Roberts, see the collection of his memoirs and materials at LARC. I describe this labor-left culture at more length in *Victor Arnautoff and the Politics of Art* (Urbana: University of Illinois Press, 2017), ch. 10. For an overview of the CLS, see John Skovgaard, "The California Labor School" (unpublished paper, 2003, Labor Archive and Research Center, San Francisco State University). See also the CLS collections at LARC, and the Urban Archives, California State University, Northridge.

55. *PW*, March 22, 1945; *Chronicle*, March 25, 1945.

56. Al Richmond, *A Long View from the Left: Memoirs of an American Revolutionary* (New York: Dell Publishing, 1974), 280–81; *Chronicle*, Dec. 17, 1943; Dec. 20, 1944.

57. Biographical note, Guide to the John Pittman Papers, Tamiment Library/Robert F. Wagner Labor Archives, New York University.

58. Jessica Mitford, *A Fine Old Conflict* (New York: Alfred A. Knopf, 1977), chs. 1, 2.

59. Mitford, *Fine Old Conflict*, chs. 3, 4; ch. 4 has a hilarious account of her confrontation with a party expectation that she come from a proletarian background in order to become county financial director; obituary, Doris Brin Walker, *San Francisco Chronicle*, Aug. 19, 2009; Robert E. Treuhaft, *Left-Wing Political Activist and Progressive Leader in the Berkeley Co-op*, interviewed by Robert G. Larsen, 1988–1989, Berkeley Oral History Project, Berkeley Historical Society, 1990, p. 30.

60. COMRAP is FBI file 100-203581; CINRAD is FBI file 100-1090625; both summary reports are available online, COMRAP at https://archive.org/details/CominternApparatus/ and CINRAD at https://archive.org/details/CINRAD/. The Venona documents are online at https://www.nsa.gov/news-features/declassified-documents/venona/. The Vassiliev notebooks are online at https://digitalarchive.wilsoncenter.org/collection/86/vassiliev-notebooks/. See also John F. Fox Jr., "What the Spiders Did: U.S. and Soviet Counterintelligence before the Cold War," *Journal of Cold War Studies* 11 (2009): 206–224, esp. 219; Robert L. Benson, *The Venona Story* (Fort George C. Meade, MD: Center for Cryptologic History, National Security Agency, n.d.), 41–42; John Earl Haynes and Harvey Klehr, *Venona: Decoding Soviet Espionage in America* (New Haven, CT: Yale University Press, 1999). A recent study, Calder Walton's *Spies: The Epic Intelligence War between East and West* (New York: Simon and Schuster, 2023), summarizes Soviet espionage and U.S. counter-espionage during World War II in chapter 4. The seven who were knowingly involved in working with the

Soviet consular officers were Steve Nelson, Isaac Folkoff, Louise Bransten, George Eltenton, James Miller, Holland Roberts, and a pharmacology instructor named or code-named Park.

61. Gregg Herken, *Brotherhood of the Bomb: The Tangled Lives and Loyalties of Robert Oppenheimer, Ernest Lawrence, and Edward Teller* (New York: Henry Holt, 2002); Kai Bird and Martin J. Sherwin, *American Prometheus: The Triumph and Tragedy of J. Robert Oppenheimer* (New York: Alfred A. Knopf, 2005); Ray Monk, *Robert Oppenheimer: A Life Inside the Center* (New York: Random House, 2012).

62. Steve Nelson, James R. Barrett, and Rob Ruck, *Steve Nelson, American Radical* (Pittsburgh: University of Pittsburgh Press, 1981), chs. 5, 8; Steve Nelson interview by Martin Sherwin, box 6, file 3, Sherwin Papers, Library of Congress.

63. Nelson et al., *Steve Nelson*, chs. 5, 8; Nelson interview by Sherwin; Historical/Biographical Note, Steve Nelson Papers, Tamiment Library and Wagner Labor Archives, NYU. Regarding his recruitment by the NKVD in 1942, see Herken, *Brotherhood*, 98, citing Nelson's conversation with Zubilin on April 10, 1943, in an FBI report on the transcribed conversation, May 7, 1943, CINRAD file (Herken, *Brotherhood*, 355n96); Report of [name redacted], Jan. 31, 1947, CINRAD, file 100-1090625, p. 30; hereafter, CINRAD report. Herken overstates Nelson's position in the CP, calling him "the Bay Area's top Communist" (p. 56).

64. Comintern Apparatus (COMRAP), Dec. 15, 1944, FBI file 100-203581, section 62, part 1, 34; hereafter, COMRAP report. For DSM as code name for the atomic bomb project, see Vincent C. Jones, *Manhattan: The Army and the Atomic Bomb* (Washington, D.C.: Center of Military History, US Army, 2007), 43. Regarding Oppenheimer, see Bird and Sherwin, *American Prometheus*, 174, 175.

65. Herken, *Brotherhood*, 161; Bird and Sherwin, *American Prometheus*, 193–99; Monk, *Oppenheimer*, 345–47. The encounter between Chevalier and Oppenheimer haunted both men and their wives through repeated investigations. See also one of Chevalier's memoirs: Haakon Chevalier, *Oppenheimer: The Story of a Friendship* (New York: George Braziller, 1965), 52–55. See also Harvey Klehr and John Earl Haynes, "Special Tasks and Sacred Secrets on Soviet Atomic Espionage," *Intelligence and National Security* 26 (2011): 5, 656–75, http://dx.doi.org/10.1080/02684527.2011.604203/.

66. CINRAD report, 4–9.

67. Herken, *Brotherhood*, 99; COMRAP report, part 3, 3–4. None of this appears in Schneiderman's FBI file.

68. Herken, *Brotherhood*, 99–110.

69. Herken, *Brotherhood*, 99, ch. 6 esp. 105–107, 122–24; Haynes and Klehr, *Venona*, 330.

70. Vassiliev White Notebook #1, https://digitalarchive.wilsoncenter.org/topics/vassiliev-notebooks, 89, 118, 133, 146, 257, 414.

71. COMRAP, part 1, 85–88, but much is redacted; summary, 15, 28; Nelson, *American Radical*, 258; Nelson interview by Sherwin. Nelson spells the name "Falkoff" rather than Folkoff. For Venona messages, see Kheifets to Moscow, Feb. 8, 1944; same March 5, 1944, https://www.nsa.gov/Helpful-Links/NSA-FOIA/Declassification-Transparency-Initiatives/Historical-Releases/Venona/.

72. Vassiliev White Notebook #1, 43, 136, 148, 414.

73. COMRAP, section 2, p. 222, and *passim*; Herkin, *Brotherhood*, 92–93. Louise Bransten was long since divorced from Richard Bransten; during World War II, Richard Bransten assisted Gregory Silvermaster and Jacob Golos to pass material collected from sources in Washington to NKVD operatives in New York. For Richard Bransten, see, COMRAP, section 2, p. 544; John Earl Haynes, Harvey Klehr, and Alexander Vassiliev, *Spies: The Rise and Fall of the NKVD in America* (New Haven, CT: Yale University Press, 2010), 43, 170.

74. Vassiliev White Notebook #1, 43, 136, 148, 414, 121, 135–36, 414–15.

75. COMRAP, section 1, 81–82; Summary, p. 27; Venona messages, San Francisco (Kheifets) to Moscow, Nov. 8, 1943; Dec. 7, 1943; Dec. 31, 1943; March 27, 1944.

76. Vassiliev White Notebook #1, 115–18, 148.

77. Venona, Apresyan to Moscow, April 6, 1945; Vladimir Pravdin to Moscow, June 4, 1945; Apresyan to Moscow, Feb. 20, 1946. The reference to "her institution" reinforces the speculation that MAP was Louise Bransten; see Haynes and Klehr, *Venona*, 356; Herken, *Brotherhood*, 119.

78. Kheifets to Moscow, Nov. 9,1943; Haynes and Klehr, *Venona*, 228–29, 428n73, 428n74.

79. Letter, George to David Jenkins, Aug. 13, 1945, box 4, file 13, Lisette and Samuel Kutnick Collection, LARC.

80. On Lambert, see unidentified clipping dated Jan. 11, 1952, probably from *PW*, in PW Research Files, box 22, file 261, LARC; Louise Todd oral history; World War II draft registration from Ancestry.com; Minutes of the San Francisco County Personnel Committee, Aug. 28, 1945, box 4, file 4, Kutnick Collection.

81. Vavilov to Moscow, Nov. 13,1945; Haynes and Klehr, *Venona*, 324, 344. The online version of this message has information about Callahan redacted. On Vavilov, see the online concordance and index to the Vassiliev notebooks, 446.

82. Schneiderman's file is filled with reports from FBI agents and informants about his movements, contacts, and conversations. He was also subject to a "mail cover," i.e., the FBI recorded and investigated his correspondents. His FBI file also includes summaries of telephone conversations attributed to "confidential informant," the FBI's usual form for presenting the results of an illegal wire tap or listening device. For an example of Schneiderman's contacts with Folkoff, see Report of R. C. Taylor, LLS, 5/29/41, which summarizes information from Dec. 1, 1940 through May 23, 1941, file 97-26-27, pp. 15–17, which lists a meeting of Schneiderman and Folkoff at Chevalier's home, at which Oppenheimer's auto was parked outside, but so was the auto of Paul Smith, editor of the *San Francisco Chronicle*, and a later visit by the Schneidermans to the Folkoffs. N.J.L. Pieper, the special agent in charge of the San Francisco field office, reported in June 1944 that the Schneidermans were "on very friendly terms" with the Folkoffs; see letter, Pieper to Director, June 5–June 18, 1944, 97-26-148, Schneiderman FBI file.

83. Joseph R. Starobin, *American Communism in Crisis, 1943–1957* (Cambridge: Harvard University Press, 1972), 45, 232.

84. *People's World*, Feb. 14, p. 1; May 22, p. 1; May 24, 1944, p. 1; Browder, *Teheran: Our Path in War and Peace* (New York: International Publishers, 1944); Starobin, *American Communism in Crisis*, 61–70; Isserman, *Which Side Are You On*, 188–91, 196; Edward P. Johanningsmeier, *Forging American Communism: The Life of William Z. Foster* (Princeton, NJ: Princeton University Press, 1994), 296–304; Ryan, *Earl Browder*, 221–25. See also *PW*

for the period between early 1942 and early 1945; and Earl Browder, *Moscow, Cairo, Teheran* (New York: Workers Library Publishers, 1944); *Teheran and America: Perspectives and Tasks* (New York: Workers Library Publishers, 1944); *Shall the Communist Party Change Its Name?* (New York: Workers Library Publishers, 1944). B. B. Jones told me on Sept. 14, 1986, that he was expelled for disagreeing with the Teheran line.

85. Minutes of County Personnel Committee, Aug. 17, and Aug. 25, 1945, box 4, file 4, Lisette and Samuel Kutnick Collection, LARC.

86. This is developed at more length in Cherny, *Bridges*, ch. 11. *PW*, May 27, 1944; press release, May 26 [1944]; telegram, Bridges to *The Times*, Chicago, May 27, 1944: Bridges, statement to *St. Louis Post Dispatch*, July 9, 1944, file "No Strike Pledge," box 2, series ILWU History, World War II-1940–45, ILWU Library. Starobin, *American Communism in Crisis*, 59, 77.

87. *PW*, April 26, 1945.

88. Jenkins interview by Cherny, May 8, 1987; *PW*, May 11, 1945; "Story of a Long Friendship," 12 (see note 9); report of Donald W. Kuno, Aug. 17, 1945, Arnautoff FBI file, vol. 1, 47–51.

Chapter 7. The Party in Crisis

1. Starobin, *American Communism in Crisis, 1943–1957*, 78, 79; John Earl Haynes and Harvey Klehr, "The 'Mental Comintern,' and the Self-Destructive Tactics of the CPUSA, 1944–8," in *Post–Cold War Revelations and the American Communist Party: Citizens, Revolutionaries, and Spies*, ed. Vernon J. Pedersen, James G. Ryan, and Katherine A. S. Sibley (London: Bloomsbury Academic, 2021), 27, 28; Duclos's article, in English, is at http://www.marxists.org/history/usa/parties/cpusa/1945/04/0400-duclos-ondissolution.pdf/.

2. Isserman, *Which Side Are You On?*, 218–33; *PW*, April 16, May 3, 24, June 4, 7, 1945; "Present Situation and the Next Tasks: Resolution of the National Convention of the Communist Party, U.S.A., Adopted July 28, 1945," 24 (1945): *Political Affairs*, 816–32, esp. 830, 832.

3. Isserman, *Which Side Are You On?*, 218–33; *PW*, July 19, 31, Aug. 1, 1945; for Darcy, see Series II, box 1, file 11, Sam Darcy Papers, Tamiment Library, Robert F. Wagner Labor Archives, New York University.

4. Minutes of the San Francisco County Personnel Committee, Aug. 7 [1945], box 4, file 4, Lisette and Sam Kutnick Collection, LARC. On Jenkins's role, see letter, Harrison George to David Jenkins, Aug. 13, 1945, box 4, file 13, Kutnick Collection, LARC.

5. Report of Leadership Review Committee San Francisco County, CP (no author, undated but ca. Sept. 1945), minutes of Aug. 10, 1945, and other minutes of individual committee meetings listing participants, box 4, file 13, Kutnick Collection.

6. Report of Leadership Review Committee San Francisco County, box 4, file 13, Kutnick Collection.

7. Minutes, Personnel Committee, Aug 24, 1945, box 4, file 13, Kutnick Collection.

8. Minutes, Personnel Committee, Aug. 28, 1945, box 4, file 13, Kutnick Collection.

9. Minutes, Personnel Committee, Sept. 1, Sept. 3, Sept. 5, 1945, box 4, file 13, Kutnick Collection.

10. Report of Leadership Review Committee San Francisco County, box 4, file 13, Kutnick Collection.

11. Report of Leadership Review Committee San Francisco County, box 4, file 13, Kutnick Collection. I was unable to find any report on the results of the county convention in *PW* between Sept. 5 and Nov. 1, 1945.

12. Loretta Starvus Stack interview by Lucy Kendall, July 1986–January 1987, LARC, https://californiarevealed.org/islandora/object/cavpp%3A15593/; hereafter, Starvus oral history. Starvus is very vague about the date she was elected to that office; she appears in the 1945 city directory with that position. Jessica Mitford described a similar situation: "A number of malcontents . . . had discovered to their joy that the full-time leadership was overloaded with ex-lawyers, ex-social workers, and other bourgeois elements of that ilk. . . . [They] launched a full-scale campaign aimed at Effecting Change, i.e., ousting the old leadership and substituting proletarians—themselves"; see Mitford, *A Fine Old Conflict* (New York: Alfred A. Knopf, 1977), 77.

13. Louise Todd Lambert interviews by Lucy Kendall, May–August 1976, California Historical Society; hereafter, Louise Todd Lambert oral history, CHS, 171; Starvus oral history. On Irving Kretchmar/Keith, see Abraham Lincoln Brigade Archives, https://alba-valb.org/volunteers/irving-keith/. Other biographical information from Ancestry.com.

14. Starvus oral history; Walter Stack CUAC card, State Archives.

15. Eva Maas, *Looking Back on a Life in the Left: A Personal History* (self-published, 1998).

16. Maas, *Looking Back*.

17. "Don Watson: Union Stalwart," in Harvey Schwartz, *Solidarity Stories: An Oral History of the ILWU* (Seattle: University of Washington Press, 2009), 288–95; Don Watson oral history, interview by Harvey Schwartz, 1994, LARC; Don Watson interview by Robert Cherny, 1996.

18. Summary report by Paul C. Fuller, April 25, 1951, 1: 210–38; Special Agent in Charge San Francisco to Director FBI, Oct. 4, 1951, 1: 248–50; Report of Paul C. Fuller, Oct. 4, 1951, 1: 240–47, all Arnautoff FBI file, available at LARC.

19. Robert E. Treuhaft, *Left-Wing Political Activist and Progressive Leader in the Berkeley Co-op*, interviews by Robert G. Larsen, 1988–1989, Berkeley Oral History Project, Berkeley Historical Society, 1990, p. 30; Dorothy Ray Healey and Maurice Isserman, *California Red: A Life in the American Communist Party* (Urbana: University of Illinois Press, 1993), 41, 45, 101. Nathan Heller, "Private Dreams and Public Ideals in San Francisco," *New Yorker* (Aug. 6 and 13, 2018), https://www.newyorker.com/magazine/2018/08/06/private-dreams-and-public-ideals-in-san-francisco/.

20. I've described this labor-left culture at more length in my *Victor Arnautoff and the Politics of Art* (Urbana: University of Illinois Press, 2017), ch. 10. For an overview of the CLS, see John Skovgaard, "The California Labor School" (unpublished paper, 2003, LARC). See also the CLS collections at LARC, and the Urban Archives, California State University, Northridge.

21. David Jenkins interview by Robert Cherny, May 8, 1987; Holland Roberts memoirs, box 1, file 17, Holland Roberts Papers, Labor Archives and Research Center, San Francisco State University. For early CP schools in San Francisco, see Lisa Jackson, "Twenty-Four-Hour Party People: A Gendered Social History of California Communism," MA thesis, San Francisco State University, 2015, ch. 2; on other CP-sponsored schools, see Marvin Gettleman, "The Lost World of United States Labor Education: Curricula at East and West Coast Communist Schools, 1944–1947," in *American Labor and the Cold War: Grassroots Politics*

and Postwar Political Culture, ed. Robert Cherny, William Issel, and Kieran Walsh Taylor (New Brunswick, NJ: Rutgers University Press, 2004), 205–215. On Jenkins, see *The Union Movement, the California Labor School, and San Francisco Politics, 1926–1988,* interviews with David Jenkins by Lisa Rubens, 1987 and 1988, University of California, Bancroft Library, Regional Oral History Office (hereafter, Jenkins oral history), 153; Pele Edises, "The Solid Scholar of Lower Market Street," *PW,* Nov. 18, 1944.

22. The early CLS catalogs listed their various endorsers and supporters in box 1, files 1–8, California Labor School Collection, LARC; on Crocker's support, see Holland Roberts memoirs, folder 8, box 1, and Jenkins oral history, p. 153; *Rosenberg Foundation, 1936–1946* (San Francisco: Rosenberg Foundation, 1947), 34. See also Edises, "Solid Scholar."

23. Course catalogs, box 1, files 1–8, CLS Collection, LARC; enrollments projected from financial data, folder c, box 4; flyers and announcements, folder 9, box 1, CLS Collection, LARC; Holland Roberts memoirs, box 1, file 17, Holland Roberts Papers, LARC; Jenkins interview by Cherny, May 8, 1987; Jenkins oral history, p. 212.

24. Jenkins interview by Robert Cherny, May 8, 1987; Holland Roberts memoirs, box 1, file 16; course catalogs, box 1, file 1, CLS Collection, both LARC.

25. Course catalogs, box 1, file 1, CLS collection, LARC.

26. Course catalogs, box 1, files 1–8, CLS Collection, LARC; Judy Nitzberg interview by Robert Cherny, March 25, 2018; "Keith Eickman: Idealism and Disappointment," in Harvey Schwartz, *Solidarity Stories: An Oral History of the ILWU* (Seattle: University of Washington Press, 2009), 274–80; Don Watson oral history, interview by Harvey Schwartz, 1994, LARC; O'Connor Yates, Richmond, Stack, Tobin CUAC cards, State Archives.

27. Carol Cuénod oral history, interview conducted by Harvey Schwartz, LARC, 1994, revised 2014; hereafter, Cuénod oral history; Jenkins oral history, p. 212.

28. Draft, Report of Sub Committee, no date, no author, six typed pages and two handwritten pages, included with other materials from the Security Commission, successor to the Control Commission, box 4, file 5, Lisette and Sam Kutnick Collection, LARC. I found no reference to this investigation in Holland Roberts's memoirs, LARC.

29. Jenkins interview by Cherny, May 8, 1987.

30. Jenkins oral history, p. 174; Leah Schneiderman interview by Cherny, April 14, 1987; Nathan Godfried, "'Voice of the People': Sidney Roger, the Labor/Left, and Broadcasting in San Francisco, 1945–1950," *American Communist History* 18 (2019): 56–78.

31. Foster, "The Struggle Against Revisionism," 782–799, esp. 796; John Williamson, "The Reconstitution of the Communist Party," 800–815, esp. 802; "Present Situation and Next Tasks," resolution of the National Convention, July 28, 1945," 815–32, esp. 820 (emphasis in original), all from *Political Affairs* 24 (Sept. 1945).

32. *PW,* Sept. 28, Oct. 5, 17, 25, 26, Nov. 3, 5, 1945; *Chronicle,* Nov. 4, 1945.

33. *PW,* April 12, 15, 17, May 2, 8, 20, 22, 29, 31, June 4, 1946.

34. *Chronicle,* May 28, June 2, 6, Aug. 6, 1946; *PW,* Oct. 25, Nov. 1, 1946.

35. *PW,* Sep. 11, 13, 15, 22, Oct. 2, 3, 4, 9, 13, 23, 24, Nov. 1, 6, 1947; *Chronicle,* Oct. 4, 6, 16, 27, Nov. 3, 6, 1947.

36. "Statement of the National Board of the Communist Party on the Recent Expulsion," *Political Affairs* 25 (Nov. 1946), 1011–1015, esp. 1011; Oleta O'Connor Yates, "The Struggle against Deviations and Factionalism in San Francisco," *Political Affairs* 25 (Dec. 1946),

1091–1103. See also Paul Costello, "Anti-Revisionist Communism in the United States," *Theoretical Review* 11 (1979): 10–17.

37. "Report on Factional Situation in San Francisco," mimeographed, no date but ca. 1946, and two fragments of drafts of the same report, all in box 4, file 1, Kutnick Collection, LARC.

38. Harrison George, *The Crisis in the CPUSA* (Los Angeles: n.p., 1947); *Supplement to The Crisis in the CPUSA* (New Jersey: n.p., 1948); https://www.marxists.org/history /erol/1946-1956/crisisinthecpusa/index.htm/ and https://www.marxists.org/history /erol/1946-1956/suppcrisisinthecpusa.htm/.

39. Untitled typed report with penciled notations, 11 typed pages with penciled corrections, box 4, file 1, Kutnick Collection, LARC.

40. Report titled "National Review Commission" and dated Dec. 25, 1950, box 4, file 5, Kutnick Collection, LARC; fragment of a draft report, box 4, file 1, Kutnick Collection, LARC.

41. National Review Commission report Dec. 25, 1950, Kutnick Collection, LARC.

42. National Review Commission report Dec. 25, 1950, Kutnick Collection, LARC; untitled list of 201 former party members, most expelled, box 5, file 36, Kutnick Collection, LARC.

43. Report on drops as of July 15, 1949, box 4, file 15, Kutnick Collection, LARC.

44. Undated list of drops, box 4, file 15; letter, Hilde Daniels to County Committee, Sept. 3, 1950, box 6, file 9; Report on drops as of July 15, 1949, box 4, file 15, Kutnick Collection, LARC.

45. National Education Department, Communist Party, "The Struggle against White Chauvinism" (Sep. 1949), box 13, folder 57, American Left Ephemera Collection, Archives Service Center, University of Pittsburgh, http://digital.library.pitt.edu/u/ulsmanuscripts /pdf/31735051655326.pdf/.

46. Healey and Isserman, *California Red*, 126; Mitford, *Fine Old Conflict*, 127–28; and see below, for the experiences of the Nitzbergs and Keith Eickman.

47. Judy Nitzberg interview by Robert Cherny, March 25, 2018, and conversations over many years.

48. "Keith Eickman: Idealism and Disappointment," in Schwartz, *Solidarity Stories*, 274–80.

49. Healy and Isserman, *California Red*, 128.

Chapter 8. The Crisis Deepens

1. Joseph Starobin, *American Communism in Crisis, 1943–1957* (Cambridge, MA: Harvard University Press, 1972), 14–19, chs. 6, 7; Bert Cochran, *Labor and Communism: The Conflict That Shaped American Unions* (Princeton, NJ: Princeton University Press, 1979), ch. 10; Harvey Klehr and John Earl Haynes, *The American Communist Movement: Storming Heaven Itself* (New York: Twayne, 1992), 103–13.

2. "United Labor Can Stop Reaction," *Political Affairs* 26 (May 1947): 387–90, esp. 390; *PW*, May 10, 21, 29. For Bryson's party membership, see Minutes of the San Francisco County Personnel Committee, Aug. 24, 1945, box 4, file 4; for Lynden, see list of members dropped or expelled, box 4, file 36, Lisette and Sam Kutnick Collection, LARC.

3. "United Labor Can Stop Reaction," *Political Affairs* 26 (May 1947): 387–90, esp. 390; Jack Stachel, "The Third Party Movement in the 1948 Elections," *Political Affairs* 26 (Sept. 1947): 780–93 esp. 785; *PW*, June 7, 25, July 25, Sept 19, Oct. 8, Oct. 14; *Dispatcher*, July 25, Aug. 8, Sept 2, Oct. 3, 17, 1947.

4. My timing of the CP decision is based on Starobin, *American Communism in Crisis*, 172–77; and Johanningsmeier, *Forging American Communism*, 319. According to Johanningsmeier, it was Eugene Dennis who was the major proponent of CP support for the Wallace campaign.

5. *Labor Herald*, March 23, April 13, 20, 1948; *PW*, April 29, Oct. 14, 21, 27, 30, 1948; *Chronicle*, Oct. 1; press release, Progressive Party, New York, Aug. 30, 1948, file Wallace, Henry, box 47, CIO Secretary Treasurer Collection, Archives of Labor History and Urban Affairs, Wayne State University.

6. Curtis MacDougall, *Gideon's Army* (New York: Marzani and Munsell, 1965), 3 vols., 1: 291. Wikipedia has county-by-county election returns for each state at https://en.wikipedia.org/wiki/1948_United_States_presidential_election_in_California/.

7. Kenny, quoted in Janet Stevenson, *The Undiminished Man: A Political Biography of Robert Wallace Kenny* (Novato, CA: Chandler & Sharp Publishers, 1980), esp. 168, 170–71; letter, Darcy to Bridges, Oct. 19, 1964, box 12, file 3, Bridges Papers, LARC; Dennis quoted in Starobin, *American Communism in Crisis*, 16–17. See also Edward L. and Frederick H. Schapsmeier, *Prophet in Politics: Henry A. Wallace and the War Years, 1940–1965* (Ames: Iowa State University Press, 1970), esp. 181; Karl M. Schmidt, *Henry A. Wallace: Quixotic Crusade 1948* (Syracuse, NY: Syracuse University Press, 1960), esp. 258–59.

8. For the California unions that were expelled, see Cherny, *Harry Bridges*, ch. 13.

9. Angela Gizzi Ward oral history interview by Sue Cobble, 1976, California Historical Society, p. 117. For 1950 election data, see Join California: Election History for the State of California, http://www.joincalifornia.com/.

10. James P. Walsh, *San Francisco's Hallinan: Toughest Lawyer in Town* (Novato, CA: Presidio Press, 1982), esp. chs. 8, 9; Vincent Hallinan, *A Lion in Court* (New York: G. P. Putnam's Sons, 1963), chs. 13–15; David Jenkins, *The Union Movement, the California Labor School, and San Francisco Politics, 1926–1988*, interviews by Lisa Rubens, 1987, 1988, Regional Oral History Office, Bancroft Library, University of California, Berkeley (hereafter, Jenkins oral history), p. 175. On the Bridges trial and defense, see Cherny, *Bridges*, ch. 13. Bass had sold the paper and moved to New York in 1951.

11. Jenkins oral history, p. 178. Election data is from Join California: Election History for the State of California, http://www.joincalifornia.com/.

12. California Legislature, *Third Report: Joint Fact-Finding Committee on Un-American Activities in California: 1947*, 77–94. For the CP schools of the early 1930s, see Lisa Jackson, "Twenty-Four-Hour Party People: A Gendered Social History of California Communism," MA thesis, San Francisco State University, 2015. All were organized as one-time events, and all focused solely on Marxist-Leninist analysis.

13. *New York Times*, Dec. 5, 1947, Aug. 13, Sept. 26, 1948; Robert W. Cherny, *Victor Arnautoff and the Politics of Art* (Urbana: University of Illinois Press, 2017), 160–62, 169–70, 178; "How to Padlock a School," flyer, box 5, file 5/4, CLS Collection, LARC.

14. Draft, Report of Sub Committee, no date, no author, six typed pages and two handwritten pages, included with other materials from the Security Commission, successor to

the Control Commission, box 4, file 5, Kutnick Collection, LARC. I found no reference to this investigation in Holland Roberts's memoirs, but in his memoirs Roberts did insist, "No official or member of the Communist Party ever told us what to say or teach." box 1, file 25, Roberts Memoirs.

15. Draft, Report of Sub Committee, no date, no author, six typed pages and two hand-written pages, included with other materials from the Security Commission, successor to the Control Commission, box 4, file 5, Kutnick Collection, LARC.

16. Draft, Report of Sub Committee, no date, no author, six typed pages and two hand-written pages, included with other materials from the Security Commission, successor to the Control Commission, box 4, file 5, Kutnick Collection, LARC.

17. Report of Leadership Review Committee San Francisco County, CP (no author, undated but ca. Sept 1945), box 4, file 13, Kutnick Collection, LARC.

18. Report, Final Perspectives for L. S., box 6, file 12, Kutnick Collection, LARC.

19. Draft, Report of Sub Committee, no date, no author, six typed pages and two handwritten pages, included with other materials from the Security Commission, successor to the Control Commission, box 4, file 5, Kutnick Collection, LARC; Holland Roberts memoirs, box 1, file 1, Roberts Papers, CLS Collection, LARC; "How to Padlock a School," flyer, box 5, file 4, CLS Collection, LARC.

20. Nathan Godfried, "'Voice of the People': Sidney Roger, the Labor/Left, and Broadcasting in San Francisco, 1945–1950," *American Communist History* 18 (2019): 56–78; Al Richmond, *A Long View from the Left: Memoirs of An American Revolutionary* (New York: Delta, 1975), esp. 300, 298ff., 382.

21. Gray Brechin, "Politics and Modernism: The Trial of the Rincon Annex Murals," in Karlstrom, ed., *On the Edge of America: California Modernist Art, 1900–1950* (Berkeley: University of California Press, 1996), 68–89.

22. *San Francisco News*, May 14, 1948; *PW*, Nov. 15, 1947; April 12, 1948; *Rincon Annex Murals: San Francisco: No. 83-5: Hearing before the Subcommittee on Public Buildings and Grounds of the Committee on Public Works, House of Representatives, May 1, 1953* (Washington: United States Government Printing Office, 1953), esp. 47, 54; Brechin, "Politics and Modernism," 77–85.

23. The Internal Security Act of 1950, among other things, specified the existence of "a world Communist movement which, in its origins, its development, and its present practice, is a world-wide revolutionary movement whose purpose it is, by treachery, deceit, infiltration into other groups (governmental and otherwise), espionage, sabotage, terrorism, and any other means deemed necessary, to establish a Communist totalitarian dictatorship in the countries throughout the world through the medium of a world-wide Communist organization." See U.S. Statues at Large, 81st Cong., II Sess., ch. 1024, 987–1031.

24. For HUAC in the late 1940s, see, e.g., Walter Goodman, *The Committee: The Extraordinary Career of the House Committee on Un-American Activities* (New York: Farrer, Strauss, and Giroux, 1968), chs. 6–9, 10–13; Victor S. Navasky, *Naming Names* (New York: Viking, 1980).

25. *Chronicle*, Dec. 1, 2, 3, 1953.

26. *Chronicle*, Dec. 4, 5, 6, 13, 1953.

27. *Chronicle*, Dec. 11, 12, 1956.

28. Data for 1940–1950 is from "CP Membership by Year 1922–1950," *Mapping American Social Movement Projects*, University of Washington, http://depts.washington.edu/moves/CP_map-members.shtml; later data from Klehr and Haynes, *American Communist Movement*, 108, 137, 147. For Halling and Heide, see list of former members, box 4, file 36, Kutnick Collection, LARC.

29. I assume the FBI had a very accurate count of party members.

30. Interview of Lincoln Fairley by Robert Cherny, 1986.

31. "Jack Olsen: Activist and Educator," in Schwartz, *Solidarity Stories*, 274–80, 280–88; Jack Olsen, obituary, *San Francisco Chronicle*, Feb. 28, 1989, B-6; Panthea Reid, *Tillie Olsen: One Woman, Many Riddles* (New Brunswick, NJ: Rutgers University Press, 2010), throughout. Where I've found a conflict between Jack Olsen's oral history in Schwartz, *Solidarity Stories*, and Reid, *Tillie Olsen*, I've accepted the version in the oral history.

32. Reid, *Tillie Olsen*, chs. 8, 9; Minutes, Personnel Committee, 1945, box 4, file 4, Kutnick Collection, LARC.

33. Stanley I. Kutler, *The American Inquisition: Justice and Injustice in the Cold War* (New York: Hill and Wang, 1982), ch. 6.

34. Accounts of the Foley Square trial and its aftermath can be found in Michal R. Belknap, *Cold War Political Justice: The Smith Act, the Communist Party, and American Civil Liberties* (Westport, CT: Greenwood, 1977), chs. 1–5; Kutler, *American Inquisition*, ch. 6; Arthur J. Sabin, *In Calmer Times: The Supreme Court and Red Monday* (Philadelphia: University of Pennsylvania Press, 1999). The Supreme Court decision was *Dennis v. United States*, 341 U.S. 494 (1951).

35. Kutler, *American Inquisition*, ch. 6; Belknap, *Cold War Political Justice*, chs. 5, 6; Colin Wark and John F. Galliher, *Progressive Lawyers under Siege: Moral Panic during the McCarthy Years* (Lanham, MD: Lexington Books, 2015), 82–85, 93–94.

36. This summary of the law firm is from the Guide to the Norman Leonard Papers, LARC. For Resner, see list of expelled or dropped members, box 5, file 36, Kutnick Collection, LARC.

37. Norman Leonard, *Life of a Leftist Labor Lawyer*, oral history conducted by Estolv Ethan Ward, 1985, Regional Oral History Office, Bancroft Library, University of California, Berkeley, (hereafter, Leonard oral history), esp. 1–25.

38. William Schneiderman, *Dissent on Trial: The Story of a Political Life* (Minneapolis: MEP Publications, 1983), 114–18, 330; Johanningsmeier, *Forging American Communism*, 324–30, fails to mention Schneiderman's role.

39. Healy and Isserman, *California Red*, 124.

40. Louise Todd Lambert oral history, interviews by Lucy Kendall, May–August 1976, California Historical Society, 214–23, 238, 255; Loretta Starvus (Stack) oral history, interviews by Lucy Kendall, 1986, 1987, Labor Archives and Research Center, San Francisco State University (hereafter, Starvus oral history), side 21. Starvus and her husband were divorced in 1972; information from Ancestry.com.

41. Oral histories by Archie Brown and Hon Brown, in Griffin Fariello, *Red Scared: Memories of the American Inquisition, An Oral History* (New York: W. W. Norton, 1995), 241–46.

42. Maas, *Looking Back*, ch. 8, 77–79; Nora Lapin, unpublished memoir, in possession of the author.

43. Jenkins oral history, 179–80.

44. Bailey, *Kid from Hoboken*, 402.

45. Starobin, *American Communism in Crisis*, 222–23.

46. Reports of William B. Dillon, Oct. 28, 1954, March 1, 1955, Arnautoff FBI file, National Archives, 3: 14–27, 54–78, esp. 16, 59–60.

47. Kutler, *American Inquisition*, 181; Belknap, *Cold War Political Justice*, ch. 6; *LAT*, July 27, Aug. 1, 1951. The *LAT*, on July 27, undoubtedly reflecting information from federal authorities, described O'Connor Yates as "California party secretary." Given Schneiderman's acting role at the national level after the *Dennis* decision, O'Connor Yates was apparently in a similar acting capacity in California.

48. Healey and Isserman, *California Red*, 136–37; Richmond, *Long View*, 324; Schneiderman, *Dissent*, 134–35; Leonard oral history, 101–102; Doris Brin Walker interview by Robert Cherny, June 29, 2007. Brin Walker told me that she had been a lifelong CP member. The Norman Leonard Collection at LARC includes the trial transcripts.

49. Healey, *California Red*, 137–38, 142; Richmond, *Long View*, 329; Leonard oral history, 105–106. Johanningsmeier, *Forging American Communism*, does not mention these discussions.

50. *LAT*, April 16, 1952; *NYT*, April 16, 1952; Starvus oral history, side 22; Starvus oral history in Fariello, *Red Scare*, 212–19. Leonard does not address this situation in his oral history.

51. *LAT*, June 11, 1952; Richmond, *Long View*, 343–49; Schneiderman, *Dissent*, 216–36; Leonard oral history, 108–110. For the Supreme Court decisions on the appeal from the contempt citations, see *Yates v. U.S.*, 355 US 66 (1957), *Yates v. U.S.*, 356 U.S. 364 (1958).

52. Healy and Isserman, *California Red*, 141; *Yates v. U.S.* 225 F.2d 146 (9th Cir. 1955).

53. Howard Ball and Phillip J. Cooper, *Of Power and Right: Hugo Black, William O. Douglas, and America's Constitutional Revolution* (New York: Oxford University Press, 1992), 148.

54. Belknap, *Cold War Political Justice*, 237–38.

55. Belknap, *Cold War Political Justice*, 241–42; Richmond, *Long View*, 359.

56. Belknap, *Cold War Political Justice*, 243–44.

57. *Yates v. U.S.*, 354 U.S. 298 (1957).

58. *Yates v. U.S.*, 354 U.S. 298 (1957); *LAT*, June 18, 1957.

59. Ball and Cooper, *Of Power and Right*, 149. *Yates v. U.S.*, 354 U.S. 298 (1957); *LAT*, June 18, 1957, 1.

60. *Washington Post*, Dec. 3, 1957.

61. There is a file of material regarding this case in box 423, file 5, of the Leonard Collection, LARC. See also *Chronicle*, Oct. 31, Nov. 20, 1959.

62. *Chronicle*, Nov. 20, 1959; copy of letter, George Andersen to John McTernan, Nov. 27, 1959, box 423, file 5, Leonard Collection, LARC. For Goodman's decision in the Bridges case, see Cherny, *Bridges*, ch. 14.

Chapter 9. The Crisis of 1956–1958, the Collapse of the Old Left, and After

1. *PW*, April 9, 1956.

2. Joseph R. Starobin, *American Communism in Crisis, 1943–1957* (Cambridge, MA: Harvard University Press, 1972), 3–17, esp. 16–17; Edward P. Johanningsmeier, *Forging*

American Communism: The Life of William Z. Foster (Princeton, NJ: Princeton University Press, 1994), 338–41.

3. *PW Magazine*, April 23, *PW*, April 19, 23, 26, 27, 30, May 7, 1956; report headed "National Review Commission," Dec. 25, 1950, box 4, file 5, Lisette and Samuel Kutnick Collection.

4. Schneiderman, unpublished final chapter to his *Dissent on Trial*, box 2, file 18, Schneiderman Papers, LARC. See also Johanningsmeier, *Forging American Communism*, 341–47.

5. Maurice Isserman, *If I Had a Hammer . . . The Death of the Old Left and the Birth of the New Left* (New York: Basic Books, 1987), 22–23; Dorothy Ray Healey and Maurice Isserman, *California Red: A Life in the American Communist Party* (1990; Urbana: University of Illinois Press, 1993), 151–53; Al Richmond, *A Long View from the Left: Memoirs of an American Revolutionary* (New York: Dell, 1972), 367–76, esp. 368.

6. *NYT*, June 5, 1956; *LAT*, June 5, 1956; *Washington Post*, June 5, 1956; *PW*, June 7, 11, 12, 13, 1956; Edith Jenkins, *Against a Field Sinister: Memoirs and Stories* (San Francisco: City Lights Books, 1991), 34; David Jenkins, *The Union Movement, the California Labor School, and San Francisco Politics, 1926–1988*, interviews by Lisa Rubens, 1987, 1988, Regional Oral History Office, Bancroft Library, University of California, Berkeley (hereafter, Jenkins oral history), 188–89, 194.

7. Jessica Mitford, *A Fine Old Conflict* (New York: Alfred A. Knopf, 1977), 268–69. That book has the pamphlet reproduced in full in the appendix, 323–33.

8. *PW*, Nov. 6, 7, 1956; biographical note, John Pittman Papers, Tamiment Library/Robert F. Wagner Labor Archives, New York University.

9. Bill Bailey with Lynn Damme, *The Kid from Hoboken: An Autobiography* (San Francisco, Circus Lithographic Prepress, 1993), 419–20; Estolv Ethan Ward, *Organizing and Reporting on Labor in the East Bay, California and the West, 1925–1987*, interviewed by Lisa Rubens, 1987, Regional Oral History Office, Bancroft Library, University of California, Berkeley (hereafter, Ward oral history), 191; Angela Gizzi Ward, oral history interview by Sue Cobble, 1976 California Historical Society (hereafter, Gizzi Ward oral history), 118–19.

10. Jenkins oral history, 194; Ward oral history, 191; Gizzi Ward oral history, 120; Bailey, *Kid from Hoboken*, 421.

11. Richmond, *Long View*, 380–81.

12. Schneiderman, unpublished final chapter to *Dissent on Trial*.

13. Eva Krupnick Lapin Maas, *Looking Back on a Life in the Left: A Personal History* (Self-published, 1998), 79.

14. Mitford, *Fine Old Conflict*, 274–76.

15. Maas, *Looking Back*, 80–81.

16. Copy of letter, Bill Sennett et al. to National Committee, March 26, 1958, attached to Louise Todd Lambert, interviews by Lucy Kendall, May–August 1976, California Historical Society (hereafter, Louise Todd Lambert oral history), following p. 295.

17. Loretta Starvus Stack interviews by Lucy Kendall, 1986, 1987, Labor Archives and Research Center, San Francisco State University (hereafter, Starvus Stack oral history), side 24; Louise Todd Lambert oral history, 256, 269, 271; William Sennett, *William Sennett: Communist Functionary and Corporate Executive*, interviews by Marshall Windmiller, 1981, 1982,

Regional Oral History Office, Bancroft Library, University of California, Berkeley (hereafter, Sennett oral history), 315, 323, 332–34; copy of letter, Bill Sennett et al. to National Committee, March 26, 1958, attached to Louise Todd Lambert oral history, following p. 295; *Chronicle*, March 3, 1964, 20; *San Francisco Examiner*, March 3, 1964; Minutes of the San Francisco County Personnel Committee, Tuesday, Aug. 24, 1945, box 4, file 4, Kutnick Collection.

18. Carol Cuénod, interviews by Harvey Schwartz, Labor Archives and Research Center, San Francisco State University, 1994, 2014 (hereafter, Cuénod oral history), 38.

19. Mitford, *Fine Old Conflict*, 279–80.

20. Gizzi Ward oral history, 201.

21. Louise Todd Lambert oral history, 133, 149, 195, 214–38; Maas, *Looking Back*, ch. 8; Reid, *Tillie Olsen*, 120, 139.

22. Louise Todd Lambert oral history, 125–26, 127, 130; Starvus Stack oral history, side 20; Reid, *Tillie Olsen*, 392n39.

23. Hobbs, *Cayton Legacy*, 172–73; Jenkins interviews by Cherny; Jenkins oral history, 179, 180; Pat Tobin interview by Cherny; Lincoln Fairley interview by Cherny; Starvus Stack oral history, sides 24, 26; Louise Todd Lambert oral history, 124, 127; Gizzi Ward oral history, 43, 61, 71.

24. Most studies of the CPUSA in the 1950s do *not* mention Soviet anti-Semitism as a factor in the resignations of the late 1950s, including Starobin, *American Communism in Crisis*; Isserman, *If I Had a Hammer*; Guenter Lewy, *The Cause That Failed* (New York: Oxford University Press, 1990); Johanningsmeier, *Forging American Communism*; Vernon L. Pedersen, *The Communist Party in Maryland, 1919–1957* (Urbana: University of Illinois Press, 2001); Gregory S. Taylor, *The History of the North Carolina Communist Party* (Columbia: University of South Carolina Press, 2009); and Ryan S. Pettengill, *Communism and Community: Activism in Detroit's Labor Movement, 1941–1956* (Philadelphia: Temple University Press, 2020). Irving Howe and Lewis Cosar, in *The American Communist Party: A Critical History* (1957; reprint with new epilogue, 1962; reprint, New York: Da Capo Press, 1974), write, regarding the Khrushchev revelations, "Still another factor speeding the disintegration of the party was the tremendous shock which the revelation of Soviet anti-Semitism . . . had upon the Jewish members in New York and other large cities" (498), but they provide no indication of the numbers who may have left the party as a result. In their 1962 epilogue (555–72), Howe and Cosar focus on factionalism in the late 1950s and early 1960s and do not mention Soviet anti-Semitism as a cause for loss of members. Harvey Klehr, in *Communist Cadre: The Social Background of the American Communist Party Elite* (Stanford, CA: Hoover Institution Press, 1978), notes, regarding the events of 1956–1958, "Revelations that anti-Semitism [in the Soviet Union], far from being eradicated, had been a state tool and that Yiddish culture had been destroyed along with many of its leading lights damaged the faith of many of the party's Jewish leaders" (90). However, in no place does Klehr attribute any significant loss of members to Soviet anti-Semitism; his list of fourteen reasons why former Central Committee members left the party (91) does not include Soviet anti-Semitism. A few studies have focused on the reactions of Jewish CPUSA members to revelations of Soviet anti-Semitism in the early 1950s. Lucy Dawidowicz, in "American Reaction to Soviet

Anti-Semitism," *American Jewish Year Book*, 55 (1954): 152, says that those revelations produced "several defections." However, reviewing the same events, Nathan Glazer, in *The Social Basis of American Communism* (New York: Harcourt, Brace, 1961), says, "Not a single Jewish leader is known to have left the party. The Jewish cadre remained solid" (154–57). Philip Mendes, "American, Australian, and other Western Jewish Communists and Soviet Anti-Semitism: Responses to the Slansky Trial and the Doctors Plot 1952–1953," *American Communist History* 10 (2011): 152, says, "Some appear to have quietly resigned, or at least drifted away from Party activity." Mendes also claims, without citation, that "many" resigned from the party after the 1956 revelations. Paul A. Appelbaum, "U.S. Jews' Reaction to Soviet 'anti-Zionism,'" *Patterns of Prejudice* 12 (1978): 21–32, does not deal directly with CP members, but notes that "American Jewry" was "mildly interested, but passive" regarding Soviet anti-Semitism until 1962 (21). Arthur Liebman, *Jews and the Left* (New York: John Wiley and Sons, 1979), 523–24, points to Soviet support for the Arab states in the Six-Day War (1967) as the source for "the collision between the Communist party and many of the remaining older and prominent Jewish Communists [that] finally occurred in 1967 and 1968." Harvey Klehr and John Earl Haynes, in *The American Communist Movement* (1992), say nothing about Soviet anti-Semitism in their treatment of the events of the mid- and late 1950s (141–47), but do say, as of the mid-1980s, "The Jewish presence in the party had also declined due to intense party hostility to Israel and denial of Soviet anti-Semitism."

25. Email, Nora Lapin to Robert Cherny, April 4, 2023.

26. Eickman interview by Robert Cherny, Feb. 9, 1993; Maas, *Looking Back*, 81–82.

27. Copy of report on Bridges sent to the State Department, other federal officials, and FBI agents abroad, attached to copy of memo, Hoover to C. Tomlin Bailey, July 28, 1958, file 39-915-3414, all Bridges FBI file.

28. California Legislature, Senate Fact-Finding Committee on Un-American Activities, *Eleventh Report, Un-American Activities in California, 1961* (Sacramento, 1961), 12–13.

29. *Chronicle*, June 14, 16, 17, 19, 21, 1957; *PW*, June 27, 1957.

30. *Chronicle*, June 6, 12, Aug. 12, 13, 22, 1959; *Dispatcher*, Aug. 28, 1959. For an excellent overview of events, see Joshua Paddison, "Summers of Worry, Summers of Defiance: San Franciscans for Academic Freedom and Education and the Bay Area Opposition to HUAC, 1959–1960," *California History* 78 (1999): 188–201, 219–21.

31. Paddison, "Summers of Worry"; *Chronicle*, May 12, 13, 1960.

32. Paddison, "Summers of Worry"; *Chronicle*, May 13, 1960.

33. Paddison, "Summers of Worry"; *Chronicle*, May 14, 1960; email from Nora Lapin to Robert Cherny.

34. Paddison, "Summers of Worry"; *Dispatcher*, May 20, 1960; *Chronicle*, May 14.

35. Memo to Mr. Nease from M. A. Jones, May 2, 1958, with attached HUAC report, *Operation Abolition* (Government Printing Office, 1957), FBI file 61-7582-3769, https://sites.google.com/site/ernie124102/home/.

36. Paddison, "Summers of Worry"; *Operation Abolition*, https://blogs.princeton.edu/reelmudd/2010/10/operation-abolition-and-operation-correction/. *Operation Correction* is on the same website. See also U.S. House of Representatives, 86th Cong., 2d Session, *The Communist-Led Riots Against the House Committee on Un-American Activities in San Francisco*,

Calif., May 12–14, 1960, Report by the Committee on Un-American Activities (Washington, D.C.: Government Printing Office, 1960), 7, 8. This published report is a slightly edited text of the film, https://babel.hathitrust.org/cgi/pt?id=uc1.aa0004039012&view=1up&seq=3/.

37. See the online films, previously cited.

38. Paddison, "Summers of Worry."

39. *Chronicle,* Oct. 21, Nov. 17, 1959.

40. *Chronicle,* Sept. 29, 1960; *Dispatcher,* Sept. 23, 1960; Remarks of Senator John F. Kennedy at Mormon Tabernacle, Salt Lake City, Utah, September 23, 1960, John F. Kennedy Presidential Library, https://www.jfklibrary.org/archives/other-resources/john-f-kennedy-speeches/salt-lake-city-ut-19600923-mormon-tabernacle/.

41. Norman Leonard, *Life of a Leftist Labor Lawyer,* oral history conducted by Estolv Ethan Ward, 1985, Regional Oral History Office, Bancroft Library, University of California, Berkeley (hereafter, Leonard oral history), 161–62; clipping, Herb Caen's column, *Examiner,* Aug. 1957, file Harry Bridges material about 1957–1958, History Collection, ILWU Library.

42. *Chronicle,* May 25–27, 1961; *NYT,* May 25, 1961; *LAT,* May 25, 1961; *Dispatcher,* June 2, 30, 1961.

43. Leonard oral history, 162–63; *Dispatcher,* Dec. 1, 1961, Nov. 15, 1963, June 26, 1964, June 11, 1965; *Chronicle,* March 31, April 4, 5, May 5, 1962, June 28, 1964, June 8, 1965; *Archie Brown v. U.S.,* 334 F2d 488 (9th Cir. 1964); *U.S. v. Brown,* 381 US 437 (1965).

44. *NYT,* July 27, 1951, *LAT,* June 11, 1989, *Chronicle,* Nov. 16, 1965; Ray Healey and Isserman, *California Red,* 165.

45. *NYT,* June 1, 1962.

46. "Albertson v. Subversive Activities Control Board," *Oyez,* www.oyez.org/cases/1965/3/. See also Dorothy Ray Healey's account of the case in Ray Healey and Isserman, *California Red,* 189–90, where she misquotes the act but explains the thinking of those who refused to register.

47. *Albertson and Proctor v. Subversive Activities Control Board,* 382 US 70 (1965).

48. Schneiderman, report to state committee, Sept. 23, 1956, box 2, file 4, Schneiderman Papers, LARC; Ray Healey and Isserman, *California Red,* 164, 165.

49. Schneiderman, handwritten biographical notes, box 2, files 13, 14, Schneiderman Papers.

50. Art Cohn's column, *San Francisco Examiner,* Feb. 12, 1958; Richmond, *Long View,* 432–33; Ray Healey and Isserman, *California Red,* 164, 342–44; Peggy Dennis, *The Autobiography of an American Communist: A Personal View of a Political Life, 1925–1975* (Westport, CT: Lawrence Hill, 1977), 269–96.

51. *Chronicle,* Dec. 10, 1999; Aug. 7, 1975. A copy of Brown's letter is in carton 20, file 255, *People's World* Research Files Collection, LARC. Danny Grossman, son of Aubrey and Hazel, sent me copies of a number of items summarizing his parents' activism in the 1950s–1980s; he plans to donate the full collection to York University in Toronto.

52. Slutsky, *Gendering Radicalism,* ch. 4.

53. *Statement of the Vote . . . 1968,* 13; *Statement of the Vote . . . 1972,* 12; *Statement of the Vote . . . 1976,* 14.

54. Pat Tobin, interviews by Robert Cherny, Feb. 9 and 25, 1987; Don Watson, "Union Stalwart," in Schwartz, *Solidarity Stories,* 288–91; Bailey, *Kid,* 391–93; Bill Bailey interview

by Robert Cherny, March 16, 1993; Hobbs, *Cayton Legacy*, 160, 162–68; Mitford, *Fine Old Conflict*, ch. 6; Maas, *Looking Back*, chs. 7–9; Jack Olsen, in Schwartz, *Solidarity Stories*, 280–81, 286–87; Reid, *Tillie Olsen*, 184, 208, 258.

55. CUAC index card summary, State Archives; testimony of Harrison George, *Hearing before the Committee on Un-American Activities, House of Representatives, 83d Congress, 1st Session, December 2, 1953* (Washington, D.C.: Government Printing Office, 1954), 3431; Ancestry.com.

56. Biographical notes, Sam Darcy Papers, Tamiment Library, New York University. For Darcy as a "renegade," see, e.g., "Statement by the National Board of the Communist Party on the Expulsions," *Political Affairs* 25 (Nov. 1946): 1011.

57. Keith Eickman, "Keith Eickman: Idealism and Disappointment," in Harvey Schwartz, *Solidarity Stories: An Oral History of the ILWU* (Seattle: University of Washington Press, 2009), 274–80 (hereafter, Eickman oral history); Eickman interview by Robert Cherny, 1993; Watson, in Schwartz, *Solidarity Stories*, 288–91; Nitzberg interview by Cherny, 2018; Bailey, *Kid from Hoboken*, 410–17; Bailey interview by Cherny, 1993; Tobin interview by Cherny, 1987; Hobbs, *Cayton Legacy*, 194–95; Carol Cuénod, interviews by Harvey Schwartz, LARC, San Francisco State University, 1994, 2014. In his oral history (p. 180), David Jenkins suggests that it was largely his own decision to do blue-collar work; when I interviewed him on May 8, 1987, he suggested that it was the party's decision.

58. Bailey, *Kid from Hoboken*, 419; Watson, in Schwartz, *Solidarity Stories*, 292; Maas, *Looking Back*, 87; *San Francisco Examiner*, March 3, 1964, 3.

59. Reid, *Olsen*, 189, 190, 194, 195; Cherny conversations with Judy Nitzberg over many years; Maas, *Looking Back*, 87–89; Jenkins, *Against a Field Sinister*, 69, 70; Edith Arnstein Jenkins obituary, *San Francisco Chronicle*, Oct. 31, 2005, 18; Cuénod interview by Schwartz, 56–57, 62–64.

60. Starvus Stack oral history, side 25; Louise Todd Lambert oral history, 272ff.

61. Maas, *Looking Back*, 87; for Lincoln Fairley, see, e.g., *Facing Mechanization: The West Coast Longshore Plan* (Los Angeles: Institute of Industrial Relations, University of California, Los Angeles, 1979); with James Haig, *Mount Tamalpais: A History* (San Francisco: Scottwall Associates, 1987); Edith Arnstein Jenkins obituary, *San Francisco Chronicle*, Oct. 31, 2005, 18; for Watson, see "Mixed Melody: Anti-Communism and the United Packinghouse Workers in California Agriculture," in *American Labor and Cold War: Grassroots Politics and Postwar Political Culture*, ed. William Issel, Robert W. Cherny, Kieran Walsh Taylor (New Brunswick, NJ: Rutgers University Press, 2004), 58–71; Watson also presented papers at a number of conferences at which I was present.

62. Thomas Mallon, "Red Sheep: How Jessica Mitford Found Her Voice," *New Yorker*, Oct. 16, 2006, 176–82; Robert Treuhaft obituary, *The Guardian*, Nov. 19, 2001; Robert Treuhaft obituary, *Los Angeles Times*, Nov. 16, 2001; Robert Treuhaft obituary, *New York Times*, Dec. 2, 2001; Jessica Mitford obituary, *London Telegraph*, July 25, 1996; Robert Farley, "She's no red," *Politifact*, Feb. 15, 2008.

63. Jesse Hamlin, "Forever Dedicated to the Cause," *San Francisco Chronicle Datebook*, Jan. 10, 2008, E1, E2; Tillie Olsen obituary, *San Francisco Chronicle*, Jan. 3, 2007, B-4.

64. Jack Olsen obituary, [San Francisco] *Dispatcher*, March 10, 1989, 6; Don Watson obituary, *Dispatcher*, April 2015, 5; Bill Bailey obituary, *Dispatcher*, April 13, 1995, 7; Pat

Tobin obituary, *Dispatcher*, Oct. 17, 1995, 5; Pat Tobin obituary, *San Francisco Chronicle*, Sept. 9, 1995; Keith Eickman obituary, *San Francisco Chronicle*, Aug. 20, 2006, B-8; Cherny conversations with Judy Nitzberg.

65. Watson, in Schwartz, *Solidarity Stories*, 292; Loretta Starvus obituary, *Chronicle*, Feb. 9, 2001; Cherny conversations with Bill Bailey and Judy Nitzberg.

66. Don Watson oral history, interviewed by Harvey Schwartz, 1994, LARC.

67. Jenkins interviews by Cherny; Jenkins oral history, 217–84 esp. 262a; Hobbs, *Cayton Legacy*, 199–200.

68. Revels Cayton obituary, *Chronicle*, Nov. 6, 1995.

69. Eickman oral history; Keith Eickman obituary, *San Francisco Chronicle*, Aug. 20, 2006, B-8.

70. Copy of letter, Bridges to R. Palme Dutt, Dec. 12, 1968, box 9, file 3, Bridges Papers, LARC, San Francisco State University.

71. Sennett oral history, 340ff, 372; William Sennett obituary, *San Francisco Chronicle*, April 3, 2003; Veterans of the Abraham Lincoln Brigade Archives, https://alba-valb.org /volunteers/william-sennett/.

72. Bailey, *Kid from Hoboken*, 423.

73. Maas, *Looking Back*, ch. 11.

74. Isserman, *If I Had a Hammer*, 33.

75. Jack Kurzweil, emails, April 14, Oct. 4, 2022. On the founding of the Committees of Correspondence, see Aptheker, *Communists in Closets*, 220.

76. Robert Treuhaft obituary, *The Guardian*, Nov. 19, 2001; Robert Treuhaft obituary, *Los Angeles Times*, Nov. 16, 2001; Robert Treuhaft obituary, *New York Times*, Dec. 2, 2001; Doris Brin Walker interview by Robert Cherny, June 29, 2007; CUAC annual reports for 1965, 112, 150, and 1966, 65, 71, 101, 194, 120, 126; *San Francisco Chronicle*, Dec. 28, 1966, Jan. 20, 1967, Jan. 9, 1994. Regarding Hillary Rodham Clinton, see Farley, "She's no red," *Politifact*, Feb. 15, 2008.

77. Biographical note, Matt N. and Evelyn Graves Crawford Papers, Emory University.

78. Ray Thompson interviews by Jesse Warr, Oct. 11, Nov. 6. 1978, History Center, San Francisco Public Library.

79. Albert Vitere Lannon, "Second String Red: The Life of Al Lannon, An American Communist," MA thesis, San Francisco State University, 1997.

80. Judy Nitzberg interview by Timothy V. Johnson, July 9, 1985, Manny Harriman Oral History Collection, Tamiment Library/Robert Wagner Labor Archives, New York University; Cherny conversations with Judy and Leo Nitzberg; Louise Todd Lambert oral history, 272, 283; Oleta O'Connor Yates obituary, *San Francisco Chronicle*, March 3, 1964; "Crags Court Community Garden," https://www.glenparkassociation.org/crags -court-community-garden-a-hidden-gem-in-glen-park/; Lincoln Fairley, CUAC card file for 1954–1968, State Archives; Bill Bailey memorial service brochure, 1995, Robert W. Cherny Research Files, LARC.

81. Schneiderman, *Dissent on Trial*, 245; Healy and Isserman, *California Red*, 131. Ray Healey says that Hudson was expelled; the Kutnick files indicate he was a "voluntary drop," box 5, file 36, Kutnick Papers, LARC.

82. Gizzi Ward oral history, 121, 129.

83. Sennett oral history, 330; Maas, *Looking Back*, 81; Bailey, *Kid from Hoboken*, 434; Eickman oral history, 280; Tobin interview by Cherny; Gizzi Ward oral history, 121; Cuénod oral history, 34.

84. Cuénod oral history, 66; Louise Todd Lambert oral history, 120–21.

85. Bailey, *Kid from Hoboken*, 423; *Dispatcher*, April 13, 1995, May 1997.

86. Brin Walker interview by Cherny; Archie Brown obituary, *Chronicle*, Nov. 24, 1990, C3; "The Old Man and the Bay," *Sports Illustrated*, Dec. 15, 1975, https://vault.si.com /vault/1975/12/15/the-old-man-and-the-bay/.

87. Biographical note, Pittman Papers, Tamiment Library; John Pittman obituary, *Chronicle*, April 12, 1993.

88. Isaac Zafrani interview by Cherny, 1987.

89. All this comes from Elaine Black's FBI file, box 5, Elaine Black Yoneda Papers, LARC.

90. City and County of San Francisco Certificate of Honor, April 4, 1983; clipping, *Examiner*, May 20, 1983, box 29, file 211, *PW* Research Files, LARC. The account of Walter Johnson's statement is from my memory of the event.

91. Leah Schneiderman interviews by Cherny, April 14, 1987; April 26, 1993; email from Jack Kurzweil, April 14, 2022.

92. Leah Schneiderman interview by Cherny, 1993.

SELECT BIBLIOGRAPHY

Primary Sources

ROBERT W. CHERNY INTERVIEWS

All have been deposited with the Labor Archives and Research Center (LARC), San Francisco State University, as part of Robert W. Cherny Research Files.

Bailey, William, 1993
Brin Walker, Doris, 2007
Brown, Archie, 1987
Darcy, Sam, 1994, 1996
Dinkin Johnson, Miriam, 1993
Eickman, Keith, 1993
Fairley, Lincoln, 1986
Green, Archie, 1986
Grossman, Aubrey, 1993
Jenkins, David, and Edith Arnstein Jenkins, 1987, 1992
Jones, B. B., 1986
Nitzberg, Judith Fried, 2018
Resner, Herbert, 1992, 1993
Schneiderman, Leah, 1987, 1993
Tobin, Pat, 1987
Watson, Don, 1996
Zafrani, Isaac, 1987

INTERVIEWS AND ORAL HISTORIES BY OTHERS

Arnstein Jenkins, Edith. Interview by Martin Sherwin, 2002. Sherwin Papers, Library of Congress.

Brown, Archie and Hon Brown, in Griffin Fariello, *Red Scared: Memories of the American Inquisition, An Oral History*. New York: W. W. Norton, 1995.

Bulcke, Germain. Longshore Leader and ILWU-Pacific Maritime Association Arbitrator. Interview by Estolv Ward, 1983. Regional Oral History Office, Bancroft Library, University of California, Berkeley, 1984.

Cuénod, Carol. Interviews by Harvey Schwartz, 1994, 2014. Labor Archives and Research Center, San Francisco State University.

Darcy, Sam. Interview by Ron Filipelli. Darcy Papers, New York University.

Darcy, Sam. Interview by Richard Wormser, 1981. Oral History of the American Left, Tamiment Library/Robert F. Wagner Labor Archives, New York University.

Decker Gladstein, Caroline. Interview by Dorothy Sue Cobble, 1976. California Historical Society.

Dinkin Carlson, Lillian. "A California Girlhood." In *Red Diapers: Growing Up in the Communist Left, edited by Judy Kaplan and Linn Shapiro*. Urbana: University of Illinois Press, 1998.

Dinkin Johnson, Miriam. "The King-Ramsay-Conner Defense Committee, 1938–1941." In *The Shipboard Murder Case: Labor, Radicalism, and Earl Warren, 1936–1941*, Vol. 2. Interviews by Miriam Feingold. Earl Warren Oral History Project, Regional Oral History Office, Bancroft Library, University of California, Berkeley, 1976.

Dinkin Johnson, Miriam. Interview by Timothy V. Johnson, May 3, 1986. Manny Harriman Oral History Collection, Tamiment Library/Robert Wagner Labor Archives, New York University.

Dolsen, James. Interview by Paul Buhle. Oral History of the American Left, Tamiment Library/Robert F. Wagner Labor Archives, New York University.

Eickman, Keith. "Keith Eickman: Idealism and Disappointment." In Harvey Schwartz, *Solidarity Stories: An Oral History of the ILWU*. Seattle: University of Washington Press, 2009.

Gizzi Ward, Angela. Oral history interview by Sue Cobble, 1976. California Historical Society.

Goldblatt, Louis. *Louis Goldblatt—Working Class Leader in the ILWU, 1935–1977*. Interviews by Estolv Ethan Ward, 1978–1979, Regional Oral History Office, Bancroft Library, University of California, Berkeley.

Grossman, Aubrey. "A Defense Attorney Assesses the King, Ramsay, Conner Case." In *The Shipboard Murder Case: Labor, Radicalism, and Earl Warren, 1936–1941*, Vol. 2. Interviews by Miriam Feingold, 1976. Earl Warren Oral History Project, Regional Oral History Office, Bancroft Library, University of California, Berkeley.

Havenner, Franck Roberts. *Reminiscences: Oral History*. Interview by Corinne Lathrop Gilb. Berkeley: Regional Oral History Office, Bancroft Library, University of California, 1953.

Jackson, Robert Houghwout. *Reminiscences of Robert Houghwout Jackson: Oral History*, 1952, Columbia University.

Jenkins, David. *The Union Movement, the California Labor School, and San Francisco Politics, 1926–1988*. Interviews by Lisa Rubens, 1987, 1988. Regional Oral History Office, Bancroft Library, University of California, Berkeley.

Leonard, Norman. *Life of a Leftist Labor Lawyer*. Oral history interview by Estolv Ethan Ward, 1985. Regional Oral History Office, Bancroft Library, University of California, Berkeley.

Nelson, Steve, and Margaret Nelson. Interview by Martin Sherwin, 1981. Sherwin Papers, Library of Congress.

Nitzberg, Judith Fried. Interview by Timothy V. Johnson, July 9, 1985. Manny Harriman Oral History Collection, Tamiment Library/Robert Wagner Labor Archives, New York University.

Olsen, Jack. "Jack Olsen: Activist and Educator." In Harvey Schwartz, *Solidarity Stories: An Oral History of the ILWU*. Seattle: University of Washington Press, 2009.

Orr, Violet. Interviews by Lucy Kendall, 1976. California Historical Society.

Resner, Herbert. "The Recollections of the Attorney for Frank Connor." In *The Shipboard Murder Case: Labor, Radicalism, and Earl Warren, 1936–1941*, Vol. 2. Interviews by Miriam Feingold, 1976. Earl Warren Oral History Project, Regional Oral History Office, Bancroft Library, University of California, Berkeley.

Schmidt, Henry. *Secondary Leadership in the ILWU, 1933–1966*. Interviews by Miriam F. Stein and Estolv Ethan Ward. Regional Oral History Office, Bancroft Library, University of California, Berkeley, 1983.

Sennett, William. *William Sennett: Communist Functionary and Corporate Executive*. Interviews by Marshall Windmiller, 1981, 1982. Regional Oral History Office, Bancroft Library, University of California, Berkeley.

Spector, Frank. Interview by George Ewart, 1972. Bancroft Library, University of California, Berkeley.

Starvus (Stack), Loretta. Interviews by Lucy Kendall, 1986, 1987. Labor Archives and Research Center, San Francisco State University.

Thompson, Ray. Interviews by Jesse Warr, Oct. 11, Nov. 6. 1978. San Francisco Public Library History Center.

Treuhaft, Robert E. *Left-Wing Political Activist and Progressive Leader in the Berkeley Co-op*. Interviews by Robert G. Larsen, 1988–1989. Berkeley Oral History Project, Berkeley Historical Society, 1990.

Todd (Lambert), Louise. Louise Todd Lambert oral history. Interviews by Lucy Kendall, May–August 1976. California Historical Society.

Ward, Estolv Ethan. *Organizing and Reporting on Labor in the East Bay, California, and the West, 1925–1987*. Interview by Lisa Rubens, 1987. Regional Oral History Office, Bancroft Library, University of California, Berkeley, 1989.

Watson, Don. "Don Watson: Union Stalwart." In Harvey Schwartz, *Solidarity Stories: An Oral History of the ILWU*. Seattle: University of Washington Press, 2009.

Watson, Don. Oral history interview by Harvey Schwartz, 1994. Labor Archives and Research Center, San Francisco State University.

Yoneda, Elaine Black. Elaine Black Yoneda oral history. Interviews by Lucy Kendall, 1976–1977. California Historical Society.

ARCHIVAL COLLECTIONS

California State Archives, Sacramento
California Un-American Activities Committee Records
Secretary of State, Election Reports

Federal Bureau of Investigation Files
  Arnautoff, Victor
  Bridges, Harry
  CINRAD, https://archive.org/details/CINRAD/
  Communist Party, Los Angles Field Office Reports, c. 1922–1925
  COMRAP, https://archive.org/details/CominternApparatus/
  Schneiderman, William, 1940–1945
Labor Archives and Research Center (LARC), San Francisco State University
  Brown, Archie, Collection
  Bedacht, Max, Memoirs
  California Labor School Collection
  Cherny, Robert W., Research Files
  Kutnick, Lisette and Sam, Collection
  Leonard, Norman, Collection
  People's World Research Files
  Roberts, Holland, California Labor School Collection
  Schneiderman, William, Papers
  Stack, Loretta Starvus, Papers
  Surveillance Papers
  Yoneda, Elaine Black, Collection
Library of Congress
  Sherwin, Martin, Papers
Lilly Library, Indiana University
  Sinclair, Upton, Papers
Russian State Archives for Social and Political History (Rossiyskiy gosudarstvennyy arkhiv
  sotsial'no-politicheskoy istorii, RGASPI), Moscow, Russia
    Fond 495, Anglo-American Secretariat of the Communist International, Papers (includ-
      ing previous American commissions)
    Fond 515, Communist Party of the United States, Papers
    State Archive of the Rostov Region, Rostov, Russia (Gosudarstvenny Arkhiv Rostovskoy
      Oblasti, GARO)
    Fonds 1485, 2563, Records of the California and Pioneer Communes
Tamiment Library/Robert F. Wagner Labor Archives, New York University, New York,
  New York
  Darcy, Sam, Papers
  Pittman, John, Papers
  See also list of interviews held by this archive.

ONLINE PRIMARY SOURCES

Communist Party Membership by Districts, 1922–1950, Mapping American Social Movement Project, University of Washington, https://depts.washington.edu/moves/CP
  _map-members.shtml/
Vassiliev Notebooks, Wilson Center, Digital Archive, https://digitalarchive.wilsoncenter
  .org/topics/vassiliev-notebooks

Venona Project, National Security Agency, Central Security Service, https://www.nsa.gov /Helpful-Links/NSA-FOIA/Declassification-Transparency-Initiatives/Historical -Releases/Venona/

PUBLISHED MEMOIRS AND AUTOBIOGRAPHIES

Arnautov, Viktor Mikhailovich, with Leonid Sanin. *Zhizn' zanovo* (*Life Anew*), 2nd ed. Donetsk: Izdatel'stvo Donbas, 1972. Translation by Lloyd Kramer, Labor Archives and Research Center, San Francisco State University.

Bailey, William, with Lynn Damme. *The Kid from Hoboken: An Autobiography*. San Francisco: Circus Lithographic Prepress, 1993.

Darcy, Sam. "The San Francisco General Strike—1934." *Hawsepipe* 1 (Sept.–Oct. 1982) 1, 7.

Darcy, Sam. "The San Francisco General Strike—1934: Part II." *Hawsepipe* 1 (Nov.–Dec. 1982): 1–2, 4–6.

Dennis, Peggy. *The Autobiography of an American Communist*. Westport, CT: Lawrence Hill, 1977.

Dolsen, James H. *Bucking the Ruling Class: Jim Dolsen's Story*. N.p.: n.p., 1984.

Hallinan, Vincent. *A Lion in Court*. New York: G. P. Putnam's Sons, 1963.

Jenkins, Edith Arnstein. *Against a Field Sinister: Memoirs and Stories*. San Francisco: City Lights Books, 1991.

Maas, Eva Krupnick Lapin. *Looking Back on a Life in the Left: A Personal History*. Self-published, 1998.

Merriman, Marion, with Warren Lerude. *American Commander in Spain: Robert Hale Merriman and the Abraham Lincoln Brigade*. Reno: University of Nevada Press, 1986.

Mitford, Jessica. *A Fine Old Conflict*. New York: Alfred A. Knopf, 1977.

Nelson, Steve, and James R. Barrett, Rob Ruck. *Steve Nelson, American Radical*. Pittsburgh: University of Pittsburgh Press, 1981.

Ray Healey, Dorothy, and Maurice Isserman. *California Red: A Life in the American Communist Party*. Urbana: University of Illinois Press, 1991.

Richmond, Al. *A Long View from the Left: Memoirs of an American Revolutionary*. New York: Dell, 1972.

Schneiderman, William. *Dissent on Trial: The Story of a Political Life*. Minneapolis: MEP Publications, 1983.

Yoneda, Karl G. *Ganbatte: Sixty-Year Struggle of a Kibei Worker*. Los Angeles: Asian American Studies Center, UCLA, 1983.

NEWSPAPERS AND JOURNALS

[*Chicago, New York*] *The Communist*
[*Chicago, New York*] *The Party Organizer*
Los Angeles Times
[*New York*] *Political Affairs*
New York Times
San Francisco Chronicle
[*San Francisco*] *Dispatcher*
[*San Francisco*] *Labor Herald*

[*San Francisco*] *Labor Unity*
San Francisco News
[*San Francisco*] *People's World*
[*San Francisco*] *Rank and File*
[*San Francisco*] *Western Worker*
Washington Post

COURT CASES

Albertson and Proctor v. Subversive Activities Control Board, 382 U.S. 70 (1965)
Archie Brown v. U.S., 334 F.2d 488 (9th Cir. 1964)
Bridges v. Wixon, 326 U.S. 135 (1945)
Communist Party v. Peek, 20 Cal.2d 536 (1942)
Dennis v. United States, 341 U.S. 49 (1951)
James v. Marinship Corp., 25 Cal.2d 721 (1944)
People v. Todd, 9 Cal. App. 2d 237 (Cal. Ct. App. 1935)
Schneiderman v. U.S., 320 U.S. 118 (1943)
U.S. v. Brown, 381 U.S. 437 (1965)
Yates v. U.S., 225 F.2d 146 (9th Cir. 1955); 354 U.S. 298 (1957); 355 U.S. 66 (1957); 356 U.S. 364 (1958)
Whitney v. California, 274 U.S. 357 (1927)

Secondary Works

Aptheker, Bettina. *Communists in Closets: Queering the History, 1930s-1990s.* New York: Routledge, 2023.

Ball, Howard, and Phillip J. Cooper. *Of Power and Right: Hugo Black, William O. Douglas, and America's Constitutional Revolution.* New York: Oxford University Press, 1992.

Belknap, Michal R. *Cold War Political Justice: The Smith Act, the Communist Party, and American Civil Liberties.* Westport, CT: Greenwood, 1977.

Benson, Robert L. *The Venona Story.* Fort George C. Meade, MD: Center for Cryptologic History, National Security Agency, n.d.

Bernstein, Seth, and Robert Cherny. "Searching for the Soviet Dream: Prosperity and Disillusionment on the Soviet Seattle Agricultural Commune, 1922–1927." *Agricultural History* 88 (2014): 22–44.

Bird, Kai, and Martin J. Sherwin. *American Prometheus: The Triumph and Tragedy of J. Robert Oppenheimer.* New York: Alfred A. Knopf, 2005.

Blaisdell, William. "Leo Eloesser: The Remarkable Story of a Medical Volunteer in Spain." *The Volunteer* (Dec. 3, 2016). https://albavolunteer.org/2016/12/leo-eloesser-the-remarkable-story-of-a-medical-volunteer-in-spain/.

Bosmajian, Haig A. *Anita Whitney, Louis Brandeis, and the First Amendment.* Madison, NJ: Fairleigh Dickinson University Press, 2010.

Brechin, Gray. "Politics and Modernism: The Trial of the Rincon Annex Murals." In *On the Edge of America: California Modernist Art, 1900–1950,* edited by Paul J. Karlstrom, 69–95. Berkeley: University of California Press, 1996.

Browder, Earl. *Teheran: Our Path in War and Peace.* New York: International Publishers, 1944.

Brown, Kathleen A. "Ella Reeve Bloor: The Politics of the Personal in the American Communist Party." PhD diss., University of Washington, 1996.

Brown, Kathleen A. "Ella Reeve Bloor: Suffragist, Trade-Unionist, Socialist, and Revolutionary in the Making, 1862–1919." MA thesis, San Francisco State University, 1987.

Carroll, Peter N. *The Odyssey of the Abraham Lincoln Brigade: Americans in the Spanish Civil War*. Stanford, CA: Stanford University Press, 1994.

Cherny, Robert W. "Anticommunist Networks and Labor: The Pacific Coast in the 1930s." In *Labor's Cold War: Local Politics in a Global Context*, edited by Shelton Stromquist, 17–48. Champaign: University of Illinois Press, 2008.

Cherny, Robert W. "The Communist Party in California, 1935–1940: From the Political Margins to the Mainstream and Back." *American Communist History* 9 (2010): 3–33.

Cherny, Robert W. *Harry Bridges: Labor Radical, Labor Legend*. Urbana: University of Illinois Press, 2022.

Cherny, Robert W. "The Party's Over: Former Communist Party Members in the San Francisco Bay Area." In *Post–Cold War Revelations in the American Communist Party: Citizens, Revolutionaries, and Spies*, edited by Vernon Pedersen, James Ryan, and Katherine Sibley, 229–54. London: Bloomsbury Academic, 2021.

Cherny, Robert W. "Prelude to the Popular Front: The Communist Party in California, 1931–1935." *American Communist History* 1 (2002): 5–37.

Cherny, Robert W. *Victor Arnautoff and the Politics of Art*. Urbana: University of Illinois Press, 2017.

Cochran, Bert. *Labor and Communism: The Conflict That Shaped American Unions*. Princeton, NJ: Princeton University Press, 1979.

Daniel, Cletus E. *Bitter Harvest: A History of California Farmworkers, 1870–1941*. Berkeley: University of California Press, 1981.

Draper, Theodore. *American Communism and Soviet Russia: The Formative Period*. 1960; New York: Vintage Books, 1986.

Dubofsky, Melvyn, and Warren Van Tine. *John L. Lewis: A Biography*. New York: Quadrangle, 1977.

Duffy, Peter. *The Agitator: William Bailey and the First American Uprising against Nazism*. New York: Public Affairs, 2019.

Eby, Cecil D. *Comrades and Commissars: The Lincoln Battalion in the Spanish Civil War*. University Park: Pennsylvania State University Press, 2007.

Eliel, Paul. *The Waterfront and General Strikes: San Francisco, 1934*. San Francisco: Hooper Printing, 1934.

Fayet, Jean-François. "VOKS: The Third Dimension of Soviet Foreign Policy." In *Searching for a Cultural Diplomacy*, edited by Jessica C. E. Glenow-Hecht and Mark C. Donfried, 33–49. New York: Berghahn Books, 2010.

Fowler, Josephine. "From East to West and West to East: Ties of Solidarity in the Pan-Pacific Revolutionary Trade Union Movement, 1923–1934." *International Labor and Working-Class History* 66 (Fall 2004): 99–117.

Frost, Richard H. *The Mooney Case*. Stanford, CA: Stanford University Press, 1968.

Gettleman, Marvin. "The Lost World of United States Labor Education: Curricula at East and West Coast Communist Schools, 1944–1947." In *American Labor and the Cold War:*

275

Grassroots Politics and Postwar Political Culture, edited by Robert Cherny, William Issel, and Kieran Walsh Taylor, 205–215. New Brunswick, NJ: Rutgers University Press, 2004.

Getty, J. Arch, and Oleg V. Naumov. *The Road to Terror: Stalin and the Self-Destruction of the Bolsheviks, 1932–1939.* New Haven, CT: Yale University Press, 1999.

Ginger, Ann Fagan. *Carol Weiss King: Human Rights Lawyer, 1895–1952.* Niwot: University Press of Colorado, 1993.

Godfried, Nathan. "'Voice of the People': Sidney Roger, the Labor/Left, and Broadcasting in San Francisco, 1945–1950." *American Communist History* 18 (2019): 56–78.

Haynes, John Earl, and Harvey Klehr. "The 'Mental Comintern' and the Self-Destructive Tactics of the CPUSA, 1944–8." In *Post–Cold War Revelations and the American Communist Party: Citizens, Revolutionaries, and Spies*, edited by Vernon J. Pedersen, James G. Ryan, and Katherine A. S. Sibley. London: Bloomsbury Academic, 2021.

Haynes, John Earl, and Harvey Klehr. *Venona: Decoding Soviet Espionage in America.* New Haven, CT: Yale University Press, 1999.

Haynes, John Earl, Harvey Klehr, and Alexander Vassiliev. *Spies: The Rise and Fall of the NKVD in America.* New Haven, CT: Yale University Press, 2010.

Healey, M. J. "Red Scare Politics: California's Campaign against Un-American Activities, 1940–1970." *Journal of American Studies* 20 (1986): 5–32.

Herken, Gregg. *Brotherhood of the Bomb: The Tangled Lives and Loyalties of Robert Oppenheimer, Ernest Lawrence, and Edward Teller.* New York: Henry Holt, 2002.

Hobbs, Richard S. *The Cayton Legacy: An African American Family.* Pullman: Washington State University Press, 2002.

Issel, William. *Church and State in the City: Catholics and Politics in Twentieth-Century San Francisco.* Philadelphia: Temple University Press, 2013.

Isserman, Maurice. *Which Side Were You On? The American Communist Party during the Second World War.* Middletown, CT: Wesleyan University Press, 1982.

Isserman, Maurice. *If I Had a Hammer . . . The Death of the Old Left and the Birth of the New Left.* New York: Basic Books, 1987.

Jackson, Lisa. "Twenty-Four-Hour Party People: A Gendered Social History of California Communism." MA thesis, San Francisco State University, 2015.

Johanningsmeier, Edward P. *Forging American Communism: The Life of William Z. Foster.* Princeton, NJ: Princeton University Press, 1994.

Kann, Kenneth L. *Comrades and Chicken Ranchers: The Story of a California Jewish Community.* Ithaca, NY: Cornell University Press, 1993.

Kimmeldorf, Howard. *Reds or Rackets: The Making of Radical and Conservative Unions on the Waterfront.* Berkeley: University of California Press, 1988.

Klehr, Harvey. *The Heyday of American Communism: The Depression Decade.* New York: Basic Books, 1984.

Klehr, Harvey, and John Earl Haynes. *The American Communist Movement: Storming Heaven Itself.* New York: Twayne, 1992.

Klehr, Harvey, and John Earl Haynes. "Oppenheimer Was a Communist." *Commentary*, Sept. 2023. https://www.commentary.org/articles/harvey-klehr/oppenheimer-was-a-communist/

Klehr, Harvey, John Earl Haynes, and Kyrill M. Anderson. *The Soviet World of American Communism.* New Haven, CT: Yale University Press, 1998.

Klehr, Harvey, John Earl Haynes, and Fridrikh Igorevich Firsov. *The Secret World of American Communism*. New Haven, CT: Yale University Press, 1995.

Kutler, Stanley I. *The American Inquisition: Justice and Injustice in the Cold War*. New York: Hill and Wang, 1982.

Lannon, Albert Vitere. "Second String Red: The Life of Al Lannon, An American Communist." MA thesis, San Francisco State University, 1997.

Liss, Jeffrey F. "The Schneiderman Case: An Inside View of the Roosevelt Court." *Michigan Law Review* 74 (1976):500–523.

MacDougall, Curtis. *Gideon's Army*, 3 vols. New York: Marzani and Munsell, 1965.

Markholt, Ottilie. *Maritime Solidarity: Pacific Coast Unionism, 1929–38*. Tacoma, WA: Pacific Coast Maritime History Committee, 1998.

McDermott, Kevin, and Jeremy Agnew. *The Comintern: A History of International Communism from Lenin to Stalin*. New York: St. Martin's, 1997.

McWilliams, Carey. *Factories in the Field: The Story of Migratory Farm Labor in California*. 1939; reprint, University of California Press, 1999.

Monk, Ray. *Robert Oppenheimer: A Life Inside the Center*. New York: Doubleday, 2012.

Nelson, Allan. *The Nelson Brothers: Finnish-American Radicals from the Mendocino Coast*. Willits, CA: Mendocino County Museum and Immigration Research History Center, University of Minnesota, 2005.

Nelson, Bruce. *Workers on the Waterfront: Seamen, Longshoremen, and Unionism in the 1930s*. Urbana: University of Illinois Press, 1988.

Paddison, Joshua. "Summers of Worry, Summers of Defiance: San Franciscans for Academic Freedom and Education and the Bay Area Opposition to HUAC, 1959–1960." *California History* 78 (1999): 188–201, 219–21.

Pedersen, Vernon L. *The Communist Party on the American Waterfront: Revolution, Reform, and the Quest for Power*. Lanham, MD: Lexington Books, 2019.

Pedersen, Vernon L. "Underfunded, Understaffed, and Underground: The History of the San Francisco Bureau of the Pan-Pacific Trade Union Secretariat." *Continuity: A Journal of History* 26 (Spring 2003): 1–20.

Pedersen, Vernon, James Ryan, and Katherine Sibley, eds. *Post–Cold War Revelations in the American Communist Party: Citizens, Revolutionaries, and Spies*. London: Bloomsbury Press, 2021.

Pritchard, Robert L. "California Un-American Activities Investigations: Subversion on the Right?" *California Historical Quarterly* 49 (1970): 309–327.

Raineri, Vivian McGuckin. *The Red Angel: The Life and Times of Elaine Black Yoneda, 1906–1988*. New York: International Publishers, 1991.

Reid, Panthea. *Tillie Olsen: One Woman, Many Riddles*. New Brunswick, NJ: Rutgers University Press, 2010.

Richmond, Al. *Native Daughter*. San Francisco: Anita Whitney 75th Anniversary Committee, 1942.

Rubens, Lisa. "The Patrician Radical: Charlotte Anita Whitney." *California History* 65 (1986): 158–71, 226–27.

Ryan, James G. *Earl Browder: The Failure of American Communism*. Tuscaloosa: University of Alabama Press, 1997.

Schreiber, Rachel. *Elaine Black Yoneda: Jewish Immigration, Labor Activism, and Japanese American Exclusion and Incarceration.* Philadelphia: Temple University Press, 2022.

Scobie, Ingrid Winther. "Jack B. Tenney and the 'Parasitic Menace': Anti-Communist Legislation in California, 1940–1949." *Pacific Historical Review* 43 (1974): 188–211.

Selvin, David F. *A Terrible Anger: The 1934 Waterfront and General Strikes in San Francisco.* Detroit: Wayne State University Press, 1996.

Shaffer, Ralph E. "Communism in California, 1919–1924: 'Orders from Moscow' or Independent Western Radicalism." *Science & Society* 34 (1970): 412–29.

Shaffer, Ralph E. "Formation of the California Communist Labor Party." *Pacific Historical Review* 36 (1976): 59–78.

Shaffer, Ralph E. "Robert Whitaker: 1919, A Crisis Year." *Southwest Economy & Society* 6 (1984): 14–27.

Schapsmeier, Edward L. and Frederick H. *Prophet in Politics: Henry A. Wallace and the War Years, 1940–1965.* Ames: Iowa State University Press, 1970.

Schmidt, Karl M. *Henry A. Wallace: Quixotic Crusade 1948.* Syracuse, NY: Syracuse University Press, 1960.

Skovgaard, John. "The California Labor School." Unpublished paper, 2003. Labor Archive and Research Center, San Francisco State University.

Slezkine, Yuri. *The House of Government: A Saga of the Russian Revolution.* Princeton, NJ: Princeton University Press, 2017.

Slutsky, Beth. *Gendering Radicalism: Women and Communism in Twentieth-Century California.* Lincoln: University of Nebraska Press, 2015.

Starobin, Joseph R. *American Communism in Crisis, 1943–1957.* Cambridge: Harvard University Press, 1972.

Stevenson, Janet, *The Undiminished Man: A Political Biography of Robert Wallace Kenny.* Novato, CA: Chandler & Sharp Publishers, 1980.

Strum, Philippa. *Speaking Freely:* Whitney v. California *and American Speech Law.* Lawrence: University Press of Kansas, 2015.

Walsh, James P. *San Francisco's Hallinan: Toughest Lawyer in Town.* Novato, CA: Presidio Press, 1982.

Walton, Calder. *Spies: The Epic Intelligence War between East and West.* New York: Simon and Schuster, 2023.

Ward, Estolv Ethan. *The Gentle Dynamiter: A Biography of Tom Mooney.* Palo Alto, CA: Ramparts Press, 1983.

Wark, Colin, and John F. Galliher. Progressive Lawyers under Siege: Moral Panic during the McCarthy Years. Lanham, MD: Lexington Books, 2015.

Weber, Devra. *Dark Sweat, White Gold: California Farm Workers, Cotton, and the New Deal.* Berkeley: University of California Press 1994.

Wollenberg, Charles. "James v. Marinship: Trouble on the New Black Frontier." *California History* 60 (1981): 262–79.

Wollenberg, Charles. *Marinship at War: Shipbuilding and Social Change in Wartime Sausalito.* Berkeley: Western Heritage Press, 1990.

Zieger, Robert H. *John L. Lewis: Labor Leader.* Boston: Twayne, 1988.

Zumoff, Jacob A. *The Communist International and US Communism, 1919–1929.* Leiden: Brill Academic Publishers, 2014.

INDEX

Koide, Joe, 24, 91
Kreichmar, Irving (Irving Keith), 149, 176–77
Kurzweil, Jack, 200–201, 206
Kutler, Stanley, 171

Labor's Non-Partisan League (LNPL), 69, 74, 75, 77, 78, 80, 82, 84, 92, 187
Labor Unity (newspaper): closes down, 9–10, 44; coverage of Farmer-Labor Party, 6; replaces *Rank and File*, 9
Labor Youth League, 203
La Follette, Robert, Jr., 77, 79
La Follette, Robert, Sr., 6, 9
Lambert, Carl Rude: biographical summary, 141, 211; Duclos article and, 147–48; leaves CPUSA, 187–88; life in the CPUSA and, 116; Smith Act and, 174–75; Soviet agents, contacts with, 140, 141; World War II and, 124
Lambert, Walter, 128, 141, 156, 187–88
Landis, James, 86
Landon, Alf, 70, 73–74, 84
Landrum-Griffin Act (1959), 192–93
Lannon, Al (Francisco Alberto Vitere), 149, 202
Lannon, Elva, 202
Lanz, Henry, 132
Lapham, Roger, 126, 156
Lapin, Adam: biographical summary, 150, 211; *Daily Worker* and, 150; leaves CPUSA, 186, 188–89; life after the CPUSA and, 196, 198; *People's World* (*PW*) and, 150, 173, 198; Smith Act and, 173, 174
Lapin, Nora, 173, 188, 190
Lapin Maas, Eva Sonenshine: biographical summary, 150, 213; CPUSA National Convention (1957) and, 185–86; leaves CPUSA, 186, 188–89; life after the CPUSA and, 197, 198, 200; life in the CPUSA and, 173, 203
Latin Americans, as CPUSA members, 20
Lawrence, Ernest, 135, 138
League for Industrial Democracy, 72
Legere, Ben, 69–70, 71
Lenin, Vladimir, 11, 12, 21, 101, 157, 206
Lenin School (Moscow), 109–11, 134, 149, 176–77, 202
Leonard, Norman: biographical summary, 172, 212; legal defense activities, 193; postwar anti-Communism and, 169, 172, 193; Smith Act and, 176, 177, 178
Lerner Olsen, Tillie, 135; biographical summary, 103–4, 212; leaves CPUSA, 188; life

after the CPUSA and, 197, 198; life in the CPUSA and, 103–4; San Francisco County Personnel Committee and, 146–47; Tehran (Teheran) line and, 148–49
lesbianism/homosexuality, 157–59, 207
Levin, Emanuel: as California DO, 10–11, 14, 15–19, 20, 22, 23, 25–28, 30; *Daily Worker* and, 20; Workers Party and, 6–7
Levinson, Sanford, 131
Lewis, John L., 68, 85
Lewis, Tom, 10, 11, 15, 16, 22
Liebknecht, Karl, 11
Lima, Albert ("Mickey"), 174–75, 176, 193–94
Liss, Jeffrey, 130–31
Lomakin, Lorissa, 120
Lomakin, Yakov Mironovich, 120
Los Angeles Chamber of Commerce, 77
Los Angeles Times, 175
Lovestone, Jay, 11, 22, 25–30, 37–38, 39, 55, 115
Lundeberg, Harry, 68–69, 95
Luxemburg, Rosa, 11
Lynden, Richard, 143, 162

Maas, Eva. *See* Lapin Maas, Eva Sonenshine
Maguire, Michael, 190–91
Malone, V. J., 98
Manuilsky, Dmitry, 72–73, 110, 112
Manus, J. G., 19, 23, 25–27, 28, 32
Marcantonio, Vito, 92–93, 162
Margolis, Ben, 86, 99, 172, 176, 178
marijuana use, 158, 165
Marine Cooks and Stewards (MC&S), 93
Marine Firemens' Union (MFOW; Pacific Coast Marine Firemen, Oilers, and Wipers Association), 67, 69, 93, 97–98, 124, 149–50, 163, 196, 204
Marine Workers Industrial Union (MWIU), 47–53, 58–61, 64–66, 90, 92, 93, 123, 202
Marinship, 125–26
Maritime Federation of the Pacific Coast (MFP), 67, 68–69, 93, 96, 98, 105, 116
Marshall, George, 161
Marshall, Thurgood, 126
Marshall Plan, 161–62, 163, 182
Martin, M., 26
Marty, André, 72–73, 107, 110
Marx, Karl, 12, 37, 157, 179
Marxism-Leninism, 55, 87, 146, 149, 151–53, 171–72, 176–77, 185–87, 202
Mason, Redfern, 69–70, 71
Mass, John, 168
Mattson, Lester, 6
May Day celebrations, 11, 12–13, 35–36, 42, 162

ROBERT W. CHERNY is a professor emeritus of history at San Francisco State University. His many books include *Harry Bridges: Labor Radical, Labor Legend* and *Victor Arnautoff and the Politics of Art.*

The University of Illinois Press
is a founding member of the
Association of University Presses.

———————————————

Composed in 10.75/13 Arno Pro
with ITC Avant Garde Gothic Std display
by Kirsten Dennison
at the University of Illinois Press

University of Illinois Press
1325 South Oak Street
Champaign, IL 61820-6903
www.press.uillinois.edu